Arthur H. (Arthur Haynesworth) Masten, Making of America Project

The History of Cohoes, New York

Arthur H. (Arthur Haynesworth) Masten, Making of America Project

The History of Cohoes, New York

ISBN/EAN: 9783744664493

Printed in Europe, USA, Canada, Australia, Japan

Cover: Foto ©ninafisch / pixelio.de

More available books at **www.hansebooks.com**

THE

HISTORY OF COHOES,

NEW YORK,

FROM ITS

EARLIEST SETTLEMENT TO THE PRESENT TIME.

ALBANY:
JOEL MUNSELL.
1877.

INTRODUCTION.

The preparation of a sketch of the history of Cohoes was commenced by the writer at the request of the Hon. D. J. Johnston, mayor of the city, made in accordance with a proclamation issued by the president, calling attention to the following resolution passed by Congress, May 13, 1876:

"It is hereby recommended to the people of the several states that they assemble in their several counties or towns on the approaching Centennial Anniversary of our National Independence, and that they cause to have delivered on such day an historical sketch of said county or town from its formation, and that a copy of said sketch be filed, in print or manuscript, in the clerk's office of said county, and an additional copy, in print or manuscript, be filed in the office of the librarian of congress, to the intent that a complete record may thus be obtained of the progress of our institutions during the first centennial of their existence."

The understanding was that the sketch should be published in one of the city papers in case it was not completed by July 4th. It was found, however, after some progress had been made, that if limited to the length suitable for production in the manner proposed, the history would in many particulars be incomplete and unsatisfactory, and it was accordingly decided to enlarge it to the form in which it now appears.

As the manufacturing interests of Cohoes have always been its most important feature, their history forms in a great measure that of the place and consequently occupies a large share of the following pages.

An effort has been made to relate in addition the principal facts in the early history of this locality, and to describe the general progress of the place since the first steps were taken, fifty years ago, towards the development of its resources, giving accounts of its various institutions and of the most important local events.

Great care has been taken to insure accuracy in all respects — especially in regard to names and dates, though in a work of this sort, abounding in details, it is of course impossible to avoid a certain number of errors. Whenever it has been necessary to depend for data upon the memory of individuals, the information thus obtained has been verified, if possible, by a comparison of the versions given by different persons, and by reference to such records as are in existence. Except in the case of chapters I and VIII, an arrangement of facts in their chronological order rather than according to subject has been adopted, in the belief that a better idea would thus be afforded of the general growth and progress of the place. Although this method makes the narrative at times disconnected, it appears preferable on the whole, since its disadvantages have been obviated as far as possible by foot notes and the full index at the close of the volume.

The materials used in the preparation of the book, aside from those obtained from private sources, have been for the greater part furnished by the files of the *Cohoes Cataract, Cohoes Daily News, Troy Times,* and *Troy Press.* Many facts have also been taken from the valuable publications of Mr. Joel Munsell concerning the history of Albany.

The writer would here express his obligations to the many friends who have assisted him in his labors, particularly to his father, James H. Masten, to whom he is indebted for constant aid and advice. Among others to whom acknowledgments are especially due may be mentioned Messrs. Joshua R. Clarke, Lucien Fitts, Henry D. Fuller and Nicholas En Earl of Cohoes; Miss E. Howe and Mr. Isaac I. Fonda of Waterford; Mr. Timothy Bailey of Ballston; Mr. Evert Van Der Mark of Lansingburg, Mr. Oliver C. Hubbard of West Troy and Mr. Chas. A. Olmsted of Lockport, N. Y., who have furnished much valuable information which could not otherwise have been obtained.

The writer is also indebted to Messrs. T. G. Younglove, D. J. Johnston and Harvey Clute of Cohoes; Mrs.

Hugh White of Waterford, Mr. A. A. Peebles of Lansingburg, and Mr. Charles Van Zandt of the Van Rensselaer office, Albany, for access to important documents, and to Mr. A. J. Weise of Troy for the use of the cut of the Van Schaick House and other favors.

ARTHUR H. MASTEN.

Cohoes, December, 1876.

HISTORY OF COHOES.

I.

EARLY ACCOUNTS OF THIS LOCALITY, FROM THE WRITINGS OF VISITORS TO THE FALLS.

IT is well known that the word *Cohoes* is of Indian origin, and has been the designation (with varied orthography) of this locality from the earliest times. Its exact derivation and meaning, however, have not been agreed upon. The different versions of Indian legends all have as their most prominent feature, a canoe carried over the Falls by the current, and this fact has furnished the derivation generally accepted. The signification — "a canoe falling"— has been given by almost every writer on the subject since Spafford, who wrote in 1813 : "The name is of indiginal origin, and like the most such, has an appropriate allusion. Cah-hoos or Ca-hoos, a canoe falling, as explained by the late learned Indian sachem, Brandt, of illustrious memory." In Morgan's *League of the Ho-de-sau-nee or Iroquois* is a list of the settlements in the different territories, and under the head of Ga-ne-a-ga-o-no-ga or Mohawk territory, the author gives "Cohoes Falls: In Mohawk dialect *Ga-ha-oose*, meaning the ship-wrecked canoe." Many persons, on the contrary, whose knowledge of the Indian dialects entitles their opinion to respect, give another interpretation to the word, which is stated as follows in an article published in the *Schenectady Reflector*, in 1857 : "The term in question is in the Mohegan language ; its signification we cannot express without circumlocution, unless we use the word pitch or plunge, or coin a new substantive, *overshoot*. The

Canadian Indians designate by the name *cahoos* those unpleasant hollows which occur in roads covered with snow, and which sleigh riders vulgarly call pitch holes or more commonly *cradle holes.*" This derivation seems perhaps the more reasonable, though the other has the sanction of long use and general acceptance. Whatever the meaning of the word, it is certain that the name of our city had its origin in something connected with the Falls. This being so, and since the town has always been more or less associated with the Falls in the public mind, it may not be amiss to give in this sketch some of the earliest references to them.

Though the history of Cohoes as a town of importance commenced barely half a century ago, the spot on which the city stands was well known both abroad and in this country at a very early day. The natural beauties of the locality brought here many of the travelers who visited America in the 17th and 18th centuries. Albany, then one of the most important cities in the country, was one of the first places visited by foreigners, and as the Falls were among the most accessible objects of interest to persons staying there, we find accounts, or at all events mention of them, in a large number of the books of American travel.

Allusions to the Falls are also frequent in the English and French documentary history of the seventeenth and eighteenth centuries, having reference generally to the navigation of the river.

The earliest account of the place which I have been able to find is that of the Rev. Johannes Megapolensis, the first minister of the gospel in Albany, who settled there in 1642. It was contained in a description which he wrote to friends in Holland of the manners and habits of the Mohawk Indians, and is as follows:

"Through this land runs an excellent river about five hundred or six hundred paces wide. This river, comes out of the Mahakas country, about four miles north of us. There it flows between two high rocky banks, and falls from a height equal to that of a church, with such a noise that we can sometimes hear it with us. In the beginning of June twelve of us took a ride to see it. When we came there we saw not only the river falling with such a noise that we could hardly hear one another, but the water boiling and dashing with such force in still weather, that it was all the time as if it were raining; and the trees on the hills there (which are as high as Schooler Duyn) had their leaves all the time wet exactly as if it rained. The water is as clear as crystal and as fresh as milk. I and another with me saw there in clear sunshine, when there was not a cloud in the sky, as we stood above upon the rocks, directly opposite where the river falls in a great abyss, the half of a rainbow, or a quarter circle of the same color with the rainbow in the sky. And when we had gone about ten or twelve rods further downwards from the fall, along the river, we saw a complete rainbow, or half a circle appearing clearly in the water just the same as if it had been in the clouds, and this is always to be seen by those who go there. In this river is great plenty of several kinds of fish, pike, eels, perch, lampreys, suckers, cat fish, sun fish, shad, bass, etc. In the spring, in May, the perch are so plenty that one man with a hook and line, can catch in one hour as many as ten or twelve can eat. My boys have caught in less than an hour, fifty, each a foot long. They have a three pronged instrument with which they fish, and draw up frequently two or three perch at once. There is also in the river a great plenty of sturgeon, which we Christians do not eat, but the Indians eat them greedily.[1] In this river, too, are very beautiful islands, containing, ten, twenty, thirty, fifty and seventy morgens[2] of land."

The *Description of New Netherlands* published in Amsterdam in 1656, by Adriaen Van Der Donck,[3] contained some interesting accounts of his explorations in this vicinity, among them the following concerning the Falls:

---

[1] Dr. Mitchill (in *Coll. N. Y. Hist. Soc.*, I, 41), says: "No particular path was selected by the *sturgeons*. They seem to have swam at large, as they do at present. But they assembled for the propagation of their kind at the bottom of the Cohoes or great falls of the Mohock." John Maude, from whose account a quotation is given further on, stated that the river then (1800) furnished pike, bass and trout.

[2] A morgen is about two acres.

[3] *New York Historical Collections.*

"The other arm of the North River runs by four sprouts as we have related to the great falls of the Maquas Kill (Mohawk River) which the Indians name the Chahoos and our nation the Great Fall, above which the river is again several hundred yards wide and the falls we estimate to be one hundred and fifty or two hundred feet high.[1] The water glides over the falls as smooth as if it ran over an even wall and fell over the same. The precipice is formed of firm blue rock ; near by and below the falls there stand several rocks, which appear splendid in the water, rising above it like high turf heaps, apparently from eight, sixteen to thirty feet high. . . . . The Indians, when they travel by water and come to trade, usually come in canoes made of the bark of trees, which they know how to construct. When they come near the falls they land and carry their boats and their lading some distance below the falls and proceed on their voyage, otherwise they would be driven over the falls and destroyed. An occurrence of this kind took place here in our time. An Indian whom I have known accompanied by his wife and child with sixty beaver skins descended the river in his canoe in the spring when the water runs rapid and the current is strongest for the purpose of selling his beavers to the Netherlanders. This Indian carelessly approached too near the Falls before he discovered his danger, and notwithstanding his utmost exertions to gain the land, his frail bark with all on board was swept over by the rapid current and down the Falls ; his wife and child were killed, his bark shattered to pieces, his cargo of furs damaged. But his life was preserved. I have frequently seen the Indian and have heard him relate the perilous occurrence or adventure."

The following version of one of the Indian legends concerning the Fall, given in the *Sentimental American Traveller*, may have had its foundation in the account of Van Der Donck, above quoted:

"Many years since, an Indian and his squaw, having made too free with the bottle, were carelessly paddling along the Mohawk in their canoe. On a sudden, perceiving themselves drawn by the current and hurried down the stream to the dreadful cataract, looking upon their fate as inevitable, they

---

[1] The correct figures, according to measurements taken by Mr. Gwynn, proprietor of the Cataract House, in 1875 are; breadth 1,140 feet, height 86 feet.

composed themselves to die with resolution, in a manner worthy their ancestors. They drank the last dregs of the intoxicating cup and began the melancholy death song. Occuna was dashed into pieces against the rocks; his faithful consort escaped, but by what miracle has never been known. The Indians of their tribe have preserved this incident by faithful tradition, and as often as any of them pass the fatal spot they make a solemn halt and commemorate the death of Occuna."

Another form of the legend is the following, which went the rounds of the newspapers in 1857:

"A squaw, being fatigued on a hot summer's day, betook herself to rest in a canoe a short distance above the Falls. She had hardly taken time to lay herself down in the bottom of the canoe before it became loosened from its moorings and the frail bark was hurled on by the current to the brink of the precipice. She gathered her blanket over her head and resigned herself to her fate, expecting to be dashed to pieces on the rocks below. Heaven had however otherwise decreed. Her boat had taken the direction which brought her to that point of the precipice where there was the greatest quantity of water. She was picked up shortly after, some distance below the Falls, senseless through fright but otherwise unscathed."

Van Der Donck said, elsewhere: "I cannot forbear to mention that in the year 1647, in the month of March, when by a great freshet, the water was fresh almost to the great bay, there were two whales of tolerable size, up the river, the one turned back, but the other stranded, and stuck not far from the great Fall of the Chahoos."[1]

The following account of this occurrence is compiled from O'Callaghan's *History of New Netherland:*

"The winter which had just terminated, was remarkably

---

[1] Judge Benson, in an article on the Dutch names of Albany and vicinity (*Annals of Albany*, vol. 2), quotes this passage and says: "The lands immediately opposite to Albany, and for a distance along and from the river, the Dutch denoted as *Het greene bosch, the pine woods,* corrupted to *Greenbush.* The *mouths* of the Mohoch they distinguished as the *Spruytes,* corrupted to, and which may also possibly pass for a translation, the *Sprouts.* The larger island formed by the sprouts they called *Walvisch Island,* Whale Island." This name, however, does not appear to have been in general use.

long and severe. The North River closed at Rensselaerswyck on the 25th November, and remained frozen some four months. A very high freshet, unequalled since 1639, followed, which destroyed a number of horses in their stables, nearly carried away the fort (Fort Orange, at Albany), and inflicted considerable other damage in the colonie. 'A certain fish of considerable size, snow white in color, round in the body, and blowing water out of its head,' made at the same time his appearance, stemming the impetuous flood. What it portended, 'God the Lord only knew.' All the inhabitants were lost in wonder, 'for at the same instant that this fish appeared to us, we had the first thunder and lightning this year.' The public astonishment had scarcely subsided when another monster of the deep, estimated at forty feet in length, was seen, of a brown color, having fins on his back, and ejecting water in like manner, high in the air. Some seafaring people 'who had been to Greenland' now pronounced the strange visitor a whale. Intelligence was shortly after received that it had grounded on an island at the mouth of the Mohawk, and the people turned out in numbers to secure the prize, which was, forthwith, subjected to the process of roasting in order to extract its oil. Though large quantities were obtained, yet so great was the mass of blubber, the river was covered with grease for three weeks afterwards, and the air infected to such a degree with the stench, as the fish lay rotting on the strand, that the smell was perceptibly offensive for two (Dutch) miles to leeward."

The journal of Jasper Dankers and Peter Sluyter, two members of the society of Labadists, who came here from Holland to procure a site for a colony of their sect, contains the following, under date of 23d April, 1660:

"Mr. Sanders having provided us with horses, we rode out about nine o'clock, to visit the Cahoos, which is the Falls of the great *Maquas Kil* (Mohawk River), which are the greatest falls not only in New Netherland, but in North America, and perhaps, as far as is known, in the whole new world. "We rode for two hours over beautiful, level, tillable land along the river when we obtained a guide who was better acquainted with the road through the woods. He rode before us on horseback. In approaching the Cahoos from this direction the roads are hilly, and in the course of half an hour you have steep hills, deep valleys and narrow paths, which run round the precipices, where you must ride with care, in order to avoid the danger of falling over them, as sometimes happens. As you come near the Falls, you can hear the roaring which makes everything tremble, but on reaching them and looking at them, you see something wonderful, a great manifestation of God's power and sovereignty, of his wisdom and glory. We arrived there about noon. They are on one of the two branches into which the North River is divided up above, of almost equal size. This one turns to the west out of the highlands, and coming here finds a blue rock which has a steep side as long as the river is broad, which, according to my calculation, is two hundred paces or more, and rather more than less, and about one hundred feet high. The river has more water at one time than another, and was now about six or eight feet deep. All this volume of water coming on this side fell headlong upon a stony bottom, this distance of an hundred feet. Any one may judge whether that was not a spectacle, and whether it would not make a noise. There is a continual spray thrown up by the dashing of the water, and when the sun shines the figure of a rainbow may be seen through it. Sometimes there are two or three of them to be seen, one above the other, according to the brightness of the sun and its parallax. There was now more water than usual in consequence of its having rained hard for several days, and the snow water having begun to run down from the high land."

In 1699, the Earl of Bellomont, who was engaged in examining the country for the best means of procuring naval supplies for the king, wrote as follows to the Lords of Trade, in a report dated Boston, Oct. 20:

"I am glad to find there are pines of eleven and twelve feet about, for either of those sizes is big enough for a first-rate ship, as I am informed, and I am satisfied the trees might be floated down the great Fall (which I have been at) and then they will be the cheapest in the world, for they may be floated all down Hudson's River to the ship's sides that take 'em in to carry them to England. In summer, when there is not a flood in the river, I grant it would hazard the breaking such heavy trees to let them tumble down that great Fall, but in winter I cannot believe there's the least hazard. I stood looking a good while at that

Fall. It is at least six hundred yards broad and in the highest place about fifty foot high. Tis eight miles above Albany due north. The river while I was there was shallow for about a mile below the Fall, and rocky except just under the Fall which the people that were my guides assured me was six fathom deep, and the mighty and continual fall of water seems to have made the cavity in the rock, for that it was solid rock, I could plainly perceive ; to be sure the season of the year must be watched when there are floods in the river and then I am confident those trees may be safely floated, especially if the water be so deep at the foot of the Fall as I was told, for then the depth of the water will break the fall of the trees, besides there is an art to save one of those great trees from breaking with its fall by binding lesser trees about it."

Another report on the same subject was made May 13, 1701, by Robert Livingston, who wrote from New York:

"As to the production of masts and other naval stores in this province I beg leave to inform your Lordships that I am told those that are already cut are not so large as the dimensions the Earl did notify, but are much less, and are now on ground above the Falls, and cannot be got down until the fall of the leafe, that the rivers are up ; that there is no experiment made of getting any down the Fall. Some are of opinion that the fall will spoil them, some otherwise. It is about forty foot perpendicular and for two miles above it, shelving ; which makes the stream so rapid that none dare come near it with a canoe. I doubt the masts will receive injury in the falling."

In the report made to Queen Anne in 1709, by the Board of Trade, in regard to the settlement of a colony of Palatines (afterwards established near Little Falls) the country about the Mohawk is recommended as being eligible, and, it is added :

"The objection that may be made to the seating of the Palatines on the fore mentioned Mohaques River is the Falls that are on the said river between Schenectady and Albany which will be an interruption in the water carriage, but that may be easily helped by a short land carriage of about three miles at the west."

It was decided on this account to locate the colony elsewhere, as appears from a report of Perry, Keill and Du Pré made to the London Board of Trade 11th Dec., 1711, in which it is stated that the country of the Maquaas was not selected "because their lands are distant from the river nearly twenty miles, and Schenectady besides a waterfall of six hundred feet high, hath the same inconveniency upon which account the carriage of anything would cost as much if not more than its worth."

The obstruction afforded by the Falls to navigation is thus noticed in a report dated 1757, found in the Paris documents :

"Going from Chenectedi (Schenectady) to Orange (Albany) there is a Great Fall which prevents the passage of batteaux so that everything on the river going from Chenectedi to Orange passes over the high road that leads there direct."

In the *Memoirs of an American Lady* by Mrs. Anne Grant, who was living in Albany between 1757 and 1768, appears the following on the same subject, with reference to the journeys of the traders from Albany into the Indian country :

" There commenced their toils and dangers at the famous water fall called the Cohoes, ten miles above Albany . . . . This was the Rubicon which they had to pass before they plunged into pathless woods, ingulphing swamps and lakes, the opposite shores of which the eye could not reach. At the Cohoes, on account of the obstruction formed by the torrent, they unloaded their canoe, and carried it above a mile further on their shoulders, returning again for the cargo, which they were obliged to transport in the same manner."

In 1760, the Falls were visited by Gov. Thos. Pownall, a man who held several positions of importance in this country, and was prominent among those Englishmen who at home a few years later, defended the action of the colonies in revolting from the crown. Among several interesting volumes which he published in regard to America was one

(London, 1776), which contained a map of this country, and topographical descriptions of the parts he had visited. In this he describes at considerable length the appearance of the Falls, saying that he had seen them once before when the rocks were almost entirely bare, but at this time, June 25th, the volume of water was immense. After speaking of the grandeur and beauty of the sight he says :

"In other parts, where it shoots over in a sheet of water, there is a peculiar circumstance which struck me, and which I will endeavor to explain ; there are every now and then violent explosions of air which burst through the surface of the torrent, and as I considered it attentively on the spot, I explained it as follows to myself : The air which is contained and pent in between the rock and the arch of the torrent must, by the violent motion of this torrent, be heated and rarefied, and if so will of course break out in explosions. The vapors which fly off from this Fall disperse themselves, and fall in heavy showers for near half a mile round the place. These Falls the Indians call by the expressive name Cohoes."

Gov. Pownall made a sketch of the Falls at this time, which he took back to England, and there had it painted, engraved and published. One of the original prints, which are now extremely rare, is in the possession of Joseph Chadwick, Esq., of this city, and is remarkably well preserved.

The title of the picture is as follows : "A view of the great Cohoes Falls on the Mohawk River. The Fall about seventy feet, the river near a quarter of a mile broad. Sketched on the spot by his excellency Gov. Pownall, painted by Paul Sanby, and engraved by William Elliott, May, 1761." A steel engraving of this print, much smaller than the original, forms the frontispiece to this volume. Gov. Pownall mentions another sketch of the Falls, taken when the water was low, and published some years previous by an English traveler named Calm, which he says was an inferior production, and so poorly done as to give the Falls the general appearance of a mill-dam.

The interruption to navigation before spoken of, was the means of adding considerably to the business of Schenectady, as appears from the following taken from the papers of the *Mass. Historical Coll.*, and dated 1792. "It (Schenectady) stands upon the Mohawk River about nine miles above the Falls called the Cohoes, but this I take to be the Indian name for falls; its chief business is to receive the merchandize from Albany and put into batteaux, to go up the river and forward to Albany such produce of the back country as is sent to market."

It will be observed that of the writers who have been quoted nearly all speak of the Falls in terms of the highest admiration. The Duke de la Rochefoucault Liancourt, an exile of the French revolution, who visited this place in 1795, does not, however, appear to have been particularly impressed. Concerning the Falls (which he called *Xohos*, and his translator corrected to *Cohoez*) he said:

"But the river contains not at present sufficient water to support the Falls. In many places the rocks are quite dry; but in others they afford a fine prospect. The perpendicular height of the Falls may amount to about fifty feet, and the river is about an eighth of a mile in width. But upon the whole the view is not strikingly wild, romantic or pleasant, though the Falls are much celebrated throughout America."

The following description of this neighborhood, from *Travels in the United States and Canada*, 1795-97, by Isaac Weld Jr., though giving no new observations in regard to the Falls, is worthy of notice as containing a reference, one of the earliest on record, to the existence of a settlement here:

"Early the next morning we set off and in about two hours arrived at the small village of Cohoz close to which is the remarkable Fall in the Mohawk River. * * The appearance of this Fall varies very much according to the quantity of water; when the river is full the water descends in an unbroken sheet from one bank to the other whilst at other times the greater part of the rocks are left uncovered.

The rocks are of a remarkable dark color and so also is the earth in the banks which rise to a great height on either side. There is a very pleasing view of this Cataract as you pass over the bridge across the river, about three-quarters of a mile lower down."

A very inferior drawing of the Falls (referred to by Moore, see note below) was published by Mr. Weld.

In 1800, the Falls were visited by John Maude, an Englishman, who writes in his journal as follows :

"Cross the Mohawk, over the bridge at the foot of the Cohoes Falls, near which I breakfasted at Forth's tavern.[1] After breakfast I visited the celebrated cataract of the Cohoes, and strange to say, I was more pleased with it now that I had seen Niagara, than I was five years ago when I beheld it with disappointment."

The visit of Thomas Moore to the Falls, during 1804, has become famous as suggesting the composition of the following poem, which is widely known and quoted.

LINES.

"WRITTEN AT THE COHOS, OR FALLS OF THE MOHAWK RIVER."[2]

" Gia era in loco ove s'udia 'l rimbombo.
Del acqua . . . "— *Dante.*

From rise of morn till set of sun
I have seen the mighty Mohawk run,
And as I marked the woods of pine
Along his mirror darkly shine,
Like tall and gloomy forms that pass
Before the wizard's midnight glass :
And as I viewed the hurrying pace
With which he ran his turbid race,
Rushing, alike untir'd and wild,
Through shades that frowned and flowers that smiled,
Flying by every green recess

---

[1] I have been unable to ascertain positively the locality of this tavern. There was an inn kept by a man named *Ford*, just this side of Gibbonsville (now West Troy), and on the north side of the river were settled several families of *Forts*, one at Fort's Ferry, another at the *Halve Maan*.

[2] " There is a dreary and savage character in the country immediately about these Falls, which is more in harmony with the wildness of such a scene, than the cultivated lands in the neighborhood of Niagara. See the drawing of them in Mr. Weld's book. According to him the perpendicular height of the Cohos Falls is fifty feet, but the Marquis de Chastellux makes it seventy-six. The fine rainbow which is continually forming and dissolving as the spray rises with the light of the sun, is perhaps the most interesting beauty which these wonderful cataracts exhibit."

> That woo'd him to its calm caress,
> Yet, sometimes turning with the wind,
> As if to leave one look behind !
> Oh ! I have thought, and thinking sigh'd—
> How like to thee, thou restless tide !
> May be the lot, the life of him,
> Who roams along thy water's brim !
> Through what alternate shades of woe,
> And flowers of joy my path may go !
> How many a humble, still retreat
> May rise to court my weary feet,
> While still pursuing, still unblest,
> I wander on, nor dare to rest !
> But urgent as the doom that calls
> Thy water to its destined falls,
> I see the world's bewildering force
> Hurry my heart's devoted course
> From lapse to lapse, till life be done,
> And the last current cease to run !
> Oh, may my falls be bright as thine !
> May heaven's forgiving rainbow shine
> Upon the mist that circles me,
> As soft, as now it hangs o'er thee !

It has been stated, but with what authority I cannot say, that the house occupied by Moore during his stay here, was afterward owned by G. M. Cropsey, and was standing until recently at Northside. In relation to this, the following, published in the *Albany Evening Journal* in 1859, will be of interest: " About the 5th of June, 1839, Moore received a letter from some person, a resident of the village of Cohoes, which so attracted his notice that he spoke of it to Daniel Webster, whom, on the 9th of June, he met at dinner. The point in the letter of interest now is that the writer claimed to have identified and visited the cottage occupied by Moore when at Cohoes, and the walk near the Falls frequented by him." In a letter from Moore to his mother, written from Saratoga, July 10th, 1804, is the following reference to his visit.

"Two or three days ago I was to see the Coho Falls on the Mohawk River, and was truly gratified. The immense fall of the river over a natural dam of thirty or forty feet high, its roar among the rocks, and the illuminated mist of spray which rises from its foam, were to me objects all new, beautiful, and impressive. I never can forget the scenery of this country, and if it had but any endearing associations of the heart (to diffuse that charm over it, without which the fairest features of nature are but faintly interesting), I should regret very keenly that I cannot renew often the enjoyment of its beauties. But it has none such for me, and I defy the barbarous natives to forge one chain of attachment for any heart, that has ever felt the sweets of delicacy, or refinement. I believe I must except the *women* from this denunciation ; they are certainly flowers of every climate and here waste their sweetness most deplorably."[1]

Among the latest descriptions of the Falls in which new points of interest are touched upon, is that of Timothy Dwight, president of Yale College, who was in the habit of making annual tours through this neighborhood. Writing in 1811, he said : " The river was low, but I was better pleased with the appearance of the cataract than at any time heretofore. The face of the precipice was sensibly worn since 1802, and presented more and bolder varieties to the view than at that time. A great deal of the precipice was naked."

When, with the progress of the present century, the lines of travel in this country became extended, Niagara and other cataracts by their superior grandeur rendered the Cohoes Falls less an object of interest, and the number of tourists thither decreased. To visitors in this neighborhood of later years, other features of the place have seemed more important, and the Falls, once the sole attraction, have received but passing mention.

---

[1] *Memoirs, Journal and Correspondence of Thomas Moore, Edited by the Rt. Hon. Lord John Russell, M.P.*, vol. i, London, 1853.

II.
COHOES AS A FARMING HAMLET.

THE greater part of the land on which the city of Cohoes now stands was originally in the Manor of Rensselaerswyck, and was purchased from the Indians in 1630. A charter of privileges and exemptions had been granted in the preceding year, for the encouragement of patroons to settle colonies, and Kiliaen Van Rensselaer, a pearl merchant in Amsterdam, and a director of the Dutch West India Company, was one of those who availed themselves of its advantages.

At different times during the next seven years the agents of this gentleman purchased for him tracts of land in this vicinity, until his domain extended twenty-four miles along the Hudson River, and twenty-four miles on each side of the river, east and west, embracing the land which now composes the counties of Albany, Rensselaer, and part of Columbia. The northern boundary of this manor was on the line of the Cohoes Falls, running along what was afterward known as *Cohoes Lane* and still later as the *Boght Road* and *Manor Avenue*. The land north of this manor line, which is now within the city limits, was given by the Indians to Illetie or Hilletie (Alice), the wife of Pieter Danielse Van Olinde. She was the daughter of Cornelis Antonissen Van Slyck, and was a half-breed, her mother being a Mohawk woman. She acted for many years as interpretess for the province, and as such was frequently mentioned in the journals of Dankers and Sluyter, before quoted. The Mohawk sachems gave her, in 1667, the Great Island at Niskayuna, and also land at Willow Flat, below Port Jackson and at the Boght, in Watervliet.[1]

The islands at the mouth of the Mohawk, which were in

---

[1] The land northwest of the city, which was settled at an early day by the Van Denberg and other families, was originally included in a patent granted to Peter Hendrickse De Haas in 1697.

early years a favorite resort of the Indians — one of their strong holds, Moenimines Castle, being situated on Haver Island — came into possession of Capt. Goosen Gerritse Van Schaick, brewer, of Albany. In 1664, he, together with Philip Pieterse Schuyler, was granted permission to purchase the *Halve Maan* from the Indians " to prevent those of Connecticut purchasing it." This grant, commonly known as the Van Schaick or Half-Moon patent, included the present village of Waterford, and part of Half-Moon. Its name is derived from the crescent shape of the land lying between the Hudson and the Mohawk at that point.[1]

Under the terms of the charter it became the duty of Mr. Van Rensselaer to encourage the settlement of the tract of which he was possessor, and in 1630, and succeeding years, numbers of colonists came over from Holland and were provided with good farms and comfortable homes in Fort Orange (Albany) and vicinity. The first settlers in the neighborhood of Cohoes belonged to or were descended from those families and were located on the *Halve Maan*, at Waterford, or on the Mohawk Flats near Niskayuna — then called *Nestigione* or *Conistigione*.

Of the land which is now within the limits of the city, Cohoes Island, afterwards known as Van Schaick's and Adams' Island, appears to have been the part first placed under cultivation. This, together with Haver Island (*Haver* being the Dutch for oats), which adjoins it on the north, was occupied at an early day, and references to them in the old records are frequent. Capt. Van Schaick, the original owner, died about 1676, and some of his property was disposed of by his widow, as appears from the following and other deeds among the early records of Albany county:

" Appeared before me Robert Livingston, secretary etc., and in presence of the after named witnesses, Annetie Lie-

---

[1] This tract, it will be seen, was of considerable size, and as many of the farmers living in this vicinity were described in the old records merely as living at the *Halve Maan*, it leads to some difficulty in preserving the identity of the different families. Waterford was taken off from the original township in 1816, and Clifton Park in 1828.

vens widow of Goose Gerritse Van Schaick deceased, of the one side, and Jan Jacobse Van Noortstrant of the other side, who declared that they had in amity and friendship made a bargain with each other for the sale of a piece of land lying to the north of the fourth branch or fork [*Spruyt*] of the Mohawk River above the colony Rensselaerswyck, being a part of a parcel of land called the foreland of the Half Moon, and by the Indians Mathahenaach, together with about two morgens of cleared land lying on the island which lies directly over against the aforesaid parcel of land, commonly called Haver [Oats] Island, . . . for which two parcels of land Jan Jacobse Van Noortstrant promises to deliver the sum of sixty and six whole beavers,[1] to be paid in wheat, oats, or other grain, cattle, work, etc., at market prices. . . . Thus done in Albany the 26th of June, 1677, in presence of Mr. Gerrit Banker and Harme Rutgers as witnesses hereto invited."

Van Schaick's Island, however, remained in possession of the family, who, though not residing there, appear to have rented it to different parties living in the vicinity. Thus, Guert Hendrickse Van Schoonhoven, spoken of as belonging at the *Halve Maan* in 1675, had a farm on the island in 1681, as did also Harmon Lieviense or Lieverse, while Roeloff Gerritse Van Der Werken was an occupant of it in 1680.

The first settlement on this side of the river was somewhat later, though the exact date cannot be ascertained, and was made in the neighborhood of *the Boght* at the northwest of the city.[2]

---

[1] A beaver skin was worth about eight guilders or $3.20 in our currency.

[2] "Boght, *het boght*, is a locality situated within the town of Watervliet. Spafford, in his Gazetteer, says this word means a cove or bay. This is wrong. The Dutch Dictionary tells us the signification is a 'bend or turn,' so this place. It was settled by branches of the Fort and Fonda families at a very early period; we regret that we have not been able to ascertain the precise time. Exploring and hunting parties from Albany for many years after its settlement made the Boght as well as Niskayuna and Schenectady places of frequent resort. Those Albanians too, dealt in contraband goods, and carried on a trade in furs with the Mohawks at Schenectady contrary to the ordinance of the common council of Albany, and passed through this place and Niskayuna on their way to Schenectady to avoid suspicion."— *Prof. Pearson.*

During the first half of the eighteenth century the land adjoining the river which now forms the principal part of the city, and a tract near its western boundaries, about a mile from the river, was settled by several families of Lansings, and the families of Heamstreet (Heemstraat or Von Heemstraaten), Ouderkirk, Liverse (Lieverse or Lievense), Fonda and Clute; of whom the Lansings appear to have come from Albany, and the others from Niskayuna or the Half Moon.

The date at which that part of the land which was within the manor was first occupied cannot be definitely ascertained; for as it was under the jurisdiction of the patroon, no public record was made of leases or conveyances to farmers. Deeds are in existence, however, of the lands north of the manor line which belonged to the Van Olinde family, showing the dates at which they were sold to other parties, and it is probable that all the families above named settled here about the same time. Among the earliest of these transfers was one of a woodland lot of over one hundred acres situated just north of the manor line which was sold by Daniel Van Olinde, eldest son of Pieter and Illetie Van Olinde, to Walran Clut or Clute.

The following is an abstract of the deed :

"THIS INDENTURE, made and Concluded on the four and Twentieth day of November in the Seventh Yeare of The Reign of our Sovereing Lord George. By the Grace of God of Great Britain franc and Ireland KING defender of The faith, etc., and In the year of our Lord, one Thousand Seven hundred and Twenty by and Between Daniel Van Olinde of the County of Albany in the province of New Yorke Yeoman of the one part, and Walran Clut of the same county of the other part WITNESSETH THAT HE THE SAID Daniell Van Olinde, for and In consideration of fourty Two pounds of currant Lawfull money of New Yorke to him In hand paid Before the Ensealing and Delivery of This presents the Receipt Whereof he The Said Daniel Van Olinde

Doth hereby acknowledge and him Self therewith full Satisfied and Contented and Thereof and of every part and parcell Thereof Doth fully and absolutely Exonerate and Discharge The Said Walran Clut his heirs executors administrators and assigns By These presents hath Granted Released and Confirmed . . Bargained and sold . . . and doth hereby sell unto the Said Walran Clute his heirs and assigns for Ever All That Certain Tract or Pacall of Wood Land Scituate Lying and Being within the county off Albany aforesaid on The South Side of The Mohaks or Schaneghtendy River between Cahoos and Canastojoind [Conistigione or Niskayuna] is Bounded, etc. One The East End Thereof by the Great fall caled the Cahoos aforesaid and on the West Running along The Line of the manner of Renselaers Wick Till you come by a Kill which is called the boghts' Kly Kuyll or Kly Kill by the land of one Hendrik Rider which land is also (illegible) * * transported by the aforesaid Danell Van Olinde Into him The Said Hendrik Rider, and so along that Said Land Till you come again upon The Aforesaid Kly Kill and Then along The Said Kill Till you come To The River aforesaid and So along The Said River To The Cahoos where first begon — provided alwais and for Ever hereafter that he The said Walran Clut and his heirs and assigns Shall Leave one wagon road along the river for The Use of The Neighbourhood, ... It is further agreed by and between the Said Daniel Van Olinde and Walran Clut for theire Self and there heirs for ever that he the Said Clute has free Liberty to build one or more Saw Mills or Grind Mills and To Ly Dams provided that in Case The aforesaid Walran Clute his heirs or assigns Shall come to buld a Saw mill and Saw Loggs out of the right of him the said Daniel his heirs and assigns that Then and In such case he the said Walran Clute his heirs and assigns shall pay to him the said Daniel his heirs and assigns ten Boards yearly and Every year forever, and In case a Grind Mill That Then and In such case he the said Walran Clut and his heirs and assigns shall forever grind for Daniel Van Olinde and his heirs and assigns, for one famaly that Shall Life upon the Land where the said Daniel now Lifes on . . .

. . . IN WITNESS WHEREOF THE parties To These presents

Indenture have Interchangeabley put their hands and Seald The Day and Year first above writting

Signed Scald and Delivered   DANIEL VAN OLINDE [L. S.]
    In the presence of
        Mynders Schuyler Justice
        John De Peyster
        Evert Wendell.

The farm directly north of this, embracing about two hundred acres, was sold by Daniel Van Olinde to Gerret Lansing in May, 1740. The dates of these transfers and other facts in regard to the matter which are accessible, afford fair evidence that the first general settlement of the place was made between 1725 and 1750.

It is almost impossible to obtain in detail an accurate account of the early inhabitants; in most cases there is nothing to show the date at which their farms were cleared or their houses built, and with one or two exceptions but few facts can be given in regard to their family history. Under these circumstances the history of Cohoes, while it was but a farming community, must necessarily be incomplete. From records in existence, however, it is possible to identify the different farm houses, some of which still remain, and to give the boundaries of the principal farms as they were held by the original settlers.

In a map of the manor of Rensselaerswyck made for the patroon by John R. Bleeker, surveyor, in 1767, the following houses appear on the land now included within the city limits, most of them near the river, and the main road, now Saratoga street:

Henry Lansing's, opposite the upper end of Green Island. This house, situated a short distance below the *Old Junction* near the canal, is now occupied by Lucius Alexander. It has been altered and enlarged from time to time, and the original building is still in good condition.[1]

---

[1] The property of Henry or Hendrik Lansing was afterwards sold to Jacob H. Lansing who occupied the farm-house for many years. William Lansing, his son, occupied the house on the opposite side of the road, and it is said, kept a tavern

Lansing's, on the opposite (west) side of the road from the above and a little to the south. This house is said to have been burned, but at what date is not known.

Cornelis Ouderkerk's,[1] opposite the lower end of Van Schaick's Island. This house was last occupied by a family named Conaughty, after having been for some years occupied as a tavern. It stood on the west bank of the Champlain Canal, a short distance below Tighes' brewery near Newark street, and was torn down in 1865.

Derek Heamstreet's,[2] a few rods north of Ouderkerk's. Part of this building, located between the canal and the river, directly east of the brewery, still remains, and is now in possession of John P. Weber. It was partially destroyed by fire, Dec. 2, 1868. The lower part of the building remains the same as before, but the Dutch gable roof was burned, and replaced by the flat roof now seen. This, like all the other old farm houses in the neighborhood, was built to last, and none of its material was light or flimsy. The old barn, which stood near the house, was a most massive structure. It was built throughout of the heaviest and best selected timber; the flooring was of five inch plank hewn by hand, and the roof was covered with four feet cedar shingles, secured by wrought nails. The building was purchased some years since by George E. Simmons, and when it was torn down enough material was found in it to serve for the construction of two barns of modern style.

---

there in the early part of the present century. Descendants of the family, among them Abraham F. Lansing of this city, and Dow F. Lansing of Albany, are yet living.

[1] The Ouderkerk family do not appear to have long resided here, and in accounts which are found in old records they are mentioned as being from the Half Moon. Several marriages between this family and the Fondas are recorded in the middle of the last century, which may account for the fact that the farm afterwards came into possession of the Fonda family. The house was occupied in 1815, by Harmon Fonda, who owned the farm together with his brother Dow I. Fonda. Their descendants still live in this vicinity, some of them in Watervliet.

[2] Derek Heamstreet was succeeded by Charles Heamstreet, who became one of the principal farmers in the neighborhood. He had five sons: Richard, Albert, John,

John Lansing's,[1] on the west side of the highway, a short distance south of the manor line. This was destroyed a number of years ago, and the house at present occupied by Egbert W. Lansing erected nearly on its site.

Frederick Clute's.[2] Outside of the manor, and a few rods north of the Lansing house, on the brow of the hill. This was a log house. A frame house was afterwards built by Gerret Clute, son of the above, on the bank of the river, a short distance above the Falls, where traces of it are still discernible. It was destroyed during the progress of the Cohoes Company's improvements in 1832 or thereabouts.

Frans Lansing's, Dow Fonda's and Wm. Liverse's. These were located at different points some distance west of the river, and nearly on the line of the present western boundary of the city.

Van Schaick's House,[3] on Van Schaick Island. This

Jacob and Philip. Richard occupied the farm known as the Gerret Witbeck farm; and John built the small yellow house yet standing on Saratoga street, opposite the brewery. Richard had four sons: Garret, Charles, William and Stephen, of whom one (Charles) is now living in Clifton Park. Albert had four sons: Charles, Henry, Jacob and Abraham. The name is given above as it appears on the patroon's books. It is now spelled *Hemstreet*.

[1] John (or *Johannes*) J. Lansing was born in 1719, and died in 1813. He had ten children, one of whom, Andrew (born 1760, died 1835), succeeded him in possession of the farm. Andrew had four sons: John, Jacob, Evert and Abram, the latter of whom (born 1790, died 1867), was a well known citizen. Two of his sons, Egbert W., and John V. S. Lansing, are now living in Cohoes, the former occupying the old farm.

[2] Frederick Clute was the son of Walraven or Waldron Clute, who bought the farm from Daniel Van Olinda. His grandfather, also named Frederick Clute, came from Kingston about 1703, and settled at Niskayuna, where he bought land of Johannes Clute.
Frederick the younger was born 1724, and married Maria De Ridder, Nov., 1754. His oldest son, Gerret Clute, was born Feb. 29, 1761, and occupied the farm until the early part of the present century. Gerret Clute had ten children, as follows: Maria, wife of Richard Hemstreet, Getty, wife of John Hemstreet, Anna, wife of James Ostrander, William, Kate, Matthew, Rachel, Henrietta, wife of John Johnson, Charles, and ———. The oldest son William, was the father of ex-Justice Harvey Clute now of this city.

[3] Sybrant, the second son, of Capt. Goosen Gerritse Van Schaick, was born 1653, and died about 1685. He had four children, of whom the third, Anthony, was born in 1681, and lived in Albany, being by trade a glazier. His second son, Wessel, was

house, which is the best preserved of the old buildings now in the city, was erected in 1762, and has since been altered but little. The only change in the front of the house is a new porch which was built by Mr. Adams a year or two ago. The old windows, with their heavy sashes and diminutive panes, and the old fashioned divided door with its massive brass knocker and ponderous iron bar still remain. The bricks of which the house was built were made on the island, with the exception of a few of peculiar curved shape, which form a sort of ridge or coping extending around the body of the house about four feet from the ground — those having been brought from Holland. The wooden house now standing a few rods south of the old mansion was built certainly over a century ago, and perhaps before the brick building.

The homestead of Gerret Lansing,[1] on the farm just north of Frederick Clute's, though not marked on this map, was in existence at the time. It was located near the site of the red brick house (built by Rutger Lansing, son of Gerret, in 1790), which yet stands near the Cohoes Company's dam.

The boundaries between the different farms do not appear to have been definitely fixed by the patroon, nor were leases for them regularly drawn until towards the close of the last century. This may be accounted for on the ground that as the Van Rensselaers were desirous of encouraging the settlement of their domain, no rents were at first exacted, and owing to the vast extent of the manor, farmers were allowed to settle in different parts of it and occupy the land for many years before arrangements were made for the regular collection of tithes.

The maps of the original farms in this neighborhood, as

---

born in 1712. He had five children. His second son, John Gerritse, was born Oct. 23, 1748. In 1805, he had a house and store on the west side of Broadway, Albany. He died on Van Schaick's Island, July 7, 1828. His youngest son, Henry, died at Lansingburgh, Oct. 7, 1829, aged 33 years. The last member of the Van Schaicks to occupy the island was the first husband of Mrs. Wm. L. Adams.

[1] Gerret Rutger Lansing was the son of Rutger. After his death the farm came itno the possession of his son, Isaac D. F. Lansing, born 1790, died Nov. 12, 1874.

surveyed under direction of the patroon, are preserved in the Van Rensselaer office. A map showing the relation of the farm boundaries to the streets, as at present laid out, would be of interest, but the preparation of one which would be suitable for publication with this sketch has not seemed feasible. The following description of the outlines of the principal farms, with references to streets and localities which are now familiar, giving the names of their occupants as recorded in the patroon's books, and a sketch of the subsequent disposition of the property, will, it is hoped, be sufficient to give a general idea of the way in which the land was divided.

Commencing at the lower part of the settlement, the first farm was one which formed part of the tract disposed of by the patroon to Col. Schuyler, and was known in later years as the Jacob H. Lansing farm. It extended on the south to a line which is now the southern limit of the city (near Cedar Grove) and had for part of its boundary the *Soult Kill* (Salt Brook). Its northern limit was a line running nearly parallel with the brook which flows eastward through the ravine south of the residence of Samuel Bilbrough on Main street, and is carried under Saratoga street a short distance below its junction with Main street. This land, the farm house on which, occupied by Henry Lansing, has been before mentioned, had been sold by Killian Van Rensselaer to Col. Philip Schuyler, May 10, 1708, and was held by him until 1731, when it was sold to Hendrick Lansing. On January 15th, 1774, " the fourteenth year of the reign of our sovereign King George the Third" it was sold by "Hendrick Lansing, mason or bricklayer of the Boght, county of Albany and province of New York unto Jacob H. Lansing, yeoman, for the consideration of four hundred pounds, lawful money." In his possession it remained until 1822, when it was sold to R. P. Hart, and has been since disposed of in lots to various parties, though some yet remains in the hands of the Hart estate.

Next was the Jacob D. Fonda farm, bounded on the south by the Lansing farm above described and having for its northern limit a line which commenced at the river and ran northwest, passing the south end of the brewery (on Saratoga street below Newark) reaching Columbia street near where it is crossed by the Central rail road and extending along the old line of that street to a point near the cemetery. The house on this farm was that which was occupied by Cornelis Ouderkirk in 1767. The land, comprising 136½ acres, was leased to Jacob D. Fonda, Dec. 16th, 1794, for the consideration of "fifteen bushels wheat, four hens and one day's service."

Early in the present century it was bought by Abraham G. Lansing, who built about 1820, as a country residence, the house afterwards occupied by Wm. N. Chadwick and at present by Samuel Bilbrough. A large part of the farm afterward came into possession of Messrs. Bayard Clark and Wm. N. Chadwick, by whom it was sold to Gould & Tracy, who disposed of it to various parties. A number of lots in the western part of the city, beyond the Central rail road, have remained until within a few years in possession of the Lansing heirs.

Above the Fonda farm was that of Charles Heamstreet, the northern boundary of which was very irregular. A portion of it ran nearly parallel with White street as at present laid out; commencing at a point on Mohawk street in rear of the school house now built on the corner of White and Mohawk streets, it ran westward until it reached Sargent street, near the site of Bogue's block. This was the boundary of the middle portion of the farm. On both sides, however, it extended much further to the north. On the right, commencing at White street, the line ran up Mohawk street almost to Oneida, when it turned to the northeast, striking the river a few rods west of the present rail road bridge.

---

[1] These farms were granted from the patroon on perpetual leases.

On the other (western side) the line, commencing at Sargent street, ran north until it reached a point near Lock 14, and then ran west about to the location of the bridge over the Central rail road, at Johnston avenue. This farm, which originally comprised 205½ acres, was leased to Charles Heamstreet, April 15, 1793, for the annual rent of "twenty-seven bushels of wheat, four fat fowls and a day's service with carriage and horses."

It was sold in part in 1822, for $8,500 to R. P. Hart, with whom Ebenezer Wiswall, Philip Schuyler and Jno. P. Cushman afterward held a joint interest, and by them was disposed of to various parties. One section, embracing the land near White street, was for some time in possession of Hugh White.

North of the Heamstreet farm was one comprising seventy-three acres which was leased in January, 1794, to Gerrit Witbeck, concerning whose residence nothing has been ascertained. The annual rental was "three bushels and three pecks of wheat, four fat fowls, and one day's service with carriage and horses." The boundary of this farm ran about northeast along by the present Erie Canal, until it reached a point near Harmony Mill No. 2, when it turned to the east and followed the *Diepe gat*, or *Diepe-gat Kil*,[1] which emptied into the river a short distance below Harmony Mill No. 3. The lease of this farm was assigned to Lucas G. Witbeck, in 1801. It soon afterward came into the possession of the Heamstreet family and was assigned to Derek Heamstreet, in 1802. The farm was occupied for a number of years by Richard Heamstreet, whose house was situated on Mohawk street between Oneida and Factory streets, on the site now occupied by

---

[1] This *Diepe gat* or *deep cut* which has since been so completely filled in and covered that all traces of it have been obliterated, was a rocky gorge, so dark and gloomy that it was the terror of the children of the neighborhood. The brook which flowed through it was called by them *Spook kil* and the bridge which crossed it became known among the farmers as the Spook's bridge.

the south part of Witbeck's block.[1] It was sold by the sheriff to Ebenezer Wiswall, Oct. 2, 1819, and was purchased from him by Canvass White, March 17, 1824, from whose hands it passed into the possession of the Cohoes Company.

The next farm was that of Andrew Lansing, comprising 211 acres, which was leased to him March 24th, 1813, at an annual rent of eighteen bushels of wheat, with the usual consideration of fowls and service. It was bounded on the north by the manor line, or present Boght road, and on the south by the lines of the Witbeck and Heamstreet farms. A large portion of this farm, comprising much of the land now occupied by the Harmony Company, was sold to the Cohoes Company by Mr. Lansing in 1831; and other parts of it are still in possession of the family. The eastern boundary of this farm was the old road, which ran nearly the same as the present Mohawk street. The strip between the road and the river, extending from the *Diepe gat* to the Falls, remained in possession of the patroon, until it was sold to the Cohoes Company in 1836.[2]

The eastern limits of these five farms, with the exception in the case of Andrew Lansing's just mentioned, was the river. Their western boundaries were irregular and as they extended in most cases beyond the limits which now mark the thickly settled portions of the city, need not be particularly described. Taking the Gerret Witbeck lot as part of the Heamstreet farm (as it was in effect for many years), it may be said that all the farms extended at least as far west as the present Cohoes Cemetery, while those of Andrew

---

[1] This building was destroyed by fire February 13, 1858, having been for some time unoccupied.

[2] It is said that this strip was offered, in the early part of the century, to Evert Lansing, and his brother, if they would pay the back rent upon it, but as they declined to do so it was kept by the Van Rensselaers and on the formation of the Cohoes Company, was transferred by Stephen Van Rensselaer, as part payment for his stock.

Lansing and Jacob Fonda were still deeper. The farms lying to the west of those above described, were, according to the patroon's maps, as follows: West of Andrew Lansing were the farms of Peter and Henry Fero, and Peter Lieverse; west of Charles Heamstreet and Jacob D. Fonda was the farm of Douw A. Fonda; and west of Jacob H. Lansing was a farm occupied at different times by branches of the Lansing and Fonda families. The Lieverse and Fonda farm houses have been before mentioned.

But little is to be said concerning the lands outside of the manor, which are now within the city limits, as they have been occupied as farm lands until within a few years. The Clute farm, lately known as Mrs. Miller's, situated just above the manor line and extending on the west to the present Erie Canal, remained for the greater part in possession of the family until some years ago. A portion of it in the southwest corner was, however, leased to the Van Der Mark family early in the present century, and other parts near the river were afterward sold to the Cohoes Company.

Nearly all of the Lansing farm, just north of Clute's, still remains the property of the heirs of I. D. F. Lansing, although part has been sold to the Cohoes Company.

Van Schaick's Island, comprising about 320 acres, remained the property of the family until it came into the possession of Wm. L. Adams, the present owner, about forty years since.

These farms of course furnished the principal employment of their occupants, but some of the inhabitants were also engaged, in a small way, in other business. The Lansing family, as early as 1740, were the owners of a saw mill, located a short distance north of the present site of the Cohoes Straw Board Mill, near the Cohoes Company's dam. A grist mill was afterwards built, just south of the saw mill, and the two establishments were run in partnership by Gerret and Rutger Lansing for many years. On the Clute farm a grist mill was also erected, which was located a short distance above the Falls. The establishment of a mill of some sort, evidently contemplated when the deed of the farm was drawn, may have transpired soon after the sale, but there is no record of its existence until the time of Gerret Clute, who remained for some time the proprietor. Another grist mill, which was afterwards converted into a carding mill, was located on the Heamstreet farm, on the flats just opposite Simmons's Island. It was originally conducted by Charles Heamstreet and afterwards by his son Albert.[1] The power for each of these mills was furnished by means of a wing dam extending some yards into the river, that of the Heamstreet mill being built out to a large rock in the channel which is still a prominent feature of that locality.

It will be seen that the early inhabitants of Cohoes were in comfortable circumstances. All were possessed of large and productive farms on which substantial and comfortable houses had been erected, and some in addition had their mills, which were probably well patronized by their neighbors of the Boght and other parts of Watervliet.

They were fair types of the thrifty and prosperous Dutch farmers who were the early settlers of this portion of the state, and the features of their social life were similar to those which existed throughout this neighborhood and have been often described. Among the customs which prevailed here as in other Dutch settlements was slave-holding, and from the extent of the negro burial places of which traces remain on the Heamstreet, Lansing and other farms, it is evident that each family possessed quite a number.

The following document from among the papers of the Clute family will be of interest in this connection:

"Know all men by these presents that I, Isaac J. Fonda

---

[1] The lease of the mill privilege was granted by the patroon to Charles Heamstreet Dec. 22, 1794, at an annual rental of $12.50.

of the Bought in the town of Watervleet County of Albany and State of New York for and in consideration of the sum of twenty pounds of lawful Money of the State aforementioned to me in hand paid by Gerret Clute of said place County and state above mentioned at or before the sealing and delivery of these presents the Receipt Whereof I the said Isaac J. Fonda do hereby acknowledge have granted bargained and sold and by these presents do grant bargain and sell unto the said Gerret Clute his Executors, Administrators and Asigns a Negro Boy Named Ben or Benjamin to have and to hold the said Negro Boy to the said Gerret Clute His executors administrators forever and I the said Isaac J. Fonda for myself my heirs executors and Administrators and Assigns against the said Isaac J. Fonda, my Heirs Executors and Administrators and against all and every other person and persons whatsoever shall and will warrant and forever defend by these presents the said Negro I the said Isaac J. Fonda have put the said Gerret Clute in full possession of at the sealing and delivery of these presents. In witness whereof I have hereunto set my hand and seal this day of June in the year of Our Lord one thousand seven hundred and ninety-three.

"N. B. The date of the month and the word three at the bottom or in the last line of the presents were interlined and altered before the sealing and delivery of the said presents.

"Present at the sealing and delivery Bought June Received of Mr. Gerrit Clute twenty pounds, In full for a Negro bought by the said Gerrit Clute, received by me." [1]

It is probable that until the revolution there was but little interruption to the quiet monotony of the life in this farming hamlet. The neighboring settlements being difficult of access, communication with them was limited to market days, and the inhabitants, busied from day to day with the duties of their farms or mills, were little affected by the course of events in the outside world. With the outbreak of war, however, this peaceful routine was disturbed. A number of men from this vicinity joined the

---

[1] The number of slaves in Watervliet, in 1810, was 123. All slaves in the state were emancipated in 1827.

companies which were raised in adjoining towns,[1] and this, together with the proximity of the place to the scene of many of the important events of the war, must have caused the inhabitants to regard the progress of the struggle with the deepest interest. The main road to the north, on this side of the river, passed over the islands at the mouth of the Mohawk, since the sprouts could be forded more easily than the main stream, and traces of it still remain on Adams's Island. Over this road many of the troops marched during the campaigns in this vicinity. The islands were occupied from July to October, 1777, by a force of from 4,000 to 6,000 men, stationed there by Gen. Gates, after the retreat of his army from the neighborhood of Lake Champlain. The men remained there during the operations near Saratoga and Stillwater, for the purpose of covering the rear of the American army and securing a position to fall back upon in case Burgoyne should compel a retreat. It is said that the Van Schaick house was used for the headquarters of the officers during the occupation. Fortifications were erected on Haver Island, remains of which are still visible.

In 1784, the first church in the vicinity was established. The Reformed Dutch church of the Boght, said to have been the first north of Albany, was organized by the Classis of Albany, on the petition of forty-two members of the Dutch church of that city, presented February 22. The original church building, which stood on the road running north and south at the present western limits of the city, was doubtless erected some time before the organization of the church. The first elders were David Fero and Isaac Fonda, and the first deacons were Abraham D. Fonda and Gerret I. Lansing. The first pastor called was the Rev. John Demarest who began his ministry in 1790, taking charge of the Boght church in connection with that at Nis-

---

[1] Among them were Gerret Clute, and members of the Lansing and Fonda families, but no complete list of their names can be obtained.

kayuna. He preached in Dutch, and all the records of the church during his ministry were kept in that language. The membership of the church in 1791 was 121. Rutger Lansing became one of the deacons in 1789, and Gerret R. Lansing was a deacon in 1794. This church was for many years the only one attended by the inhabitants of Cohoes, and had an important part in the early history of the place.[1]

In 1795 the first bridge across the Mohawk at Cohoes was erected. The increase in the number of inhabitants in the Half Moon and this vicinity had made the necessity of a bridge at this point for some time apparent, and as early as January, 1771, the following resolution in regard to it was passed by the common council of Albany:

---

[1] The following sketch of its history since 1800, which, together with the above facts, has been kindly furnished by the present pastor, will be of interest.

Mr. Demarest closed his ministry in 1803.

In 1805, the Rev. Dr. J. Bassett was called who remained until 1811.

In the beginning of his ministry a subscription was circulated for the purchase and erection of a stove in the church. The stove was placed upon an elevated platform in order that it might heat the church more effectually. In the ministry of Dr. Bassett the services and the church records began to be in the English language.

In 1807, a new church building was erected.

Rev. Robert Bronk became pastor in 1814. He ministered also to the church of Washington and Gibbonsville, now the South Reformed church of West Troy. Mr. Bronk resigned his charges in 1823.

In 1824, Rev. John B. Steele, of Waterford, became pastor and continued until 1833.

Rev. Cornelius Bogardus was pastor from 1833 to 1838.

Rev. William Pitcher became pastor in 1840. During his ministry, it was proposed to build a new church, and after much discussion with reference to the site, the present church was erected on the parsonage ground in 1847. At this time twenty-two members left the church and were organized as the Church of Rensselaer, and another church edifice was built at Van Vranken's Corners.

Mr. Pitcher left in 1854, and Rev. John Dubois was called who remained until 1859. Rev. John W. Major was pastor from 1860 to 1864.

In 1864, the church of the Boght united with the church of Rensselaer and called Rev. H. A. Raymond as pastor. He remained until 1871.

The present pastor, Rev. George I. Taylor, began his ministry Jan. 1st, 1874. The present members of consistory are, Elders: Gerardus Clute, Douw Lansing, Jacob Van Denberg. Deacons: Jesse Fonda, Benjamin Reamer, Wm. Lambert.

"*Resolved,* That it is the unanimous opinion of this Board that it is practicable to be done, and that considering the inconveniences the inhabitants and travelers are under at certain seasons of the year, we conceive that it will be of great use to have a bridge about that place and well worthy the Legislaters consideration. Ordered, that the Clerk of this Board enclose a Copy of this Resolution in a letter to the Members for the County of Albany. We the Mayor, Aldermen and Comonalty of the city of Albany do certify and declare that we conceive that the erecting of a Bridge below the Cahos will greatly tend for the benefit and conveniency of the publick & will in particular encourage the Settlements to the Northward of the said Bridge."

The bridge was first opened for travel July 24, 1795. It was 900 feet long, twenty-four feet wide, fifteen feet above the bed of the river and rested on thirteen stone piers. Its cost was $12,000. It was located several hundred feet west of the site of the rail road bridge, the Cohoes end being a short distance north of the present termination of Remsen street. An excavation in the rock, yet visible, marks the place where it rested upon the Waterford side. The gate house, which was on this side of the river, was for many years tended by Jacob Winnie, a blacksmith. The bridge was one of the best then existing in this part of the country, and was frequently mentioned in books of travel.

In the writings of the Count Rochefoucauld Liancourt, from which a quotation has previously been made, it was described as follows :

"This bridge is erected on the spot where the Cohoez Falls appear to the greatest advantage. It is constructed of timber and rests on stone pillars about twenty-five or thirty feet distant from each other. The masonry is not remarkable for solidity or neatness ; but the carpenter's work is exceedingly well done."

An act in regard to the bridge was passed by the legislature, April 3, 1797, in which the rates of toll were fixed as follows :

"To make adequate provision for keeping the bridge in

good repair, it is enacted: That from and after the first day of June next, the following toll shall be collected from every person crossing said bridge, viz : For every carriage crossing the said bridge and drawn by a single horse, six cents ; for every wheel carriage or sled crossing said bridge and drawn by two horses, mules, or other working cattle, the sum of eight cents ; for every carriage or sled drawn by more than two horses, two mules, or two other working cattle, at and after the rate of two cents for each additional creature ; for a man and horse or mule the sum of four cents ; for every single horse, mare, colt or mule the sum of one cent ; for every bull, ox, cow, heifer or calf, the sum of two cents, and for sheep and hogs, at and after the rate of ten cents per score."

The toll house and gates were to be erected and the collector of tolls to be appointed by "the supervisor of the town of Watervliet, and the supervisor of the town of Half Moon," who were also directed to apply the surplus money " to the clearing away and removing the rock at the northeast corner of the said bridge, and in repairing and amending the highways in the said counties of Albany and Saratoga, leading to and from the said bridge."

This act was amended by the passage of an act March 30, 1798, which appointed John Hazard of the town of Half Moon and Peter S. Schuyler of the town of Watervliet, as commissioners " with full power yearly and every year hereafter, on the first Tuesday in May to sell at public vendue the toll of the bridge together with the toll house belonging to the same for the term of one year then next ensuing." By this act, also, a penalty was established of $15, to be imposed upon any one who should break open the toll gates, and it was declared unlawful for any one to keep a tavern or inn at the toll house.

On petition of Matthew Gregory and Gradus Van Schoonhoven, then lessees of the bridge, who set forth that as it had been much injured by ice and water, the tolls were insufficient to pay for the necessary repairs, the legislature, in an act passed April 4, 1801, authorized the commissioners to increase the rates of toll to the requisite figure, with the restriction that the increase should not be over 33⅓ per cent. or be continued more than four years.

The Cohoes Bridge Company, consisting of Samuel Stewart, Ira Scott, John I. Close, Guert Van Schoonhoven, Moses Scott, Henry Davis and Samuel Demarest, was incorporated April 4, 1806, "for the purpose of rebuilding the state bridge over the Mohawk River," it having been severely damaged by the ice. The stock of the company was limited to three hundred shares of twenty-five dollars each. New rates of toll were fixed, considerably higher than those of 1797.

The completion of the bridge was of course followed by some little change in the life of the inhabitants. A means of communication was furnished to parts of the adjoining country which had previously been difficult of access, and as the amount of travel by the new route was considerable, the hamlet doubtless assumed a slight appearance of activity. The road, beside being generally used by the farmers in the vicinity, became one of the main routes to the north, and in later years was traversed by the stage coaches running from Albany to Ballston Spa and other points. A tavern was established in the house on the farm before described as Gerret Witbeck's, Richard Heamstreet being proprietor.

III.

From the Incorporation of the Cohoes Manufacturing Company, 1811, to the Commencement of Operations by the Cohoes Company, 1830.

Thus far in the history of Cohoes, there had been no indications of the importance which it was destined to assume as a manufacturing town. As at other points along the river, several small mills had been established, but they were comparatively unimportant, and there was little to distinguish the place from other farming settlements in the neighborhood. Early in the present century, however, the advantages of this locality for manufacturing purposes were recognized, and on a small scale the first attempt was made to utilize them.

In 1811, the *Cohoes Manufacturing Company*, composed entirely of gentlemen from Lansingburg, was incorporated, being one of the first corporations formed under the " general act" of that year. A tract of sixty acres on the bank of the river, which was part of the Heamstreet farm,[1] together with the water privilege, was secured, and land was also purchased from Jacobus Van Schoonhoven on the opposite side of the river, embracing what is now known as Simmons's Island. The property belonging to the patroon was transferred to Gerret Peebles, one of the trustees of the company,

---

[1] This tract, known for some years as the *Factory lot*, and which afterward came into possession of the Cohoes Company, comprised all that part of the Heamstreet farm which lay east of Mohawk street, down to a point near Columbia street. The southern limit may be described according to landmarks now in existence, as a line extending from the Rensselaer and Saratoga rail road crossing (near Steenberg's carriage shop) to the river, passing by Geo. Ducharme's house and the new gas works. The annual rental was seven bushels of wheat. A new lease was at the same time executed to Charles Heamstreet for the remainder of his farm, **145½ acres.**

May 20. The certificate of incorporation, filed June 18 in the office of the secretary of state, was as follows :

"This may certify that Timothy Leonard, Elijah Janes, Garret Peebles, Calvin Barker, Elias Parmelee, Sylvanus J. Penniman, Ebenezer W. Walbridge, John Stewart, Joseph Fox, Jacob L. Lansing, James Adams, Elisha Janes, John Pierce and Seth Seelye, in the village of Lansingburg in the county of Rensselaer, and state of New York, have associated and formed themselves into a company according to the act entitled 'an act relative to Incorporations for manufacturing purposes, passed March 22, 1811,' by the name of 'The Cohoes Manufacturing Company,' for the purposes of manufacturing Cotton, Woolen and Linen goods, making bar-iron, Anchors, Mill Irons, nail rods, Hoop-iron and Iron Mongery. That the Capital Stock of said company shall be *One Hundred Thousand Dollars* and the number of shares *two thousand*. The stock, property and concerns of the said company shall be conducted and managed by seven trustees, and Timothy Leonard, Calvin Barker, Gerrit Peebles, Elias Parmelee, Elijah Janes, Ebenezer W. Walbridge and Seth Seelye, shall be the Trustees to manage the concerns of said company for the first year, commencing on the day of the filing of this certificate in the Secretary's office of this State. The operations of the said Company will be carried on at Cohoesville in the town of Watervliet, in the county of Albany and state aforesaid, on the west Bank of the Mohawk River, a little distance southeast of the Cohoes bridge."

The first enterprise in which the company engaged was the manufacture of screws ; a wing dam was built, and a building (on the site now occupied by Weed & Becker's axe factory) was erected soon after the incorporation.

It was the intention of the company, in purchasing so large a tract of land, to lay it out and improve it so as to afford sites for further manufacturing establishments which in time could be disposed of to other parties, but no movement of the sort appears to have been made, and for some years, at least, the operations of the Company were confined to this factory. The operatives employed were mostly from New York. Several large wooden tenements, still standing, (between Saratoga street and the canal) were built for their accommodation, on the knoll at the west of the factory.

The first superintendent employed by the company was named Pierce, who was succeeded in 1813 by Col. Prescott.

Horatio Spafford, who was a resident of Lansingburg, and was doubtless acquainted with his townsmen who were engaged in this enterprise, appears to have been the first writer to mention the wonderful facilities offered by this locality for manufacturing purposes. In his *Gazetteer of New York State* (1st ed., 1813), he said, under the head of *Half-Moon:*

"The Cahoos Falls of the Mohawk, near its mouth, are between this town and Watervliet, and will supply a vast profusion of sites when the surrounding population shall need extensive works. There are now mills erected upon the upper sprout or delta of that river just at Waterford Point where it meets the Hudson."

Under the title of *Watervliet*, the following appeared in regard to Cohoes:

"About three miles N. of Gibbonsville (West Troy) there is a bridge across the Mohawk, a short distance below the Cahoos Falls. The roads are numerous in the interior, but they are rather paths than highways. The Cahoos, being the principal falls of the Mohawk, are between Watervliet and Half Moon in Saratoga Co. The whole waters of the Mohawk descend in one sheet at high water, about 70 feet. In the vicinity of the Cahoos is a Dutch church and farming neighborhood commonly called the Boght. Since the above was written, a manufactory of screws of iron for woodwork, erected on the lower sprout of the Mohawk near the Cahoos bridge, has got into successful operation.

Works are about to be added for drawing the wire from which the screws are formed, when the iron will be taken in the bar, and manufactured into screws, now made of foreign wire. The machinery is all driven by water, and is said to be very ingenious, the invention of a self-taught artist, Mr. Wm. C. Penniman. Some samples of the screws which I have seen appear to be well formed, and they are cut with great dispatch. These works are owned by an incorporated company with a sufficient capital, and are situated directly opposite Lansingburg, and about two miles below Waterford."[1]

It is probable that the establishment of this factory made little difference in the general life of the hamlet. It was situated some distance from the main road, accessible only by a rough path through the woods (now Oneida street), its proprietors and operatives were all strangers, and beyond the interest naturally awakened by the first operations, the enterprise received but slight attention from the inhabitants.

One event, however, which was of general importance, was perhaps brought about by the accession of the families of the factory operatives. The only school house in the neighborhood previously, had been located at the Boght, but another was established about this time, which was more accessible to many of the inhabitants. The school was first located in a building on the main road, afterwards occupied as a residence by Israel Anthony, a shoe-maker, and still later by Wm. Link.[2] The first teacher was a man named O'Neil. About the same time or soon afterward, a school building was erected a short distance above the Heamstreet farm house.[3] Supply F. Wilson was one of the early teachers.

About this time the manufacture of writing paper was commenced in Gerret Clute's mill near the Falls. The building had not been used as a grist mill for some time, and was occupied for several years as a cloth establishment for dressing common farmers' flannel. The proprietor of the paper mill was Elisha Sheldon, who employed a man

---

[1] John M. King, who as a boy was employed in the screw factory, is now living in Lansingburg.

[2] Near the corner of Oneida and Mohawk streets, on the site of the residence of M. S. Younglove.

[3] On Saratoga street on the site occupied by the *Red* or *State-yard* school house.

named Ensign as his superintendent. Two wooden tenements were erected near the mill.[1]

In 1815 or 1816, the screw factory was burned, and this appears to have interrupted for a time the operations of the company. A great part of the stock changed hands, most of it coming into possession of Benjamin and Samuel De Milt of New York, and after some delay a new building was erected, which was occupied as a cotton factory. In connection with it a small factory was afterward established for the manufacture of shovels and other tools which was conducted by Collin and Jones. Few particulars in regard to it can be obtained.

About the year 1820, the first church building within the present limits of Cohoes was erected. It was a small wooden structure, located above the north line of the Charles Heamstreet farm, near what is now the northwest corner of Mohawk and White streets. But little can be ascertained in regard to the history of the church. It was of the Methodist denomination, and was organized mainly through the efforts of the different Heamstreet families. The services were conducted by Jacob Heamstreet and a man named Whipple of Lansingburg, as *exhorters*, but there is no record that a clergyman was ever regularly settled. The building was only used about two years, when disputes of some sort arose and the services were abandoned. It remained for some time unoccupied, and was afterward converted into a dwelling house. Directly in front of this church was located the ninth mile stone from Albany. The eighth mile stone was near Jacob II. Lansing's house.

The construction of the Erie and Champlain Canals, which was begun in 1817, and completed, at least in this vicinity, in 1823, was the first event to cause a noticeable change in

---

[1] The mill was destroyed about 1832, when the improvements of the Cohoes Company were in progress.

the character of the place. It may well be imagined that the equanimity of its quiet Dutch inhabitants was seriously disturbed by the projection of these improvements, and that they regarded the invasion of their domains with a disfavor which no awards of land damages could remove. Every farm was traversed by one or both of the canals. Both passed directly in front of the residence of Abram G. Lansing, marring the lawn which extended from the house to the river, and destroying much of the beauty of his country place — while the next farm on the north, belonging to Charles Heamstreet, was damaged almost as greatly. The front yard of the farm house was cut off by the Champlain Canal, leaving no means of access to the highway, except by a bridge which was built a short distance above the house, and soon afterward Mr. Heamstreet disposed of the farm, and moved away, his reason being, it is said, disgust at this mutilation of his property. The other farmers, whose lands were all more or less injured, appear to have been more resigned to the innovation, though it was doubtless equally unwelcome.

The junction of the Erie and Champlain Canals (located near the site of the stables of the Troy and Cohoes Horse Rail Road Company on Saratoga street north of the *dyke*), gave this locality some little importance in the early days of canal navigation. On the occasion of the canal celebration Oct. 8th, 1823, the *Dewitt Clinton*, the first boat to pass from the Erie Canal into the Hudson, was here met by the joint committee of the common council and citizens of Albany, who escorted to that city the passengers, consisting of Gov. Yates, the canal commissioners, and other prominent officials. It was at this point that the slight activity in the place, which followed the regular opening of navigation, was chiefly manifested. The construction of the canals brought to Cohoes quite a number of new inhabitants, some of whom came during the progress of the work and others soon after its completion. Houses were built, and canal groceries, stables, and similar concerns established at different points. The most important of these were at the junction, at which place the principal settlers were Messrs. Crowner, Waterman and Phelps. The house of Mr. Waterman, who was the first justice of the peace in the neighborhood, was situated on the hill just south of the ravine at the northwest of the junction, and those of Crowner and Phelps were by the canal north of the site of the horse rail road stables. Among other families which came to Cohoes about this time were those of Messrs. Henry En Earl, Flannigan, Beecher, Wolcott and Herkimer.

The boats at this time only ran during the day and there was consequently a demand for lodgings for the boatmen and stabling for their horses, which was the means of supporting several small taverns; of these the most important was the one which had been established by Richard Heamstreet, and was then kept by Andrews. Another was located in the old Ouderkirk or Fonda farm-house, which was kept by ——— Dyer and afterward by ——— Williams. Connected with this was a large barn (burned a few years since) which stood on the flats between the canal and the river, and furnished accommodations for a number of canal teams. On the hill was the Cohoes House owned by the Van Der Marks, who had leased the southwest portion of the Clute farm. This was located near the bridge which crosses the present Erie Canal by the Boght road.[1]

With the exception of some alterations made three years since, near the old junction, the course of the Champlain Canal, near Cohoes, has remained as originally laid out. The old Erie Canal ran north from the junction, passing over the ground now occupied by Main street, and the third and second levels of the Cohoes Company's canals. Above the Falls it ran in a north westerly direction, being at the west of

---

[1] This was torn down in 1875. In later years it was called the *Old House at Home*, and was kept by Geo. Bray.

the present location of the Cohoes Company's upper level. Within the space now included between the northern and southern boundaries of the city were nineteen locks, following each other in rapid succession. Two of these were below the junction, and seven between the junction and the road to Watervliet, now Columbia street. The next one was located near what is now White street, and the old lock house (on the east side of Main street), is still standing; three more were situated near the site now occupied by the jute mill (formerly paper mill) on Mohawk street, and two others occupied the ground near where the pump house now stands. Between the *Three Locks* and the *Two Locks*, near the site of the *Harmony Mills*, was a large basin, capable of holding thirty or forty boats, which at night was often filled. A canal grocery, owned by Oliver C. Hubbard, was, about 1828, located on one of the *Two Locks*. The last locks, four in number, were near the present northern boundary of the city.

These locks were an object of great dislike to travelers and boatmen, whose progress was seriously impeded by them in busy seasons when boats were numerous. To avoid wasting the time which would have been employed in the tedious journey from Albany to the upper locks, a line of stage coaches was established by ——— Allen, a few years after the opening of the canals, which connected with the packets just above the locks. These coaches, on some days five or six in number, came up from Albany every morning bringing westward bound passengers and returned at night with those who had come in from the opposite direction. The horses were stabled during the day at the Van Der Mark tavern.

In Spafford's *Canal Guide*, published 1824 and 1825, the following objects of interest in Cohoes at that time were mentioned:

"Between Albany and Schenectady, twenty-eight and a

half miles, a day is employed, there being so many locks to pass; but every person is well compensated for the time and expense of at least one trip, passing twenty-seven locks, two aqueducts, and an interesting variety of natural scenery. . . . .

Miles from Albany.

8½ Juncta, or the junction where the Erie receives the Champlain Canal by a navigable feeder from the Mohawk, below which there is a basin and 2 locks, Nos. 3 and 4, 2 of the *Nine Locks*. No. 3 to 11, in about half a mile rise 78 feet. Here are two locks the commencement of a double set now building of the white marble of Westchester Co.

r. from Juncta by Champlain Canal to Waterford, 2 miles.

l. A. G. Lansing's at lock No. 6.

9 Lock No. 12, rise 8 feet.

9¼ The *Three Locks*, Nos. 13, 14 and 15, rise 26 ft., opposite *Cahoos Bridge*.

9½ The *Two Locks*, Nos. 16 and 17 rise 18 ft., Nos. 13, 14, 15, 16, the 4 *Marble Locks*.

10 Deep cutting, 26 ft., 40 rods, transition argillite

r. Cahoos Falls, perpendicular descent 78 ft.

10¼ r. Paper Mill on Mohawk River.

10½ The *Four Locks*, Nos. 18, 19, 20, 21, rise 32 ft.

r. Wing dam, and grist saw and plaster mill.[1]"

The points mentioned on the Champlain Canal were Whiting's factory,[2] the cotton factory and the dam, the latter of which is thus described. "½ m. Dam, Mohawk River, 7 ft. pond 1600 ft. wide, back water 53 rods, navigation through the pond, guard locks, feeder for Erie Canal."

In the second edition of Spafford's *Gazetteer*, published 1824, the place was described as follows:

---

[1] The plaster mill, belonging to the Lansing family, had not been long in operation. It was located in an addition which was built at the south of the original saw and grist mills. The building was used a few years later for the manufacture of coarse wrapping paper.

[2] This was the mill which had been conducted by John Heamstreet. It came into the possession of the Whitings of Troy, and was used some years as a candle factory. The frame of the mill remained standing as late as 1837. The house occupied by the Whitings, and in later years known as the *Alcombrack house*, is still standing, near the site of the old mill.

"The detention of boats in passing the numerous locks near here will help the proprietors towards making this a place of business, particularly if they connect it with mill works and factories, as they may well do. . . . . . I have perhaps rather whimsically named the new town which the proprietors mean to have at the place where the Erie Canal receives the Champlain Canal, *Juncta*, but if they make a town or village there, I may at least make a name for it until they give it one. It is a pretty spot, and if they give it water power and hydraulic works, there will soon collect about it people enough to make a handsome little village."

The cotton factory of the Cohoes Manufacturing Company, of which ——— Sayres was at the time agent, was spoken of as *Prescott's factory*, "a stone building, near the Cahoos bridge and the ruins of the screw factory mentioned in the first edition of this work. It is owned principally in Lansingburg."

It was at the time the only cotton factory in the county. The design of the company to establish here a manufacturing village, referred to in the above extract, is described at greater length in a memorial drawn up for presentation to the canal commissioners by the trustees, soon after the opening of the canal. In this it was stated that they had purchased lands and water privileges from Stephen Van Rensselaer and Jacobus Van Schoonhoven "for which lands and water privileges there has been paid by the trustees of the Cohoes Manufacturing Company to the aforesaid persons the sum of four thousand six hundred and seventy-one dollars. Your memorialists further represent that at the time of making the above purchases they had ascertained that the lands so purchased, together with the water privileges, would furnish sites and power for twenty-two manufacturing establishments; that the ultimate value of so many sites for hydraulic machinery your memorialists calculated would indemnify them for the extraordinary price paid for the aforesaid premises, and the expenses which they might incur in commencing operations which were yet new in this country; that with the view of disposing of sites to purchasers, they have had their land surveyed and laid out into proper lots, and have excavated a canal nearly through their land, forty feet wide, at an expense of three thousand four hundred and sixty dollars; that after practicing every economy, which the nature of their business would admit, they have expended on the premises the sum of seventy-five thousand dollars, for which or for the interest that has accrued thereon, they have as yet received no return. Your memorialists beg leave further to suggest that they conceive they had acquired a perfect title to all the above mentioned premises; that they are entitled to an adequate compensation for the damages they sustain by the loss of land and improvements by means of the canal operation, and by loss of privileges occasioned by the use and diversion of the waters of the Mohawk, and your memorialists beg leave further to suggest the propriety of their claim to the waters of the Mohawk, beyond what is necessary for supplying the northern and western locks and canals; and your memorialists respectfully solicit your honorable body to fix upon certain regulations under which your memorialists may have leave to take and use such of the waters of the Mohawk as shall not be wanted for canal purposes."

From various reasons, chiefly lack of capital, the plans of this company never approached completion. The opening of the canal had, however, drawn the attention of other parties to the feasibility of a similar enterprise, and in 1826, with the incorporation of the *Cohoes Company*, the first steps were taken towards the development, on a large scale, of the wonderful natural resources of the place, and the foundation was laid for the establishment of a thriving town.

The honor of originating the first design for the complete and systematic utilization of the water power belongs to Canvass White, of whom an extended notice is given elsewhere. He first became interested in the project while engaged as engineer in the construction of the Erie Canal, and being convinced of its importance, devoted himself earnestly to obtaining means for its execution. Not being a man of large property himself, he sought the coöperation of a number of capitalists with whom he had acquaintance — prominent among them being Stephen Van Rensselaer of Albany, and the members of the firm of Peter Remsen & Co. of New York, and without difficulty gained their aid in the enterprise. A company was formed, which was incorporated March 28th, the directors named in the charter being as follows: Peter Remsen, Chas. E. Dudley, Stephen Van-Rensselaer Jr., Francis Olmstead, Canvass White, Henry J. Wyckoff and David Wilkinson. Their election held in that year resulted in the choice of Mr. White as president, and Mr. Van Rensselaer as vice president. The first secretary, Mr. Wyckoff, was not elected until the following year. The powers of the company in regard to improvements were thus stated in the charter:

"It shall and may be lawful for the said corporation to erect and maintain a dam across the Mohawk River, opposite the lands belonging to said corporation above the great Cohoes Falls for supplying water for the purpose of said corporation. . . . The said corporation shall have full right, power and authority to cut, construct and make a canal or canals from said river upon the lands of said corporation, to supply water for all the purposes of said corporation ; and to cut, construct and make upon the lands of said corporation as many lateral canals connected therewith as may be necessary to supply water for the manufacturing establishments which may be erected, and also to afford such water communication with the Erie and Champlain Canals as shall be approved by the canal commissioners or such other person or persons as may hereafter be appointed by the legislature, having the superintendence and management of said canals ; and may also at any time hereafter purchase, build, or hire for the use and in the name of the said corporation, houses, factories, warehouses, wharves and other necessary buildings and to sell or lease any part or the whole of the above mentioned property, and also any surplus water of their canals, in such manner as they may think most conducive to the interest of said corporation."

The capital of the company was $250,000.[1]

---

[1] Increased in 1835, to $500,000 with the proviso that none of the additional capital should be employed in manufacturing operations.

The incorporation of this company, the most important event thus far in the history of Cohoes, had no immediate effect upon the place. Time was required for the perfection of plans and the completion of necessary arrangements, so no active operations were at once commenced, and for the next few years but little is to be recorded concerning the history of the village.

During the winter of 1825-26, the locks at the junction, which had proved insufficient to accommodate the rapidly increasing number of boats, were doubled. A new bridge (on the site of the present one) across the Mohawk above the dam was constructed by the Cohoes Bridge Company, which was authorized to contract with the canal commissioners for building and sustaining a tow path bridge for the benefit of the Champlain Canal, and was empowered to change the location of the old structure, and take such lands of the adjoining shores as might be necessary. The new bridge, built by ——— Hayward, was of wood, and had latticed sides, being one of the first so constructed in the neighborhood.[1] The toll collector was Jacob Van Der Werken, who had been the last collector at the upper bridge.

After the completion of this bridge, efforts were made for the establishment of a suitable approach to it, and a survey of the road from the junction north was made by Wm. Roberts Jr., March 22, 1828, as follows :

"The road is laid out four rods wide in all places, measured at right angles with the course thereof. Beginning at a point in the centre of the road bearing north seventy-five degrees and fifty minutes west thirty-nine links from the southwest corner of the tavern house owned by A. G. Lansing, and now occupied by Henry En Earl and running thence upon the centre of the road north fourteen degrees and ten minutes east to the centre of the new Cohoes bridge at the south end thereof."

For some reason this survey was never recorded, and in

---

[1] It was partially destroyed by ice, in 1832, but remained in use until March, 1853 when it was burned. The last toll collector was John G. Bonce.

later years various parties have been able to encroach upon the street with impunity. When the state buildings were erected, about eight years later, the fence projected some distance into the street. Remonstrance was made by Hugh White, then president of the Cohoes Bridge Company, and he was assured by Clark Sumner, canal superintendent, that the land should be restored any time it was needed for public purposes. This, however, has never been done.

In 1828, a new school district was formed, all this neighborhood having been previously included in one district, having for its only accommodation the *Red School House.* The new school was located in a building which had been used as a boarding house during the construction of the bridge, and stood near the site of the old freight house of the Rensselaer and Saratoga Rail Road Company, on Oneida street.

In 1829, the cotton factory burned, and the Cohoes Manufacturing Company was broken up. The last agent of the company was Otis Sprague, and its trustees at the time of its dissolution were : B. De Milt, Edward Taylor, John Sayre, Calvin Barker, Joseph Curtis, Wm. M. Morrell and Samuel De Milt. The enterprise had not been particularly successful, financially, and the proprietors made no effort to rebuild and continue business, probably seeing that their concern would be completely overshadowed in the progress of the operations then about to be commenced by the Cohoes Company.

IV.

1831 TO 1836.

WITH the completion, in 1831, of the first actual improvements of the Cohoes Company, commenced a new era in the history of Cohoes.

Though this neighborhood had been settled at an early day, and had been increased in population and activity by the establishment of the factory of 1811, and the opening of the canals, there had never been any movement toward a regular development of the place. The early inhabitants, occupied only with their farms or their traffic with passing boatmen, had no local interests in common which would stimulate them to an effort for the establishment of a village, and previous to this time, the place, hardly entitled to be even called a hamlet, had consisted (aside from the factory) of the half dozen farm houses at intervals along the banks of the river, and a few scattered canal groceries. The advent of new inhabitants, however, all engaged directly or indirectly in putting to practical use the natural advantages of the place, and having a common interest in its growth and improvement, infused a new life into Cohoes, and its active career was then entered upon.

Early in the season a wooden dam was constructed above the Falls, not far from the location of the present one. At the same time the company purchased from I. D. F. Lansing a large tract of land in that vicinity, together with a portion of the mill privilege which had been the property of his family since their first settlement in the neighborhood. Mr. Lansing reserved the right of using enough water for four run of stone, and transferred to the company the remainder of the water power, together with the privilege of constructing the dam and the necessary canals, for the sum of $12,495. Further accessions had been made by the purchase of lands on the opposite or Waterford side of the river. A strip one rod in width, extending from the Falls to the dam, was purchased from Garret Van Schoonhoven in 1826, for $5,000, thus enabling the company to control the entire power of the river except that reserved by Mr. Lansing. Other tracts, embracing a large part of what is now known as *Northside* and extending beyond the *Shatemuck Mill* property on the Champlain Canal, were purchased from Joshua Blower at different times from 1826 to 1838.[1]

The officers of the company made an arrangement by which they were permitted to use the Erie Canal for the purpose of supplying water to factories until the company could complete a canal of its own. The water from above the dam was conveyed into the Erie Canal just below the *Four Locks*, by means of a wooden trunk which passed under the highway near I. D. F. Lansing's grist mill.

Having thus prepared for the utilization of its facilities the company began to invite the attention of capitalists to the locality, and take measures for the establishment of a village. These efforts, though not resulting as favorably as had been hoped, still had the effect of bringing a number of new inhabitants.

One of the first settlers led here in consequence of the organization of the Cohoes Company, was Hugh White, who had arrived with his family in April, 1830. He had made previous arrangements for settling here, and his house on the Waterford road (the lumber for which had been prepared in Chittenango, N. Y., and was shipped on the canal ready to be put up), was nearly completed on his arrival. Mr. White took the place of his brother Canvass, who was often away attending to other business, in superintending the early improvements of the company. Early in the year David Wilkinson, of Pawtucket, R. I., one of

---

[1] This land was originally in the old Van Schaick Patent.

the Cohoes Company, after urgent solicitation and liberal offers on the part of his fellow members, decided to take up his residence here, and arrived in April, being followed the next month by his brother-in-law, Hezekiah Howe. These gentlemen, together with the friends who accompanied them, had a most important part in shaping the history of the town. Mr. Wilkinson was one of the foremost mechanics and inventors in the country, and was widely known to manufacturers and capitalists. Having suffered heavily in the business depression of 1829, he, with his partner Mr. Howe, determined to avail himself of the opportunity offered for trying his fortunes in a new locality. The result proved how well grounded were the expectations of the company in regard to the effect of his ability and enterprise on the growth of Cohoes.

Among the friends of Messrs. Wilkinson and Howe, who arrived here about the same time, were Joshua R. Clarke, John Baker, Nathaniel Wheeler, Samuel Baldwin, Pardon Whitman, Robert Leckie, Geo. H. Kimball, and John Tillinghast.

The prospects for the new comers were not particularly encouraging. The best accommodations to be had were afforded by Mr. Faulkner, who then kept the Richard Heamstreet tavern, and they were of the most limited description. Mr. Howe and his family, after boarding for some little time at this place, took up their residence in the house on the southwest corner of Oneida and Saratoga streets, which had previously been occupied by employés of the Cohoes Manufacturing Company; Mr. Wilkinson took possession of the Whiting house, near the river; Mr. Clarke occupied half of another of the factory houses, below Saratoga street near Ontario, and the other families found accommodations, for the most part temporary, in different localities in the neighborhood. At this time there were not over twenty or twenty-five buildings standing on the ground which is now the most thickly settled portion of the city, and mention has already been made of the greater part of them. Among the most important were the old farm houses on the Lansing and Heamstreet properties, the dwellings of Crowner, Waterman, Phelps, and En Earl at the junction, and the factory tenements near the state dam. On the west side of Mohawk street, near its junction with Oneida,[1] was quite a settlement, the principal house being that of Jacob Van Der Werken; opposite to this, and nearly on the site of the present residence of Geo. Lawrence, lived a man named Rice. Next door to Van Der Werken's was the dwelling of Washington Cavan, which now forms part of the offices of P. D. Niver, and Justice Redmond. South of this was the dwelling of Wm. Link, which has been before referred to as occupied by Israel Anthony. On Mohawk street, opposite the present City Hotel (the site of which was then occupied by a large Dutch barn belonging to the Richard Heamstreet farm), was a small cottage occupied by Mr. Robinson; on the bank of the river the gate house of the old bridge was still standing, and was occupied by Capt. Andrews. On the hill, besides the Lansing farm houses and the Van Der Mark tavern or *Cohoes House*, there was nothing except the canal groceries of Hubbard and Revels.

The first house south of Link's was that of Isaac Fletcher, on the southeast corner of Mohawk and Pine; adjoining this were two or three small buildings, one of which was occupied by a man named Crabbe. The Methodist church, on the opposite side of the street, was then unoccupied; Dr. Tracy, the first physician, it is said, who settled in Cohoes, had a house on the north side of Columbia street, between Main and Remsen streets, and near the junction of Mohawk and Saratoga (on the site of the residence of Malachi Weidman), stood a small dwelling occupied by

---

[1] In speaking of these localities, I am compelled to use the names of our present streets, though of course they were not in existence at that time.

Isaac Van Der Werken. Along the canal may have been a few small groceries, and here and there an occasional shanty, but so far as I have been able to ascertain, there were no buildings of importance then standing in the main part of the village besides those already mentioned. All the land west of the Erie Canal was yet uncleared; on the east a great part of it was unfit for farming purposes and had been neglected. Between the canal and Remsen street was a swamp which, for a number of years, was put to no use except as a cow pasture. The character of the land, marshy and full of quicksands, proved a serious obstacle in later years to many who were building in that locality. Between Remsen and Mohawk streets the soil was better adapted for cultivation, and on part of it a crop of corn had been raised in the previous year. The block between Factory and Oneida streets was occupied by an orchard belonging to the Richard Heamstreet farm. A deep ravine, through which had once flowed a brook of considerable size, passed from the canal down Ontario street across Remsen, and then in a northeast direction to Mohawk street.

At this time, and for a number of years later, there was a beautiful pine grove on the land through which the Rensselaer and Saratoga Rail Road now passes, extending from the bridge nearly to Howard street, and smaller groves were scattered at intervals between the Falls and the junction.

For the accommodation of the people at the factory, a narrow road (now Oneida street) had been cut through from the state dam to the main road, with which it connected near Jacob Van Der Werken's house. Besides this and the main highway there were no other public roads, except the one which is now Columbia street. This had been in use from a very early day. The farmers from the Boght, instead of turning into the main road near the Falls, often chose the lower road in preference, and came down that way when they drove to Troy and Albany with their produce, or went to Heamstreet's mill.

Such was Cohoes in 1831. A description of life in the place during that year, from some of those who were pioneers in its settlement and improvement, gives one a striking sense of the inconveniences and annoyances they must have suffered. Until they could become settled in business, and make arrangements for building or hiring suitable houses, their accommodations were restricted; there were no facilities of any account for communication with the outside world, the only public conveyance to neighboring towns being the canal boats, which often consumed two hours in making the trip from here to Troy, though the people were in the habit of saving time by walking to the junction and taking the boat at that point, thus avoiding the delay of the locks; it was almost impossible to obtain the commonest necessities of life; groceries, and those of an inferior description, could only be procured at the canal stores, at either extremity of the village, and fresh meat was a luxury only to be found occasionally at the junction; the nearest post office was at Waterford.

When, in addition to these discomforts, the fact is taken into account that the business prospects of the inhabitants were by no means bright, that the influx of capitalists and new population which had been expected was slow in coming, and the golden dreams which had been cherished in regard to the growth of the place were realized in but a slight degree, we can understand how much credit is due to the energy and perseverance of these early settlers and those who followed them within the next decade. Notwithstanding the obstacles in their way, the new-comers commenced at once their efforts for the improvement of the place. Messrs. Wilkinson and Howe were both active churchmen, and their first step was to procure accommodations for holding public worship. On May 2d, the day after Mr. Howe's arrival, St. John's Episcopal church was organized, and having secured the assistance of Rev. Orange Clark of Waterford, services were held the next Sunday in the school house of District No. 5, on Oneida street.

A Sunday school was at the same time organized under direction of Miss Wilkinson and Miss Maria Howe. The church services, which were held in the afternoon, were well attended and continued regularly during the year.

The first church officers were as follows: Wardens: David Wilkinson, Hugh White. Vestrymen: Hezekiah Howe, Otis Sprague, Albert S. Wilkinson, John Van Der Werken, Matthias Williams, Samuel H. Baldwin, Luther M. Tracy.

Mr. Wilkinson commenced business operations at once, and his machine shop, located on Mohawk street on the site of the present Empire Mill, was erected and in full operation within a few months after his arrival. The power was obtained from the Erie Canal by means of a waste gate, located near the north end of the present Harmony Mills carpenter shop, from which the water was conveyed to the machine shop by a small ditch. During the year Mr. Wilkinson was occupied chiefly in constructing machinery for cotton manufacture, some of which was shipped to Seneca Falls. Another establishment, which was completed in the fall, was a saw mill belonging to Hugh White, which stood at the *Two Locks* where is now the picker room of No. 1 mill. It was built by Sylvester Van Der Mark, who had in his employ, as an apprentice, Dennis Flannigan. Mr. Van Der Mark and Joshua R. Clarke were the principal carpenters here, and most of the buildings erected for a number of years following were under the supervision of one or the other.[1]

About the same time Mr. Howe established the first store of any importance in the place. It was located in a build-

---

[1] This mill was run by Mr. White alone for a few years, and afterwards with J. R. Clarke as a partner. In August, 1836, it was sold to the Harmony Manufacturing Company, which was then being organized.

ing erected for the purpose at the middle one of the Three Locks, near the present Jute mill, at the place where Mr. Howe landed from the canal boat which brought him to Cohoes. The business, which was that of a general country store, was conducted by his son.

On the 23d of February 1832, the first postmaster, Frederick Y. Waterman, was appointed. The office was located at the junction, and as it was not much more convenient of access than the one at Waterford, many people continued to have their mail sent to the latter place until Mr. Howe was appointed in the following year, when the office was transferred to his new store on the canal bank. The mail was carried by Wright Mallery, in later years a well-known resident of this city, who had at that time a bakery in West Troy. He made daily trips in this direction, visiting the groceries along the line of the canal, and brought the Cohoes mail in his bread cart — no heavy burden — for it consisted some days of but one or two letters. Mr. Mallery moved here in 1834, but went to Troy on business every day and continued to carry the mail for some time.

During 1832, the Cohoes Company was actively engaged. The first dam was carried away by ice on January 10, and was immediately rebuilt. During the spring, also, the first two canals of the company, which had been commenced in the previous year, were completed; the contractors for the work being Oliver C. Hubbard and Captain Andrews. The principal one, *Basin A*, extended from a point in the rear of the present Harmony Mills carpenter shop, on Mohawk street, to a short distance north of Factory street. The other, *Basin B*, was of less importance, serving principally to receive the water from Basin A and convey it to the river. It is on Remsen street and forms the fourth level of the Cohoes Company's present system. The first factory to obtain its power from Basin A was one (now occupied by Holsapple's bedstead factory) which was erected in the early part of the year by E. L. Miller, a wealthy gentleman of Charleston, S. C., who intended to engage in cotton manufacture. At the same time he tore down the old Heamstreet barn, on the corner of Factory and Mohawk streets, and commenced building a commodious residence, while directly opposite, on the east side of Mohawk street, he erected a small wooden building afterward occupied as a store by his nephew, Mr. Whiting, and in later years by the post office. The mill and residence were built by Joshua R. Clarke, and the masons employed were Elihu and John Stevenson, for many years well known citizens, who had come to Cohoes a few months previous.

The buildings were hardly completed, however, when Mr. Miller fell into ill health, and changed all his plans. He became dissatisfied with his investments here, abandoned his idea of engaging in business, and went to New York, leaving his property to be disposed of for what it would bring. His house, directly after its completion, was converted into a hotel, which was first conducted by a man named Fuller, who came here from Watertown, and it has ever since been used for that purpose. It has been so altered and enlarged from time to time, however, that the present City Hotel bears but little resemblance to the original structure. In the mill, the machinery, which had been made by Mr. Wilkinson, was set up and ready for use, but soon after Mr. Miller's removal, it was sent to New Jersey to be sold. Another factory was erected during this season, by two gentlemen from New York for the purpose of manufacturing carpets. It was situated on Mohawk street, on the site now occupied by Gregory and Hiller's mill, and the power was obtained from Basin B.

Soon after the mill was completed it was sold to Messrs. Roach and Jones, of West Troy.[1]

---

[1] It is said that the cause of this sudden abandonment of their enterprise by the original proprietors was the Asiatic cholera, then alarmingly prevalent. They took

One of the most memorable buildings of the year was St. John's church, erected by Joshua R. Clarke, which stood on the south side of Oneida street, between Remsen and Mohawk streets; the structure was of wood, thirty-eight by forty-eight feet in size. The interior was finished in the plainest possible manner, and upon the ladies of the parish devolved the work of adorning it with such decorations as their limited resources would allow. The church bell, destined to remain in use nearly forty years, was a gift from David Wilkinson. The entire cost of the edifice did not exceed $1,500, of which $500 were contributed by the Cohoes Company, who also gave the lot upon which it was erected, the latter being a stipulation made by Mr. Wilkinson before he consented to come here. Notwithstanding this assistance, it was by no means easy to raise the necessary amount, for the members of the parish were few in number and nearly all of limited means. The work was one, however, to which all were earnestly devoted and in its accomplishment they were assisted by the cordial efforts of almost every one in the place, without regard to theological differences. The zeal of those who had labored so faithfully in its behalf met with deserved success, and St. John's church, the organization of which had been one of the first steps towards the improvement of the village, became permanently established. The building was consecrated on May 12th of the following year by Bishop Onderdonk, Rev. Mr. Whipple of Lansingburg assisting.

Other buildings erected during this year were Mr. Wilkinson's house on the northwest corner of Oneida and Mohawk streets, the most imposing residence the village had yet seen, and the brick building west of the church,

---

it for granted that the race would soon become extinct, and that it would be useless to make any business arrangements.

The building was in later years used for the manufacture of white lead by Mr. Underwood, who had commenced that business in part of the Wilkinson machine shop.

which was owned by Hugh White. The bricks used in the construction of the latter were made by a man named Welch and are said to have been the first made in the place, aside from those found in the old farm houses.[1]

The event which marks this year as one of particular importance in the history of the place was the establishment by Egberts and Bailey of the first factory in which knitting machinery was successfully run by power.[2] Mr. Egberts, who had been keeping a store with his brother in Albany, became interested in 1831 in the process of making knit goods, and gave the subject considerable attention. After inspecting the clumsy hand machines then in use, the idea was suggested that improvements might be made by which a knitting frame could be made to run by power. Mr. Egberts himself was not a practical mechanic, and could do nothing towards perfecting any such apparatus ; but while he was talking on the subject with Dr. Williams, his family physician, the latter suggested that Timothy Bailey, who was then in the employ of Alfred Cooke, a cabinet maker, was a young man of remarkable mechanical ability, who could accomplish almost anything he turned his hand to, and would doubtless be able to carry out the idea if it were possible. Mr. Bailey was accordingly consulted, and after a careful examination of the knitting frame then

---

[1] Bricks were afterwards made in considerable quantity by Mason Sawyer. About 1842, Patrick Rogers, who has for some years had a monopoly of this branch of business here, commenced operations. His brick yard was located on the flats south of Columbia street, afterwards on Mohawk street near Columbia and another has been of late years established on Harmony Hill.

[2] "The art of knitting is said to have been invented in Scotland, but the first machine for making knitted fabrics was the invention of Wm. Lee of England about two centuries ago. This machine remained in nearly the same condition in which Lee left it for almost two centuries and the first introduced into America was the old heavy hand frame, which required the strength of a pretty strong man to operate it with advantage. Immense sums of money had been expended in England to adapt the knitting frame for operation by steam or water power, like the carpet loom, but this achievement was left for the perseverance and skill of American inventors."— Aiken's *History of the Art of Knitting.*

used, concluded that he would undertake the task, on the understanding that Mr. Egberts was to provide the necessary funds. The first thing requisite was a knitting machine on which experiments could be commenced, and as this could not be obtained in Albany, Mr. Bailey went to Philadelphia, arriving there April 1, 1831. After some search he succeeded in finding a disused machine, which he purchased for $55, and returned, prepared to commence operations at once. Within six days after its arrival in Albany he had the apparatus so arranged that it would knit by turning a crank at the side, and preparations were accordingly made for perfecting its operation. Mr. Egberts procured an upper story in a store near the foot of State street, to which Mr. Bailey moved his tools and machinery, and there continued his labors. In time he succeeded in making a machine which would make four shirt bodies, and knit thirty times back and across per minute, by the simple revolution of a crank, and steps were then taken to put the invention to practical use. In the meantime, Joshua Bailey, an elder brother of Timothy, had become interested in the machine, and selling out his farm, came to Albany to take part in the enterprise. In the fall of 1832, the partners came to Cohoes, and established themselves in the lower story of the cotton factory which was then being finished, the wheel having been just put in when they moved into the building. Their operations at first were of course on a very small scale, owing to their lack of facilities. Mr. Bailey's time was given almost altogether to making new machinery, in which he was at first assisted by Edward Gleason, who had been in his employ some time while engaged in the first frame in Albany. Eight machines were made in succession and after a time Mr. Bailey arranged machinery for carding and spinning, the first goods having been made from yarn bought of outside parties. Thus was laid the foundation of that branch of industry which has since become a distinguishing feature of Cohoes, and to which it is largely indebted for its present importance.[1]

Egberts and Bailey did not occupy all of the cotton factory until some years later, and in the meantime several other concerns were located in the building. One of the earliest was the machine shop of Russell Phelps, established soon after the factory was completed. S. D. Fairbank, afterwards a prominent citizen, came to Cohoes with Mr. Phelps, and engaged in business with him.

Early in 1833 John Tillinghast commenced the manufacture of satinet warps, but did not long continue; the late Wm. Leckie of this city was in his employ. In the fall of the year the first building of importance on Remsen street, the first one north of the present Music Hall, was erected by John Stevenson, who sold it soon afterward to Mr. Mudge. On Mohawk street below the site of Root's Mill the first office of the Cohoes Company, a small brick structure, was built. During this year the company commenced the construction of the upper canal, one and three-quarter miles long, with a fall of eighteen feet, by which the water from the dam was brought directly into use in the lower levels. The work, done under direction of Chas. A. Olmsted, Geo. Strover of Schuylerville being contractor, was completed in the following year. It ran on the east side of the Erie Canal and parallel with it, to a point a few hundred feet above the *Two Locks*, near School street, where it was taken under the canal by means of two wooden trunks about four or five feet in diameter, and then continued in its present course, terminating near the middle lock of the *Three Locks*, in the rear of the present Harmony Mill No. 2. The water was then let into the upper end of Basin A, being again taken under the Erie Canal by means of wooden

---

[1] The Bailey Brothers secured lodgings for a time in the village, and afterwards occupied different parts of the wooden block which was erected by the firm about 1835, on the corner of White and Remsen streets. Mr. Egberts was in the habit of driving up from Albany every day, and for some years boarded at the Cohoes Hotel.

trunks. At this point, on the site of the Harmony Mills carpenter shop, was located the Cohoes Iron Foundry, conducted by John L. Wilkinson and Nathaniel Wheeler, which for many years did a large business.[1]

A factory for the manufacture of axes and edge tools, established during this and the following year by Daniel Simmons, was the foundation of a branch of business which has since become one of the most important in Cohoes. Mr. Simmons began life as a blacksmith and had a forge in the lower part of the city of Albany. Here he commenced making axes by hand for an occasional customer, using for the cutting edges German or blister steel, which was then supposed to be the only kind that could be successfully welded to iron. About 1825 it was found that by the use of refined borax as a flux, cast steel could be made to answer the purpose, and Mr. Simmons promptly took advantage of the discovery, being one of the first to put it to practical use. His axes soon became favorably known, and the demand for them was so increased that greater facilities for production became necessary. Accordingly in 1826, he removed to Berne, Albany County, where he secured a small water power, erected rude buildings, and put up trip hammers and other machinery. In time these accommodations proved insufficient, and Mr. Simmons came to Cohoes, where he founded the establishment, one of the earliest in the country, which, under years of successful management, has made the *Simmons Axe* familiar in all parts of the globe. His partner for two years was Levi Silliman.[2] The

---

[1] Though Mr. David Wilkinson was interested in the establishment of this foundery and of the machine shop, the business of both was conducted by his son. Mr. Wheeler's connection with the foundery ceased in 1844. Its subsequent proprietors were Chas. A. Olmsted, the Cohoes Company and Fuller & Safely (1858), by whom it was destroyed in 1867.

[2] In 1848, Mr. Simmons associated with him, under the firm name of D. Simmons & Co., Messrs. Wm. H. Weed of New York and Storm A. Becker of Cohoes. Hiram St. John, of New York, was subsequently admitted, to the partnership. After Mr. Simmons's death in Dec. 1860, the firm of Weed, Becker & Co., was formed, which gave place to the present company in Feb. 1874.

first building (destroyed by fire in 1875), and the office of the present company which was built a few years later, were erected on the foundations of the establishments of the Cohoes Manufacturing Company.

Another business enterprise was the establishment of the veneering and sawing mill of Hawes and Baker which was built near the junction of Remsen and Mohawk streets on the site at present occupied by the Star Knitting Company. The concern had been started in the preceding year, in an upper story of Mr. Wilkinson's machine shop, by Hawes and Goodwin, the latter of whom was one of the pioneers in the business of sawing veneers. His interest was bought by John Baker.

Among the private residences erected during the year was that of Joshua R. Clarke, on the corner of Mohawk street and Cataract alley, now occupied by H. S. Bogue.

During the next few years but little progress seems to have been made. The increase of population was slight, and there were but few additions to the business of the place, as appears from the following account of the village and its manufactures published in 1836 :

"The property of the Cohoes Company, of which the village is part, at the mouths of the Mohawk, includes the Falls and the banks on both sides of the river, and extends within a few rods of the junction of the Erie and Champlain Canals. The property around the Falls has, from the first settlement of the country, been in the Van Rensselaer family who, with a just regard to its future value, had refused to part with it. The great hydraulic power here was first developed by Mr. Canvass White, during the progress of the Erie Canal ; at whose instance it was arranged with Peter Remsen & Co., of New York, and Mr. Van Rensselaer to commence its improvement on a large scale ; a liberal charter was obtained from the state in 1826, authorizing the investment of $250,000 and subsequently of half a million. By an independent canal, nearly two miles long, supplied with water by a dam in the river, half a mile above the Falls where the stream is three hundred yards wide, unconnected with the state works, the company are enabled to avail themselves of the whole water of the river, yielding power for mills as durable and constant as the rocks and the stream. The entire head and fall thus gained is one hundred and twenty feet, permitting the use of the water under *six* successive falls of from eighteen to twenty-three feet above the level of the state dam, below which it may be used under a head of eleven feet, and may be carried on these levels to almost any point on the company's estate. The minimum supply of water is one thousand cubic feet, the second, competent to drive from three to four millions of cotton spindles. The upper canal, excavated for a great part of its course in the slate rock, passes from the dam on the east side of the Erie Canal and thence by a tunnel under that canal to the west side. The advantages of this position for manufactures are unquestionably the greatest in the state. By the Erie Canal and the North River it communicates directly with the great marts on the Hudson and with the ocean, by that canal with the interior of the state and the lakes and the *Great West;* and by the Champlain Canal with the northern portion of the state and the basin of the St. Lawrence; obtaining readily from the south all that may be required from abroad, and from the west and north a never-failing supply of provisions, lumber and iron, upon the cheapest terms. . . . . . . The village now contains one factory for cotton and woolen machinery, one for edge tools, one for cotton, linen and woolen hosiery made on newly invented looms, a mill driving turning lathes, an iron foundry, a carpet factory, an Episcopal church, two hotels, three stores, many shops of various kinds on the canals, and sixty dwellings, whose number is rapidly increasing."— Gordon's *Gazetteer of New York.*

V.
1837 TO 1847.

AFTER two comparatively uneventful years, an important addition which was made to its business interests gave an impetus to the activity of the place. In 1837, the Harmony Manufacturing Company, composed of New York capitalists, commenced the erection of a large cotton factory on Harmony Hill, the germ of the immense establishment which is now foremost among the manufacturing concerns of Cohoes. The company had been incorporated under the general act, in the previous year, by the following stockholders: Peter Harmony, Henry Punnett, Peter Remsen, Francis Olmsted, H. J. Wyckoff, P. H. Schenck & Co., James Stevenson, Joseph D. Constant, William Sinclair, Van Wyck Wickes, Eliphalet Wickes, LeBron & Ives, Teunis Van Vechten, Joab Houghton, Charles O. Handy, Francis Griffin, Jacob H. Ten Eyck, Illis Winne, Jr., Hugh White, Henry Dudley, Stephen Van Rensselaer, Jr., and Benjamin Knower. The capital was $100,000 which was increased in 1839, to $150,000. The building (which is now standing immediately south of No. 1 mill, of which it forms a part according to the present arrangement of the company), was erected by Joshua R. Clarke and was completed in the following year. A report made in August of that year by Peter Schenck and Hugh White, the building committee, described it as follows:

"It appears by accurate accounts kept of expenditures that the cotton mill which is of very stout brick walls and slated roofs, four stories in height, one hundred and sixty-five feet long and fifty feet wide, with wheel houses at each end of the building of two stories, about thirty-nine and twenty-five feet each, with the flumes, water wheels, driving pullies, etc., etc., has cost the sum of about $60,000 Aug. 1,

1838. That the sum of $12,000 or thereabouts, will be required to finish the Cotton House, put up steam boiler and pipes for heating, two forcing pumps, hose, etc., and complete the tail race, with other small items that appertain to factory (not machinery)."

At the same time the company erected beyond the canal three brick tenements for the use of their operatives, containing each two stories and a basement, at the average cost of $3,000, and arranged for completing another in the following year.

In the same report it was stated that the saw mill, which had cost $6,000, had been kept in constant employ and at a profit on the investment though it would require $4,000 to purchase timber to make it a profitable concern. The managers had at this time three thousand spindles in the mill and were on the point of commencing operations. They had contracted with the Matteawan Company for the purchase of six thousand spindles, but the cost of the building was so much more than had been anticipated, that the company were prevailed upon to alter the contract, and furnished only five thousand, all of which were in operation in the following spring.

In this year were made the first preparations for the enlargement of the Erie Canal, and the changing of its course through the village.

It was the intention of the Cohoes Company to continue their first canal, running it further west, around the base of Prospect Hill in about the direction now taken by the Erie Canal, but the appropriation by the state of this land as the site for its improvements, made this impossible. The company of course sought compensation at once, and an arrangement for exchange was made, as set forth in the following act of the legislature, passed May 16, 1837.

"The canal board are authorized in this discretion to grant and convey to the Cohoes Company so much of the present Erie Canal (except the stone of which the locks and bridge abutments are constructed) as may be abandoned after the completion of the enlarged Erie Canal in satisfaction of the damages sustained by the said company by reason of the enlargement and alteration of the line of the present Erie Canal. Such grant shall be made upon such conditions and under such restrictions and reservations as the said board may deem proper."

The establishment of a large factory, and the commencement of work on the canal improvement brought here a number of new inhabitants, adding largely of course, to the business activity of the place, and making necessary a number of local improvements.

A change in the proprietorship of the Cohoes Hotel, during 1838, established, on a sound basis, an institution which for many years after played a prominent part in the history of the village. The first proprietor had been succeeded in a short time by Willard Jenks (known by the nick-name of *Quid*), who was followed by Messrs. Alby and Lyons. This firm had no better success than its predecessors, and was sold out by the sheriff. Up to this time, it is said, no rent had been paid for the building, the owners of which were so well satisfied in having it occupied as a hotel, that they asked no further remuneration — an instance of remarkable public spirit. After the failure of Alby and Lyons the property came into possession of Henry D. Fuller, who moved here from Waterford, and was afterwards joined by his brother, Edward W. Fuller.[1] Under the new management the hotel was greatly improved, and became one of the most important local institutions. For a number of years all the public entertainments and exhibitions were held in its dining room; the elections took place there at various times, and it was the scene of all the public meetings for different purposes which were held until some time after the incorporation of the village. If an improvement

---

[1] The subsequent proprietors have been Jacob Anthony, 1843-18—, Robert Williams, 1848. A. C. Bentley, 1848-50, Wm. Schouten, 1850-51, J. R. Wilkins, 1851-57, A. Van Der Mark, 1857-60, Oscar O Finney, 1860-65, Hulet Lake, 1865-70, *City Hotel*, Geo. Z. Dockstader, 1871-76, M. L. Crocker.

was to be suggested, or a remonstrance to be made, or money to be raised, or any matter of importance to the public in general to be considered, "A meeting of our citizens, to be held at the Cohoes Hotel," was invariably called, as the first proceeding.[1]

Among the improvements of the proprietors was the establishment of a regular mail stage, running between Waterford and Albany and making one round trip daily. The first public conveyance had been started about three years before by John Brown (a brother of Thos. V. Brown, now residing in this city) ; it was a vehicle of the simplest kind, and far from comfortable, being merely an ordinary box wagon, with an oil cloth top. Mr. Brown sold out to the Messrs. Fuller, who put on the road a new coach, of the kind we now call *old-fashioned stage coach*, but then regarded as a model of elegance and comfort.

There were few changes of importance during this year in the business interests of the place. Messrs. Hawes & Baker sold out their veneering and sawing mill to Levi Silliman, the former partner of Daniel Simmons, and commenced the manufacture of stoves, which they continued for some years, the only Cohoes firm, it is said, ever engaged in that business. Their castings were at first made in the Cohoes foundery, and afterwards in West Troy and Green Island.

Among the private residences built were those of Hezekiah Howe and Wm. J. McAlpine, both under direction of

---

[1] For many years the only places in town at which liquor was sold (except the canal groceries) were the hotel and Van Der Werken's grocery on the corner of Oneida and Mohawk streets. The latter establishment was a well known resort in the earlier days of Cohoes. It was originally kept by Jacob Van Der Werken, and afterward by his son, John B., known to the citizens respectively as *Yaupy*, and *John Yaupy*, both of whom were prominent in local affairs. The property on this corner came into the possession of Jacob Van Der Werken about sixty years ago and remained in possession of his family until quite recently, part having been bought by John Larkins in 1864, and a lot in the rear of the old grocery by Wm. Triebel, in 1865.

Joshua R. Clarke. The former, on the south-west corner of Seneca and Mohawk streets, now occupied by Dr. Moore, has since been considerably altered; the house of Mr. McAlpine (who was engineer of this division of the canal), on the opposite side of the street, is now occupied by W. N. Chadwick, and is one of the best preserved of the older residences of Cohoes. The valuation of land in the village, at this time, as appears from a memorandum in the patroon's office, was $1,000 per acre.

An important evidence of the growth of the village was the establishment of new churches. The Reformed Dutch church had been organized in November of the previous year, with the following members, of whom only the last two are now living: Nicolas Lighthall, Rosetta Lighthall, James Safely, Janet Safely, John Schoonmaker, Gitty Schoonmaker, Abram Weidman, Elizabeth Weidman, John Van Der Werken, Daniel Simmons, William Renwick, Isabella Renwick.

The corner stone of the first church, which stood on the same site as the one now in use, was laid on Sept. 4, 1838, by Hon. Tunis Van Vechten, mayor of Albany. A hymn was sung, composed for the occasion by Rev. Wm. Lockhead, first pastor of the church, and prayers were offered by Rev. Drs. Yates of Schenectady and Vermilyea, then of the North Dutch church, Albany.

In 1839 the Methodist church was organized by Rev. E. Crawford, under direction of Rev. Chas. Sherman. The original members were twenty in number, among them being Jas. Hemstreet and wife, Joseph Mudge and wife, Mrs. Timothy Bailey, James Shannon, Jonas Simmons, Sr., and wife, Baltheus Simmons, Mrs. Fuller, Joseph Gould, Sr., and wife, Wm. Dodge and wife, Silas Owen, Sr., Gideon Longley and Mr. Rhodes. The first services were held in the school house on Oneida street, in which the Episcopal church had been organized.

In May of the same year, the first Baptist church was organized, and the Rev. John Duncan ordained as pastor, the sermon of ordination being preached by Rev. I. Westcott, of Stillwater. These services were held in Harmony Mill, No. 1, and the church as then constituted consisted of twenty-four members, of whom Thomas Lansing is the sole survivor. Among them were Josiah H. Beach and wife, Alanson Cook and wife, Ebenezer Bartlett, wife and four children, Mr. and Mrs. Castleton, Peter Link, Rebecca Steenberg and Mrs. Duncan. The first deacons were Ebenezer Bartlett and Alanson Cook. For nearly a year the meetings were held in a boarding house, on the West Harmony, and afterwards in a building on Mohawk street, below Oneida, recently occupied by Peter Smith.

On the 10th of August the Presbyterian church was established under direction of Rev. Mr. Chamberlin, with the following members : Levi Silliman, Mrs. Clarissa Silliman, Timothy Bailey, Joshua Bailey, Joshua Bailey, Jr., Mrs. Almira Bailey, Augustus J. Goff, Asahel Goff, Mrs. Lucy Goff, Mrs. Melinda Goodsell, Maltby Howell, Mrs. Mary Howell, Mrs. Eliza Ann Tremain and Miss Fanny A. Hamilton. Of these, only one, Mrs. Clarissa Silliman, is now living in Cohoes, and only three are living elsewhere. Levi Silliman and Timothy Bailey were chosen to be the first elders of the church, and Maltby Howell was chosen as deacon. The church was organized in the house of Levi Silliman, in the northern half of the house now occupied by H. B. Silliman, on Saratoga street. That part of the house was not then finished as a dwelling, and could easily accommodate the infant church. The society then worshiped for a time in the building erected for a carpet factory which stood on the site of Gregory & Hiller's mill. The first church, a small wooden structure, was erected in the following year, on the northeast corner of Remsen and Factory streets. The building, which has since been used for a variety of purposes, is still standing, one door east of the corner, and is now used as a second-hand store.

In 1840, also, the Baptist church, was built on Remsen street opposite the Presbyterian church, on the site now occupied by J. H. Parsons & Co.'s mill. The building, the cost of which was $521, was afterwards moved to Canvass street opposite the Catholic church, and is now used as a dwelling.

In January 1839 the Cohoes Company's dam had been severely damaged by a freshet, which washed away about three hundred feet of the structure. The work of rebuilding it was completed during this year at a cost of $40,000, Oliver C. Hubbard being one of the contractors. The new dam was of timber, filled in with stone and concrete masonry, 1500 feet long and nine feet high.

The commercial depression from which the whole country suffered about this time was severely felt in Cohoes and between 1840 and 1842 the place made slight progress. Business of every kind was very dull, and many of the manufacturing establishments suspended operations. During this period the enlarged Erie Canal and the Troy and Schenectady Rail Road were in process of construction, and these alone kept the village from utter stagnation. The presence of numbers of men who were engaged upon them gave the neighborhood at times some little air of activity, and made brisk a few branches of business.

By this time quite a number of buildings had been erected on Remsen street ; most of them were dwellings, however, and there was yet no indication that it would ever become a favorite location for business, the universal supposition being that as the village increased, Mohawk street, to which business was then confined, would continue to be the principal thoroughfare.

In 1841 the first Methodist church, which stood on the west side of the street near the site of the present Clifton mill, was completed and was dedicated by Bishop Peck.

The building was of wood, cost $550, and had a seating capacity of two hundred. The principal buildings on the street at this time, aside from the three churches, and the factories which were near its intersection with Mohawk street, may be briefly mentioned. Between Factory and Oneida streets was the dwelling of Mr. Mudge, before mentioned; between Seneca and Ontario streets, on the west side, that of Thos. Hitchens,[1] a contractor on the enlarged canal; on the site of Adams's block was a row of tenements which had been erected a few years before by Oliver C. Hubbard; at the northeast corner of Remsen and White streets was the block of tenements owned by Egberts & Bailey; on the southeast corner the residence of Jno. P. Steenberg, and on the southwest corner that of Jacob I. Lansing, south of which was a small house owned by Samuel Cook; between White and Howard streets, on the east side were the residences of John Judge (now Mrs. FitzPatrick's) Henry Rockfellow, Mrs. Doyle and Jas. Shannon, and on the northwest corner of Howard and Remsen streets was that of Chas. O'Brien. Below Howard street, in the region long known as Cork Hill, the buildings were unimportant, most of them being shanties built and occupied by the laborers on the canal. On the corner of Remsen and Columbia streets, however, was a building of some size, owned by Patrick Judge.

The Troy and Schenectady Rail Road, built by the city of Troy, was completed in 1842. It was the first rail road which at all affected the interests of Cohoes people, though not the first in the vicinity, for the one from Saratoga to Troy, passing over Adams's Island, had been constructed in 1835. Judging from the opposition which was afterwards manifested when a second road (the Albany and Cohoes) was proposed, we may conclude that this enterprise met with little approval, especially from those older

---

[1] The building is now owned by Jno. Orelup. It was enlarged and converted into a store in 1870.

inhabitants whose land was called into requisition. At all events there is no record that the completion of the road was hailed with particular satisfaction, or celebrated by any unusual demonstration on the part of the citizens generally, though they at once proceeded to avail themselves of its advantages.

During this year the manufacture of bedsteads, which has since always been an important branch of Cohoes industry, was commenced by Orson Parkhurst.[1] His factory was located in a small building which had been used by Egberts and Bailey as a dye house, and was situated between their mill and that of Hawes and Baker. The power was obtained from a waste weir. All the work of the establishment was done by two men, and the quarters were so restricted that there was no room for the planing machine, which Mr. Parkhurst was compelled to place in the Wilkinson machine shop.

Another new enterprise was a flouring mill established by Messrs. Slocum & Granger in the carpet factory building, which they enlarged and remodelled for the purpose.[2]

The winter of 1842–43 was one of great severity. An unusual depth of snow covered the ground for many months and remarkably cold weather continued until the spring was well advanced — the date at which the Hudson River was opened, April 13, being the latest on record. An accurate account of the weather in Cohoes was kept by Postmaster Howe, from which, as containing several interesting local allusions, extracts are given below:

"*March* 17*th*. Snow fell this day about ten inches and is two feet six inches deep on the level at least in the vicinity of Cohoes. The mercury has several times during this month thus far fallen down to zero.

"18*th*. Road impassible for sleighs from Cohoes to Troy

---

[1] The firm afterwards became O. & D. Parkhurst, and later, Parkhursts & Fullers.

[2] The building burned a few years later and the lot remained vacant until the building of Smith, Gregory & Co.'s mill.

on account of snow drifts. The mail was brought from Troy on horseback in the forenoon of this day — was forwarded in sleigh in the afternoon to Albany. Snow three feet deep on the level.

"23*d*. Snow continued falling all day, high winds and cold. Roads impassible in many places. The mail stage worked its way down to West Troy and Albany in the afternoon. On the return left stage at West Troy and the driver and passengers returned thence on horseback.

"24*th*. Col. F. Lansing and others from his neighborhood made out to reach Cohoes this day by shovelling their way. Snow on the level between three and four feet deep, and continued cold as in February.

"*April* 4*th*. Many of the roads near Cohoes yet impassible.

11*th*. Snow is nearly melted away in Mohawk street. Town meeting this day at Yearsley's. Some went with sleighs, some with wagons and many on foot. The road is blocked with snow for two and three and some places four feet deep.

"14*th*. This is the most extraordinary season on record; the long continuance of winter weather (from the middle of November to the middle of April) and the depths of snow still lying not only in the country but in our streets, are unprecedented."

The enlarged Erie Canal, which under the direction of different contractors had occupied five years in construction, was finally completed in 1843, and it then became possible to increase the manufacturing facilities of the place. Deeds were duly executed, conveying the Cohoes Company's land to the state and the abandoned canal to the company, and the latter at once commenced operations. That part of the canal which ran east of the Harmony Mill, between the Two Locks and the Three Locks, became the second level, in the system of the Cohoes Company, and may now be described as extending from just below the pump-house to the jute mill. The level of the Erie Canal between the Three Locks and the One Lock (White street) became the third of the present system, having been united with the old Basin A, at a point near Factory street, and the level now extends from above the Strong Mill to the rear of the Clifton Mill. The remainder of the canal bed, from the latter point to the junction, became by degrees filled up, and some years later became a highway under the name of Canal street.

An important addition this year to the business of the place was a second axe and edge tool factory, established in February by Messrs. White, Olmstead & Co. The firm erected a small building at the head of Remsen street, on the site of Griffins' sash factory, and also rented a portion of the Wilkinson machine shop. At first but six or eight men were employed, but the business increased rapidly, and in later years the concern was one of the foremost in the place. The senior partner, Miles White, had been for some time in the employ of Daniel Simmons as traveling agent, and besides a knowledge of the business had gained an extensive acquaintance among dealers.

One of the first firms to take advantage of the improvements of the Cohoes Company was Egberts & Bailey, who commenced the erection of the mill on Ontario street (since greatly enlarged) which is now occupied by the Troy Manufacturing Company. For the first eight or nine years the operations of this firm had been limited ; the machinery was not entirely perfected, and it was some time before sufficient could be constructed to enable the production of goods to any amount. A carefully detailed history of their business during this time, showing the discouragements which attended the establishment and growth of what is now so important a branch of our manufactures, would be invaluable. At this date, however, the preparation of such a sketch is almost impossible, and of the accounts which have been published at different times many have been found to be so incorrect that they are not worthy of quotation. An outline of the history is all that can be satisfactorily obtained. The following published in the Bennington *Banner* in Nov. 1870, though inaccurate in some particulars, may be of interest:

"Twenty-five years ago, the writer, after going through as much circumlocution and full as many assurances as are required to work one's way into a Masonic Lodge, visited the knitting room of Messrs. Egberts & Bailey at Cohoes, N. Y., who were then the most extensive and successful and almost the exclusive machinery knitters in this country. Their machinery was an improvement on any then in use and was not patented. They preferred keeping it so secret that the monopoly which they enjoyed, would be, as it proved to be, more profitable and surer to bring them a fortune than to run the risks of improvements, infringements and impositions which then, as now, were sure to follow the public exposure of specifications and explanations necessary to be made in procuring letters patent. They employed only the most reliable workmen, kept their doors constantly fastened with spring locks, and allowed no man in their knitting room without first putting him under the most sacred obligations to divulge nothing which they might *learn* or *find* within those mystic walls. One Gen. Geo. S. Bradford ran the Cohoes mill by contract for two years, it being a stipulation in the contract *that he should not enter the knitting room*, and he did not until a defection on the part of the foreman made it necessary that some man should take charge in there. Timothy Bailey who was the inventor of the machinery then used, and the foreman Van Dwyer who had always run it, were the only persons who knew anything about it, and although they had come to have much confidence in Gen. Bradford's knowledge and management of machinery, the company could hardly suppose that he could run a set of knitters which he had never seen, and which were of an entirely different style, and far more complicated than the frames since in use, and turn out the usual and necessary quantity of goods. The sequel proved, as all who have since known the general would expect, that he did run it most successfully, and turned out, not only an excess over the usual amount of goods, but a much improved article. For many years this Cohoes mill was the only knitting mill of importance in the country, and was claimed to be the only one in the world where all the knitting of shirts and drawers was done by machinery."

The following is from an address delivered in 1866 before the National Association of knit goods manufacturers by Hon. C. H. Adams, then president of that body :

"I can remember, among the recollections of my boyish days, when the principle of knitting by power was first successfully applied in this country. It was first attained in 1832, although nothing of importance was accomplished until 1841. In those days the inventor and manufacturer, now one of our honorary members, was wont to wander through the streets of New York, urging the merchants to permit him to leave a sample of goods for sale. The whole production of that time did not exceed $40,000, now we estimate our production at half as many millions."

For some years, although the production of the mill was so slight, it could not all be disposed of in the New York market, so part of it was sold in small lots to Troy and Albany merchants and among the country stores in the vicinity. In Troy, it is said, Mr. Bailey would go from one dry-goods dealer to another, carrying packages of shirts and drawers and taking in return for their sale orders payable in goods, and with these the female operatives in the mill were paid.

In time, however, as Egberts & Bailey's goods grew into favor, the increased demand made such efforts as these unnecessary, and their business became established on a sound basis. When the building of the mill was commenced it was in a prosperous condition; the dullness of 1840 and 1844, had on the passage of the protective tariff act been succeeded by great activity, and during the previous year the firm had cleared $22,000. The mill was the first in the village, and it is said, in this country, erected especially for knitting purposes. The building, which was of brick, was originally one hundred and twenty-four by forty-five feet, and three stories high. Four sets of machinery were put in operation at first, and two more afterward added when the seaming room was completed — a brick building twenty-five by seventy feet and two and a half stories high, extending to the corner of Ontario and Remsen streets.[1] The builder of the mill was

---

[1] This was converted into a store by F. E. Pennock in 1859.

Joshua R. Clarke, and the wheelwright Jacob I. Lansing. Soon after it was finished the partnership was dissolved, Timothy Bailey remaining in the Miller building, while Mr. Egberts and Joshua Bailey took possession of the new mill. When this factory was erected, the Cohoes Company made use of the ravine at Ontario street, before mentioned, as a water-course; and the first bridge over it on Remsen street, a slight wooden structure, was built. The only means of crossing it before had been by two planks stretched side by side from one bank to the other.

In 1844 was built the sawing and veneering mill of Wm. Burton & Co., who for many years were among the most prominent firms of Cohoes. For some time previous Mr. Burton had been in business with John M. Tremain, their establishment being located in an upper story of the Wilkinson machine shop.[1] In this year he bought Mr. Tremain's interest, and also the machinery and fixtures of Levi Silliman, who had succeeded Hawes & Baker, thus securing a monopoly in Cohoes of that branch of manufacture. The building (now occupied as a knitting mill by Thompson & Horrocks), was of brick and stone, thirty by sixty feet, and had three stories including the basement. An upper story was occupied by Parkhurst's bedstead factory.

From this time there is nothing of importance to be recorded until the year 1846, which was one of marked growth in the business interests of the place. Among the most important accessions were two establishments for the manufacture of cotton cloth, the largest one being the *Ogden Mills*. The Ogden Mill, No. 1, the foundations of which had been laid in 1844, was completed in the following year. It was of brick, two hundred and six by fifty-one feet, and had three stories and a basement. Directly north of this was the No. 2 mill built in 1846, which was two hundred

---

[1] Tremain's predecessor in that building was an Englishman named Mills who had commenced the sawing business about 1835.

and fourteen by fifty-two feet and three stories high. These buildings have since been united. The two brick blocks across the canal west of the mills, were built at the same time for the accommodation of the operatives. The proprietors were Messrs. Tenney & Cowles, of Boston, whose agent in Cohoes was Luke Bemis.[1]

The Strong Mill, situated near Mohawk street at the head of the Cohoes Company's third level, was built in the latter part of the year, by Wm. N. Chadwick. The machinery was not put in until the following season. The building was of brick, eighty-three by forty-three feet, and had three stories and a basement. South of the mill, on Mohawk street, were erected three wooden tenements. Both of these mills were built by John B. Colgrove, then one of the principal carpenters of the place. With their completion, cotton manufacture took the foremost rank among the industries of Cohoes. The capacity of the Harmony Manufacturing Company's mills had been increased in 1844. The president's report for 1846, contained the following account of their transactions:

"The amount of goods made during the past year are 53,045 cuts of print cloths, averaging thirty-two yards each, containing 1,692,125 yards, showing an increase over the products of the preceding year of 5,400 cuts or 172,400 yards of cloth. 723 bales, containing 338,786 lbs. of cotton have been used during the past year."

In the spring of the year the Cohoes Worsted Company was incorporated, with a capital of $50,000, and commenced the manufacture of carpet and lace yarns in the building (on the site of the Star Mill) which had been erected by Hawes and Baker. Since this mill was vacated by Levi Silliman it had been occupied by Mr. Roy of West Troy as a butt factory, and by Alex. Rogers as a woolen mill,

---

[1] In February, 1847, a joint stock company was formed of which the trustees were Amos Tenney, John Tenney, Luke Bemis, Robert Curtis and Chas. A. Olmsted. Capital $100,000, which was increased February, 1848, to $200,000 and in April, 1850, to $275,000. C. A. Olmsted was agent.

the latter having possession of it in 1845. The Worsted Company built for its operatives the wooden structure on the upper end of Remsen street known as the *Mouslin de Laine Block*, which was destroyed in 1873. The agent of the company was Wm. Cockroft, who continued in business after its failure, which occurred a short time later.[1]

Two new concerns were located in the Wilkinson machine shop. On the third floor was the sash and blind factory of James Salisbury & Co.,[2] the first establishment of the kind in the place; in the fourth story or attic was the sofa and cabinet ware manufactory of Jacob Dodge, who employed as his superintendent R. T. Briggs. The two lower stories of the building, were then occupied by White, Olmsted & Co., the Wilkinson machinery having been moved by Mr. Olmsted, part to his foundery, and the balance to a machine shop which he started in the basement of Ogden Mill No. 1. In these two establishments, and in the shop of Baldwin and Baker, much of the machinery for the Ogden Mill was constructed.

A new building was erected by Samuel N. Baldwin on the corner of Ontario and Remsen streets (now Chadwick's Mill), and occupied by him as a machine shop. It was completed in the latter part of the year, and the first work of importance was the manufacture of machinery for the Ogden Mills. The wood work for the looms was made by John Baker, who was established in an upper story of the building.

The improvements of the past few years, and the consequent increase of population had fairly entitled Cohoes to

---

[1] He subsequently entered into partnership with Richard Hurst and Ephraim French. The partnership was dissolved in March, 1854, and the business succeeded to Mr. Hurst, who continued it until the premises came into possession of the Star Knitting Company. Mr. Cockroft was engaged for some time in the grocery business in the store at the junction of Mohawk and Remsen streets, but disposed of his interest in 1853, to Geo. Wood.

[2] Afterward Loveland and Palmer.

rank as a growing town, and as such one of her first requisites was a newspaper. This want was supplied by the establishment of *The Cohoes Advertiser*, a weekly journal, the first number of which was issued February 9th, 1847, by Ayres & Co.[1] The firm was composed of Alexis Ayres and Wm. H. S. Winans, two young printers from Troy, the editorial department being under control of the former. The paper was twenty by twenty-eight inches, and contained twenty-four columns, about half of which were occupied by advertisements. The first and fourth pages contained miscellaneous literary matter; the second page was devoted to general news, editorial articles and local items — the latter being sadly in the minority. This arrangement was continued for a number of years, and until communication with Troy and Albany became easier, and the newspapers of those places acquired a large circulation here, general news occupied a great part of the local paper. The supposition was, doubtless, that as the place was small, everybody would know of home matters without being told, and would prefer a paper which gave them information of the outside world. This deficiency in the local columns, though probably satisfactory to the subscribers, is not entirely so to one who is searching for facts in the early history of the place.

After the establishment of this newspaper, however, the growth and history of Cohoes can be much more easily followed — valuable information being often found in a mere paragraph, or an advertisement ; and as the materials for this sketch for ensuing years have been taken almost entirely from its files, it would be ungrateful to make any com-

---

[1] The office of the paper was first established in a building in the south part of the Ogden mill yard, which has since been removed, and now stands near the rail road bridge. In April it was removed to Factory street, "first door below the old canal." In July it was again moved to the southwest corner of Factory and Remsen streets, over the store now occupied by Geo. E. Thompson, and at that time by E. G. Mussey. From there it was taken to the Wilkinson building occupied by White. Olmsted & Co.

plaints, especially since it is fair to presume that however meager the local columns may have occasionally been, all matters of particular importance were recorded.

The leading article of the first *Advertiser* was a salutatory, over a column in length, in which were stated the politics of the proprietors (whig), their motives for establishing the paper and their expectations in regard to it. Another column was devoted to a comparison of the tariff of 1846 with that of 1842, with coments on an article which had appeared in the *Troy Budget* in regard to the establishment of the Ogden mills. There were only two local items, both in reference to a fire on Mohawk street, which was thus described:

"On Thursday night last our village was visited by a fire which for a time threatened great destruction, but through the indomitable exertions of our citizens its onward progress was arrested. It originated in a two story building, the lower part of which was occupied by Messrs. Howe & Ross as a drug store, the upper part by S. H. Foster, Esq., and Messrs. Miller & Van Santvoord, attorneys, and Dr. Goss, as dentist. The building was owned by the Cohoes Company, and not insured. Howe & Ross were insured for about $900. S. H. Foster, Esq., loss about $200, no insurance. Messrs. Miller & Van Santvoord's loss about $1000, no insurance. Dr. Goss's loss $100, no insurance. The fire soon communicated with the post office building owned by D. W. Leland, Esq. The contents of the office were saved — building insured in the Saratoga Co. Mutual for $300. Here the progress of the flames, which for a time threatened destruction to a row of wooden buildings south, was arrested by the persevering exertions of our citizens, who with ropes and axes succeeded in razing it to the ground, preventing its further extension." The Cohoes advertisers in this number were as follows:

Lawyers: S. H. Foster, Miller & Van Santvoord.

Dealers in Dry Goods and Groceries: Wm. H. Hollister & Co., Caw & Quackenbush, White, Olmsted & Co., Jones & Southworth, Jno. P. Steenberg, P. Kendrick & Son, F. W. Farnam, J. G. Burnap, W. D. Russell & Co., **Patrick Mc Entee.**

Clothing, etc.: E. C. Howe, Twining & Alden, Waring & Robbins.

Stoves, etc.: John D. Luffman.

Drugs, etc.: Howe & Ross.

Cohoes Hotel: Robert Williams.

Dentist: O. P. Yates.

Axes, etc.: White, Olmsted & Co.

Cohoes Foundery: Chas. A. Olmsted.

Cabinet Ware: Jacob Dodge.

Of these business men only one, Isaac Quackenbush, is now remaining in the place.

In the next issue, a number of new advertisers appeared, among them Wm. Burton & Co., saw mill, John M. Coon, boots and shoes, James G. Foster, leather, and A. L. Phelps, hair dresser.

The editor announced his intention, in the issue of Feb. 23d, of publishing a series of articles on the "History and Manufactures of Cohoes, from its earliest infancy," and added " We shall have no objection to mix with it a bit of the romantic, and for that purpose invite the ladies of our village to exercise their imaginations in penning a tale of 'love and daring' by some Indian maid of the Valley of the Mohawk." Several prizes were offered for contributions of this kind, but none ever appeared. The articles on the manufactures were published, however, and afford us an interesting glimpse of the state of Cohoes industry at that time. The first of the series, from which extracts are given below, appeared March 9th.

" The oldest inhabitant informs us that when he came to this place, sixteen years ago, the number and quality of the buildings were neither worth computing or placing a value upon. There were five tenements constructed of the most rude material, and in the one story building now occupied as the justice's office (the Richard Heamstreet tavern), he obtained his board and lodging until he secured a home in the suburbs. This was only sixteen years ago ; now, with its magnificent water power improved, extensive manufactories, behold, how great the change. While its sister village of Waterford has hardly held its own, Cohoes has been extending its borders until it now boasts of a population of 4,000. . . . . The first cotton factory was built in 1837. There are now 4 extensive cotton factories, 2 factories for making cotton and woolen shirts and drawers, 1 factory for making worsted yarn and mouselin de laine, 2 extensive axe factories, 2 grist mills, 1 saw mill for making veneer and looking glass backs, 1 paper mill, 1 iron foundry, 1 paint mill, 2 machine shops, 1 bedstead factory, 1 sofa factory, 1 scythe and edge tool factory. Axes and edge tools are also manufactured at the extensive manufactories of Messrs. Simmons and White, Olmsted & Co. . . . . The increase in population during the last year is about 1000. . . .

"There are now in Cohoes 15 stores and groceries, two stove and tin ware establishments, 2 drug stores, 3 clothing stores, 1 leather store, 1 dentist, 4 physicians, 3 lawyers, 5 places of public worship, 1 large hotel, 2 shoe stores."

The figures given in descriptions of the different establishments, which were published during the next few weeks, are quoted below. A comparison of them with the industrial statistics of the present day is interesting, as affording one of the best means of judging the growth of the place.

"The Harmony Mill has nearly 8,000 mule and throstle spindles and 220 looms in operation, producing over 1,500,000 yards of printing cloths annually. The annual consumption of cotton is over 700 bales averaging 450 lbs. each; 250 to 260 operatives are employed in this factory, of whom about 60 or 70 are girls occupied in the weaving rooms. Upwards of $3,000 are disbursed monthly to operatives alone.

"The Strong Mill has 2,700 spindles which supply yarn for 80 looms. The annual production is estimated at 750,000 yards. The number of hands employed is 69. The consumption of cotton is nearly 300 bales per year."

"The Ogden Mill, No. 1, contains 7,000 spindles (self actor mule), and 180 looms. Warp No. 30, filling No. 32, 70 ends warp and 78 picks filling to the inch. 20,000 yards of 41 and 36 inch goods are manufactured weekly. About 5,500 lbs. cotton used weekly. No. 2 mill contains 8,500 mule and throstle spindles and 200 looms, and will when in full operation turn out 3,500 yards weekly. 250 hands are now employed in each mill. Pay roll about $3,000 monthly for each mill.

"The Cohoes Iron Foundry. Mr. Olmsted now employs in these works about 60 operatives.

"Dodge's Sofa Manufactory. This establishment is capable of manufacturing from 15 to 20 sofas per week.

"Simmons's Axe and Edge Tool Manufactory. About 200 men are employed in this manufactory, and when on their way to and from their work look like an army. 600 tons of iron and 100 tons of cast steel are manufactured up yearly, and 1,200 tons of coal are consumed. 50 doz. axes besides tools, are manufactured daily.

"Messrs. White, Olmsted & Co. now employ about 60 men and are making from 250 to 300 axes per day.

Messrs. O. and D. Parkhurst's Bedstead Factory is capable of manufacturing from 100 to 150 bedsteads per week, from the common rope bedstead to the most finished article in use.

"Sash and Blind Factory, by Jas. Salisbury & Co. They enjoy facilities for making sash for 50 windows per day, and a proportionate number of venetian shutter blinds. From 6 to 8 men are employed.

"The Cohoes Worsted Co. The number of spindles in operation is 2,000. Combing machines 2. 30 men are employed in combing by hand. The whole number of operatives employed is 130. Amount paid per month $1,000. 500 lbs. of wool are manufactured up per day.

William Burton employs 8 or 9 hands.

"The Cohoes Knitting Factory, by Timothy Bailey. Mr. B. employs about 50 operatives. In this factory are 18 knitting frames in operation, 800 spindles and 3 sets of cards. About 1800 pairs shirts and drawers can be manufactured per week by this machinery. About 1000 lbs. wool and the same amount of cotton are manufactured up each week. Egberts & Bailey work up about 400 lbs. wool a day employing about 250 operatives."

A creditable feature of the early numbers of the *Advertiser* was the poetical column, sustained by local talent. The chief contributors were S. H. Foster, for years a prominent lawyer of the place, and Wm. G. Caw, of the firm of Caw & Quackenbush.

In the issue of April 27th is first mentioned the Young Men's Association, an organization which had been formed a short time previous and afterwards became a prominent institution of the place. Its objects were the formation of a library, and the support of a lecture course, in which it had a fair degree of success. The officers, as elected this year, were: Luke Bemis, president; Henry D. Fuller, first vice president; Geo. Abbott, second vice president; Jacob W. Miller, corresponding secretary; Andrew Alexander, recording secretary; Joshua R. Clarke, treasurer. Managers: J. M. Brown, H. En Earl Jr., Wm. Leckie, Daniel McElwain, Charles O'Brien, S. H. Foster, J. Van Santvoord, C. A. Olmsted, C. A. Stevens, Darius Parkhurst, Wm. H. S. Winans.

The first allusion in the columns of the paper to means of communication between Cohoes and Troy was the following advertisement:

"COHOES AND TROY RAIL ROAD.
New arrangement.

On and after March 10th, the cars on this road will run as follows:

Leave Cohoes	Leave Troy
¼—6	7—¼
¼—8	10—½
¼—11	1
¼—2	5
5—¼	6½

Perham and Pettis[1]

Cohoes, March 7, 1847."

This Cohoes and Troy Rail Road was an institution established several years after the opening of the Troy and Schenectady road. Perham and Pettis, who had succeeded the Messrs. Fuller as proprietors of the stage line in 1843, made an arrangement with the rail road officials by which an extra car was attached to the westward bound trains.

---

[1] The fare, as stated in a later advertisement, was 6¼ cts. to Troy and 18¾ cts. to Albany.

This car was dropped at Cohoes, and as the grade was heavy between here and Troy, could be started on the downward trip by simply loosening the brakes, and would acquire sufficient momentum to carry it to the Troy bridge; it was then drawn to the station by horses. This method of travel proved popular, and the investment doubtless paid. In the *Advertiser* of July 6, it was stated that "1700 passengers were carried over the Cohoes and Troy Rail Road yesterday." Beside the above route Messrs. Perham and Pettis kept possession of the stage line, and for some time enjoyed a monopoly of the business. On June 8th, the following advertisement appeared:

"COHOES AND ALBANY, SUMMER ARRANGEMENT."

Mail Stages.

The subscribers have placed upon the route a new and commodious stage with four horses and will run for the accommodation of passengers as follows: Leave Cohoes post office at 1½ P. M. Leave Albany Museum at 4 P. M. Fare 25 cents.

PERHAM and PETTIS."

However restricted in former years, Cohoes people appear now to have had abundant facilities for travel. Another stage line was announced soon after as follows:

"CLEAR THE TRACK!

NEW MAIL LINE.

Waterford, Cohoes, West Troy and Albany —
The undersigned having fitted up a neat coach for the accommodation of the traveling public, and also for carrying the mail, respectfully gives notice that he will, on and after the 5th of October, run as follows:
Leave Cohoes for West Troy at 8 A. M., returning at 9 A. M.
" " " Waterford at 10 A. M., returning at 12½.
" " at 1½ P. M., passing through West Troy at 2 P. M.
Returning, will leave Albany at 4 P. M.

Fare from Waterford to Albany, 25 cts.
"   "   Cohoes   "   "   25 "
"   "   "   " Troy 12½cts.
"   "   Troy   " Albany, 12½cts.

The undersigned trusts that by punctuality and a fervent desire to please, to merit a share of public patronage.

JAMES HUBBARD.

Cohoes, Sept. 29, 1847."

The project of connecting Van Schaick's Island with Cohoes, which has been but recently carried out, has been under discussion for many years. One of the earliest suggestions on record in regard to it is the following from the *Advertiser* Nov. 14 :

"Some time since we called the attention of the people to a proposed route for a railway between here and Troy which would cost comparatively a small sum. The route was to connect Van Schaick's Island to the main land at a point east of the Dutch church by means of an open bridge, and thus reach the line of the Saratoga and Troy rail road. . . . The cheapness of this route and the fact of its decreasing the present traveled distance between our village and Troy, with which city our business relations are so extensive, are conclusive in its favor."

The citizens of Cohoes have always responded liberally to any call for aid to those in need, and the sufferings of the Irish people from the famine of this year, for the relief of which so much was done in this country, did not pass unnoticed here. An Irish Relief Association was formed, which raised money sufficient for the purchase of fifty barrels of meal, which were sent to the sufferers. The following report, from G. J. Slocum, who furnished the meal, shows the amounts contributed by different individuals as chairmen of committees, etc.

D. P. McDonald,	$33 00
Michael Donovan,	14 00
J. M. Brownson,	3 50
H. D. Fuller,	21 75
G. J. Slocum,	8 00

H. En Earl,	3 00
C. A. Olmsted,	37 50
Miles White,	23 50
Geo. Abbott,	2 50
Mr. Connaughty,	1 00
Luke Bemis,	62 50
Egberts & Bailey,	8 00
Egbert Egberts,	20 00
	$238 25

A fire on the morning of Nov. 28th, destroyed the paint mill belonging to Jeremiah Clute,[1] situated near Courtland street east of Mohawk, at a loss of $2,000. The *Advertiser* took occasion to again urge the necessity of the organization of a fire department, saying that if it had not been for several inches of snow which fell during the previous night severe damage would have been done to adjacent property.

An important addition to the religious bodies of Cohoes, was St. Bernard's Catholic church, organized in the early part of the year, by Rev. Bernard Van Reeth, a Belgian. Mass was first said in an old shop, located on what was then known as the *Flats*, and later, the services were held in a carpenter's shop on the east side of Remsen street, just below Howard. This building has since been moved to the rear of the block now owned by Wm. Healey, and is now used as a dwelling. The Catholics in Cohoes, of all nationalities, numbered at that time 300.

The corner stone of the church was laid Nov. 18th by Bishop McCloskey, assisted by Rev. Father Van Reeth and several other clergymen. The *Advertiser*, after describing the ceremony, said: "We congratulate our citizens in the prospect of having another handsome building to adorn our

---

[1] This mill had not been long established. Another was soon afterward built by Mr. Clute on the bank of a ravine about half way between the Cataract House and the present East Harmony school-house. This was burned Feb. 21, 1850, and then rebuilt, and then again burned March 3, 1852.

village. We understand that the new church is to be a gothic structure forty-five by eighty feet, with a tower and spire. For ourselves, we wish the projectors every success."

During the year about forty buildings — stores and dwellings — were erected ; many of them being on Remsen street, which within a short time had considerably increased in importance. During 1846, the residence of Luke Bemis (now S. A. Becker's) on the corner of Seneca and Remsen streets, and the store and dwelling of W. H. Hollister, on the northeast corner of Remsen and Oneida streets, had been built; the principal additions in the following year were the Granite Hall Block, built by Mr. Baker, corner of Ontario and Remsen streets ; the block of Caw & Quackenbush, southwest corner of Oneida and Remsen streets, and the building adjoining it owned by Miller & Van Santvoord, the two last named now forming Silliman's Block. Another important structure, was a four story building, forty by one hundred feet, erected by H. C. Billings of Schenectady, just north of Seneca street, on the site of Johnston's Block. This was used as a hotel, the ground floor being occupied by stores, and the upper story as a public hall. It was to be called the *Claxton House*, after Col. F. S. Claxton, agent of the Cohoes Company, but the name finally adopted was the *Van Rensselaer House*. It was described in the *Advertiser*, as " similar to the Delavan House, in Albany." "This," said the editor, " in addition to the buildings of Mr. Baker, Miller & Van Santvoord and Caw & Quackenbush, the new Presbyterian and Methodist churches, will render Remsen street the Broadway of Cohoes."

In the rear of the hotel Mr. Billings commenced the erection of a factory, in later years known as the Mohawk Mill, the first story of which was completed in the latter part of the year, but for some reason the building was not finished until some time after.

Other new structures were the bedstead factory of Messrs. Parkhurst, a brick building thirty-five by seventy feet, and three stories high, which stood near the north end of the present jute mill; a brick store on the opposite side of the street owned by Wm. N. Chadwick, which the editor described as the "handsomest store in the village," and a brick school house on the corner of Canvass and Oneida streets, which was built by A. L. Ferguson. Its erection was procured mainly through the efforts of Messrs. J. W. Miller and C. A. Olmsted, then school trustees.[1] Preparations were also made by F. W. Farnam for the erection of the three story brick store on Mohawk street, foot of Factory, which now forms part of North's Block. A small wooden store on its site, which had been occupied by the Messrs. Fuller, was moved to the south corner of Remsen street and St. John's alley, and used by J. M. Brown as a shoe store. It is now owned and occupied by Mrs. Ira Terry. These improvements, indicating a good degree of prosperity, were made the subject of frequent congratulations by the editor of the *Advertiser*. One article, entitled "CANT HELP CROWING," after stating that "Cohoes and *improvement* are synonymous" and enumerating the buildings then in progress, concluded as follows:

"Now for a village charter — for the water works — three or four good engines — clean streets — and a law limiting the number of dogs in each family to two, a law also prohibiting swine running at large, and we are a made community."

---

[1] This building remained in use until March, 1871, when it was sold to A. J. Griffin, who converted it into a dwelling house.

VI.
1848 TO 1854.

SINCE 1840, there had been a wonderful increase in the activity of Cohoes. The establishment of two large cotton factories, a new knitting mill, and a number of miscellaneous concerns added greatly to the population and business importance of the place. The hamlet of fifteen years before, containing a score of houses, had now become a thriving village, with every prospect of rapid growth; its development, after a long struggle, was well under way, and the time had come for the inhabitants to take measures for its systematic organization and improvement.

The necessity of incorporating the village had been for some time felt by many citizens, but the project was agitated for a year or more before the general feeling in its favor was strong enough to carry it into effect.

In April 1847, the six weeks notice for application to the legislature for a charter was filed, but nothing further was accomplished. Agitation of the matter continued during the year, and it was made the subject of numerous articles in the *Advertiser* setting forth the benefits which would result from incorporation. The following is a specimen:

"The annual tax consequent upon it is nothing in comparison with its manifold advantages. We should then have comfortable and convenient sidewalks and not be subjected to the disagreeable necessity of traveling through mud, ankle deep, or being ship-wrecked in any one of the many ditches and puddles which are too abundant by half, or of being brought up "all standing," as the term is, against some stump or post placed out of line. In the event of being incorporated, some little degree of pride would be evinced by our law makers, and an efficient Fire Department would be organized. Send in the petitions, then; press them upon the attention of the legislature, and let us have some laws by which to be governed in future, the observance of which will tend to beautify and improve the appearance of our growing village."

Such appeals from the editor, and the continued efforts of the friends of incorporation seem to have had their effect. A meeting of the electors at the hotel was called Feb. 3d, of which notice was given in the paper as follows: "Reader, dear reader, dear indulgent reader, in view of the past let us do something for the future. There is to be a meeting to-morrow evening at mine host Williams's to take into consideration the first steps towards getting a charter for this village. Several worthy individuals have been missing during this latter " thaw." Come to the meeting, and go it strong for a charter or a line of life boats."

The following is a copy of the proceedings of this meeting: "Chas. A. Olmsted was appointed chairman, and Leonard Van Dercar secretary.

"The secretary then read part of the act relating to incorporations. John Van Santvoord, Esq., submitted the following resolution which was adopted :

"*Resolved*, That in the opinion of this meeting it is expedient that we take the necessary steps to incorporate the village of Cohoes.

"On motion of Egbert Egberts, Esq., that a committee of five be appointed by the chair to take the necessary steps for the incorporation, the chair appointed as such committee Egbert Egberts, Wm. N. Chadwick, John Van Santvoord, Jeremiah Clute, and Henry D. Fuller. It was moved and adopted that the chairman, Chas. A. Olmsted, be added to the committee, and that the committee have discretionary power to determine on the boundary of such charter and also to call further meeting."

The matter was then pressed rapidly forward, and the charter was drawn up by John Van Santvoord, who had been from the first one of the most active men in its favor.

A map of the territory to be incorporated (now on file in the county clerk's office) was made by John P. Steenberg, April 15th, in which the area of the village is given in 1603.22 acres. On June 5th the application for incorporation was granted by the court of sessions at Albany, which appointed as inspectors of election, to canvass the vote of the electors upon the measure, Chas. A. Olmsted, Origen S. Brigham and Alfred Phelps. The election was held on the 1st July with the following result:

   In favor, ... 346
   Against, ... 26
              ─────
              372

The first charter election was held at the Cohoes Hotel a week later. The officers voted for were: five trustees, three assessors, a treasurer, collector, clerk, and poundmaster. The number of voters was 521. The first session of the trustees was held Aug. 4th, in Miller & Van Santvoord's law office on Remsen street, which was the place of meeting until the completion of the engine house in the following year.

Almost the first business done by the trustees was to take steps for the organization of a fire department. Up to 1847 the village had enjoyed a singular exemption from fires, but the occurrence of several disastrous conflagrations during that year awoke the citizens to the necessity of being better provided for accidents of this kind. Accordingly Miles White went to Albany, and on his own responsibility borrowed from the authorities an old hand-engine — No. 6 in the Albany department — which had been discarded because unfit for use. A small amount was spent in repairs, and the machine was brought to Cohoes, and though by no means in good working order, was used for some time. The only fire apparatus prior to this of which Cohoes could boast was a small rotary hand engine called the Excelsior No. 1, which had been purchased in 1834 or 1835 by subscriptions from a number of citizens, among whom were Joshua R. Clarke, Oliver Hubbard and David Wilkinson. Its insignificance may be inferred from the fact that in a report made to the trustees on the condition of the fire department, it was stated that "your committee would report that *they cannot find* the Excelsior engine No. 1." The machine had done good service, however, considering its size and power, for a number of years, and at one time was the means of checking a large fire in Waterford which threatened to consume the entire village. In later years, however, it was treated with a contempt which the memory of its past services should have restrained, and was kicked about from one place to another, the plaything of several generations of boys.[1]

After the fire on Mohawk street which is chronicled in the first number of the *Advertiser* it became evident that the village fire apparatus was greatly deficient, and a meeting of the citizens at the hotel was accordingly called for the purpose of arranging for better protection. A committee consisting of Luke Bemis, Egbert Egberts, Miles White, H. D. Fuller, G. A. Slocum, L. S. Fonda, Wm. N. Chadwick, Chas. A. Olmsted, S. F. Wilson and W. H. S. Winans was appointed to take the necessary steps and Luke Bemis was chosen to act as chief engineer in case of the occurrence of a fire. The result of this meeting was the purchase by Messrs. Fuller, Wilkinson and Olmsted of the Cataract hand engine, and the formation of a company, of which H. D. Fuller was captain. An entrance fee of $3 was charged each member, and the proceeds were devoted to the purchase of a hose-cart.

On August 11th, 1848, it was resolved "that the corporate authorities of the village of Cohoes purchase from S. Wilkinson, G. T. Olmstead and H. D. Fuller the fire engine, hose carriage and hose purchased by them from L. Button & Co., and to pay to them or their order the sum of $675." The department was regularly organized at the meeting

---

[1] It is said that the wheels and axles of the old engine are still in existence and form part of a cart used in moving iron about Morrison, Colwell & Page's mill.

of Oct. 4, 1848, from the minutes of which the following is an extract :

"*Resolved*, That two fire companies be organized in this village for the extinguishment of fires, and that one of the said companies be known and styled as the Parmelee Engine Co., No. 2, and that the other company be styled Cataract Engine Co., No. 3,[1] and that said companies be composed of not more than fifty men each.

"*Resolved*, That the engine known as Excelsior Engine No. 1, be placed in charge of the fire wardens to be and to remain under their direction and control, subject to the action of the trustees.

"On motion of Mr. Abbott, the following were appointed members of Cataract Engine Company No. 3 :

Wm. T. Palmer,
Samuel Wilkinson,
Chas. E. St. John,
Henry E. Robbins,
Henry L. Landon,
Julius Robbins,
Patrick H. Moore,
Wm. Green,
John Van DerMark,
Wm. Ferrell,
Joseph Hahn,
Alexander Hay,
Joseph M. Brown,
Marcus S. Deyo,
George Jackson,
Alonzo Wilmot,
John Eastwood,
S. M. Swart,
Jacob I. Lansing,
Isaac D. Ayres,
Sherman D. Fairbank,
Thos. H. Kendrick,
Joseph B. Prescott,
Wm. Manning,
Lucien Fitts,
I. F. Overpaugh,
Wm. H. Doty,
John P. Warwick,
George W. Miller,
Darius Parkhurst,
Wm. B. Barrett.

The following of Parmelee No. 2 :
Jacob J. Lansing,
Wm. L. Freeman,
Jos. C. Kittle,
J. H. Johnson,
Wm. H. Van Der Werken,
Henry Hall, Jr.,
John A. Miller,
Benjamin Franklin,
Malachi Ball,
Alex. McCalla,
A. F. Rockwell,
Wm. Shannon,
John McEnerny,
Herman D. Felthousen,
John Van Santvoord."

The Parmelee Engine Company took charge of the Albany

---

[1] On petition of the company the name was in 1850 changed to No. 1.

machine, which became No. 2, in the Cohoes department, and when this was returned in August of the following year, the company "ran with" the old Excelsior No. 1, chiefly for the purpose of creating a little healthful opposition. Arrangements were soon after made for an engine house. A report was submitted to the trustees Oct. 16, that "Mr. John Hays offers to sell to the village a lot twenty-five by thirty situated near the Methodist church for $350," and at the next meeting the president was authorized to purchase it. The price paid was $312, of which $112 were paid down and bonds of $100 each, payable in one and two years, executed for the balance.

The building (which is now occupied by the Campbell Hose Company), was erected in the same year by Henry Van Auken, the contract price being $750. Until its completion the Cataract was kept in a shed belonging to the Cohoes Company on Mohawk street on the site of Bilbrough's Mill. A barn which stood on the east side of Remsen street, south of Factory street, was also used for an engine house, the Excelsior having been kept there for some time.

In February of this year, the village paper changed hands, Alexis Ayres retiring, and his place being taken by Isaac D. Ayres, formerly of the Troy *Telegraph*. It was published for the next year under the title of the Cohoes *Journal*. The files during that time unfortunately cannot be obtained; which is especially to be regretted, since the incorporation of the village, the organization of a fire department, the construction of water works, and other important local matters doubtless furnished abundant material for interesting discussion.

The question of supplying the village with water by means of the Cohoes Company's Canal had been agitated during 1847. The first public movement in the matter was in response to the following:

NOTICE.

"The occupants of dwellings in this village are requested to meet at the Cohoes Hotel, Wednesday Eve, next, 23d inst., at 8 o'clock, to ascertain what encouragement can be given to the Cohoes Company for the establishment of hydrants in the principal streets and the introduction of water from their Summit Canal into the dwellings of those who desire it.

Chas. A. Olmsted,	L. Bemis,
Wm. P. Israel Jr.,	H. Howe,
Egberts & Bailey,	Miles White,
J. Van Santvoord,	Sam'l Wilkinson,
F. W. Farnam,	John D. Luffman,
O. & D. Parkhurst,	H. D. Fuller.

Dated Cohoes, June 19, 1847."

The result of this and subsequent meetings was an agreement, prepared in September, between the citizens and the Cohoes Company in which were stated the terms and conditions upon which the latter would commence operations. This was signed by a large number of citizens. The work was completed in 1848, and pipes were laid through the principal streets under the direction of Col. F. S. Claxton. The water was drawn from the Cohoes Company's upper level, the reservoir being near the point in the canal from which the water for Harmony Mill No. 2 is now taken.

A rail road between Albany and Cohoes had been talked of for some years. A movement in its favor had been made as early as 1846, but it met with some opposition, as appears from the following remonstrance to the legislature which was signed by a number of Cohoes citizens:

"The undersigned citizens of Cohoes in the county of Albany respectfully remonstrate against any act authorizing any rail road either to or through the village of Cohoes. Our citizens are generally opposed to the project, for the following among other reasons:

"1st. Such a rail road is entirely unnecessary.

"2d. The object is to divert the trade from a growing country village to an already opulent city.

"3d. The village is already cut up with roads and canals.

"4th. The effect would be to depreciate the value of property in the village and vicinity.

"5th. A rail road would be a great inconvenience to the farming community and needlessly expose property and life.

"6th. It is a project for the exclusive benefit of a large city without regard to the interests or convenience to the community in general who ride along the route of the proposed road. All of which is respectfully submitted.

"Cohoes, February 28, 1846."

In the following year a bill incorporating a company was introduced, but nothing came of it.

In the winter of 1848 the Albany and Cohoes Rail Road Company was formed, the following commissioners being named in the bill: John Stewart and John Cramer of Waterford; Hugh White and Egbert Egberts of Cohoes; David Hamilton and Wm. N. Chadwick of Watervliet; Jas. Horner, C. Van Benthuysen, S. Stevens, J. L. Schoolcraft, J. K. Paige, J. D. Wasson, Jas. Edwards, E. P. Prentice, Archibald McClure, Theo. Olcott, Wm. Smith, Peter Cagger, Ellis Baker, James Kidd and Stephen Van Rensselaer of Albany. The capital stock of the company was $250,000 divided into shares of $50 each. After many delays its books were opened for subscriptions, but the stock did not sell readily, and the company accomplished no more than its predecessors.

A number of new buildings were erected during the year, prominent among them being the new Methodist and Presbyterian churches. The former was a brick building, on Remsen street, on the site of the present church, and cost $12,000. The Presbyterian church on Seneca street (which has been greatly enlarged) was built by Joshua R. Clarke at a cost of $5,500, the lot, valued at $2,000, having been presented to the society by the Cohoes Company.

Among the additions to the business of the place was a machine shop in which steam power was used, established by Doncaster and Hay, on Remsen street, below Columbia, near the site of the residence of Wm. T. Horrobin. The firm did not continue long in business.

On January 1st, 1849, the village paper came into the possession of Chauncey Stow, Horace B. Silliman and Stephen C. Miller, who conducted the business under the firm name of C. Stow & Co., until March, when, on retirement of Mr. Stow, the firm became Silliman & Miller. Messrs. Stow & Co. changed the name of the paper to that which it now bears, *The Cohoes Cataract*, and made several alterations in its arrangement. On the first page, between the words "Cohoes" and "Cataract" appeared a woodcut of the Falls, with the motto underneath, "Goes sparkling, dashing, foaming on." The editorial column on the second page was embellished by another cut, representing the interior of the sanctum, in which three very jovial looking gentlemen (supposed to be the editors) were seen sitting at a table, which was covered with writing materials. The columns on the same page, devoted to news items, editorial notes, etc., were headed with titles appropriate to the name of the paper, such as *Cataract Foam*, *Floating Straws and Drift-Wood*.

There appear to have been few local events of importance during the year, and the editors were indebted to the streets and sidewalks for many an item. Complaints in regard to their bad condition with humorous or sarcastic comments, and appeals to the authorities to have railings erected in dangerous localities, were a prominent feature of the paper.

With the labor of perfecting the organization of the village government the trustees had found time during 1848, to do but little, except the establishment of a fire department, towards accomplishing those results which the editor of the *Advertiser* had hoped would follow incorporation. In the succeeding year, however, they were able to devote more attention to general improvements. M. McKernan was appointed engineer, and under his direction grades were established for streets and sidewalks throughout the village.

A number of streets were opened and declared public highways according to his surveys, among them Remsen, Pine and White streets and Trojan, Rock, and Cataract alleys.

The following list of moneys necessary to meet the expenses of the village for the year, which was voted for at the electors' meeting, in March, affords an interesting contrast to the city budgets of the present time :

1. "For the second installment of the purchase moneys of the Engine Lot, ... $100 00
2. For 1 year's interest on the village bonds given for the balance unpaid on the Engine Lot, 14 00
3. For furnishing and painting Engine house, 200 00
4. For furnishing Engine house and Trustees' Room with stoves, pipe and furniture, ... 75 00
5. For the hire of barn for safe keeping of Engine No. 3, ... 20 00
6. For paying expenses of the Fire Department,... 75 00
7. For an additional hose cart, ... 40 00
8. For the completing the establishment of grades for sidewalks, ... 100 00
9. For the expenses of laying cross walks, ... 100 00
10. For the compensation of the village assessors for the next year, ... 25 00
11. For the compensation of the village clerk for the next year, ... 50 00
12. For the compensation of the street commissioners for the next year, ... 50 00
13. For printing, ... 75 00
14. For books and stationery, ... 10 00
15. For paying the expenses of the annual meeting for 1849, and of special meetings,............ 25 00
16. For a fund for paying the expenses of enforcing the laws and other contingent expenses, 50 00
17. For the annual rent of water for fire hydrants, 25 00
18. For the fund for the compensation of the collector at 4 *per centum* for the next year, 44 00

And which said several sums in the whole amount to ten hundred and ninety (1,090) dollars."

The prevalence of the cholera during the summer caused some uneasiness, and several precautionary measures were taken by the trustees. The first Board of Health, appointed June 11th, in accordance with a proclamation by the governor, was as follows: Egbert Egberts, Francis S. Claxton, Miles White, Chas A. Olmsted, Samuel H. Foster; Health Officer, Wm. F. Carter, M.D.

On July 11th, the knitting factory of Timothy Bailey (now Holsapple's bedstead factory) was burned, the two upper stories being completely destroyed. The fire, which was one of the most disastrous that had yet visited Cohoes, was spoken of in the *Cataract* as follows:

"It is supposed to have been caused by spontaneous combustion of the wool and cotton. . . The building was owned by Mr. Haggerty of New York, and was insured sufficiently to cover the loss. Mr. Bailey's loss upon the machinery is estimated to exceed $5,000. How much stock was lost we did not ascertain. He was fully insured on all losses, but no insurance can compensate to him for the loss by suspension of his business at this most pressing season of the year when he was running night and day to meet his orders. The loss falls upon one of our most worthy citizens who has the heartfelt sympathy of all. And it is moreover a great calamity to our village, throwing out of employment nearly two hundred persons, whose main support was derived from this establishment."

Fire companies from Waterford and Troy were in attendance, and excellent service was done by the Cataract engine — of which it was said, "she has in this one instance well repaid her cost and the members of her company deserve the thanks of our citizens generally." Some of the machinery was saved, and with this Mr. Bailey removed in the following month to Ballston, where he established a mill. Another fire, in November, destroyed part of the building in the rear of the Van Rensselaer House, which had been erected for a factory by H. C. Billings.

"The building was occupied for a number of different purposes, having a Bat Factory, a Sash & Blind Factory in one end, and the large Saloon of the Van Rensselaer House in the other. The fire originated in the Bat Factory which was entirely consumed. The end containing the Saloon was saved. The Cataract Engine was on hand in good season and did nobly. The two force pumps in the Ogden Mills also threw a large quantity of water."

The saloon or ball room, referred to, was in the southern part of the building, and was entered by a passage from the dining room in the second story of the hotel. Under the ball room was a bowling alley. The cotton bat and sash and blind factories were in the north end of the building, and were owned, the former by Nicholas Coyle, and the latter by Overpaugh and Childs, who had moved from the Wilkinson machine shop the machinery formerly used by Loveland and Palmer, whom they succeeded.

A new business establishment of the year was B. R. Peck's Sash and Blind Factory, located in the Baldwin machine shop building, corner of Ontario and Remsen streets, occupying half of one floor. In later years as the business increased, Mr. Peck took possession of the entire main part of the building.[1]

In September a strike occurred in the Ogden Mills, which caused considerable excitement. The cause was a fifteen per cent reduction of wages. The agent, Mr. Chas. A. Olmsted, advertised at once for outside help, which was procured, and work resumed after a stoppage of three weeks. The Cohoes Worsted Company earlier in the same year had trouble with their operatives, and a public meeting of workingmen was called which condemned their action in most emphatic terms. Among their employés was Michael McKernon, who ran for surveyor-general on the workingmen's state ticket of that year. Other Cohoes workingmen, among

---

[1] The firm of Peck & Van Der Mark was formed in 1856, to which A. J. Goffe was subsequently admmitted, but retired in 1859. The business was disposed of in 1861 to Messrs. Falardo and DeVilliers, who conducted at until the buieding changed ahnds and was converted into a knitting mill.

them Wm. Manning, H. E. Higley and Joseph M. Brown, were prominent in that campaign, the last two named being on the state central committee.

The plank road fever was then at its height in this vicinity and a company was formed in which several Cohoes parties was interested, to build a road from here to West Troy. It was completed during the fall.

At different times during the year, local items on "Improvements" showed that the growth of the place was considerable. The following is from the *Cataract* of May 26:

"There are at present thirty or forty buildings going up, besides numerous other improvements. Somebody had better begin to think about a bill to make Cohoes a city — if we don't hold on a little we shall be big enough for two before the next session."

Among the most important buildings erected were the block of Egberts & Bailey, on the west side of Remsen street, north of Cataract alley, and the block on Mohawk street south of Ontario, which was built by F. S. Claxton, and is now owned by W. T. Dodge.

Among the matters of public importance during 1850, was a movement to change the school arrangements of the village, which were then under control of the town authorities. The village was divided into three districts, in each of which scholars of all ages and degrees of advancement were taught in the same building, and by the same teachers. The change proposed was to constitute the village one school district, which was to be divided into five wards. From each of these two trustees whose term of office was two years, were to be elected, under whose supervision the schools were to be properly graded, and by whom their affairs were to be managed. At a meeting held February 5th, to take action upon the matter, "A committee was appointed to draft a bill in conformity with the plan, and to circulate petitions for the passage of the same by the legislature. The committee nominated was: H. B. Silliman and J. M. Brown, from District No. 5; Wm. Manning and

Henry Van Auken from District No. 15 ; John McGill and Henry Howarth, from District No. 19. On motion, John Van Santvoord, Henry D. Fuller and Patrick Judge were added to the committee." The original plan met with some opposition ; at a meeting held the next week, a remonstrance was presented by Mr. Cary, signed by one hundred persons in District No. 15, against the passage of such a law. It was subsequently modified in some particulars, however, and the bill passed the legislature April 10th.

The *Cataract* during this year was frequently enlivened by spicy paragraphs on local topics, many of which, though affording an interesting glimpse of life in Cohoes at that time, can scarcely be considered as historical material. One matter, however, which was made the subject of much humorous comment, was deemed of sufficient importance to merit the attention of the trustees, which it received in the following resolution passed February 11th:

"Complaint having been made that Wm. H. Bortell has a bear near his house which is not safely secured, therefore

"*Resolved :* That the police constable be, and he is hereby ordered to direct the said Bortell in the name of the village to secure the said bear or remove him so as children and passengers shall not be exposed any longer."

Although a number of sidewalks had been constructed during 1849, there was still enough ground for complaint in this respect to justify the appearances of many editorial squibs. A rough wood cut, of which an outline is given below, was published in the issue of June 8th, under the heading, "A Cut on our Sidewalks," and illustrates the manner of grading which prevailed at that time.

The erection of a structure to be used as a court room by Justice Daw was chronicled as follows:

"THE NEW COURT HOUSE. This elegant structure, the

corner stone of which was laid on Tuesday of this week and which is now nearly completed, stands upon the corner of Remsen and Seneca streets[1] and just on the other side of a vacant lot commonly occupied by a large pile of hogs, in a great state of discomfort, for the purpose of rubbing off fleas against each other, in which they seem to do a large business. We think this a circumstance highly favorable to the rapid dispensation of justice and likely to give a new impulse to the progressive march of law and order through our village. This magnificent erection is about fifteen by twenty and about eight or ten high ; it is built of the best three by four joists and is, we understand, to be shingled with shad scales, both because they are the best to shed water and are also the most appropriate symbols of justice. . . . But joking aside, we are glad that we have at last got a convenient place for the administration of justice exclusively. Now who'll build a lock up ?"

Another subject which furnished abundant material for the local columns, during the years 1849, and '50, and at different times later, was the disagreement between the Cohoes Company and the village authorities in regard to the construction of railings, etc., and repairs of bridges on the property belonging to the former. The trustees claimed that those bridges within the village limits which were made necessary in consequence of the existence of the company's water courses, should be kept in repair by them, while the company insisted that as the bridges were used as a part of the public highways, all bills for repairing them should be paid by the village. The bridges had been for a long time in very bad condition, and complaints were so numerous that the authorities made some repairs on them, presenting the bill to the Cohoes Company with their assessment for highway tax. Payment was refused, and a long dispute ensued. In the trustees' proceedings of June 12th, 1850, " on motion of Mr. Caw, the president was authorized to enter into an arrangement with the Cohoes Company to have the bridge question decided by the Supreme Court,

---

[1] On the site of Musgrove's store.

and to enter into an agreement with them that in the meantime all necessary repairs to bridges and all necessary new bridges, should be made by the village and the company together, each paying half the expense, and that the losing party in the decision of the court refund to the other all such advances."

In July the bridge on Seneca street (which is now replaced by a stone arch) fell — not with a crash, said the editor, because it was too rotten — to the bottom of the ravine, while the Troy omnibus, filled with passengers, was not more than ten feet away. This occurrence, and the very bad condition of the bridge over Basin A, furnished subjects for fresh complaints. The matter was settled for the time being by an agreement in the following year on the part of the company to pay $1,225, in full of their taxes for 1848, each party to settle its own costs.[1]

The Fourth of July celebration of this year was the largest Cohoes had yet seen, and was entered into with great enthusiasm. The second page of the *Cataract* of June 29 was almost entirely occupied by the programme, printed in large type, from which the following extract may be made:

"The Baptist, Presbyterian and Reformed Dutch Sunday Schools, the Boght Sunday School, and the Sunday School at Mr. I. D. F. Lansing's, together with the Roman Catholic Sunday School, the Fire Company No. 3, and the citizens at large will celebrate the 74th Anniversary of American Independence at the Grove southerly from Prospect Hill. The several societies and associations, and the citizens generally, are cordially invited to participate in the festivities.

Mr. Pettis will be at the Dutch church with carriages to carry the clergy, the surviving heroes of the Revolution, teachers, and the younger scholars to Dickey's Grove. The remainder of the scholars and teachers, the various societies,

---

[1] The question was again opened in 1863, and occupied the attention of the trustees for some weeks. Propositions were made to refer the matter to an outside party for decision, but nothing was accomplished in this way. Some of the trustees were strongly in favor of suing the company. This course was finally adopted, and the village was beaten.

the gentlemen and ladies of the village, and all strangers will follow the carriages in procession with martial music. The other schools above named will reach the grove at the same time. The business of the day will be wholly subject to the marshal and his assistants.

MARSHAL OF THE DAY — Luman Dowd.

EXERCISES.

Prayer, by Rev. Mr. Pitcher.

Music, Anniversary Hymn, by all the schools.
Reading of the Declaration, by Andrew Lansing, Esq.
Short Oration, by Henry D. Fuller, Esq.

Music.

Poem, by S. C. Miller, Esq.
Hymn, "The Golden Rule," by all the schools.
Short Oration, by Chas. H. Adams, Esq.

Music.

Short Oration, by Joseph M. Brown, Esq.

Music.

Short Address, by Rev. Mr. Round.
The Long Meter Doxology, by the audience.
Benediction, by Rev. Mr. Waldron."

The refreshments were contributed by the citizens, and were collected under the direction of the Committee of Arrangements, which consisted of Wm. H. Hollister, John Van Santvoord, Jacob I. Lansing, Wm. Leckie, Stephen H. Adams and Miles White. In the evening a large display of fireworks was made from Prospect Hill, after which, said the *Cataract*, "the people were astonished and gratified at the unusual sight of a balloon ascension by night," for which they were indebted to Dr. C. F. Goss.

The question of extending Remsen street to Saratoga street was agitated early in the year, and the heirs of Abram G. Lansing offered to give the land necessary, if they could be released from assessment. A meeting of the tax payers, called June 20th, of which Egbert Egberts was chairman, and H. L. Landon secretary, decided that "at present it was inexpedient to open Remsen street below Newark." So the matter rested, and at a meeting of the trustees, a week or two later, Newark street (which had formerly been called Lansing street) was declared opened as a public highway.

A prominent addition to the manufacturing establishments of the place was the new knitting mill (now occupied by Parsons & Co.), erected by Egbert Egberts on the corner of Factory and Remsen streets. The building was of brick, fifty by one hundred and fifty feet and five stories high. The work was done mainly by Cohoes mechanics, as follows: Joshua R. Clarke, architect and builder; Wolford & Stephenson, masons; Jacob I. Lansing, wheelwright; Isaac F. Fletcher, marble cutter; and W. T. Palmer, painter.

The block of stores on the southeast corner of Remsen and Oneida streets, built by Dr. Carter, was completed about the same time.

An event destined to be of great importance to the interests of Cohoes was the change during this year in the proprietorship of the Harmony Mills. The career of the old corporation had been anything but successful. No dividends had ever been paid to the stockholders, and when the company sold out they had floating debts to the amount of their capital. The stock had changed owners from time to time, until in the last years of its existence the management of the company was in almost entirely different hands. For some time the company had no resident agent, but on the election of Mr Wm. N. Chadwick as president in 1841, an effort was made to induce him to make his residence here and supervise the business, which he afterward decided to do. Under his administration in 1844 additional machinery was put into the mill, which had previously been but partly occupied. In that and the following year some $64,000 were cleared — all the money the company ever made — and it was of course needed to meet the deficiency of preceding years. In 1846 Mr. Chadwick resigned, and his successor as president was Wm. C. Haggerty, who continued to be the active man of the concern until it was sold.

With the advent of Mr. Robert Johnston, however, the present superintendent, a new condition of affairs began, and the career of the company since that time has been one of steady and growing prosperity. Mr. Johnston was born in Carlisle, England, in 1807, and in that country had his first training in cotton manufacture. He came to the United States in 1833, and was for a time connected with the Providence Steam Mills at Providence, R. I., where he succeeded in accomplishing what had previously been thought impossible, the spinning of warps on mules. Soon after he removed to Valatie, N. Y., where he took charge of the cotton mill of Nathan Wild, and it was at his suggestion that Alfred Wild, the son of his employer, and Mr. Thomas Garner of New York, purchased the Harmony Mill. With the inauguration of the new management the mill was greatly improved, and its capacity increased to 8,000 spindles.

An amendment to the village charter passed early in 1851, provided for the election of a police justice, whose term of office was to be four years, and increased the powers of the trustees in several particulars. The amendment seems to have given general satisfaction, and was thus commented upon by the *Cataract:* "It will be seen that provision is made for the establishment of a municipal government which can effect everything desired in the way of law and order." The first justice under this act was Alfred Phelps, elected July 29. At the regular village election in March, the first school trustees were chosen, according to the act passed in 1850. On the organization of the board, Wm. G. Caw was elected president, and John Van Santvoord, clerk. The following committees were appointed : Finance : Burton and Parkhurst ; Library: Foster and Caw ; School houses: Travis and McGill; Text books: Caw and Travis; Teachers: Foster, Burton and Caw ; Tuition of non residents: McGill and Parkhurst; Select committee for organizing and grading schools : Caw, Foster and McGill. At a meeting held April 4th, arrangements were made to procure further accommodations. The basement of the Reformed church was hired at a rental of $40 per annum, and negotiations were commenced with the Messrs. Fuller for the erection of a two story school house in Remsen street, the yearly rent to be $85. The teachers were assigned as follows: District No. 9 (Harmony Hill), Henry Dubois ; District No. 5 (depot school house), E. H. Johnston and C. Allen, Miss Van Schaick, assistant ; District No. 13 (state yard school house), Mr. Landon. J. M. Brown's store on Remsen street was selected as a proper place for keeping the libraries of the district and it was engaged for $50 per annum, Mr. Brown to act as librarian.

In April, an act was passed incorporating the Cohoes Savings Institution, of which the corporators were: Chas. A. Olmsted, Truman G. Younglove, Egbert Egberts, Hugh White, Daniel Simmons, Isaac D. F. Lansing, Henry D. Fuller, Wm. F. Carter, Abraham Lansing, Joshua Bailey, Wm. N. Chadwick, Teunis Van Vechten, Andrew D. Lansing, Harmon Pumpelly, Edward E. Kendrick, Wm. Burton, Joshua R. Clarke, Jeremiah Clute, Miles White.

With the rapid growth of the place since its incorporation, the fire department was soon found to be inadequate, and it was accordingly voted at the annual meeting of this year to purchase a new engine at a cost of $600.

At the trustees' meeting held Sept. 23, a petition was presented from "Jacob J. Lansing and others, mainly persons who were members of the Engine Company, known as the Parmelee Company, asking to be organized into a fire company under the authority of the board." The prayer was granted, and the following persons were enrolled as the first members of Engine Company No. 2, afterwards known as the Mohawk :

Jacob Lansing, foreman ; John Fulton, 1st assistant ; Michael Larkins, 2d assistant ; John Doyle, treasurer; Wm. Shannon, Lewis Wells, J. Eastwood, Benjamin Hutchins, Malachi Ball, John Henry, John Larkins, Peter Moran, Robert B. Moore, Edward Hitchcock, Louis Savoid, Isaac Van Vliet, Isaac F. Runkle, Elihu M. Stevenson, Jacob H. Hallenbeck, Patrick Hines, Henry C. Rider, Joseph Gould, Henry Shepard, Franklin Waring, Timothy McGray, Henry Brown. In December the contract for building the new engine house was let to Aaron Ferguson. This was a low wooden structure, situated on Mohawk street south of the present Miller House, and stood directly over the Cohoes Company's canal.

Since 1847, there had been a number of changes in the proprietorship of the public conveyances. The Accommodation Stage to Troy was run in 1848 by J. A. Simons, in 1849 by S. C. Moore and in 1850 by J. A. Simons until September when the partnership of Simons & Ives was formed. The Cohoes and Troy Rail Road was conducted by C. O. Perham in 1849, and by John Dearborn in the following year, which was the last of its existence as a separate institution. After Nov. 1, 1850, the stages and cars were combined, under proprietorship of Dearborn and Ives, and made hourly trips to Troy. The Albany Mail Stage was conducted by H. N. Pettis. It made in 1849 three trips, and in 1850 two trips, daily each way. In the spring of 1851, both the Albany and Troy lines changed hands, and were run by Dearborn, Simons & Co., who continued in business until the stage lines were abandoned, Mr. Simons being in later years sole proprietor.

Several manufacturing establishments were started in this year. In March Thomas Fowler rented the building formerly occupied by Timothy Bailey, repaired the damage done by the fire, and put in knitting machinery. In the building in rear of the Van Rensselaer block which was afterwards known as the Mohawk Mill, Messrs. F. W. Farnam & Co. established a factory for making linen thread from American flax, G. K. White being manager. The *Cataract* of Aug. 16th said : " The establishment will when in full operation be the largest flax manufactory in the United States and the only one where the finer branches of the work are executed. It will employ 300 hands and consume 600 tons of flax per annum."

Another new enterprise was the wheel factory of Messrs. Wightman & Youmans, established in a building erected for them on Basin A, just south of where Brockway's mill now stands. They manufactured omnibus wheels for the New York and Philadelphia markets. The works of D. Simmons & Co., (which had been enlarged in 1845), were still further improved by the erection of new buildings. Additions were also made to Miles White's axe factory. In January, 1852, the partnership between Egberts & Bailey was dissolved, Mr. Egberts taking the new or Watervliet Mill, and Mr. Bailey the mill on Ontario street. The latter gentleman organized the Bailey Manufacturing Company, with a capital of $100,000, and Mr. Egberts transferred his mill to Chas. H. Adams.[1] These establishments and Fowler's were until some years later the only knitting mills in the place.

The Baptist church, which had stood on the site of the Watervliet mill, was demolished when that structure was built in 1850. The society at once commenced the erection

---

[1] The Bailey Manufacturing Company, of which the capital was reduced in 1856 to $50,000, continued in business till 1863, when the mill and machinery were sold to the Troy Manufacturing Company. Mr. Adams remained proprietor of the Watervliet mill until 1862.

of their present edifice on Mohawk street, foot of White, which was finished in 1851, at a cost of about $6,000. It was dedicated April 28th, 1852, the sermon being preached by Rev. Dr. Warren, of Troy. Addresses were also delivered in the afternoon and evening by Revs. G. C. Baldwin, of Troy, and H. G. Day, of Schenectady. The music was under direction of Lester Allen.

A number of public improvements had been made of late in the village, and newspaper complaints about sidewalks and railings became less frequent. New grades were established for Remsen, Oneida and other important streets, and Canal (now Main), Canvass White (now Canvass), and Howard streets, were opened as public highways. Street lamps, which had long been needed, were placed by several citizens in front of their dwellings, the example having been set by Miles White. Sidewalks were laid in many parts of the village and the Cohoes Company's water course on Ontario street, which had previously been crossed by a wooden bridge at Remsen street, was covered at that point by a substantial stone arch.

In October, the block known as the Van Rensselaer House was torn down by its owners, the Cohoes Company. The existence of quicksands under the foundation of the structure rendered it unsafe, and as tenants were with difficulty induced to occupy it, the investment had never been profitable. The first proprietor was J. H. Crane, of Schenectady, who sold in 1849 to John Parker, who continued in business little more than a year, and was then sold out by the sheriff. The arrangement of the ground floor of the building was similar to that of the present Johnston block; the bar-room was in the corner corresponding to that now occupied by A. M. Harmon's store; next to that was the main entrance, north of which were three stores. A brick block three stories high was built on the site. Cohoes during this year was rather quiet, if we may judge by the local columns of the paper. In December considerable excitement was caused by the failure of Miles White, with liabilities of nearly $200,000, which threw one hundred and fifty men out of employment. This was the first failure which had seriously affected the place, and afforded material for discussion for some time.

During 1853, however, there was no lack of subjects for local comment. Early in the year the rail road from Albany, work on which had been for some time in progress, was completed. As before mentioned, several companies which had been organized were unable to make any progress with the enterprise, and the people began to believe it was never to be carried out, but when, under the auspices of the Albany Northern Rail Road Company, the contracts were actually let, the prospect was more reassuring, and the satisfaction was general. The last rail was laid March 24th, and business could have been then commenced but the bridge was not completed. The *Cataract* commented as follows: "The rails having fairly been laid as far as the station house it may be safely affirmed that this old-new road is completed from Albany to Cohoes. Having struggled on under a hundred unfortunate accidents and been a laughing stock for years, it seems almost incredible that it has at last accomplished the original task."

The station-house, which was described as "one of the finest in the state," had been completed in the previous December. A trial trip was made as far as Cohoes, April 9. Two days afterward the road was formally opened. The afternoon train from Albany brought the president and directors of the road, and several prominent citizens, and was received here with ringing of bells and firing of cannon. The party was met by the board of trustees and a large number of citizens. T. G. Younglove, on behalf of the trustees, made the following address:

"Gentlemen: In behalf of the citizens of Cohoes, we

welcome you and congratulate you, that by patience, perseverance and energy a long desired object has been accomplished. The snorting and puffing of the iron horse in our streets, mingling as it does with the roar of our cataract, the sound of our hammers, the ring of our anvils, and the hum of our spindles, is an era in our history which we too, gladly receive congratulation for, and we say to you that we not only congratulate you, but we congratulate ourselves, and rejoice in the increased facilities you have given us for sending to market more than one and a half millions of dollars — the annual product of our labor and our capital. We rejoice, then, in the establishment of this new connecting link between our embryo, and your venerable city. I think I may say without exaggeration that our water power when its locality and extent are taken into account is the most valuable in the United States. We have the power to drive all your manufacturing establishments, even to your printing presses, and we will do it provided you give us the chance. Who can say that in the progress of the arts and manufactures, Cohoes may not be a great center of industrial pursuits, annually sending forth her products, to enrich and comfort thousands nay, even millions of the inhabitants of the earth? But I have digressed. Do not mistake the roar and din you hear around you for any other than that of friendly and cordial greeting. Even the waters of the Mohawk join in our greetings to you. Again I say, *we welcome you*."

Robert H. Pruyn, one of the directors, replied on behalf of the company. Speeches were also made by Judge Cheever, Mr. Wasson, and Col. J. W. Miller. After the excursionists had visited the Falls, the factories and other objects of interest, they assembled at the Cohoes Hotel, where, said the *Cataract*, " an ample and handsome collation was prepared which was thoroughly taken care of, and which prompted a pleasant interchange of sentiment on the part of those present."

The regular trains commenced running at once, eight daily between here and Albany, and were well patronized. An Albany paper of the 16 inst. said : " The Cohoes factories were to-day closed, in order to afford the female operatives an opportunity to visit Albany by the new rail road, which they availed themselves of in great numbers." The first ticket agent at this station was Chas. T. Carter.

The Cohoes Gas Light Company was organized in January under the general law, and had its buildings ready to commence operations in July.[1] The capital of the company was $50,000 and the first officers were T. G. Younglove, president, R. Merrifield, secretary. The other trustees were Egbert Egberts, H. D. Fuller, W. F. Carter, J. Bailey, H. Pumpelly and J. Battin.

On August 15th, the Cohoes Savings Institution, which had been incorporated some time before, commenced to receive deposits at the office, which was on Remsen street near Oneida, in the store at present occupied by Wm. Bell, dry goods dealer. The officers were, Egbert Egberts, president ; W. F. Carter, vice president ; Truman G. Younglove, tseasurer ; Edward W. Fuller, assistant treasurer.

Several articles were published in the local paper during the year on the manufacturing interests of the place, which indicated a fair degree of prosperity.

There were three knitting mills, run respectively by the Bailey Manufacturing Company, C. H. Adams, and G. Steer, agent for Thomas Fowler. They employed 750 hands, and produced 45,000 dozen goods annually. The production of the cotton mills was as follows:

Harmony Mills,	2,652,000	yards *per annum*.
Ogden Mills,	4,090,000	" " "
Strong "	800,000	" " "

The total number of hands employed was about 800.

In October a new mill was completed by the Harmony Company, adjoining their first building. It was 274 by 75

---

[1] These works, which were on Sargent street, continued in use until 1869, when the company needed more room, and erected the buildings occupied by them at present on the east side of the Champlain Canal, the producing capacity of which is 250,000 cubic feet per day, five times that of the old works.

feet and five stories high, with an L, 50 by 75 feet, which made the dimensions of the whole building 493 by 75 feet.

Other establishments described were Simmons's axe factory, Hurst's worsted mill, the Cohoes Iron Foundery (then superintended by Joshua R. Clarke), the bedstead factory of Parkhursts & Fullers (formerly O. & D. Parkhurst), Wightman & Youman's wheel factory, Burton's veneering mill, Peck's sash and blind factory, and John Baker's bobbin factory, situated in the same building. There were also several new firms. The Mohawk Mill, Samuel Bilbrough proprietor, and Wm. Baxter superintendent, which had been established the previous year, was located in the building formerly used as Farnam's thread factory,[1] and employed one hundred hands, producing 500,000 pounds of carpet warp and fine yarns per year. The Novelty Works, Joseph Haskins proprietor, were in the same building and employed twenty-five hands in the manufacture of twine. This concern soon afterward failed and Mr. Bilbrough took possession of the entire building. On Courtland street, east of Mohawk, a tobacco and cigar factory employing fifty hands was established by D. Cady Hollister & Co., and in the Miles White axe factory building on Mohawk street, a woolen mill commenced operations, ——— Hartness proprietor, and Jonathan Hiller superintendent.

A cotton flax mill on Ontario street, near the site of Brockway's Mill had been erected in the Spring by Bailey, Payson and Younglove. It was burned in October, however, at a loss of $6000, before operations had been fairly commenced.

The flourishing state of business was commented upon as follows by the *Cataract:*

"In proportion to its size, there is probably no place in the state of greater enterprise or business capacity than the

---

[1] After remaining in operation a short time this establishment had been removed to Mechanicsville.

village of Cohoes. To strangers, the statistics, if they could be obtained, would seem incredible, and would undoubtedly be thought exaggerated even by citizens. When we consider that it is scarcely more than ten years since this place was little better than a wilderness, the wonder becomes still greater, and forces upon the mind the conviction that in half, perhaps a quarter of a century, Cork Hill and Codfish Flats will be near the centre of a large and wealthy city."

The changes of time were thus spoken of in the issue of Oct. 1:

"Our village is not old enough to have an extended history but we must confess our surprise in looking over a copy of the *Advertiser*, published in 1847, to note the changes which time has wrought in this village even in so short time. Of all the persons and firms advertising their business in the place there are but *six* who are now residing here and continuing the same business. Many have moved away, some have changed their avocations, and many have gone to that bourne whence no traveler returns. And this is only six years, but yesterday!"

The Young Men's Association, before referred to, was in flourishing condition this year. The lecture committee, consisting of Wm. Manning, T. C. Carter, and Wm. G. Caw, provided an excellent course, which was well supported. Among the speakers of the season were Profs. John Foster, Lowell Mason, and L. N. Fowler, Hon. Ira Harris, Isaac Edwards Esq., and Mrs. E. Oakes Smith.

Among the chief topics of public interest was the Free Bridge question, which occupied a large share of the local columns of the *Cataract* for some months. The Waterford bridge, together with the residence of the gate keeper, Mr. Bonce, was entirely destroyed by fire March 13th. A meeting was soon afterward called, of which T. G. Younglove was president and John Fulton secretary, to take measures for the construction of a free bridge, and a committee was appointed to confer with the legislature on the subject. Considerable difficulty was experienced in procuring the passage of a suitable bill, as it was held by some parties that the state should construct nothing but a towing path bridge. Arrangements were finally concluded, however, by which the state was to build the main body of the bridge, and be entitled to the right of a towing path, while the piers and abutments were to be paid for by subscriptions from the citizens of Cohoes and vicinity. The contract was let in January, 1854, to Messrs. Smith and Bogue.

In the *Cataract* of May 20, at which time the bridge was nearly completed it was stated that "a large meeting of the friends of a free bridge across the Mohawk at this place was held this week, pursuant to a call of the citizens of Cohoes and Waterford, at the house of David Lamb of the latter place. Moses Bedell was appointed to solicit subscriptions in Saratoga County, and Adam Van Der Werken to perform the same duties in the county of Albany. John Fulton, Esq., of Waterford was appointed treasurer." The bridge was completed so that wagons passed over on the 4th of July. It cost originally about $25,000 and $15,000 more were afterward expended in repairs.

Another matter frequently discussed in the newspaper at that time (and in fact at intervals ever since) was the bad condition of the cemetery. This first received public attention at the annual meeting in 1852, when on motion of Mr. H. D. Fuller $400 were voted for purchasing and improving the grounds. No action was taken until the following year, when at the citizen's meeting held March 3d, it was resolved, "that a committee be appointed for the purpose of making a selection of grounds suitable for a village cemetery, said committee to consist of one person from each of the religious congregations of the village, and two from the village at large." The report of this committee was published in the *Cataract*, from which the following extract is taken: "They report that the wooded land south of Mr. Gage's, and belonging to Douw A. Fonda, can be purchased with right of way included for $200 per acre and is a very desirable location; that the present grounds can be obtained of the Cohoes Company for $100, and about eight acres north of and adjoining them can be purchased for $150 per acre. The committee recommend the purchase of the former in case the village wishes to expend five or six thousand dollars in clearing and beautifying the grounds, but if not, then they recommend the latter and say that the judicious expenditure of $400, in improving the old cemetery, will make it a very good place." Nothing was done after this report until 1854, when the condition of the cemetery became so bad as to call forth the severest comments. At the annual meeting a further appropriation of $300 was voted, and the following resolutions passed:

"*Resolved*, That the village accept the offer of T. G. Younglove in behalf of the Cohoes Company, of the cemetery grounds as a gift to the village by said Cohoes Company for a merely nominal sum.

"*Resolved*, That the thanks of this village be tendered to the Cohoes Company for their liberality in bestowing the cemetery grounds to the village of Cohoes."

A committee was appointed to superintend the improvements, consisting of Egbert Egberts, H. D. Fuller, H. B. Silliman, Jacob Travis and Matthew Fitzpatrick.

During the winter of 1853–54 the foundation was laid for the establishment of the Harmony Hill Union Sabbath School, an institution which has since been the means of doing great good in the place. It was organized originally as a branch of the Baptist Sunday School with Jas. Lansing as superintendent. The first regular election was held May 7, 1854, and resulted in the choice of Stephen Slocum as superintendent. At this meeting the total attendance was eighteen, as follows — four officers, three teachers, eleven scholars.

On July 8, the Strong Mill was burned. The original building, together with an addition of about the same size which was nearly completed, was almost entirely destroyed. Some of the machinery and most of the stock was saved, the entire loss not exceeding $16,000. One person was killed and several seriously injured by the falling of a wall during the progress of the fire.

The growth of the village continued to be rapid, and preparations were made for a number of new business enterprises. Among the buildings erected for manufacturing purposes were the bedstead factory of Jeremiah Clute on Mohawk street (on the site of Campbell & Clute's block) ; the flouring mill of J. M. Hayward, corner of Remsen and Ontario streets, into which Mr. H. moved from the Baldwin machine shop, and the rolling mill (now Morrison, Colwell & Page's), built by Mr. Simmons. The *Cataract* commented as follows on the improvements of the year:

"In three years Cohoes may apply for a city charter. The present population cannot be far from 6,000, and when the factories now in progress get into operation it will probably go up to 10,000. About 100 dwellings will be erected during the season, and rumor is busy about several other large manufacturing establishments. Hundreds of thousands of dollars are being invested here which cannot but prove profitable to the owners and give our village an impulse such as she has never before received."

VII.

1855 TO 1860.

THE census of 1855 showed that the population of Cohoes had been trebled within the past decade. The results of this began now to be shown in a demand for further improvements, for a different organization of the local government, and numerous other changes made necessary by the increased size of the village. For the next few years the steady growth of the place was manifested not so much by a large influx of new inhabitants, but by constant additions to its wealth, business importance and material improvements.

An act was passed May 12th which amended the charter in several important particulars. The village was divided into three wards; provision was made for the election of the presidents of the village and board of education, from the village at large; two trustees from each ward were to be voted for at the first election, one for the term of one, and the other for two years, and at each annual election thereafter one was to be elected to hold two years; in the same manner two school commissioners from each ward were to be chosen; the school law of 1850 was repealed and a new one enacted, similar in its provisions; the levying of a poll tax for school purposes was directed, new powers and duties were assigned to the trustees, and several minor changes in regard to the duties of village officials were made. The first election under the act was to be held on the third Tuesday of April, in the following year.

Since the passage of the act of 1850, the schools of the village had been greatly improved. At times there was discussion or complaint about some objectionable feature, but the system on the whole was better than those in vogue elsewhere. The following, published in the Albany *Knickerbocker* in January, shows how its workings were regarded in neighboring cities:

"The advantage of having our public schools entirely free is shown by the experience of Cohoes. Under the part pay system the number of pupils who attended school was less than four hundred. At present it is over eight hundred. This fact should not be lost on the legislature. It shows that what is done in Cohoes, should be done in every town in the state."

Besides the schools under control of the village there were also in operation the parish school connected with St. John's church, and a private school under the direction of Rev. Stephen Bush, who erected a building for the purpose on Mohawk street near the foot of Seneca street.[1]

The following list of the village schools and teachers for this year, compared with that of 1851, shows the extent of the improvements in educational facilities:

"*Brick School House* (Oneida street). Mr. H. B. Thayer, Miss M. Hildreth, Miss A. Caldwell, Miss Van Der Werken.

Catholic Church. Mr. J. Eccles, Miss L. Goffe, Miss E. Brooks.

Dutch Church. Miss M. Henderson.

Egberts' House (Columbia street.[2]) Mr. R. Thompson, Miss L. Benedict, Miss L. Van Schaick, Miss Moe.

Red School House.[3] Miss M. Jefferson.

East Harmony Hill.[3] Miss Caroline Brown.

West Harmony Hill. Miss S. H. Bannard."

---

[1] It afterward came under control of the board of education. It was in 1861 removed to a lot just north of the Reformed church, and was destroyed in 1873.

[2] This was a building belonging to Mr. Egberts on the corner of Columbia and Main streets, which had been erected some years before by —— Crandell. It stood near the site of the present brick school house which was erected soon afterward. The original building was for some time rented as a tenement.

[3] These buildings were erected during 1854 and '55. The first was on School street, near the site of the present school house, for which it was exchanged with the Harmony Company. The second was on Vliet street near Willow. Previous to its erection the only school house on the Harmony Hill was an old wooden building nearly opposite, on the site now occupied by the boarding houses. The West Harmony School House remained in use until 1863, when it was sold, the building on Mangam street now in use having been completed.

The erection during the year of a large number of dwellings and several buildings for manufacturing purposes, gave further evidence of the growth of the place. The *Cataract* said : "There has not been a season for several years when business was as promising in Cohoes as this spring." Prominent among the new business concerns were The Mohawk River Mills on Remsen street. The company, of which Joshua Bailey was president, had been organized in March of the previous year, with a capital of $150,000. Their building, 350 by 75 feet and four stories high, was described as the largest knitting mill in the world, and cost with the machinery $120,000. The company employed 600 hands and operated eleven sets of machinery.[1]

Another new firm was the Albany Pin Company, also incorporated in 1854, with a capital of $35,000. The officers were L. S. Parsons, president ; Louis Spanier, treasurer ; C. W. Bender, secretary. The company manufactured solid headed pins, using twenty-seven machines.[2]

In March the knitting mill of Thomas Fowler was bought by J. G. Root of Albany, who, with L. S. Parsons established the Tivoli Hosiery Mill, under the firm name of J. G. Root & Co. Mr. Egberts erected the buildings on Remsen street now known as the Diamond and Globe Mills,

---

[1] In July, 1859, the name of the establishment was changed to Clifton Mills and a new company was formed, of which A. E. Stimson of Albany was the principal stockholder, and Winsor Stone ¦agent. In Oct., 1861, the Clifton Company was organized with a capital of $100,000, the officers being as follows: president, T. G. Younglove; treasurer and general manager, A. E. Stimson ; secretary, E. L. Stimson. The company suffered reverses in the late panic, and the business was discontinued in Oct. 1875.

[2] This establishment was in June, 1862, sold to T. G. Younglove, having been idle over a year. In August, he sold to Arthur T. Becker, who commenced operations at once, Robert Johnston becoming a partner soon after. Mr. Johnston sold his interest in Nov., 1863, to Heber T. Lyon. This firm was succeeded June, 1865, by the American Pin Company, and Cohoes Pin Company, followed later by the Empire Pin Company of which E. S. & W. H. Harris of Albany, were principal proprietors, and G. M. Morris, superintendent. The business was in 1874 removed to Winsted, Conn., and the new building of the company on Courtland street sold to Tubbs & Severson in May 1876.

the middle one of which was occupied by the Pin Company, and also by Root & Co. who still retained possession however, of the old Fowler Mill.

Another knitting mill, the Halcyon, was established by Barber and Leckie in a building on Ontario street which has since become part of Brockway's Mill. This building was erected at the same time as the Mohawk River Mills and had been used among other purposes as a shop for the construction of some of the machinery of the mill.[1]

The census of this year gave the following statement of Cohoes industries :

6 Knitting mills, value of product,	$647 100
2[2] Cotton factories,	618 000
1 Axe and edge tool factory,	210 000
2 Bedstead factories,	45 000
1 Veneering factory,	42 000
2 Mills,	28 000
1 Machine shop and foundry,	34 200
1 Tobacco factory,	21 450
1 Shoddy mill,	21 840
1 Wheel factory,	9 000
1 Straw paper factory,	9 000
1 Bobbin factory,	6 000

Among the improvements made necessary by the growth of the place was a new system of water works. On April 10th a bill was passed incorporating the Cohoes Water Works Company, of which Alfred Wild was president. The following were named as commissioners : Chas. M. Jenkins, Hugh White, Alfred Wild, Egbert Egberts, Jas. Brown, Joshua Bailey, Wm. N. Chadwick, Wm. Burton, Henry D. Fuller, Andrew D. Lansing, Jenks Brown and Truman G.

---

[1] In 1857, this firm was succeeded by the Halcyon Knitting Company, and the business removed to the new factory on Erie street.

[2] The Strong mill was rebuilt during the year, but did not commence operations till 1857.

Younglove. By the terms of the charter the capital stock was $50,000, which might be increased to $250,000. The company was authorized to make agreements with the Cohoes Company for the use of water or the purchase of its works, and the latter corporation was authorized to take stock in the water works company to an amount not exceeding $20,000.

The subscription books were opened in August. Mr. James Slade was employed as engineer to make estimates on the cost of a new reservoir and reported as follows: "A reservoir on Prospect Hill, of a size to contain 1,000,000 gallons of water, will cost $12,507, exclusive of the land and earth of which the banks may be built. The hill belonging to Mr. Lansing (Abraham), near lock No. 17, Erie Canal, contains 8 acres. A reservoir on this hill to contain 3,000,000 gallons of water will cost $12,727, exclusive of the land." [1]

Some dissatisfaction arose among the citizens in regard to the organization of this company. The opinion of many was that the water works should be the property of the village, and not of any private corporation. Out of respect for this feeling against a monopoly, the project was abandoned, no active steps having as yet been taken. The pressing necessity of having a more adequate water supply still remained, however, and demanded immediate action. A new plan was accordingly set on foot, which resulted in the preparation, early in 1856, of the first draft of the "Act to provide for a supply of water in the village of Cohoes," still in force. The commissioners named in the bill were Alfred Wild, Chas. H. Adams, Henry D. Fuller, Wm. F. Carter,

---

[1] It is worthy of notice that one of the projects for supplying Albany with water, which were submitted by F. S. Claxton, engineer, to the authorities of that city in 1849, embraced the idea of a reservoir on Prospect Hill. The water was to be raised from the Cohoes Company's canals to a reservoir on the hill which was to cover two acres of ground, and to be thence conveyed to the distributing reservoir in Albany, by means of an indestructible pipe three feet in diameter.

Joshua Bailey and Truman G. Younglove. They were authorized to take all necessary steps for securing an abundant and reliable supply of water, and to meet their expenditures the trustees were authorized to issue the bonds of the village to an amount not exceeding $60,000; the commissioners were directed to purchase the pipes and hydrants belonging to the Cohoes Company, and then in use, and were authorized if they found best, to enter into arrangements for a supply of water from the company's canals. The bill at first met with some opposition and a meeting was called March 13 to remonstrate against its introduction. The chief objections urged were in regard to the term of office of the commissioners, the appraisal of lands, and the manner of letting contracts. Chas. H. Adams addressed the meeting in favor of the measure, and satisfactorily explained some of the obnoxious passages, and after the appointment of a committee to hear arguments for and against it, an adjournment was moved. The committee reported the following week in favor of the passage of the bill, which had been amended in several particulars, and a resolution was passed urging its presentation. It was passed April 12th, but new difficulties arose, which prevented the commencement of any work until the following year.

The chief obstacle was a disagreement between the commissioners and the Cohoes Company, which asked $6,000 for its works, as established, while the commissioners proposed to pay but $3,000. The company's reason for asking $6,000, was that under the new arrangement it would be obliged to pay for the use of water in its works which it was then drawing from its own canals, a sum equal to the interest on that amount. An understanding was reached in May, 1857, and the agreement between the parties was drawn up and signed by the representative of the company. A number of citizens objected, however, claiming that the village could be supplied with water at cheaper rates, and another series of public meetings followed. A committee, consisting of I. F. Fletcher, J. F. Crawford, D. J. Johnston, I. Quackenbush, Wm. Burton, H. B. Silliman and G. L. Witbeck, was appointed to investigate the subject. Upon the presentation of their report June 27th, which stated that the best course was to fall back on the proposal of the Cohoes Company, the matter was arranged without further controversy. The other plans which the committee had considered were : 1st, to purchase a water privilege in Crescent, and distribute directly from thence ; 2d, to purchase the mill privilege owned by I. D. F. Lansing near the Cohoes Company's dam ; both of which would entail an expense far exceeding the price asked by the Cohoes Company for its works, and water rent. Work was accordingly commenced on the new reservoir at once, and the contract was let in July. The ceremony of breaking ground took place August 13, and was thus spoken of in the *Cataract:* "The water commissioners and village trustees together with a large number of citizens were present, each trying his hand at the plow. After the ceremonies on the grounds, the company was invited by Mr. L. VanDercar, the contractor, to partake of a collation served up at the Hotel in Mr. Wilkins's best style ; after which appropriate speeches were made and sentiments offered, making it altogether an occasion of unusual interest."

The most noticeable fact in the history of Cohoes manufactures since 1854, was the sudden increase of knitting mills. The only accessions of importance to the business interests of the place during 1856 were of this character. In February of that year Messrs. Willard Bingham and Alden & Frink purchased "the vacant lot south of G. L. Witbeck's store," on Mohawk street, and erected thereon the knitting mill now standing between Campbell & Clute's and North's Block. The building was pushed rapidly forward, and the mill, containing three sets of machinery, was in operation in July of the same year. Another mill was established by Messrs. L. W. Mansfield, John Maxwell and Chas. Hay, who took possession of the building on Courtland street which had previously been occupied by Hollister & Co., as a tobacco factory, and put in operation two sets of machinery.[1] Messrs. Maxwell & Hay did not remain long in the firm, and the business was subsequently carried on by Mr. Mansfield alone.

In 1857 still further additions to this branch of business were made. The building on Erie street, now occupied by the Ranken Knitting Company, was erected by Wm. Burton and taken possession of by the Halcyon Knitting Company, C. P. Barber, agent, which ran four sets of machinery. The building, 60 by 60 feet, and five stories high, was described by the *Cataract* as one of the finest mills in the place. Another large mill, 46 by 80 feet, and four stories high, was erected by Smith, Gregory & Co., who put in operation three sets of machinery. The parties interested were Wm. Smith, Wm. M. and Alex. M. Gregory, of Albany, and J. R. Bullock, of Cohoes.[2] Knitting machinery was also introduced by R. Hurst, in his mill at the junction of Remsen and Mohawk streets.

Concerning inventions made in knitting machinery by Cohoes mechanics, the *Cataract* of August 16, contained the following :

"We notice by the last number of the *Scientific American*, that Augustus J. and Demas Goffe of this village have obtained a patent for a new rotary knitting machine. This makes the sixth invention of the kind by citizens of Cohoes. The first was the old "reciprocating frame," by Timothy Bailey, which is still used in the Adams and Mohawk River Mills. This was the first power knitting machine ever invented, but it was never patented. The next

---

[1] The subsequent occupants of this mill were Alden, Frink & Weston, 1862–66; Ward & Robinson, 1866–67; Scott & Stewart, 1867–73. It was destroyed by fire in 1873.

[2] Mr. Bullock remained a partner for about two years. Mr. Smith died in 1869, and his interest was bought by Jonathan Hiller, the firm name being Gregorys & Hiller. After the death of Alex. Gregory, in 1875, the remaining partners became sole proprietors.

is that of John Maxwell, which is somewhat similar in construction and operation to that of Bailey. Then came the " warp " machine of S. D. Fairbank, which was followed by John Jackson's, also a " warp " machine. These were succeeded by a new rotary knitter by Mr. Bailey (the inventor above spoken of), which has been in operation only a few months. The last is that of the Messrs. Goffe."

A department of industry connected with the knitting business was the manufacture of knitting needles, commenced by Henry Dawson, who located in the latter part of the year, in the foundery building on Mohawk street.

The importance of the cotton interest here was increased during the year by the erection of part of the Harmony Mill No. 2, having a capacity of 20,000 spindles, and giving employment to nearly 500 operatives. It was about this time, too, that the hill began to share in the general growth of the village. In 1856 the Harmony Company had purchased from Hugh White his farm of seventy acres on Prospect Hill, and laid it out into building lots. The erection of tenements and private residences followed rapidly. The *Cataract* of Jan. 31st noted the awarding of a contract to John Blair and E. Wolford " for twenty-two brick buildings on Harmony Hill which will require 1,300,000 bricks."

In August the Cohoes and Troy telegraph, built by W. C. Enos and J. C. Elmore, went into operation. It was managed by a stock company, with a capital of $1000, the officers of which were: president, Daniel Simmons; secretary and treasurer, E. W. Fuller; directors, Dr. H. L. Landon, Ira Terry and Joseph Chadwick. The telegraph office, Henry E. Lasell operator, was established in the rail road depot. The first despatch passed over the wires August 31st. In October H. R. Grant became operator and the office was located in his store on Remsen street.

Besides the factories already spoken of, a number of new buildings were erected, many of them residences. Several new stores appeared on Remsen street, among them one owned by Joshua Bailey (now by C. H. Adams), adjoining Hayward's building, and one owned by Patrick Gugerty (now by Thos. Cartwright), north of the Van Rensselaer Block. The latter was noticed in the *Cataract* as "the first marble front in the village." The following statistics of buildings in Cohoes are from the town assessment roll of 1857:

"The whole number of dwellings is 733, of which 567 are wood and 166 of brick.

No. of stores 56. No. of furnaces 1.
" " factories 21. " " forges 1.
" " saw-mills 2. " " coal and wood yards 5.
" " grist-mills 2. " " lumber yards 1."

In the latter part of the year the great financial panic which passed over the country commenced to be felt in Cohoes, and had for a time a paralyzing effect on the industries of the place. In the *Cataract* of October 10th, an account of the condition of the different manufacturing concerns was given. The three cotton mills were running on part time, the wages remaining the same except in the Harmony Mills, where a reduction of ten per cent had been made ; of the knitting mills, four were stopped entirely and the remainder were running on reduced time, with the intention of closing as soon as the stock on hand was finished ; S. Bilbrough was running on half time and D. Simmons & Co. had discharged one-third of their men. The article concluded as follows :

"It is unnecessary to add that with 2000 of our citizens almost entirely out of employment, and the gloomy prospect before us, Cohoes presents anything but an agreeable picture." The following paragraph appeared Nov. 28th. "At present there is no definite prospect that the various mills of this village will run full time before spring. With the exception of Messrs. Alden, Frink & Bingham's establishment, the knitting mills are either finishing up their old stock or are stopped entirely. Their mill is running two-thirds of the time. In the cotton mills no material change has taken place. They are running about two-thirds of the time." Elsewhere it was said: "Notwithstanding the tightness of the times, the Harmony Company are finishing up the extensive buildings connected with their mills. When they are completed and the plans connected therewith executed, their mills will be the most extensive and the most perfectly arranged of any in the state." It was feared that the embarrassments of Garner & Co., of New York, might have a disastrous effect on the Harmony Company, but such was not the case. The honorable reputation of the house made it an easy matter to secure the necessary extensions, and in the early part of 1858 arrangements were made with the creditors of the firm by which all their mills could be started on full time. Concerning Mr. Garner the following appeared in the New York *Mirror* in October of that year: "The splendid carriage and horses which were seen in Broadway a few days since with a ticket on their backs 'For sale,' belonged to Mr. Garner, who recently failed for millions. He has moved from his splendid residence in the Avenue to a small two story house in the seventh ward. This is an example of the right sort."

The stringency of the times was especially felt by the laboring classes, who found it impossible to obtain work. The announcement in the early part of November that the junction locks were to be rebuilt was hailed with satisfaction, as it promised to give employment to a number of men.

But in spite of this and the other enterprises which were in progress here, hundreds of laborers were idle during the winter, and the suffering was very great. A meeting was called February 1st, 1858, to take measures for the relief of the poor. The sum of $125 was raised at once, and committees were appointed to disburse the same and make further arrangements. The following gentlemen were designated to receive contributions: D. J. Johnston, E. W. Fuller, Jacob Travis, H. B. Silliman, Jenks Brown, Francis

Henderson, T. G. Younglove, H. R. Grant, James Hemstreet, J. R. Clarke, Wm. Acheson, Joseph Chadwick, S. Hayward, G. L. Witbeck. Among the measures taken by the committee for the aid of the poor, was the establishment of a soup-house at the engine rooms in Cataract alley which remained in operation some time, and afforded relief during the months of February and March to five hundred sufferers.

In the spring the prospect began to improve. The new mills, into which machinery had been placed during the latter part of 1857, commenced operations, and several of the factories which had been for some months closed were started up on full time. During March strikes occurred among the operatives in the Harmony and Ogden Mills and D. Simmons & Co.'s axe factory, the cause being that the reduction in wages made the previous autumn had not been completely restored. The differences were settled without much difficulty however, and work was resumed in a few weeks.

On March 5th an act introduced by Hon. C. H. Adams, assemblyman from this district, was passed by the legislature, "enabling the electors of the town of Watervliet to vote by districts for the election of town officers." The third district constituted by this law embraced Cohoes, and the citizens were no longer compelled to go out to Van Vranken's Corners to vote — a change which gave great satisfaction, for the country roads were generally in an almost impassable condition at the time of holding town elections.

On the 19th of April, a fire broke out in the picking room of the Harmony Mills which for a time threatened the destruction of the entire establishment, but was fortunately kept under control by the exertions of the firemen, who were assisted by Nos. 4 and 5 of Lansingburg. The damage to machinery and building amounted to $10,000. The Lansingburg firemen were hospitably entertained by the village department, and their services were handsomely **rewarded by the Harmony Company.**

Another fire, on the night of May 8th, destroyed the "Wilkinson machine shop" with several small outbuildings which had been used in connection with the axe factory. The building had played an important part in the early history of Cohoes manufactures, having been the location at different times, of a dozen business enterprises. The occupants at this date were: Charles M. Carleton, silk weaver, John Baker, bobbin turner, G. R. Archer, picker manufacturer, Mr. O'Hare, wagon maker and Porter & Hall, file cutters. The total loss was $7,000, of which $4,000 were insured. The property was owned by Mrs. C. A. Olmsted of New York. The *Cataract* in describing the fire said: "Our firemen were promptly on hand and did most efficient service in subduing and preventing the flames from communicating to the adjoining buildings. They are a body of men of whom we may be justly proud. Although many excellent companies were here from abroad, our noble firemen proved themselves equal to any on the ground."

Another loser by this fire was A. J. Griffin, who had machinery and stock stored in the building to the value of $500 or $600, and intended soon to commence the manufacture of sashes and blinds. After the fire his establishment was located in the mill on Ontario street (now Brockway's) which had been recently vacated by Barber & Leckie. Another concern occupying the same building at this time was the bedstead factory established by Scott & Miner, the firm soon afterward being changed to Scott & Hildreth.[1]

The *Cataract* for June 5th, contained the following: "*Our Sprinkler.* Any one who contemplates writing up the rise and progress of Cohoes, will please bear in mind that on Monday, May 31st, 1858, Thos. Van Dercar, an

---

[1] Soon after the death of Mr. Scott in 1863, the business was sold by Mr. Hildreth to L. Greenman. The latter had for some time as his superintendent, Wm. Foote, who had been connected formerly with the bedstead factory established by Jeremiah Clute. In 1865, P. S. Holsapple, the present proprietor, became interested in the business and assumed sole control February 1869.

enterprising citizen, introduced the first street sprinkler, to the infinite delight and satisfaction of the citizens, who could hardly be restrained from manifesting their gratification by forming a procession and marching in the rear of the perambulating shower."

The block on the corner of Remsen and White streets, which had been commenced by Mr. Egberts in April of the previous year, was completed this spring. The hall in the third story was formally opened on the evening of July 8th, by a concert given by "the choir of St. Paul's church, Troy, and other eminent artists," under the direction of the ladies of St. John's church of this place. The programme of the evening, which was described as the most attractive ever presented to a Cohoes audience, was prefaced by the reading of some dedicatory verses, by Mr. Dunham of West Troy. The erection of the building, which was then one of the finest in the place, was a source of great satisfaction to the community, who had long suffered from the lack of a proper hall for entertainments. The room in the second story, now occupied by the common council chamber, was leased in May by the trustees for village purposes, according to a recommendation made by President Landon in his annual report, in which he stated that, "the trustees will be under the necessity of asking at the annual meeting for an appropriation to rent a suitable room in some convenient locality for the purpose of meeting, the present room being entirely too small for the ordinary transaction of business, it being used as a trustees' room, and a room for the board of education, as also for a village library room, and as a place for the board of health to meet. Adding the tables, desks and book cases of these several departments, renders it totally inadequate for the necessities required. The room adjoining, occupied by engine company No. 1, is altogether too contracted for the use of that company."

On the evening of Sept. 10th, a meeting was called at the Methodist church for the purpose of organizing a Young

Men's Christian Association, of which H. B. Silliman was chosen chairman and W. T. Dodge, secretary. The following were appointed as a committee to draft a constitution: Herbert Hastings, Peter LeBoeuf, H. B. Silliman, A. Peck, D. H. Van Auken, D. J. Johnston, Jas. H. Masten, Wm. Nuttall, Wm. Williams, Joseph Chadwick. The first officers of the association, who were elected Sept. 27, were as follows: president, H. B. Silliman; vice presidents, Jno. V. S. Lansing, I. Quackenbush, C. N. Gregory, H. Hastings and Wm. Nuttall; corresponding secretary, C. F. Ingraham; recording secretary, W. T. Dodge ; treasurer, D. J. Johnston; managers, Wm. Benedict, F. Thompson, Silas Whitney, J. H. Masten.

The completion of the water works received the following comment in the *Cataract* of Dec. 4. " On Wednesday last, December 1st, the water from the new reservoir was, for the first time, let into the pipes, and with the most gratifying results. A trial being had for the purpose of determining the pressure of the water in the pipes, a stream was thrown completely over Root's knitting mill without difficulty, and a stream was also thrown in a horizontal direction one hundred feet. There was but one break in the whole length of the pipes laid down and that was not a serious one. We consider this an event of local importance second to none in the history of our village, and its citizens may justly pride themselves on so valuable an acquisition as the Cohoes Water Works." The reservoir, which has a capacity of 3,000,000 gallons, covers two acres of ground. Under the arrangements then made the water was raised one hundred feet from the upper level of the Cohoes Company's Canal to the reservoir at the rate of 35,000 gallons per hour, passing through 1200 feet of ten inch pipe. A large number of pipes were laid, so that including those which had belonged to the Cohoes Company, there were then five miles of pipes of sheet-iron and cement, from two to ten inches in diameter laid throughout the village; additional fire hydrants were also placed at various points at an average distance of four hundred feet apart. The pump house, containing accommodations for a hose company, was built by P. B. Ferguson and John McEnerny, under direction of Joshua R. Clarke. Wm. Dickey had the contract for street excavations, and Robert Safely that for hydrants and gates. The pump was driven by a forty-five horse power wheel, designed by E. Geyelin of Philadelphia, and constructed by Fuller & Safely of Cohoes who were builders of all the pumping machinery. It was put in place under superintendence of D. H. Van Auken, engineer. The entire cost of the works was $60,000.

In February, 1859, measures were taken for the establishment of a bank, an institution much needed, and one which had been talked of ever since the incorporation of the village. The stock, $100,000, was taken almost entirely by citizens of the place. The first officers, who were elected in March, were as follows: president, Egbert Egberts; cashier, James M. Sill, of Albany; directors, Egbert Egberts, Daniel Simmons, T. G. Younglove, Wm. Orelup, Jr., Wm. G. Caw, W. F. Carter, J. G. Root, John Sill and C. H. Adams.

The death of Dr. Henry L. Landon, March 11th, made vacant the office of president of the village. An election was accordingly held by the trustees, which resulted in the choice of Jenks Brown to fill the vacancy.

In April the Reformed Dutch church was torn down to give place to the one now standing on the site. In demolishing the building, the tin box was found which had been placed there at the laying of the corner stone in Sept. 1838. Among the documents it was found to contain was a copy of the Bible, of the constitution of the United States and of the different states in the union, the catechisms, constitution and articles of faith of the Reformed Dutch church, a list of those who formed the first consistory and the first building committee — a copy of the Albany *Argus* and the *Christian Intelligencer*, and a record of the exercises which took place at the time.

The corner stone of the new church was laid on June 22d, with the following ceremonies: "The stone was laid by Rev. O. H. Gregory, D.D., of West Troy. The scriptures were read by Rev. Dr. Pohlman of Albany, and addresses were made by Rev. R. Van Brunt of Waterford, Rev. Dr. Gregory, and by the pastor Rev. C. N. Waldron. The choir of the church, under the direction of Mr. Alden, sang several appropriate hymns, and the sabbath school children of the church sang one of their favorite pieces."

The corner stone of the present Methodist church was laid June 21st, with appropriate ceremonies.

Among the subjects which received frequent attention in the local columns of the *Cataract* was base-ball, a game then just coming into favor, and one which awakened considerable interest among the young men here. The Vanguard Base Ball Club, followed in later years by the Joe Leggett Club, was for some time a flourishing institution of Cohoes. Among the most prominent members of the Vanguard were A. T. Becker, Dr. G. H. Billings, P. D. Niver, John McDermott, Isaac V. Fletcher, Joseph Almy, Jr., Daniel McElwain, Joseph Chadwick, Wm. Arthur, Jr., and Joseph Damond. A number of match games were played with neighboring clubs, in which the Vanguards had their share of victory. The ground for a number of years was on the hill north of Columbia street beyond the Central Rail Road.

During the summer D. Simmons & Co. commenced the building of the dyke across the sprout of the river from their lower forge to Simmons's (formerly called Demilt's) Island. It was constructed for the purpose of relieving their wheel from backwater and also with a view to opening the island to the public. The *Cataract* said, "Mr. Simmons could not have engaged in an enterprise that promises better, as it only needs the improvement contemplated to make the island lots eagerly sought after, and greatly increase the value of his water lots in that vicinity." Other improvements during this year were thus spoken of in the *Cataract* of July 30 : " Good walks are now laid nearly all the way on both sides of Remsen street from Factory to Columbia streets ; on Mohawk street, from its junction with Remsen near Hurst's Mill to A. Ferguson's residence in the lower ward (corner of Howard street) and also on White street from its intersection with Mohawk to the Erie Canal, together with many others on the less important thoroughfares. The most of these improvements have been made during the past year, and are a commendable evidence of local pride and thrift. Besides the above, many places of business have been changed, enlarged and greatly improved, and many new ones erected."

The principal new factories of the year were those built by T. G. Younglove, on the site of Miles White's axe factory. The larger one, which has since been remodelled and is now known as the Empire Mill, was commenced early in the season. It was of brick, 100 by 40 feet and five stories high, and was built by Henry Howarth. It was occupied soon after its completion by the Albany Pin Company. The building near the river now occupied by A. J. Griffin was completed in July. The first story was occupied by Griffin & Co. (B. A. Glines having been admitted as partner), the second story by Scott & Hildreth's bedstead factory, and the third story by North's and Ten Eyck's bobbin shop, which had been moved from Parkhurst's bedstead factory.[1] In the building vacated by Scott & Hildreth, and Griffin & Co., a knitting mill was

---

[1] This firm had bought of John Baker. It was succeeded by North & Chesebro, January, 1860 ; North & Bogue, July, 1860 ; Bogue & Clark, 1866, and Asa Clark & Son, the last proprietors.

established by Henry Brockway, who has since made large additions to the original structure.[1]

Among the new firms of the year was Wild & Younglove, who bought the mill belonging to Isaac D. F. Lansing near the Cohoes Company's dam, and established the straw board manufactory with which Mr. Younglove has ever since been connected. The mill had been for some time occupied for a similar purpose. In 1830 coarse wrapping paper was manufactured there by a man named Bryce, and some years later Gerret R. Lansing (who was succeeded by I. D. F. Lansing) commenced making straw board, but neither of these establishments were on an extensive scale.[2]

The proper line of Mohawk street had from the earliest days of the village been a subject of controversy, and as in the case of Saratoga street, encroachments by various parties were numerous. Before 1833 the Cohoes Company owned only the land on the west of the old highway, but when in that year they purchased the Demilt tract or Factory lot, they proceeded to straighten the line of the street in several places. Near Cataract alley the old road ran so far to the west that it passed close by the front of the present residence of H. S. Bogue, and between Seneca and Oneida streets it made a deep bend toward the east. Mr. Olmsted, who occupied at one time the present residence of M. S. Younglove, extended his wooden sidewalk to the corrected line of the Cohoes Company, and it made such a prominent object in the street that it was known as Olmsted's dock, and Olmsted's raft. The efforts of the company were of little avail, however, and nearly all the houses on the west

---

[1] Mr. Brockway sold out in 1863, but rebought the property in the fall of '64, commencing operations the following spring.

[2] A new mill was built in 1863, and in 1866 Mr. Wild retired. The present company, with a capital of $85,000, was incorporated June 23, 1875, with the following officers: president, T. G. Younglove; secretary and treasurer, D. H. Van Auken; trustees, T. G. Younglove, Geo. Z. Collins, M. S. Younglove, D. T. Lamb, D. H. Van Auken, Geo. H. Stewart, Levi Dodge.

side of Mohawk street between Seneca and Oneida, extend into the street as it was laid out. The following in regard to the matter is from the *Cataract* of April 7, 1860 : "It will be remembered that a short time since the village authorized the corporation counsel, Jas. F. Crawford, Esq., to commence legal proceedings against several property owners whose buildings projected several feet into Mohawk street near its intersection with Oneida. The first suit, that against H. Bortel, was tried before Squire Hubbard, on Wednesday last and resulted adversely to the village ; it being proved that Mohawk street was a highway under control of the town of Watervliet, and that therefore, the village had nothing to do with its boundaries. This will probably settle the matter for the present, at least."

Another suit in which the village was interested, concerning the appointment of water commissioners, was decided in the following month. It had been pending since 1858, and had excited much local interest. It was necessary for the board of trustees of that year to appoint water commissioners in place of Messrs. Wild and Carter, whose terms of office then expired. As the board was equally divided in politics it was evident that no appointments could be made unless a compromise could be effected. According to the water act, vacancies in the water board were to be filled by a two-thirds vote of the trustees ; but some of the trustees were advised by Judge Parker that a majority vote would suffice, and accordingly at a meeting held May 3, when one of the board was absent, a motion was carried that Messrs. J. F. Crawford and Jno. W. Frink be appointed to fill the vacancies. This was vetoed the next day by President Landon, and at a meeting of the full board, held the same evening, Messrs. Wild and Carter were declared re-appointed. The matter was carried to the courts, where it remained for two years. The final decision of Judge Hogeboom was that Messrs. Crawford and Frink were rightfully appointed, and they served the remainder of their term.

A marked improvement of this year was the increase of church accommodations. In January, the alterations in St. John's church which had been for some weeks in progress, were completed, and were thus noticed in the *Cataract* : " An addition of thirty feet has been made to its length, the outside has been neatly painted and new blinds have been put up. In the interior a much needed change has taken place. The increased length of the house gives several additional seats and has much improved its general appearance, while the decorations of the ceilings together with the beautiful stained glass window in the rear produce a fine effect."

The new Methodist church was dedicated on Feb. 22d. Rev. Dr. Haven, editor of *Zion's Herald*, preached the opening sermon in the morning, which was followed by the dedicatory services, participated in by the presiding elder, Rev. Mr. Seymour of Waterford, assisted by several eminent clergymen from abroad. In the evening a sermon was preached by Rev. Wm. P. Corbitt of New York. Subscriptions towards liquidating the debt of the church were taken after each service, amounting in the morning to $1,700, and in the evening to $800. The church, which has a seating capacity of 800, cost about $30,000.

The Reformed church was dedicated April 11th. The dedicatory sermon was preached by Rev. Dr. Rogers of Albany, and was followed by the prayer of dedication, offered by Rev. I. N. Wyckoff of the same place. Rev. Mr. Dickson, Rev. Dr. Gregory and Rev. Mr. Van Brunt of Albany were also present and took part in the services. Rev. Mr. Seelye of Schenectady occupied the pulpit in the evening. The building, which is 98 by 74 feet, and capable of seating 850 persons, was erected at a cost of $30,000. The architect was L. A. Gouch of Yonkers. The building committee were Egbert Egberts, S. A. Becker and Jacob I. Lansing.

In June the Sisters of St. Joseph, an order established

the preceding year in connection with the Catholic church, took possession of the dwelling on Mohawk street north of Cataract alley, now owned by Solomon Stimson, where they established the parish school. After the completion of the new parsonage of St. Bernard's they removed to the building next the old church, which they now occupy.

There were during this year several important business changes. The Ogden Mills property was purchased by the Harmony Company, who enlarged and improved the buildings at a cost of $200,000, giving them a capacity of 30,000 spindles.[1]

The partnership between Root and Parsons was dissolved, Mr. Parsons, with J. H. Parsons as partner, retaining the old establishment,[2] and Mr. Root commencing the erection of a new mill on Mohawk street which was one of the most complete in the place. The latter admitted his sons Messrs. A. J. and S. G. Root to partnership, and the business was conducted under the firm name of Root & Sons.[3]

A new enterprise was Blake & Son's saw works, which occupied the first, second and third stories of T. G. Younglove's new building on Mohawk street. The polishing and grinding machine in use was the joint invention of Messrs. Blake & Dodge of Cohoes. Between forty and fifty dozen wood saws were sent to market daily.

An axe factory was subsequently established by this firm in the rear of the saw works which did not, however, continue long in operation.

In the latter part of the year the flour mill near the old

---

[1] The stock company which had been organized in 1847 failed in 1851, and in the following year the business came under control of Brown Bros. & Co., who had been heavy creditors of the old firm. The buildings passed into the possession of the Cohoes Company. The agent under the new management was Waterman Smith who was succeeded in 1853, by Jenks Brown.

[2] After the death of Mr. L. S. Parsons in 1864, the present firm was organized.

[3] Mr. Root retired in 1869, and the firm became J. G. Root's Sons, and so remained until the formation of the present company, January 1st, 1875.

junction, owned by G. M. Cropsey & Co., was completed. The building was 55 by 30 feet and three stories high.[1]

The manufacture of soap was commenced by Walter Campbell in the building on Oneida street east of the rail road, which had some time before been occupied for that purpose.[2]

The *Cataract* during the year contained a number of communications and articles on the water rents, concerning which dissatisfaction had arisen. In one of these, which gave some interesting figures in regard to mill property in Cohoes, it was shown that the total assessed valuation of such property for the preceding year was $476,000, and its owners paid a water tax of $780.25, and that during the preceding ten years twenty-one fires had occurred in mill property.

The census taken during the year showed an increase in population since 1855 of 2,694. The number of deaths reported for the last year was 183. The statistics of manufactures were as follows :

Am't capital employed in manf'g,.................. $2,078,500
Operatives employed in factories,............ 3,728
Wages paid monthly to operatives, ... $53,862

The remarkable increase in the business activity of Cohoes and its material improvement in many particulars, which had been the chief characteristics of the period just described, became less noticeable after the outbreak of the rebellion in the spring of 1861. Instead of recording constant evidences of growth, the local columns of the village newspaper were devoted mainly to matters connected with the war, and items of this sort furnish the principal materials for the history of the place during the next few years.

---

[1] This property was bought by Bills and Sage of Troy, March 1864. In the following year it came into the possession of Mills and McMartin of Albany, and subsequently Jas. McMartin, the present owner, became sole proprietor.

[2] The subsequent proprietors have been ; M. M. Wilson & Co., 1868, P. D. Niver, 1874, F. W. Grant, 1875, Mrs. H. R. Grant.

VIII.

THE PART TAKEN BY COHOES IN THE WAR.

AT the opening of the war, Cohoes was not behind neighboring towns in manifestations of patriotism, and was prompt in the contribution of funds and recruits. The first public demonstration was a meeting held in Egberts Hall April 25, to raise money for the support of the families of volunteers. Egbert Egberts was called to the chair, and the following gentlemen were chosen vice presidents : Sidney Alden, C. H. Adams, Wm. Burton, Joshua Bailey, John Lyons, T. G. Younglove, H. D. Fuller, W. N. Chadwick, Jas. Hayden, Robert Johnston, Abram Lansing, Henry Brockway, Wm. G. Caw. The secretaries were as follows : D. J. Johnston, Jas. H. Masten, Murray Hubbard, M. Monahon, S. V. Trull, H. S. Bogue. After prayer by Rev. Mr. Spor, a series of patriotic resolutions was read and adopted. The president then stated the object of the meeting, after which stirring addresses were made by S. W. Lovejoy, Jacob W. Miller, Rev. Thos. Keveney, Rev. Dr. Reed, Rev. Mr. Spor, H. B. Silliman, T. G. Younglove and H. D. Fuller. Collectors were then appointed, and the following finance committee : S. A. Becker, J. R. Clarke, F. Henderson, Edward O'Reilly, I. Quackenbush and Wm. Burton; Edward W. Fuller was chosen treasurer and the books were opened, the subscriptions of those present amounting to $3,135. Further contributions were made until within a few weeks the fund amounted to nearly $5,000.

Another evidence of loyalty in a less substantial form was spoken of as follows in the *Cataract* of April 27 :

"If displaying colors is a manifestation of patriotism the people of Cohoes are not wanting in devotion to our glorious union, for the national banner floats from every prominent building in the place, while nearly every man, woman and child wears the red white and blue rosette. On Saturday last a beautiful flag was raised over the mill of J. G. Root & Co., and impressive speeches were made by L. Sprague Parsons, J. W. Miller, C. H. Adams, S. H. Foster, and H. B. Silliman, Esqs., while Green's Cornet Band enlivened the occasion by playing a number of national airs. A large crowd was in attendance whose repeated cheers gave evidence of their heartfelt appreciation of the sentiments uttered by the speakers."

During the same week flags were raised on nearly every factory and store in the village, in many instances with similar exercises.

The first detachment of volunteers, consisting of 84 men under F. Temple, left here for Camp Willard, Troy, May 11th. Unfortunately the number of companies called for in the state had been offered and accepted before Capt. Temple could muster a full complement of men, and instead of going as a company from Cohoes, his men were forced to join companies already formed, or else stay at home. Many of them accordingly enlisted in the different companies stationed at Camp Willard, and went with Col. Carr's regiment from Troy. About 45 men went from Cohoes, who enlisted in Waterford in Co. A., Capt. J. L. Yates, which was assigned to the 22d regiment, and 25 more went with the 5th regiment, Gen. Sickles's brigade. A large number of men were enrolled in other out of town companies during the year. In August recruits were enlisted for the U. S. Vanguard Reg't, organized in New York, and for the Cameron Light Infantry, Capt. P. R. Chadwick, formerly of the 7th Reg't, of New York, being agent for the latter. Recruiting offices were also opened in September by Egbert J. Wilkins and Peter Manton, and in October by Lieut. Frank Keating, each of which did a large business. A number of men who had enlisted in the 4th Heavy Artillery, Col. Doubleday, left Cohoes in the latter part of January, 1862.

On May 10th, the Ladies Aid Society effected a permanent organization. Much useful work had been done during the preceding year by many ladies who belonged to it, in connection with the Ladies Central Association for the Relief of the Army, the headquarters of which were in New York. During the year regular meetings were held for the purpose of making articles needed by the soldiers, and contributions from private parties or business firms were packed and sent to their destination.

Recruiting continued during the summer. In July, an office was opened by Wm. Shannon, who enrolled some sixty men.[1] A number of Cohoes men also enlisted in Co. H. of the 115th Reg't, then being organized in Crescent by Capt. Smith — which drew forth the following comment from the *Cataract:* "While we have none but the best wishes for Capt. Smith's success, we regret that Albany county loses so many from its quota. It seems unfortunate for Cohoes that her volunteers are scattered among so many foreign companies, when if they had enlisted together they might have numbered a half regiment." Even at this early stage of the war it was seen that it would be very difficult to obtain accurately the number of soldiers which Cohoes had furnished. Frequent requests were made in the editorial columns to friends of men who had enlisted to hand in their names for publication, and in August a notice was published urging the preparation of a complete list of soldiers and sailors, and requesting that names be left with Postmaster Chesebro. The call of Secretary Stanton for 300,000 men was issued August 4, and steps were immediately taken to fill the quota of the town, so that a draft might not be necessary. A recruiting office was opened by S. V. Trull, and some 80 men were enrolled, who joined

---

[1] Most of the men enrolled by Capt. Shannon joined the 113th N. Y. Vols., which was afterwards known as the 7th N. Y. V. Artillery, to which they are credited in the list at the close of this chapter.

the 30th Reg't;[1] by the efforts of Wm. Conliss, some 12 more enlisted in the Corcoran Legion, and a number of other recruits joined different companies.

The militia enrollment of Cohoes, for which the draft was to be taken, was as follows:

Total number enrolled,		768
Affidavits of persons whose names were enrolled:		
Active firemen,	63	
Exempt,	5	
All other claims for exemption,	15	83
		685

On Aug. 21st, the board of supervisors voted to continue the county bounty to every man who enlisted until the quota of the county was made up.

An enthusiastic war meeting was held at the Cohoes Hotel during the same week of which Wm. Leckie was president and Michael Monahon, secretary. Addresses were made by Prof. Baerman of Troy, Wm. M. White of Canaseraga, and L. S. Parsons of Cohoes. Among the resolutions passed was the following:

"*Resolved*, That we recommend to the committee (at Albany) to offer an additional bounty of $20 to each man who shall be enlisted in any company and accepted, and that for that object we pledge our liberal contributions."

A town meeting was held Sept. 6, at which it was voted to raise by tax $60,000 to enable the payment of a town bounty of $100 to every man enlisting until the quota was filled. Committees were appointed to make arrangements

---

[1] This company joined the regiment at Sharpsburg, Md., Oct. 14th. In May, 1863, it was transferred to the 76th Regt. N. Y. Vols. Having made the campaigns of '63 and '64, the men were transferred to the 147th N. Y. Vols., Feb. 1st, '65, the term of the 76th having expired. With this regiment they made the campaign of '65, ending in Lee's surrender. On June 5th, they were mustered into the 9th Reg't N. Y. Vet. Vols., with which they returned to Albany, July 6th. In the list of soldiers at the end of the chapter the men who enlisted under Capt. Trull are all credited to the 76th Reg't, with which they were longest connected.

for procuring the funds at once — that from Cohoes consisting of Egbert Egberts, Wm. G. Caw, L. S. Parsons and Wm. Burton. Besides these bounties, extra inducements to volunteers were offered by numerous private parties ; among whom may be mentioned T. G. Younglove, who agreed to pay John Stephens of Wm. Shannon's Company $10 per month for three years, and paid $10 each to the first ten recruits of Capt. Smith's company, and Alfred Wild, who furnished six men, two for Albany and four for Columbia Co. regiments. The result of these efforts was that the town of Watervliet was exempt from the draft which was made Nov. 10th, having furnished over 800 men since July 2, and paid a town bounty of over $35,000.

The local columns of the *Cataract* at this time contained much interesting matter. Letters from soldiers and sailors, either to the editor, or published by permission of friends, were a prominent feature and continued to be so during the war.[1] Considerable space was also occupied with reports of relief committees, lists of subscriptions and other matters of the kind. Among the enterprises mentioned were two promenade concerts and festivals, held in September by the ladies of the Aid Association, Miss E. Howe manager, which cleared $260 for the Soldiers' Relief Fund. Such efforts as these, however, were but a part of the work in which the ladies were engaged. Boxes of goods or provisions were being continually packed and sent to the Washington hospitals, the headquarters of committees in New York, or the soldiers in camp ; money was raised in large amounts for contribution to the U. S. Christian Commission and similar patriotic funds, and in fact every call on their benevolence and industry was liberally answered.

Material for pleasant paragraphs was furnished when

---

[1] Among the contributors at different times were Messrs. Joseph and P. R. Chadwick, Myron and James D. Van Benthuysen, L. H. Vermilyea, J. W. Himes, Almon E. Stone, Zalmon Van Ness and A. C. Musgrove.

popular officers were presented with swords by their friends, an event of quite frequent occurrence. Among those thus favored were Messrs. Hiram Clute, Silas Owen, Jas. O'Hare, Wm. Shannon, Frank Temple, A. T. Calkins and Malachi Weidman.

Another subject for items was the scarcity of small change, which began to be felt here early in the summer and by fall had become a serious inconvenience. A number of business firms, among them Alden & Frink and H. Thompson & Son, issued *shinplasters* for fractional amounts redeemable at their establishments and at different localities in Troy and Albany. Smaller concerns issued pasteboard tickets, or tokens, and these, together with postage stamps, were made to answer the purpose of specie.

During the early part of 1863, few volunteers left Cohoes, the ordinary course of business was resumed, and aside from correspondence, war matters occupied a comparatively small space in the columns of the local paper. It was announced March 7th, that at a meeting of the supervisors it was found that there was a surplus of $18,000 remaining in the fund which had been raised for payment of extra bounties, and it was voted to appropriate this sum to the support of families of needy volunteers. The amount to which Cohoes was entitled under the allotment was $782.

The return of the regiments which had enlisted in 1861, was made the occasion of public demonstrations. The 2d Reg't of Troy, under command of Col. Carr, which had enlisted with 900 men, reached home May 16th with less than 300, having been engaged in fourteen battles. The Cohoes members received a hearty welcome from the citizens, which was described as follows :

"In anticipation of the arrival of the regiment our citizens determined to give the Cohoes boys such a reception as would prove to them that their gallant deeds in defence of their country were appreciated. Messrs. Wm. Burton, Peter Manton, H. B. Silliman, D. J. Johnston and the officers of the fire department acted as a committee of reception and in their arrangements spared no pains to give our brave soldiers a most cordial welcome ; while our citizens generally suspended business to give all an opportunity to join in the festivities. Early on Thursday morning Mohawk and Cataract engine companies, headed by the Cohoes Cornet Band and accompanied by large numbers of our citizens marched to Troy to take part in the reception there and escort our heroes home. A special train was chartered on the Central Road and about four o'clock they left Troy, arriving at our station at half past four, where hundreds of friends had gathered to greet them. They were received amid the booming of cannon, the ringing of bells, and the most earnest manifestations of joy."

On June 5th the 22d Reg't, which had been organized May 14, 1861, under Col. Phelps, and left Albany 825 strong, returned with 500 men, having been engaged in ten battles. Company A, composed of men from Waterford and Cohoes, arrived in the former village in the afternoon and was hospitably entertained. In the evening the company was formally received by the people of Cohoes. The train was met at the depot by an immense concourse of citizens, and the fire department bearing torches. A procession was formed, that paraded through the principal streets, which were brilliantly illuminated. The exercises were concluded with an address of welcome, delivered by H. B. Silliman. The return of the 10th (or 177th) Reg't was spoken of as follows in the *Cataract*, Sept. 5th:

"The anticipated joy with which the return of the 10th Reg't was to be welcomed was sadly marred when they appeared on Tuesday, by their wretched condition. Worn out, decimated by battles and fevers, sick and dying, tottering feebly or borne by others to their homes, it was almost impossible to believe that the splendid regiment which left Albany nine months ago over 1,000 strong had indeed returned. Not over 250 men could be numbered who were in the enjoyment of even moderate health."

In the latter part of September announcement was made of a draft, the quota from Cohoes being given as 93, though the enrollment was made for 140 to make allowance for all who might be exempt. The *Cataract* made the following comment :

"Cohoes, like all other wide-awake towns, has its periods of local excitement, which she enjoys or disrelishes, according to their character, with the same zest or repugnance as other large towns or cities. The fact that the draft was to take place, and had actually commenced, threw many into consternation who had lulled themselves into a sort of uneasy security because it had been so long in coming; others took the matter philosophically and began to cast about for some expedient to relieve themselves from its worst consequences. Early last week an association was formed, pledged to pay $75 each for the relief of such of its members as should be drawn. This organization grew rapidly in numbers, and before the result was announced, had secured a membership of thirty-two. Of this number eleven were drawn. If from these the usual proportion are exempted the amount pledged will cover the commutations."

The drafted men, 138 in number, were as follows :[1]

John Trim,	Alexander H. Frink,	John Clute,
Silas Owen,	Edward Nichols,	John Cahill,
John Thompson,	John Webber,	John Bisconner,
Thomas Dallas,	Joseph Chadwick,	John A. Lynch,
James Acheson,	Michael Higgins,	Charles Maguirk,
Alonzo Van Arnum,	Charles W. Orelup,	Joseph Parker,
G. Vandermark,	Ammond Winnie,	George TenEyck,
William F. Jones,	James L. N. Cranston,	Sylvian Pattric,
Albert Ten Eyck,	William Claffey,	Robert Jackson,
William Walsh,	Lorenzo D. Sanborn,	Robert Cleachem,
Thomas Mahar,	Jacob Bishop,	James McMurray,
Patrick Fay,	Frank Lebard,	John Maguire,
John S. Crane,	Elias David,	Louis Solon,
John Mitchell,	William Smith,	Patrick Gilligan,
Francis Leboeuf,	Thomas Scott,	Peter Masta,
John Cassidy,	John Brian,	David Colegrove,
John McCoun,	Levi W. Lamb,	Charles Gregory,
Henry Hunt,	George Brider,	John Condley,
William Fonda,	Thomas Hogg,	Isaac Auringer,
Joseph Booth,	James Kemp,	William Sheridan,

---

[1] Up to January 1st, 1864, the following disposition had been made of the drafted men:

Held to service, 40, of whom 1 procured substitute, and 4 paid $300.

Discharged for disability, ...	16
Aliens, ...	13
Only sons, ...	10
Over age, ...	8
Other causes, ...	8

Daniel Lanegan,	Edward Kenney	Malachi Ball,
Henry Bedford,	Edward Bullock,	John Galvin,
Artemus Pennock,	Fred. Brigamuel,	James Miggins,
John Johnson,	John Robertson,	Samuel Lemerick,
John Purdy,	George Grierson,	Kearan Agan,
Alvin Clark,	Peter D. Niver,	William Benedict,
Cilem Labe,	Daniel Simpson,	Richard Wilcox,
Daniel McIntosh,	L. Underhill,	David Wheelwright,
Daniel Seiler,	James Lackey,	William Smead,
Edward Ryan,	James McGafferney,	Samuel Maguire,
Patrick Lacy,	Matthew Sinophy,	George Thomson,
William Williams,	Hugh Johnson,	Albert Carr,
William Keffa,	David H. VanAuken,	Francis Staats,
William Wild,	John Childs,	James Finigan,
Frank McMarr,	Timothy Moore,	John Daymond,
Michael Carter,	Maurice Whitney,	Thomas Jackson,
Patrick Rabbett,	Alexander McElroy,	William Kinder,
Charles Sims,	Adolphus Juber,	John Fulton,
George Hume,	James Traver,	Albert M. Brown,
Charles Webber,	George H. Wager,	W. Irving Blakely,
Michael McGuire,	Patrick Cane,	Robert Boler,
Charles Vail,	Joseph Stephens,	Thomas Griffenty,
Sidney Deitz,	Samuel Jackson,	William Conliss,
Thomas Nuttal,	Samuel Candly,	Edward Bumhower,
Patrick Scully,	Lawrence Fitzgerald,	William Mulcahy,
John Hude,	John Johnson,	Theophilus Fountain.

The reason of such a large draft being levied in Cohoes, was that no especial inducements were made to encourage volunteers, so that many men from here enlisted in Troy where large bounties were offered. In the latter place no draft was made, their quota being filled, with a hundred men to spare.

Another call was issued in October by the president for 300,000 men to be furnished before January 1st, 1864, and earnest efforts were made to enroll sufficient volunteers in the town to avoid the necessity of another draft. New recruiting agents were appointed by the committee at Albany, Malachi Weidman and John Doyle being among those in Cohoes, and additional inducements were offered. The bounty for veteran recruits was fixed at $552, and for new recruits at $377. In addition to this, the supervisors offered an extra bounty to volunteers of $300. A town meeting was held Dec. 10, recommending the raising by tax of a sufficient sum to enable the payment of the same allowance to those who had been drafted, as to those who might be drafted under the new call. A meeting was held in Cohoes a week later, of which W. F. Carter was president and D. H. Van Auken, secretary, to protest against such action as unjust, since in many cases the extra compensation would be unnecessary. The citizens were in favor, however, of granting such relief as might be needed by men drafted from this village, and, among others, passed the following resolution : " On motion of Wm. G. Caw, seconded by S. A. Becker, the sum of ten thousand dollars (the amount recommended by the trustees for the relief of the drafted men of this village), be and the same is hereby ordered to be raised by tax upon the taxable property of this village." A committee of six was appointed to ascertain the number of enlisted men which should be credited to the village quota, and see that their names were duly entered. The quota under the new call was 71, one-third of which had been secured by enlistments since the last draft.

In January, 1864, a call was made for 200,000 more men, the quota for Albany county being 993. The county bounty of $300 was continued, and the efforts to obtain recruits renewed with vigor ; and on March 1st it was announced that the quota of the county was filled, with a surplus of several hundred.

In July 500,000 men were called for, to be furnished before Sept. 1st. Under this call the quota of Albany county after deducting the surplus above mentioned was 1,600. Messrs. Weidman & Doyle were reappointed recruiting agents in Cohoes, and the work commenced in earnest. The supervisors offered a bounty of $900, for volunteers for one year, and the sum of $100 to every person who should bring forward an accepted recruit. This proved a strong inducement, and the county escaped the draft, Cohoes having done her full share in contributing recruits. Eighty-six men left in the 91st Reg't, about ten in the 12th N. Y. Cavalry, and a number of others in different regiments.

The continued successes of the Union army during the campaigns of the ensuing fall and winter, and the series of brilliant victories in the spring of 1865 which marked the overthrow of the rebellion, awoke general enthusiasm. The news of each triumph was received here, as elsewhere, with the greatest rejoicings. The demonstrations on the occasion of the capture of Richmond were thus described in the *Troy Daily Times*, April 3d.

"Yesterday's war news so completely surprised the people of Cohoes that they were unable to control themselves. In honor of the occasion the flags were raised from nearly every staff, and some of the mills hung flags from their roofs. Bells were rung and whistles blown for about half an hour. In the evening there was a grand demonstration by the citizens generally. They formed a procession headed by a band and paraded the principal streets, the band playing patriotic airs. Illuminations and bonfires in the evening. The operatives in some of the mills turned out to help honor the event. Richmond is ours!"

Similar demonstrations followed the announcement of Lee's surrender, April 7. Another public meeting was held, and appropriate speeches were made by H. B. Silliman and other citizens. The village was yet in the midst of these rejoicings, when like a thunderbolt came the news of the assassination of the president, which cast a gloom throughout the place. Private residences, stores and factories were draped in mourning, and on the day of Mr. Lincoln's funeral there was a general suspension of business, and services were held in the different churches. On April 25th, when the remains lay in state in the Capitol at Albany, they were visited by hundreds of our citizens.

The restoration of peace added unusual interest and significance to the celebration this year of the 4th of July, and in Cohoes the demonstration was unusually large. The following is a summary of the account of the exercises given in the *Cataract:*

"The weather was all that could be desired, clear and pleasant. As no pains had been spared by the Hon. C. H. Adams, president of the day, and the committee of arrangements, the details of the celebration were perfect, and nothing occurred to mar the harmony of the occasion. The day was ushered in by the national salute and ringing of bells. At half past ten, the procession, under direction of the marshal, H. Brockway, Esq., and his assistants, Adj't Malachi Weidman, Capt. Thomas Calkins, Capt. F. Keating, Capt. Wm. Shannon, W. Mallery, Wm. Manning, Wm. Conliss, C. Houlihan, Jas. Acheson and Michael Monahon, commenced moving in the following order:

1. *Co. I, 7th Heavy Artillery, N. Y. V.*

This veteran company under command of Capt. Jas. O'Hare, made a fine appearance and commanded the plaudits of the citizens along the entire line of march.

2. *The Car of Liberty.*

This contained the Goddess of Liberty, surrounded by her guardians, art, science, agriculture, etc., and thirty-six young ladies representing the states.

3. *Fire Department.*
4. *Committee of Arrangements, Orator, Reader and Village Officials.*
5. *St. Bernard's Sunday School.*
6. *The Trades.*

The exercises on the island were opened with prayer by Rev. A. J. Bingham. The Declaration was then read by P. D. Niver, and an oration delivered by Rev. A. T. Pierson, of Waterford."

Soon after the close of the war, a number of prominent citizens of Albany commenced making efforts to procure the erection in that city of a Hall of Military Record, in which should be preserved the names of all soldiers who had enlisted from this state, accounts of the services of individuals and regiments, and all documents, relics or mementoes in any way connected with the war. Circulars were addressed to the different supervisors, and contributions solicited. The *Cataract*, in commenting on the enterprise, said: "We trust and believe that this town, which occupies so prominent a place among those that contributed largely in men and in money to bringing the late struggle to a successful and glorious close, will not be behind in an undertaking, the design of which is to perpetuate in memory not only the noble deeds of her heroes, but also those of the entire state." The project, which was carried out, was in many particulars very successful. It was found impossible, however, to obtain accurate records of the soldiers, and in spite of years of labor the lists of many places are to this day imperfect— Cohoes, unfortunately, being among the number. The census of the village in 1865, gave the number of soldiers residing here at the time of their enlistment as 514, but no complete record of their names and the regiments to which they belonged has been preserved. As before mentioned, Cohoes received no credit for much that she did towards the suppression of the rebellion ; many men, because no company was forming here, or for the sake of large bounties, went to other places — in some cases out of the state — to enlist, while others who were enrolled in Cohoes, are credited to Waterford, Albany or Troy, and very often under the general head of Watervliet.

The names given below have been obtained, for the greater part, from scattered notices in the columns of the *Cataract;* some in response to advertisements published in the city papers during the past autumn, and a number of others from miscellaneous sources. The list is very far from being complete, and it seems impossible at present to obtain one which shall be so. The preparation of a full and accurate record will demand a great deal of time, and careful research, and it is to be hoped that some one with leisure to devote to it, will undertake the labor:

Albion, James, Aug. 1862, Co. I, 7th Vol. Artillery.
Alston, Wm.,   "   "   "   "   "   " also 2d Regt. N. Y. Vols.
Ablett, James W.,   "   "   "   "   "
Augsburg, David, Sept. 1864, Co. K, 91st N. Y. Vols.
Adams, Daniel M.,   "   "   "   "   "   "
Arthur, Wm. Jr.,   "   "   Co. H, 4th Heavy Artillery.
Arnold, Jonathan D.,"   "   "   "   "   "
Abbey, Chas. E.,   "   "   "   "   "   "
Ablett, Wm. H.,   1863, 4th N. Y.   "   "
Adams, George M., Co. A, 119th Reg't N. Y. Vols.

Abbey, Wm., May, 1861, Co. E, 2d N. Y. Vols.
Aberhart, John, " " " " " "
Acheson, John, " " " " " "
Austin, Geo., Sept., 1862, Co. A., 7?. 1 N. Y. Vols.
Ashdown, Arthur, Jan. 18, 1862, Co. K., 93d N. Y. Vols.
Atridge, Thomas C. Nov., 1862, Co. D, 177th N. Y. Vols. ; also Sept., 1863, in 95th N. Y. Vols. ; also Nov., 1866, in Co. H, 69th U. S. Infantry.
Adams, Cortland, Pioneer, June, 1861, Co. A, 22d N. Y. Vols. ; also 12th N. Y. Cavalry.
Andrae, Michael, fall of 1861, in 88th N. Y. Vols., Navy in 1863, and in 1864, in 175th N. Y, Vols.
Ackley, Oscar L.,[1] Aug., 1862, Co. H, 115th N. Y. Vols.
Agan, John, " " 125th or 192d Regiment.
Alcombrack, Jacob, Griswold Cavalry.
Bray, Joseph, Aug., 1862, Co. I, 7th Vol. Artillery.
Bailey, Joshua, " " " " " "
Blum, Wm. H., " " " " " "
Baker, Chas. H., Sept., 1864, Co. K, 91st N. Y. Vols.
Bentley, Chas., " " " " " "
Bennett, Napoleon, " " " " " "
Bush, Lewis, Aug. 1862, 125th or 192d Reg't.
Bulson, Geo., " " " " "
Bayard, Augustus Willard,[1]" " Co. H, 115th N. Y. Vols.
Brockway, Geo. E., " " " "
Blair, Fred'k, Co. H, 4th N. Y. Heavy Artillery.
Bennett, John, " " " " " "
Bagley, Wm., " " " " " "
Buckley, Jas., Co. I, " " " "
Bannon, Jas., " " " " " "
Brooks, Wm., " " " " " "
Buchanan, Wm. Lieut.,[1] Aug., 1862, 76th N. Y. Vols.
Brown, Peter A., " " " " "
Buchanan, John C., " " " " "
Brierly, John,[1] " " " " "
Boss, Chas., " " " " "
Baker, John A., " " " " "
Bradshaw, Geo., " " " " "
Brodt, Wesley,[1] " " " " "
Ball, Jerome, " " " " "
Boucher, Geo., " " " " "
Brower, Geo., " " " " "
Barlow, Samuel, " " " " "
Brennan, Dennis, May, 1861, Co. E, 2d N. Y. Vols.
Bray, Wm., " " " " "
Buchanan, Geo., " " Co. L, " " " also Co. A, 22d N. Y. Vols.
Buregard, Oliver, Co. H, 56th N. Y. Vols.
Brown, Albert, 9th Heavy Artillery.
Bryan, Hugh, May, 1861, Co. A, 22d N. Y. Vols.
Benson, Egbert C., " Co. H, 10th or 177th N. Y. Vols.

---

[1] Dead.

Beaver, Lawrence, Co. F, 30th N. Y. Vols.
Bump, Alonzo, 1861, 77th Saratoga Battalion.
Bouchard, Frank, 2d N. Y. Cavalry.
Barrett, John, Jan. 14, 1862, Co. D, 4th N. Y. Heavy Artillery.
Barrett, Edward S., 1861, Co. D, 90th N. Y. Vols.
Clark, J. B.,   Aug. 18, 1862, Co. I, 7th N. Y. V. Artillery.
Corcoran, J.,   "   "   "   "   "   "   "   "
Carpenter, Philip H., "   "   "   "   "   "   "   "
Christie, James,   "   "   "   "   "   "   "   "
Connolly, Samuel,   "   "   "   "   "   "   "   "
Connolly, James,   "   "   "   "   "   "   "   "
Connolly, Edward,   "   "   "   "   "   "   "   "
Calkins, A. T., Serg't, May 19, 1861, Co. A, 22d N. Y. Vols.
Clute, Hiram, Lieut.,[1]   "   "   "   "   "
Condron, Wm., Sept. 17, 1862, 175th N. Y. Vols.
Cowden, Geo.,   "   "   "   "   "
Connors, John, Sept. 28, "   "   "   "
Cranston, Jas. L. N., Sept., 1864, Co. K, 91st N. Y. Vols.
Craig, F. B.,   "   "   "   "   "   "
Condron, James,   "   "   "   "   "   "
Cahill, James,   "   "   "   "   "   "
Cole, Lorenzo S., Co. H, 4th N. Y. Heavy Artillery.
Cline, Wm. H.,   "   "   "   "   "
Cranston, Wm. H.,[1] Aug., 1862, 76th N. Y. Vols.
Caisse, Joseph,   "   "   "   "   "
Craig, Wm.,   "   "   "   "   "
Cole, James,[1]   "   "   "   "   "
Crossley, Robert,   "   "   "   "   "
Carpenter, Wm. G., "   "   "   "   "
Carpenter, Albert F., "   "   "   "   "
Cain, John,   "   "   "   "   "
Chambers, John,   "   "   "   "   "
Collier, Wm.,   "   "   "   "   "
Chadwick, Joseph,   "   "   "   "   "
Carr, T.,   May 17, 1861, Co. E, 2d N. Y. Vols.
Costello, Joseph,   "   "   "   "   "   "
Casey, Thos. B.,   "   "   "   "   "
Cole, Geo.,   "   "   "
Clark, Joseph, Co. L., 12th N. Y. Cavalry.
Cope, Wm.,   "   "   "   "   "
Cox, Andrew, Aug. 9, 1861, 88th Illinois Vols.
Cole, Abram V., 93d N. Y. Vols.
Carroll, John C., Lieut.,[1] 1862, Co. D, 6th N. Y. Cavalry.
Cavenagh, John V., U. S. Navy.
Carpenter, Lorenzo, 43d N. Y. Vols.
Coleman, Silas B., U. S. Navy.
Crandall, Burton H., Aug., '62, Co. I, 52d N. Y. Vols.
Cady, Peter V.,   "   " 125th or 192d N. Y. Vols.
Clute, Adam,   1861, Co. B, 10th or 177th N. Y. Vols.
Chadwick, P. Remsen,   1861, 7th Reg't of N. Y.; entered service same year as adj't of 100th N. Y. Infantry from Buffalo; promoted

---

[1] Dead.

to be ass't adj't gen. in 1862; appointed provost marshal gen. of Florida, 1863.
Cole, Aaron, 42d N. Y. Vols.
Chadwick, Joseph, 1861, U. S. Navy; served on the Wyandank, of the Potomac flotilla, and on the sloop of war Ossipee.
Coleman, Joseph, 12th Reg't Ohio Vols.
Coleman, John, May 22, 1861, Co. A, 30th Reg't N. Y. Vols.; also May 4, '66, in Regular Army.
Coleman, Morris, 6th New Hampshire Vols.
Coleman, Thomas, Co. A, 30th Reg't N. Y. Vols.
Drysdale, Geo., Aug., 1862, Co. I, 7th N. Y. V. Artillery.
Doyle, M., " " " " " "
Darrow, David M., " " " " " " " also 12th N. Y. Cavalry.
Dailey, Jeremiah A., Corporal, Aug., '62, Co. I, 7th N. Y. V. Artillery.
Danaher, Maurice, Sept. 17, 1862, 175th N. Y. Vols.
Donovan, Michael, " " " " "
Deroche, James, 1864, " " "
Donahue, Wm., Aug., 1863, 21st N. Y. Griswold Cavalry.
Davis, Thos., " " " "
Drysdale, John, Sept., 1864, Co. K, 91st N. Y. Vols.; also 169th N. Y. Vols.
Dorr, David, Sept., 1864, Co. K, 91st N. Y. Vols.
Deroche, ———, 4th N. Y. Heavy Artillery.
Dietz, Stephen, " " " "
DeLancy, John, Aug., 1862, 76th N. Y. Vols.
Downing, Michael, " " " " "
Deuel, George, " " " " "
Denio, Henry, " " " " "
Dennis, Nicholas, " " " " "
Dunn, Thomas, " " " " "
Dowd, Patrick, " " " " "
Derby, Wm., May 17, 1861, Co. E, 2d N. Y. Vols.
Dunn, Edward, " " " " " " "
Dodge, Joseph C., 1861, Co. H, 10th or 177th N. Y. Vols.
Doyle, Geo. H., " " " " " "
Doyle, Chas. F., " " " " " "
Durham, Henry, 1862, 25th N. Y. Vols., Capt. Kingsley's Co.
Driscoll, Simon P., 42d N. Y. Vols.
Durham, James,[1] 3d N. Y. Vols.
Diehl, Geo.,[1] 77th N. Y. Vols.
Dumell, Alfred, Feb., '65, Co. A, 47th N. Y. Vols.
Daley, Dennis, 1864, Co. K, 91st N. Y. Vols.
Daley, John, 1863, Battery B, 55th Ohio.
Davenport, Geo, 1861, 77th Saratoga Battalion.
Davenport, John, " " " "
Davenport, Chas., " " " "
Davenport, James, " " " "
Eastham, Thos.,[1] Aug., '62, Co. I, 7th N. Y. V. Artillery.
Eccles, Francis T., " " " " " " "
Eccles, Samuel P., " " " " " " "

---

[1] Dead.

En Earl, Merrit D., Sept., 1864, Co. K, 91st N. Y. Vols.
Evans, Joel,   "   "   "   "   "   "
Everts, J. D.,   Co. I, 4th N. Y. Heavy Artillery.
Egan, Owen,   "   "   "   "
Egnesperry, Francis, Aug., 1862, 76th N. Y. Vols.
Ebah, John,[1]   "   "   "   "   "
En Earl, John H.,   "   "   "   "   "
Eastham, Henry,   "   "   "   "   "
Eagan, Kyran,   "   "   "   "   "
Ensign, H. A., Musician, Hancock Brigade.
Eastwood, John H.,[1] May, '61, Co. A, 22d N. Y. Vols.
Ellison, Robert,   "   " Co. E, 2d N. Y. Vols.
Ellis, Elihu, Dec. 9, '61, Co. D, 1st N. Y., Heavy Artillery.
Falardo, Dennis L., Jan. 18, 1865, Co. G, Vermont 7th Vet. Vols.
Falardo, Daniel,   "   "   "   "   "   "   "   "
Frost, James,   Aug., 1862, Co. I, 7th N. Y. V. Artillery.
Farthing, F. E.,   "   "   "   "   "   "   "
Frost, Robert,   "   "   "   "   "   "   "
Flannigan, ——,   "   "   "   "   "   "   "
Finlay, John,   "   "   "   "   "   "   "
Fonda, Geo. F., Serg't   May, '61, Co. A, 22d N. Y. Vols.
Fletcher, Leonard G., Corporal, "   "   "   "   "   "
Fairbank, J. W., Q. M. Serg't, "   "   "   "   "   "
Foster, Wm.,   "   "   "   "   "   "
Flannigan, Geo.,   "   "   "   "   "   "
Fry, Edwin A.,   Sept., 1864, Co. K, 91st N. Y. Vols.
Fitzpatrick, Daniel. "   "   "   "   "   "
Farrell, Matt,   4th N. Y. Heavy Artillery.
Ferguson, Wm.,   "   "   "   "
Fallon, Peter,   Aug., '62, 76th N. Y. Vols.
Fabyan, H. G.,   "   "   "   "   "
Falardo, John   "   "   "   "   "
Fonda, Gilbert M., "   "   "   "   "
Flynn, John,[1]   1861, Co. H, 10th or 177th N. Y. Vols.
Frisby, Robert W.,[1] "   "   "   "   "   "
Fletcher, Wm.,   "   "   "   "   "   "
Fairbank, David,   "   "   "   "   "   "
Finlay, John,   2d N. Y. Vols.
Fletcher, Thos., May, '61, Co. E, 2d N. Y. Vols.
Frost, Norman W., U. S. Navy.
Forward, John,   "   "
Farrell, Edward, Sept., 28, 1862, 175th N. Y. Vols.
Fonda, E. Raymond,[1] Aug., 1862, Co. H, 115th N. Y. Vols.
Falardo, Onesime,   "   "   125th   "   "
Fletcher, Jerome,   122d   "   "
Frazier, P., Hancock Brigade.
Fowler, T. S., Lieut., 77th N.Y. Vols.
Finlay, Charles.
Fowler, Ralph, 1st U.S. Engineers.
Gooch, Thomas,[1] Aug. 18, 1862, Co. I, 7th N. Y. V. Artillery.
Gauthier, Joseph,   "   "   "   "   "   "   "

---

[1] Dead.

Gauthier, F., Aug. 18, 1862, Co. I, 7th N. Y. V. Artillery.
Green, Chas. D.,[1] " " " " " " "
Gillis, J., " " " " " " "
Gormley, Robt.,[1] " " " " " " "
Goodfellow, Jas. H., May, 1861, Co. A, 22d N.Y. Vols.
Gordon, Van Olinda, " " " " "
Green, Geo., Musician, Hancock Brigade.
Green, Otis, R. " " "
Greason, Egbert, 4th N.Y. Heavy Artillery.
Gallapo, Joseph, Co. H, " " " "
Genore, J. H., Co. E, " " " "
Gauthier, Peter, " " " "
Greason, Edward,[1] Aug., '62, 76th N. Y. Vols.
Greer, John,[1] " " " " "
Greenwood, Wm., May, '61, Co. E, 2d N. Y. Vols.
Goodwater, Vital, Co. H, " " "
Green, John, died in Andersonville.
Goodrich, Fred. S., 115th N. Y. Vols.
Gould, Alfred, Aug., 1862, Co. H, 115th N. Y. Vols.
Green, Chas. N., Sept., '64, Co. K, 91st N. Y Vols.
Galbraith, James.[1]
Gage, William H. L., Jan'y 4, 1864, Co. B, 16th Regt. N. Y. Heavy Artillery.
Hart, Richard, Jr., Aug., 1862, Co. I, 7th N. Y. V. Artillery.
Howarth, John, " " " " " "
Halpin, James, " " " " " "
Hastings, Herbert,[1] " " " " " "
House, Rosen J., May, 1861, Co. A, 22d N. Y. Vols.; also Sept. '64' Co. K, 91st N.Y. Vols.
Hemphill, Henry, May, 1861, Co. E, 2d N. Y. Vols; also 1864 in 71st N. Y. Vols. Sickles's Brigade.
Hatcher, Thomas, Musician, Hancock Brigade.
Harvey, Ruel, Sept., 1864, Co. K, 91st N. Y. Vols.
Hill, Joseph, " " " " " "
Hemstreet, Russell, " " " " " "
Hemphill, Jas. T., " " " " " "
Higgins, Michael, " " " " " "
Hayward, John, " " " " " "
Hayward, Chas., " " " " " "
Hughes, Michael, " " " " " "
Haley, Joseph, Aug., 1862, 76th N. Y. Vols.
Helmrick, Joseph, " " " " "
Howard, Geo. W., " " " " "
Hay, John W., " " " " "
Heffern, Christopher, " " " " "
Hibbert, Henry C., " " " " "
Hopkins, John, " " " " "
Handy, Isaac F., 1861, Co. H, 10th or 177th N. Y. Vols.
House, Theodore M., " " " " " "
Hewson, Edward, " " " " " "
Himes, Jehial W., " " " " " "
Hardenbrook, Chas. C., " " " " " "

---
[1] Dead.

Harvey, James,[1] 128th N. Y. Vols.
Hartnett, Daniel, Jr., March 30, 1865, Co. C, 192d N. Y. Vols.
Hay, Francis, 9th Artillery.
Himes, Jas. K. P.,[1] Aug., 1862, Co. H, 115th N. Y. Vols.
Hodgson, Kendall, " " 2d N. Y. Vols.
Hodgson, Lester,[1] May 14, 1861, " " "
Hemphill, John, May, 1861, Co. E, 2d N. Y. Vols.; also Co. H, 22d Vols.
Heady, Wm., " " " " " "
Hanson, G. W., Co. I, 4th N. Y. Heavy Artillery.
Hudson, Benj., 1861, 77th N. Y. Vols.
Henderson, John, June, 1861, Co. B, 30th N. Y. Infantry.
Hodgson, John,[1] Oct. 11, 1861, Co. B, 93d Regt., N. Y. Vols.
Hill, Barney, Co. F, 30th N. Y. Vols.
Hemphill, Thomas, 1864, 169th N. Y. Vols.
Jerome, Louis, Co. H, 4th N. Y. Heavy Artillery.
Jump, Joseph E., " " " " also in 10th or 177th Regt., also in 25th Regt.
Jackson, John, Aug., 62, Co. I, 7th N. Y. V. Artillery.
Johnson, Samuel, May, 1861, Co. A, 22d N. Y. Vols.
Jackson, Wm. B.,[1] Sept., 1864, Co. K, 91st N. Y. Vols.
Johnson, Michael H.,[1] 1860, flag ship Sabine, U. S. N.
Jerome, Joseph, 1861, 10th or 177th Regt.
Jump, Jos., " " "
Keegan, F., Co. I, 4th N. Y. Heavy Artillery.
Kelly, Michael, " " " "
Keeler, Philip,[1] 50th N. Y. Vols.
Keefe, Thomas, Aug., 1862, Co. I, 7th N. Y. V. Artillery.
Kelly, Patrick, Sept., 1864, Co. K, 91st N. Y. Vols.
Keefe, John, May, 1861, Co. E, 2d N. Y. Vols.
Knox, Geo., 10th Regt., N. Y. Vols.
Keating, Francis, Lieut,[1] 25th " " "
Kelly, John, Aug. 12, 1862, Co. H, 10th N. Y. Vols.; also 1863, Co. H, 4th Heavy Artillery.
Lanahan, John, Co. F, 30th N. Y. Vols.
Lefferts, Geo., Aug., 1862, Co. I, 7th N. Y. V. Artillery.
Long, Wm.,[1] " " " " " "
Lannigan, M., " " " " " "
Lawrence, Robt. W., Sept., '64, Co. K., 91st N. Y., Vols.
Linnen, Thos., " " " " "
Loughery, Hugh,[1] Aug., 1862, 76th N. Y. Vols.
Lee, John, " " " " "
Lannigan, Thos., May, 1861, Co. E, 2d N. Y. Vols.
Latta, Thos., " " " " " "
Latta, John, " " " " " "
Lefferts, Geo., Jr., " " " " " "
Lowe, Chas., 1861, Co. H, 10th or 177th N. Y. Vols.
Lansing, F. A., " " B, " " " "
Lounsberry, Nicholas D.,[1] 30th N. Y. Vols.
Lynch, John, May 19, 1861, Co. A, 22d N. Y. Vols.
Land, John E., April, 1861, 14th N. Y. Vols., 5th Brigade.

---

[1] Dead.

Lounsberry, Charles.
Long, Michael.
Lounsberry, Jas.
Lounsberry, Robt., Aug., 1862, 125th or 192d N. Y. Vols.
Lynch, Bartholomew, Co. H, 4th N. Y. Heavy Artillery.
Lamey, Michael,   77th N. Y. Vols.
Mangham, Michael, Aug., 1862, Co. I, 7th N. Y. V. Artillery.
McCusker, John,   "   "   "   "   "   "   "
McDonald, James,   "   "   "   "   "   "   "
McManus, James,   "   "   "   "   "   "   "
McCarty, John,[1]   May, 1861, Co. A, 22d N. Y. Vols.
McCready, John,   "   "   "   "   "   "
Manning, Egbert A.,   "   "   "   "   "   "
Monk, Oliver,   "   "   "   "   "   "
McDowell, Rob't,   "   "   "   "   "   "
Murphey, Thos. A.,   Co. H, "   "   "   Promoted to orderly serg't June 9, '63, and to be major of colored troops May, '64.
McVey, Patrick, Aug., 1863, 21st N. Y. Griswold Cavalry.
Mooney, Peter,   "   "   "   "   "   "   "
Moore, John,   "   "   "   "   "   "   "
Mahar, John,   "   "   "   "   "   "   "
Manning, Daniel F., Sept. '64, Co. K, 91st N. Y. Vols.
Mallery, Willard,   "   "   "   "   "   "
McCulloch, Chas.,   "   "   "   "   "   "
McGovern, Rob't,   "   "   "   "   "   "
McCready, Geo. B.,   "   "   "   "   "   "
McDermott, Patrick,   "   "   "   "   "   "
Molamphy, Hugh,   "   "   "   "   "   "
Morrison, Wm.,   "   "   "   "   "   "
Murphy, Wm.,   "   "   "   "   "   "
McManus, James, Co. H, 4th N. Y. Heavy Artillery ; also 7th Artillery.
Mayhew, Geo., Sr.,   "   "   "   "   "
Murray, M.,   Co. I,   "   "   "   "
Miggins, James,   "   "   "   "   "
Molamphy, Rody,   "   "   "   "
Mills, Wm.,   Aug., 1862, '76th N. Y. Vols.
Melahy, Michael,   "   "   "   "   "
Manning, Wm.,   "   "   "   "   "
Miller, Lyman,   "   "   "   "   "
Manning, James F.,   "   "   "   "   "
McKinnon, Wm. R.,   "   "   "   "   "
Murphy, Martin,   "   "   "   "   "
McGaffin, James,   May, 1861, Co. E, 2d N. Y. Vols.
Mooney, Daniel,   "   "   "   "   "   "
McMahon, Patrick,   "   "   "   "   "   "
Murray, Michael,   "   "   "   "   "   "
McCullock, Wm.,   "   "   "   "   "   "
Murray, Henry,   "   " Co. D, "   "   "
McGaffin, John,[1]   1861, Co. H, 10th or 177th N. Y. Vols.
Mather, Geo.,   "   "   "   "   "

---

[1] Dead.

McDonald, Frederick, 25th N.Y. Vols.
Mayhew, Geo., May 31, 1862, 25th N. Y. Vols.; also Oct. 20, '62, in 177th N. Y. V.; also Jan. 4, '64, in N. Y. Artillery.
Monk, Edward, 12th N. Y. Cavalry.
McCleary, Daniel B., "   "   "
Mooney, Peter B., Sept. 17, 1862, 175th N. Y. Vols.
Manton, Patrick, "   "   "   "   "   "
Monroe, Gordon, Musician, May 1, 1861, 2d Vt. Vols.
Mangham, J.[1]
Moran, Jas., Battery D, 1st Artillery.
McGuire Thos., Aug. 12, 1862, 48th Mass. Vols.
McGuire, John, "   "   "   "   "   "
McCready, Edward, enlisted at Albany as substitute.
McCarthy, John, 8th N. Y., Cavalry.
Musgrove, Abbot C.,[1] Aug., 1862, Co. H., 115th N. Y. Vols.
McMullen, ———, Aug., 1862, 125th or 192d "   "
Munro, Thos., U. S. Navy.
McCabe, ———, 42d N. Y., Vols.
Moore, J. W., was the first volunteer officer who left Cohoes, having received his commission as surgeon, April 28, 1861. Was assigned to Col. Frisby's regiment and resigned soon after to take a position in the Navy, sailing from New York, May 25th, as fleet surgeon of the Chesapeake flotilla. In 1862, was transferred to the U. S. S. Vermont, doing duty in the North Atlantic blockade. In 1863, was allowed to resign his position, to accept an appointment as physician in the Philadelphia U. S. Gen. Hospital, where he remained one year.
Monk, J. H., 10th N. Y.
Monk, George, N. Y. Regiment.
McCormick, John, enlisted 1862, Co I, 10th N. Y. Cavalry.
Mooney, Thos., 2d N. Y. Vols.
Notman, James, April 18, 1861, 2d N. Y. Militia; also Aug. 10, '61, Cameron Dragoons.
Nugent, Thomas, engineer 52d Mass.
Nichols, A., Aug., '62, Co. I, 7th N. Y. V. Artillery.
Nelson, Nicholas, May, 1861, Co. A, 22d N. Y. Vols.
Nolan, John B., Sept. 17, 1862, 175th N. Y. Vols.
Nichols, Edw'd, Aug., 1863, 21st N. Y. Griswold Cavalry.
Naery, Peter, Sept., '64, Co. K, 91st N. Y. Vols.
Norton, Geo. H., Co. D, 30th N. Y. Vols.
Norton, Hiram C., Co. H, 2d N. Y. Vols.
Norton, Wm. P., Co. C, 177th "   "
O'Hare, Jas., Lieut., Aug., 1862, Co. I, 7th N. Y. V. Artillery.
O'Brien, J., "   "   "   "   "   "
O'Day, Simon,[1] "   "   "   "   "   "
O'Hearn, Timothy, Sept. 17, 1862, 175th N. Y. Vols.
O'Donnel, Thos., "   "   "   "   "   "
O'Hare, Hugh, U. S. Navy.
O'Neil, John, May, 1861, Co. E, 2d N. Y. Vols.
Osterhout, Henry,[1] 1861, Co. H, 10th or 177th N. Y. Vols.
Ostrander, Lorenzo, 1861, "   "   "   "
O'Neil, Thos., 25th N. Y. Vols.

---

[1] Dead.

O'Brien, Wm, enlisted on field at Gettysburg, 93d Indiana, having deserted from the rebel army.
O'Brien, Patrick, 112th N. Y. Vols.
O'Brien, Michael, 63d " "
Owen, Silas, U. S. Navy, went to sea in May, 1855, as third apprentice. Ordered to the Memphis in 1861, and as master's mate, served two years. Was promoted to be ensign in 1863, and was transferred to the Potomac flotilla, having command of the Primrose. Discharged Nov. 25th, 1865, with the rank of acting master.
Parks, Robert, Aug., 1862, 76th N. Y. Vols,
Parks, James, " " " " "
Pindar, John, " " " " "
Plantz, Geo. H., Sept., 1864, Co. K, 91st N. Y. Vols.
Peck, Wm., " " " " "
Paisley, Thos., 5th Artillery, N. Y.
Paisley, John, " " "
Pynes, Thos., Co. D, 25th N. Y. Vols.
Porter, Jonathan G., May, 1861, Co. A, 22d N. Y. Vols.
Powers, David, Sept. 17, 1862, 175th N. Y. Vols.
Putnam, Lewis, Corporal, Co. I, 4th N. Y. Heavy Artillery.
Pulver, Wm. H., May, 1861, Co. E, 2d N. Y. Vols.
Pitcher, D., 1861, Co. H, 10th or 177th N. Y. Vols.
Paxton, Thos., June 15, 1861, Co. E, 1st Long Island Reg't.
Potter, Lewis, June 4th, 1861, 2d Vet. N. Y. Cavalry.
Quinliven, Michael, 30th Reg't and in Aug., 1862, transferred to 76th N.Y. Vols.
Ryan, James, 1st N. Y. Mounted Rifles.
Reed, Wm., May, 1861, Co. E, 2d N. Y. Vols.
Robinson, Joseph, " " " " "
Rooney, Bryan, " " " " "
Redmond, Michael, Serg't, " " " " "
Russell, Joseph, " " " " "
Reinhart, Harvey, Sept., 1864, Co. K, 91st N. Y. Vols.
Roberts, Henry, " " " " " "
Rider, Earl D., " " " " " "
Rider, Geo. H., " " " " " "
Rafferty, John,[1] " " " " " "
Robinson, James, Aug., 1862, 76th N. Y. Vols.
Riley, Hugh, " " " " "
Richards, Henry, " " " " "
Rollowine, Fred'k, Co. H, 4th N. Y. Heavy Artillery; also as substitute in Albany.
Riley, James, Aug., 1862, Co. I, 7th N. Y. V. Artillery,
Roberts, Wm., " " " " " "
Redmond, J., " " " " " "
Rignor, Alfred, May 19, 1861, Co. A, 22d N. Y. Vols.
Riley, Lawrence, Aug., 1863, 21st N. Y. Griswold Cavalry.
Reynolds, John.
Riley, Jeremiah, Co. F, 30th N. Y. Vols.
Russell, James, Serg't, May, 1861, Co. B, 2d N. Y. Vols.
Russell, John, Pioneer Corps.

---

[1] Dead.

Syms, Thos. J.,   Aug. 18, 1862, Co. I, 7th N. Y. V. Artillery.
Shannon, Wm., Captain,   "   "   "   "   "
Scully, M. H.,   "   "   "   "   "
Shipley, Geo.[1]   "   "   "   "   "
Stevens, John,   "   "   "   "   "
Shaughnessy, John,   "   "   "   "   "
Scofield, Joseph,   "   "   "   "   "
Swartz, John B., 1st Serg't, May 19, 1861, Co. A, 22d N. Y. Vols.
Shaffer, Fred,   "   "   "   "   "   "   "
Spain, Roger,   "   "   "   "   "   "   "
Stevenson, Geo.,   "   "   "   "   "   "   "
Simpson, Clark,   Co. H,   "   "   "
Skinkle, Wm. L., May, 1861, Co. E, 2d N.Y. Vols.; also in 4th Heavy Artillery.
Smith, John H., May, 1861, Co. E, 2d N. Y. Vols.
Scully, John H.,   "   "   "   "   "   "
Stapleton, John,   "   "   "   "   "   "
Seaport, Christian,   "   "   "   "   "   "
Scovill, Chas,   Co. H, 4th N. Y. Heavy Artillery.
Shortsleeves, Joseph,   "   "   "   "   "   also 10th or 177th N. Y. Vols.
Shortsleeves, John, Co. H, 4th N. Y. Heavy Artillery.
Stevens, James K.,[1]   "   "   "   "   "
Shaw, Christopher,   "   "   "   "   "
Shaw, Isaac,   "   "   "   "   "
Sitterly, Martin, Co. I,   "   "   "   "
Sitterly, Henry,   "   "   "   "   "
Sitterly, G.,   "   "   "   "   "
Stacy, D. H.,   "   "   "   "   "
Shepard, Chas.,   "   "   "   "   "
St Onge, Treffle,   "   "   "   "
Sager, Staats A., Aug., 1862, 76th N. Y. Vols.
Sheridan, Bernard, "   "   "   "   "
Snell, Joseph,   "   "   "   "   "
Shaw, Albert,   "   "   "   "   "
Sitterly, Abram,   "   "   "   "   "
Sharp, A.,   1861, Co. H, 10th or 177th N. Y. Vols.
Shields, Thos.,   "   "   "   "   "   "
Safely, A. F., M.D.,[1]   "   "   "   "   "
Shepard, Joseph, Sept., 1864, Co. K, 91st N. Y. Vols.
Scott, Wm.,   "   "   "   "   "   "
Steenberg, Marvin, Aug., 1862, Co. H, 115th N. Y. Vols.
Smith, A. W.,   "   "   "   "   "
Smith, Michael, Aug. 1st, 1862, 125th or 192d N. Y. Vols.
Scott, Roger,   "   "   "   "   "   "   "
Shields, Peter, Sept. 17, 1862, 175th N. Y. Vols.
Shields, John, Aug., 1863, 21st N. Y. Griswold Cavalry.
Sager, Alexander, U. S. Navy.
Storer, Chas., 169th N. Y. Vols.
Slater, James, U. S. Navy.
Shannon, Richard, 12th N. Y. Cavalry.

---

[1] Dead.

1865. HISTORY OF COHOES. 171

Silcocks, John E., Nov. 1st, 1861, 93d Regt. N. Y. Vols., Nov. 1st, 1863, transferred to U. S. Signal Corps; re-enlisted in 192d N. Y. Vols.
Smith, Martin, Co. E, 7th N. Y. Regt. Heavy Artillery.
Tuthill, Clarence, Aug., 1862, Co. I, 7th N. Y. V. Artillery.
Tuthill, Edward,   "   "   "   "   "   "   "
Tuthill, Daniel D.,[1] "   "   "   "   "   "   " promoted to Sergt.
Turner, Adam,[1]   "   "   "   "   "   "   "
Travis, Chas. S.,   Sept., 1864, Co. K, 91st N. Y. Vols.
Tompkins, Monroe,   "   "   "   "   "   "
Tracy, Pat'k   "   "   "   "   "   "
Tracy, John,   "   "   "   "   "   "
Trull, Stevens V., Quartermaster, Aug., '62, 76th N. Y. Vols.
Taylor, Ammon,   "   "   "   "   "
Torongeau, Louis,[1]   "   "   "   "   "
Tourville, Chas.,   "   "   "   "   "
Tompkins, Wesley,[1]   "   "   "   "   "
Taylor, John H.,   "   "   "   "   "
Tripp, Wm.,   "   "   "   "   "
Taylor, Jacob A.,[1]   10th or 177th N. Y. Vols.
Taylor, Alonzo,   "   "   "   "
Tapler, Alonzo,   "   "   "   "
Torrey, Geo. W., 3d Corporal, May, '61, Co. A, 22d N. Y. Vols.
Telfair, Wm. H.,   "   "   "   "
Troy, John, Co. H, 4th N. Y. Heavy Artillery.
Tobin, Rob't,   "   "   "   "
Taylor, Robert,[1] Sept. 17, 1862, 175th N. Y. Vols.
Temple, Frank, May 1861, Co. E, 2d N. Y. Vols.
Taylor, John, 2d N. Y. Cavalry.
Travers, Michael, Dec., 1853, Co. D, 7th N. Y. H. Artillery.
Upham, Willard, Sept., 1864, Co. K, 91st N. Y. Vols.
Upham, Geo. W.,[1] "   "   "   "   "   "
Van Denberg, Wm. H.,[1] 1861, Co. B, 10th or 177th N. Y. Vols.
Van Dermark, Jas.,   "   "   "   "   "
Van Vliet, Geo. E.,[1]   "   "   "   "   "
Vincent, Hiram,   May 19, 1861, Co. A, 22d N. Y. Vols.
Van Der Werken, James, "   "   "   "   "   "
Van Der Cook, John H., Aug., 1862, Co. H, 115th N. Y. Vols.
Van Der Cook, Geo.,   "   "   "   "   "   "
Vermilyea, Le Roy, Sept., '64, Co. K, 91st N. Y. Vols.
Vanlouven, Nathaniel, "   "   "   "   "   "
Van Benthuysen, Myron, Aug., 1862, 76th N. Y. Vols.
Van Benthuysen, James, "   " Co. I, 7th N. Y. V. Artillery.
Van Steenberg, W., Oct., 1861, Ass't Surgeon, 1st N. Y. Vols.; promoted Oct. '62, to be surgeon, 55th N. Y. V.; transferred March, '63, to 120th N. Y. V.
Van Hagen, Jesse,[1] Co. K, 34th N. Y. Vols.
Westover, J., Aug., 1862, Co. I, 7th N. Y. V. Artillery.
Wormwood, C. F., "   "   "   "   "   "   "
Warhurst, Samuel, "   "   "   "   "   "   "

---

[1] Dead.

Walker, Isaac, Aug., 1862, Co. I, 7th N. Y. V. Artillery.
Welch, Michael, "   " Co. E, "   "   "   "
Welch, John,[1] "   "   "   "   "   "   "
Weidman, Malachi, May 19, 1861, Co. A, 22d N. Y. Vols.; promoted to be adjutant, 1863.
Weidman, Wm., May 19, 1861, Co. A, 22d N. Y. Vols.
Wood, Giles B.,   "   "   "   "   "   "   "
Whitney, Sheldon,"   "   " Co. H,   "   "   " also 2d N. Y. V.
Winters, John,   Aug., 1862, 76th N. Y. Vols.
Wood, John,[1]   "   "   "   "   "
Whipple, Madison, "   "   "   "   "
Whitney, James,   "   "   "   "   "
Whitney, Geo.,   "   "   "   "   "
Waterhouse, Job,   "   "   "   "   "
Welch, Nicholas,   "   "   "   "   "
Westover, Chas. E.,[1] Co. H, 4th N. Y. Heavy Artillery.
White, John, 93d N. Y. Vols.
Wall, J., Co. I, 4th N. Y. Heavy Artillery.
Wilcox, Alexander, May, 1861, Co. E, 2d N. Y. Vols.
Welton, Fred'k,   "   "   "   "   "   "
Wands, Jas. B., 10th N. Y. V., also 25th.
Welch, Michael, Sept., 1864, Co. K, 91st N. Y. Vols.
Wilson, James,[1] Aug., 1862, Co. H, 115th N. Y. Vols.
Woolhizer, Fred'k., Aug., 1863, 21st N. Y. Griswold Cavalry.
Wickham, Joseph,[1] 118th N. Y. Vols.
Walters, Thos. Lieut.,[1] Co. C, 97th N. Y. Vols.
Welch, John, prisoner.
Wildricks, Thos., Dec., 1863, flag ship Hartford, U. S. Navy.
Young, James,[1] Aug., 1862, Co. I, 7th N. Y. V. Artillery.
Yates, J. L., Captain, May, 1861, Co. A, 22d N. Y. Vols.

---

[1] Dead.

IX.

1861 TO 1865.

DURING the early years of the rebellion the local columns of the *Cataract* recorded few events of importance aside from those connected with the war. The feeling of uncertainty and apprehension which prevailed among business men prevented large investments of capital in new enterprises, and until 1863, there were but slight signs of progress in the place.

During 1861, especially, there were few notable local occurrences. A fire on the morning of March 25th destroyed the picking room of the Harmony Mills, which had been burned two years before. By the exertions of the fire department, assisted by Hudson Hose Company of Waterford, the flames were prevented from communicating to the other buildings. The damage to stock, etc., was $10,000, insured. Another fire, July 15th, destroyed the saw mill of Wm. Burton & Co., at a loss of $8,000. Engines from Lansingburg and Waterford and the Ranken steamer from Troy were in attendance and prevented the destruction of the adjoining veneering mill.

Among the new business establishments of the year was the brewery on Saratoga street below the state yard property, which afterwards was conducted by Tighe & Robinson and John Tighe. In the latter part of the year, the paper mill of Chas. Van Benthuysen, on the site of Fuller's bedstead factory, was completed and commenced operations in Jan., 1862. It was entirely destroyed by fire Feb. 15th, at a loss of $25,000. The cause was the spontaneous combustion of some cotton waste stored in the fourth story. Mr. Van Benthuysen at once made arrangements for rebuilding, but not on so extensive a scale as before.

In February a bill incorporating the Cohoes and Troy Horse Rail Road Company was introduced in the legislature by a number of Troy capitalists. John A. Griswold was elected president and O. H. Arnold vice president of the company. Considerable opposition to the project was at first manifested in Cohoes, the citizens believing that the trade of home merchants would suffer largely, and also that the laying of track through the streets would lower the value of property along the route. The friends of the bill had a hearing before the trustees, who appointed J. F. Crawford to appear in their behalf before the legislature. Mr. Crawford prepared several important amendments, which were accepted by the incorporators, and were probably satisfactory to Cohoes people, for no further remonstrance was made.

Another matter, which received considerable comment in the *Cataract* during the summer, was a dead lock in the board of trustees, which prevented the transaction of any public business from April 28th to Oct. 6th. The board was evenly divided in politics, and several members absented themselves so that a quorum could not be obtained.

A new knitting factory was established during this year by L. W. Mansfield, who rented the building now known as the Empire Mill and put in operation three sets of machinery.[1] Mr. Mansfield's establishment in the tobacco factory building on Courtland street, passed into the hands of Alden Frink and Bingham.

In January, 1863, the Cohoes Skating Association, the first institution of the sort in the place, was organized with the following officers: Winsor Stone, president; Rodney

---

[1] As a matter of interest in the history of this mill it may be mentioned that mid-day union prayer meetings were held in its seaming rooms for nearly two years, with an average attendance of forty persons. In the winter of 1865, a course of social singing was inaugurated, at each evening of which from three to five hundred persons were present.

Wilcox, vice-president; A. T. Becker, secretary; P. D. Niver, treasurer; Daniel McElwain, Edward Shepard, Joseph Chadwick, Peter Manton, Levi Dodge, directors. A lease was obtained of the pond north of Simmons's dyke, and suitable buildings and enclosures were erected.[1]

This year was marked by a number of changes in Cohoes business firms, and several important additions to the manufacturing interests of the village.

In January, Geo. Campbell, formerly of the firm of Gage, Campbell & Gage of Waterford, with John Clute as partner, leased the building formerly occupied by Jeremiah Clute's bedstead factory, and established a machine shop therein. In March, the property at the corner of Ontario and Remsen streets was purchased by Messrs. Joseph Chadwick and Geo. Warhurst, who converted it into a knitting mill.[2] In June, the erection of C. H. Adams's mill on Ontario street, one of the most complete in the place, was commenced. It is of brick, four stories high, and 50 by 100 feet. The firm of C. H. Adams & Co. was dissolved, S. D. Fairbank retiring on account of ill health, and Mr. Adams continued the business alone.[3] The Watervliet mill, which he vacated, was leased for 10 years by Alden Frink & Weston, who had also become proprietors of the Halcyon Mill in the early part of the year. Another enterprise in which this firm became engaged was the manufacture of axes. The factory belonging to Jonas Simmons, near the rolling mill,

---

[1] A skating park was established two years later on Oneida street, between Van Rensselaer and Saratoga streets, which remained for some time in successful operation. Mr. McElwain was principally interested in its management. The latest institution of the sort was established in December of the present year, by A. Paul.

[2] Mr. Warhurst retired in 1867, his interest being bought by Wm. N. Chadwick. P. R. Chadwick was subsequently admitted to partnership, and the present firm of Chadwick & Co., formed.

[3] The present proprietor, John Wakeman, succeeded Mr. Adams in January, 1870.

was purchased by them, and the firm of W. J. Ten Eyck & Co. organized, in which they held the controlling interest.[1]

A new knitting mill, Wm. Conliss and John Carter proprietors, was also started in the building formerly used by Wightman & Youmans as a wheel factory.

On August 15th the corner stone of the new St. Bernard's church, the site of which had been purchased by Father Keveney in 1861, was laid by Bishop (now Cardinal) McCloskey, with imposing ceremonies.

On August 17th Hurst's woolen mill on Mohawk street was destroyed by the most disastrous fire with which Cohoes has ever been visited. It caught in the picking room, located on the first floor near the stair case, and owing to the combustible character of the contents of the mill and a high wind which prevailed at the time, spread rapidly from floor to floor, cutting off almost every means of escape. Within five minutes after the alarm was sounded the entire east end of the building, containing the only stair case, was a sheet of flame. The stairs were very narrow, so that but few were able to pass down, and the only means of exit was by jumping from the windows, in doing which many sustained severe injuries. Three of the operatives, Margaret Downey, Anna Lyons and Catharine Donnelly, were unable to escape, and perished in the flames. The death of the latter was one of the most terrible features of the fire; she attempted to escape from a third story window, but her clothing became caught on the steam pipe under the window sill, and all efforts to free her being futile, she was burnt to death in the sight of hundreds who were powerless to aid her. Some twenty of the operatives were seriously injured.

---

[1] On the failure of Alden Frink & Weston, in 1866, the Ten Eyck M'f'g Co. was organized with the following officers: David Cowee, president; Geo. R. Seymour, treasurer; R. H. Thompson, secretary; W. J. Ten Eyck, superintendent. This company suspended in 1872, and in the following year the factory was taken by Williams, Ryan & Jones. Their successors have been, Sheehan, Jones & Co., Jones & Ryan, and (July 1st, '74), M. H. Jones & Co.

The firemen, aided by four companies from Waterford and Lansingburg, and the Ranken steamer from Troy, succeeded in preventing any serious damage to adjoining buildings. Mr. Hurst's loss was $27,000 of which $18,000 was insured. This calamity gave rise to a great deal of inquiry and newspaper comment in regard to the means provided for escape from our factories in case of such disasters, and had the good result of causing the erection of adequate fire escapes in all the mills of the place.

During this summer the horse rail road was in process of construction. It was the original intention of the company to have the Cohoes terminus located at the Cataract House, but this was abandoned, as not being feasible. The rails were laid as far as the junction on the 10th of October, and an excursion car was run over the road on that day. In the following week Mr. Simons disposed of his interest in the omnibus line to the company. He had been engaged in the business for fifteen years, and under his management the Troy stage became an institution of great convenience, 12 round trips daily having been made since 1859. The completion of the road was thus spoken of in the *Cataract:*

"It is one of the most important events that mark the progress of our village in the career of improvement. We know of no good reason why it may not be made advantageous to the place. True, it may tend to divert trade to the city, but it will also bring the patrons of our manufactures nearer and create a condition and feeling of intimacy between the business men of the two places, that has not hitherto existed."

The road was well patronized and soon took precedence over other modes of conveyance. Ever since the completion of the rail road running from Albany to the junction, the trains had entered the village of West Troy by means of a Y track, and stopped at the depot, a short distance from the ferry. The establishment of the horse railway, however, so far diminished their business that the railroad company discontinued the practice of backing down the Y after Dec.

21, 1863. The track was torn up, but has recently been relaid for the accommodation of the Albany and Troy locals.

The objections to street rail roads seem to have been speedily overcome, and the example of the Troy capitalists was contagious, for in the same year the Waterford and Cohoes Horse Rail Road Co. was organized by gentlemen from Cohoes and Waterford. The Cohoes representatives on the board of directors were Hugh White, Wm. F. Carter, Wm. G. Caw, Isaac Quackenbush and Wm. M. White. The stock, amounting to $25,000, was soon taken, articles of association were duly filed, and the right of way obtained from the village trustees. Another company, composed, with the exception of T. G. Younglove, of capitalists from Troy and Lansingburg was organized the next year, which, said the *Cataract*, "proposed to at once commence active operations." Nothing more definite, however, resulted than a quarrel between the two companies, which ended the consideration of the project for the time being.[1]

The first movement of importance towards the incorporation of Cohoes as a city was made in Jan., 1864. A meeting was held in the trustees' room on the 22d, of which L. S. Parsons was chairman and S. Hayward, secretary. Remarks were made in favor of the project by Wm. G. Caw, and on motion of Sherebiah Stiles, a committee of fourteen was appointed to ascertain the feelings of the citizens in regard to the matter, and the steps necessary to be taken. The citizens were evidently not favorably inclined, for no further mention of the project was made for some time.

The following notice of the destruction of an old house was published in the *Cataract* of Jan. 30:

"The building known as the Old Junction House below

---

[1] Still another company was organized Oct. 24, 1871, with the following directors: C. H. Adams, D. J. Johnston, H. S. Bogue, Murray Hubbard, E. L. Stimson, Jas. F. Crawford, Henry Brockway, J. W. Himes, Jas. B. McKee, N. W. Frost, C. F. North and John Wakeman of Cohoes, A. J. Griffin, of Waterford. The capital stock was $25,000.

this village, formerly owned by Alfred Phelps, Esq., took fire about 7 o'clock last Sunday evening, and was totally destroyed. It had recently been purchased by the Horse Rail Road Co., and was undergoing repairs preparatory to being converted into a residence for their employés. Loss $1,000, and no insurance. The building was one of the oldest land-marks in this neighborhood, and had a wide notoriety as the scene of operation of the Junction Banking Association of years ago."

Numerous improvements in the manufacturing establishments attested the good condition of business during the year. Mr. Van Benthuysen commenced the erection of an addition to his paper mill, south of the first building, 60 by 100 feet in size. The Troy M'f'g Co., who had become proprietors of the Bailey Mill, built an addition 50 by 125 feet, and four stories high, having a front of 50 feet on Ontario street, and thus doubled the capacity of their factory. The axe factory of Ten Eyck & Co. and Jonas Simmons's rolling mill were also materially enlarged. The latter establishment had never been in complete running order until this season. Mr. Simmons took Edward N. Page as a partner and commenced operations in the spring, employing 40 men, and manufacturing five tons of iron per day.[1]

The Harmony Company built an addition to the Ogden Mills, 60 by 80 feet, and five stories high, connecting the two original buildings. They also erected a cotton house 40 by 150 feet on Mohawk street.

The manufacture of paper boxes, which has since become quite a prominent branch of Cohoes industry, was commenced in July, by L. R. Dubuque & Co. in the second story of Egberts's Hall. On Aug. 1st, a similar establishment was started by Manning & Clute in the building on Remsen street now occupied by Targett & Co.[2]

---

[1] In March of the following year Mr. Simmons's interest was purchased by Messrs. Morrison & Colwell of Troy, who organized the present firm of Morrison, Colwell & Page.

[2] After one year this firm sold to L. R. Dubuque & Co. who continued until the spring of 1867, and then sold to Isaac Clute, the present proprietor.

It had for some time been the intention of Mr. Egbert Egberts, to whose public spirit Cohoes is indebted for a number of substantial improvements, to found an academy here which should be the leading educational institution of this vicinity. To this end a bill was introduced in the legislature, which was passed May 24, to incorporate Egberts Institute. The trustees of corporation were to be the pastors of the Protestant churches in Cohoes, the following being named in the bill as first trustees : Chas. N. Waldron, J. H. Hobart Brown, Fred'k W. Flint, Henry L. Starks, Wm. H. Maynard. Provision was made in the bill for endowment of the institution by Mr. Egberts to such amount as he might see fit. At the first meeting of the trustees, held May 18, Rev. Dr. Waldron was elected president, and committees were appointed for selection of a principal and preparation of a course of studies. Deeds were received from Mr. Egberts conveying to the Institute the building on White street, east of Egberts Hall, which had been completed some time before, and the property on Remsen street just north of the hall, which had formerly belonged to W. Twichell. The Institute, under direction of Rev. A. B. Bullions, was opened for the reception of scholars Sept. 8th.

The publication of the *Cataract* was discontinued from Jan. to Aug. 1865, and the only means of learning the local events during that time is from out of town papers. There appear to have been few occurrences of importance, however, aside from the rejoicings and excitement attending the close of the war.

A fire on June 1st, destroyed Conliss & Carter's knitting mill near Ontario street, and several small buildings adjoining, occupied by H. Thompson & Son's mill; B. Mulcahy's blacksmith shop, and Warner's needle factory. The mills of the Troy M'f'g Co., Clifton Co., and Henry Brockway, were seriously threatened at times but were saved by the exertions of the firemen, who were assisted by the Ranken

Steamer Co. of Troy. The losses were as follows: Conliss & Carter $7,000, Thompson & Son $3,000, H. Brockway $1,000, B. Mulcahy $200, Warner $300.

On July 1st, the capital police law went into effect, and was welcomed with great satisfaction as an improvement on the system of village constables formerly in vogue. The police district according to this law was divided into two parts, the Albany division and the Troy division. The latter contained six precincts, three in the city of Troy, and the remainder in adjacent villages. The Cohoes precinct embraced Cohoes, Green Island, and a part of Watervliet. The first members of the force in this village were: sergeants, Wm. Buchanan, John McDermott; patrolmen, Francis S. Staats, John Richmond, Moses Pickering, Gustavus Bailey, Wm. Hastings, Jas. Delve and Michael Long. The station house was established in Hayward's building, corner of Remsen and Ontario streets.[1]

The Young Men's Christian Association, which for some time had not been in a flourishing condition, was reorganized in March, and the first officers elected in August as follows: president, D. J. Johnston ; vice president, H. B. Silliman ; Cor. Sec'y, Wm. S. Smith; Rec. Sec'y, Albert Ten Eyck ; Treas., Jas. H. Masten. The association rented the second story of Quackenbush's building, corner of Remsen and Oneida streets, and fitted up a commodious reading room.

The necessity of improvements in the fire department had been for some time felt. It was evident that the hand engines in possession of the village were entirely inadequate in case of a conflagration of any size, and ever since the burning of Hurst's Mill the matter had been frequently agitated. The working of the Ranken steamer of Troy, which had been present at several fires here, gave general satisfaction, and there was a strong feeling in favor of purchasing a similar engine. An offer was made by the Har-

---

[1] In May, 1866, it was removed to its present location corner St. John's alley and Mohawk street.

mony Co. to furnish a first class steamer if the other manufacturers of the village would subscribe enough to purchase another; and also to furnish a house and equipments for one engine, without expense to the village. No action was immediately taken on this liberal offer, and the citizens were content for this year with the addition to the department of a Hook & Ladder Co., the organization of which had been for some time desired.

Prominent among the improvements of the year was the building of a new dam by the Cohoes Co., which is one of the finest structures of the kind in the country. Work was commenced in June and the dam was completed in about four months. It is of solid stone masonry, 1,443 feet in length, and is built directly below and in connection with, the old dam of 1840, thus acquiring additional strength. The gate house, built of brick, and containing the head gates, was not completed until some time later. It is 218 feet long; the front tower is 31, and the main towers are 43 feet in height. The cost of the dam and appurtenances was $180,000. The engineer of the work was Wm. E. Worthen, of New York, who was assisted by D. H. Van Auken, the present engineer of the Co., and T. G. Younglove, its agent. The contractor was John Bridgeford, of Albany.

Business at this time was prosperous, and several additions to manufacturing interests were made. The Erie Mill on Erie street was erected by Wm. Burton, for Messrs. Wm. Moore and Jonathan Hiller, who commenced putting in their machinery in the fall. This firm had during the year been conducting the factory in the Empire Mill, which had been established by L. W. Mansfield. The foundation for the Riverside Mill, on the site of one of the buildings of Miles White's axe factory, was laid in October by Messrs. Bogue & Wager. The Harmony Co. added largely to their facilities by the purchase of the Strong Mill, which they enlarged and remodelled at an expense of $100,000, extending the building 30 feet at the north end, and putting on a French roof which added a story to its height. Besides a number of other improvements in their property an addition to No. 2 mill was commenced, which was completed in the following year and increased the capacity of the mill to 48,000 spindles. The *Cataract* of Oct. 21, speaking of these improvements, said :

"What is true of the manufacturing interests of the place is also applicable to our local mercantile trade and other business. In the fifteen years of our residence in Cohoes we do not remember a time when so much activity and evident thrift was manifested. We have twice as many dry-goods stores as we had a year ago, and all appear to be doing a healthy and profitable trade. The same is also true of the clothing, boot and shoe and grocery establishments of the place."

The census taken this year showed a population of 8,795, a decrease of 5 since 1860. The falling off was accounted for by the census enumerators by the fact that among the ignorant classes a great fear of the draft existed, and many persons, supposing the census to be a new enrollment, refused to give any information concerning their families. The same trouble was found in other places, the population in Albany being reported as 2000 less than it was in 1860. The Albanians did not wish their city to show a retrograde movement, and took measures for procuring another census. Their example was followed in Cohoes ; a subscription paper was circulated to procure the necessary funds and a second enumeration was made by Sheffield Hayward, who reported the population as 9,765, the number of families being 1,826. In the government census the capital employed in manufacturing operations in the place was stated to be $2,840,900, and the number of operatives employed, 2,729.

X.

1866 TO 1869.

THE prosperous condition of business of every kind, described in the *Cataract* in the latter part of 1865, continued with but slight interruption for the next few years. There were many important additions to the manufacturing establishments of the place, bringing new inhabitants and stimulating every branch of trade. Building was extended in all directions, and blocks of stores and handsome residences appeared in localities which had formerly been considered almost outside of the village.

The early part of 1866 was marked by few local events of importance. On the night of Jan. 10th, the stables of the Troy & Cohoes Horse Rail Road Co., near the junction, were burned at a loss of $18,000. The fire originated in the office, and spread throughout the building in a very few minutes, so that before any aid could be received from the fire department, it was completely destroyed, together with all of its contents. Thirty-one horses, seven cars, and a large quantity of hay and feed were burned.

A suit brought by the village against the company to compel them to conform their track to the grade of Mohawk street, and to pave the same, which had been some time pending, was decided this month in favor of the plaintiffs. The following comment was made by the *Cataract:*

"This is an important decision not only because it vindicates the action of the trustees, but it reëstablishes the grades at the points of variation, greatly improves Howard street, compels the company to pave their road from White street to the old junction, reimburses the village for the expenses to which it has been subjected in sinking the gas and water pipes, and cutting down Howard street, and insures it against action on the part of adjacent land owners."

The second newspaper established in Cohoes — the *Co-*

hoes Democrat — made its first appearance Jan. 27th. It was a weekly sheet, about the size of the *Cataract*, and was owned and conducted by Michael Monahon, who had for twelve years been foreman in that office. It was evident that Cohoes was not yet ready to support two newspapers, for after a brief and troubled existence of four months the publication of the *Democrat* was discontinued.

In the latter part of May, ground was broken by the Harmony Co. for the erection of a new cotton factory, Mill No. 3, on the east side of Mohawk street, opposite their first building. While excavations for the foundation were being made, a few months later, the skeleton of a mastodon was discovered, an event which awakened great interest here, and caused Cohoes to be for some time quite prominently before the public. The foundation of the mill for nearly its entire length is laid upon a bed of slate rock. At the north end of the building it was found that the layer of rock was thin and rested upon a large bed of peat ; with a view to the removal of this, a small section was excavated to a depth of about sixty feet, and in so doing numerous relics of earlier ages were exhumed.

The first discoveries, made in the middle of September, were decayed stumps and limbs of trees which lay imbedded in the rich loam ; a week later, near the bottom of the bed, the jaw-bone of the mastodon was unearthed. The event was described as follows in the *Cataract*, Sept. 29 :

"Assuredly there are more things in heaven and earth than are dreamed of in our philosophy ! Those who, during the present generation, have trod the earth of Cohoes have never taken into their wildest imaginings the strange things that were concealed beneath the surface. But the late excavations made by the Harmony Co., have brought to light the fact that a huge mastodon once dwelt where our village now stands, in an age that has been followed by the mightiest convulsions and upheavals. Fifty feet below the surface the jaw of this monster has been found, and has created in our village such a sensation as few events ever excited. . . . The jaw is somewhat decayed and flaky but the teeth are in excellent preservation; the length of each jaw bone is thirty-two inches; the breadth across the jaw at the broadest point twenty inches and the extreme depth about twelve inches. On one side is a single tooth four inches in length and two and a half in width, and on the other two teeth one of which is six and a half inches long, the other four, and each uniform in width and shape with its neighbor opposite. The holes or cavities for the dental nerves are from an inch to an inch and a half in diameter. . . . The excavation has revealed other wonders, little less remarkable. Vast volumes of oak wood, so tender that it can be cut and removed with a shovel, are intermingled with the peat. This wood when exposed to the sun or fire until thoroughly dried, becomes as hard as if it had never decayed. On each side of the peat bed so far as traced, are perpendicular rocks into which huge semi-circular cavities, deep and smooth, have been worn by the action of water. There is but one solution of this mystery. The cavity of rock where the deposit of peat now rests, was once the bed of a stream running diagonally across the line of the street and towards the Mohawk. As the peat was covered deeply with slate rock, it is evident that the stream had a subterranean channel and outlet at this place, though perhaps an open river above. In this wonderful revelation there is a vast field for speculation both for the geologist and the zoölogist."

Further discoveries were made from time to time within the next few weeks; the skull, tusk, leg-bones, ribs and enough other bones of the animal to make the skeleton nearly complete were found, most of them in a pot-hole distant some sixty feet from the one in which the jaw bone was buried.[1] The remains of numerous beaver dams were also brought to light, containing logs and pieces of wood, cut with great precision and neatness by the teeth of their builders. The bones were kept for some time at the office of the Harmony Mills, where they were visited by hundreds of persons, among whom were Profs. Marsh of Yale college, Hall of Albany and a number of other scien-

---

[1] In the following March, while making excavations on the outside of the mill several bones of the fore-leg were found in a pot hole fifty feet south of that point.

tific men. They were also placed on exhibition in Troy, at the county fair and in Harmony Hall.

Several theories were advanced to account for the burial of the bones in the peat bed in such a manner — the one supported by the highest authority being that they were thus disposed by the action of moving water or ice. In the former case it may be supposed that the body of the animal had floated down the stream, gradually decomposing, while fragments were from time to time detached, and what remained was deposited in the hole where the bulk of the skeleton was found; in the latter, the theory was, that the remains were imbedded in a glacier from the melting edge of which they were dropped, and preserved, first by a covering of water in the depression, and afterward by an accumulation of mud, marl or peaty matter; that there may have been similar remains deposited in the gravel, but that the percolating water had entirely or for the most part destroyed them. At a discussion of the matter held by the national academy of science at Hartford, it was stated that "the facts brought out in connection with the Cohoes mastodon forever set at rest the commonly received opinion that the mastodon bones usually found in the marshes are the remains of those animals who visit these places for food and drink."

Several offers were received by the Harmony Co. from public institutions for the purchase of the remains, and it was thought at one time that they would be sold and the proceeds given to the Union Sunday School. It was finally decided, however, to present them to the state. The legislature voted an appropriation of $2,000 for completing the search for the bones, and mounting the skeleton, and passed a joint resolution tendering thanks to Mr. Wild and the Harmony Co. for their generosity. In the following year the skeleton was placed in position in the State Cabinet of Natural History, at Albany.

One of the amusing results of the discovery of the mastodon was the publication at different times of letters in several newspapers from active correspondents who had ascertained by talking with old inhabitants, that the skeleton was a humbug. The following, published in the *Rutland Herald*, in April, 1870, is a specimen of these productions, though more circumstantial than most of them:

"There is another sell in Albany, quite equal to the cardiff giant — but not got up expressly for the occasion. I mean the Cohoes mastodon, so called, now on exhibition in the Geological rooms in this city. It will be recollected that in 1866, as a party at Cohoes were digging to secure a reliable place as a foundation for a factory, the workmen struck upon the bones of a large animal, which some of the *savans* declared to be those of a mastodon, but all were not agreed upon this name. Henry M. Gaine, a geologist of Saratoga, wrote two or three articles for the newspapers in which he asserted that the teeth of this fossil were not those of the extinct mastodon. But he was ridiculed for expressing such sentiments and the term *mastodon* was applied to the skeleton of the animal when it was set up for exhibition. It seems a great pity to take away this name, for with it departs the great antiquity of these bones, and with it the finely wrought theory of their having been taken from that huge pot hole of peat by an immense glacier, that separated the different animal parts, and deposited them in many different places. But we will tell a story related to us by Mr. Wm. J. Bradley, of Ballston, N. Y., a respected and truthful citizen of that place, aged sixty-four years. He says he peddled tin for Wm. J. Benedict, of Schenectady, for two or three years, and for several years he followed a caravan — June, Titus, and Angevine's. It was his custom to travel from place to place in the night and sell his wares each day at auction near the tent of the caravan. In the fall of 1833, he was going from Schenectady to Troy, following the elephant, which in those days was taken from place to place in the night to escape observation — and when near what is now Cohoes, but which then had only a house or two, he found that the elephant had fallen dead in the road. The keeper had sawed off the tusks and was cutting the body into pieces that it might be drawn out of the road. This was no small job, for the elephant was one of the largest ever exhibited in this country. Mr. Bradley had a nice span of Canadian ponies on his peddler's cart. He took them off, and assisted by Aaron Ackley, then of Troy, who led one of the frightened horses while Mr. B. led the other, they drew the body off by piece meal, and dropped it into a bog hole some six or eight rods distant, the identical one, as Mr. B. thinks, in which this so called mastodon was found."

An important addition to the public buildings of the place was the new St. Bernard's church, which had been in progress since 1863, and was this fall completed. The church, the style of which is Romanesque, is 160 by 80 feet. It has nine rows of aisles and a transept with eight rows of pews, and will seat 1,400 persons on the floor. There is an end gallery capable of accommodating 500 children, and a gallery for the choir. The sanctuary is semi-circular, forty feet wide by twenty-six deep. The altar is of white and gold, the white being composed of marble and scagliola; under the altar is the entombment, full size, in *alto relievo*. Around the base of the sanctuary is an arcade, twelve feet in height, the space above which is occupied by handsome frescoes, done by John Hild, a native of Munich; among them are copies of Vandyke's *Descent from the Cross*, Raphael's *Assumption*, and other well known paintings. The windows, which are of stained glass, are each memorial gifts and were contributed by the following : Jno. W. Harrington, Richard Powers and children, Patrick Gugerty, Cornelius O'Leary, Michael Ivory, Wm. Healey, Dr. W. F. Carter, Mrs. Peter Manton; iron works, cotton mills, woolen mills and citizens of Cohoes, one each. The cost of the church with the lot was about $106,000. It was opened Oct. 14th, with a grand sacred concert, under direction of Dr. Guy of Troy, and was dedicated on Sunday Nov. 3. The ceremonies of consecration were performed by Bishop John J. Conroy of Albany who afterwards celebrated high mass. The sermon was preached by Rev. Jno. Loughlin, Bishop of Brooklyn. Some twenty clergymen from different points were also present who assisted in the exercises. The services, which commenced at 10 A.M. and lasted four hours, were attended by about three thousand people.

Several new firms commenced business during the year. The Riverside Mill, a brick building 50 by 100 feet and five stories high, owned by Bogue & Wager, was completed early in the season. The capacity of the mill is eight sets but only six were at first run. About the same time the Erie Mill, which had been built the preceding year, commenced operations. In August the Hurst property, consisting of the mill and adjoining tenements, was sold to Lyman Bennett of Troy, for $27,000, and the Star Knitting Co., with a capital of $50,000, was organized. The first officers were: R. H. Thurman, president, Lyman Bennett, O. G. Clark, Harvey Smith, R. H. Thurman, trustees. The Mohawk Mill, Samuel Bilbrough proprietor, which had before manufactured cotton yarns and cloths, was during this year fitted up in part with knitting machinery.

The failure of Alden, Frink & Weston with liabilities of nearly $500,000, in the latter part of October, caused great excitement in business circles. The firm was one of the most prominent in the place, being largely interested in two knitting mills, the Ten Eyck Axe M'f'g Co., and other concerns. Though most of the indebtedness was out of town a number of citizens lost heavily, and the failure was severely felt throughout the village. Aside from this, the year was one of fair prosperity for Cohoes business men, and the general activity of the place was increased. A number of buildings were erected, among them many residences. The Harmony Co. made preparations for the erection of a hundred tenements, made necessary by the number of operatives who were expected to arrive when work was commenced in the new mill. In the published statistics of the company for 1866, it was stated that their mills had during the year consumed 7,427 bales of cotton, manufacturing therefrom 23,135,652 yards of cloth, equal to 13,145¼ miles.

The close of the year was marked by a storm of wind and snow, of greater severity than any with which Cohoes had been visited, it was said, since 1836. Travel by rail road and street car was interrupted for three days, and there was no means of communication with the outside world from Thursday until Saturday night, when the mail was brought in a sleigh from near West Troy, where the train from Albany was snowed in.

In the early part of 1867 the iron bridge across the Erie Canal near White street, the contracts for which had been let in 1865, was completed. It was a very desirable improvement, affording access to the lands west of the Erie Canal, which the owners, Daniel McElwain and Judge Mann of Troy, improved and laid out in building lots, and this locality is now one of the most creditable portions of the city. The construction of the bridge had long been desired by our citizens, and was authorized by the legislature as early as 1859, but had been delayed from time to time by the state authorities, and it was finally procured mainly through the efforts of Mr. McElwain. The opening of Ontario street from its present western terminus to the Erie Canal, which would make the approach to that portion of the city much more convenient, was soon afterward proposed and the matter has been subsequently agitated several times.[1]

A number of business changes occurred in 1867, occasioned by the failure of Alden, Frink & Weston. The machinery which had belonged to them was sold : that in the Watervliet Mill to A. J. Root for $42,000 and that in the Halcyon Mill to Hugh Ranken of Troy for $16,500. The latter gentleman organized the Ranken Knitting Co., with a capital of $50,000, which commenced business Jan. 16th, the officers being as follows: Hugh Ranken, president ;

---

[1] This improvement was talked of by the common council in 1873, and the cost was reported at $20,000. It was deemed inexpedient to take action in the matter at the time, and little has been done concerning it until the present year. A petition from property owners on the street urging its opening, was presented to the common council, Dec. 4.

Giles B. Kellogg, secretary; Henry S. Ranken, treasurer. The other principal stockholders were Gen. John E. Wool, Wm. Barton, G. P. Cozzens, Geo. B. Smith, D. M. Ranken, Wm. J. Ranken, all from Troy. The Atlantic Mill was purchased by Geo. Warhurst, who retired from his partnership with Jos. Chadwick. Messrs. J. H. Parsons & Co. moved into the Watervliet Mill, and their old quarters in the Egberts & Bailey or Fowler Mill were occupied by L. Greenman, who moved from the building in which A. J. Griffin is located. Among the new buildings of the year was the iron foundery and machine shop on Canvass, Courtland and Van Rensselaer streets, erected by Fuller & Safely, whose old foundery on Mohawk street had been purchased the previous year by the Harmony Co. The machine shop is 100 by 50 feet and five stories high and the foundery 120 by 60 feet, one story high, both buildings being of brick.[1] Several other concerns were located in the building — the nut manufactory of Geo. & Thomas Brooks, the knitting needle factory of Henry Dawson — both of which had been established in the old foundery, and the Magnolia Tape Mill, owned by Thos. Duncan.[2]

Considerable discussion arose during the winter and spring concerning one or two projects relating to the town of Watervliet. In March, 1866, notice had been given in the legislature of a bill "to create the city and county of Watervliet, embracing the town of Watervliet, and constituting the villages of Cohoes, West Troy and Green Island, a city under the name of Watervliet." This plan was again revived and received some slight attention, but was soon forgotten. In April, an act was passed providing for the erection of a new town hall to cost $6,000. The commissioners named were W. J. Wheeler, supervisor, Henry D. Fuller and Geo. H. Wager of Cohoes, Francis Phelps and L.

---

[1] The business was sold to Wm. T. Horrobin, Nov. 1, 1872.

[2] Afterward by Clancy & Co.

D. Collins of West Troy, and T. E. Kirkpatrick of Green Island. Several meetings of the board were held both in Cohoes and in West Troy, to take preliminary action. A proposition was made from Messrs. E. W. Fuller and Wm. Manning to present the town with an acre of land on Lincoln avenue in Cohoes, as a site for the hall, and a lot in West Troy was offered by Hon. O. F. Potter. Little was accomplished beyond the consideration of these proposals. The commissioners from each village were naturally desirous of having the hall located in their village, and as no amicable conclusion could be reached, the matter rested.[1]

The first directory of Cohoes was published in this spring by Wm. H. Young, of Troy, in connection with the directory of that city, and has since been issued by him in the same manner.[2]

The question of purchasing a steamer, the agitation of which in 1865 has been spoken of, had been of late vigorously renewed, and at the tax payers' meeting held for the purpose of voting upon the sums to be raised by tax during the ensuing year the item of $5,000 for a steamer was included in the estimate. When in reading the list this was reached, a letter was handed the clerk from Hon. C. H. Adams, in which he proposed to present such an engine to the village — " as an expression of my personal interest in the welfare of this community, where I have resided for nearly a score of years." At the same time a statement was made, on behalf of the Harmony Co., to the effect that they had ordered a steamer, which, though it would of course remain in possession of the company, would always

---

[1] In the following year, the West Trojans, foreseeing that if the hall ever was built it must be in Cohoes, introduced a bill to repeal the above act.

[2] The following table shows the number of names in each years' issue since Cohoes became a city:

1870,....3120.	1873,....4766.
1871,....4146.	1875,....5124.
1872,....4630.	1876,....5376.

be ready to protect all the property of the village. An appropriation of $6,000 was at once voted for the erection of a suitable house for the Adams steamer, and with this slight expense to the citizens in general, the place was provided by the liberality of private individuals with means of protection against fire second to none in the state. The engine made its first appearance on the afternoon of July 6th, and was then formally presented by Mr. Adams to the trustees. Murray Hubbard, president of the village, responded on behalf of the board. Henry Brockway then presented the captain and his assistants with silver trumpets of elaborate workmanship. The speeches of acceptance were made by H. B. Silliman, representing the company. The *C. H. Adams* Steamer Co., which had effected an organization June 17th, contained 36 members, and elected the following as its first officers : president, H. B. Silliman; vice pres't, Jno. V. S. Lansing ; captain, Laban Vredenberg; ass't capt., Edwin Hitchcock; secretary, W. Frank Jones; treasurer, Geo. Campbell; chief engineer, S. G. Root; 1st ass't, John Clute; 2d ass't, Samuel Nuttall; 3d ass't, Joseph Delehanty.

The steamer purchased by the Harmony Mills, named the *Robert Johnston*, made its appearance here in December. It is of the same size and power as the *C. H. Adams* and finished like it, with the exception of the silver mountings. The Steamer Company, composed of operatives of the Harmony Mills, was organized Feb. 25th, 1868, and the following officers elected: president, Robert Johnston; vice pres't, A. C. Spencer ; captain, Dan'l Simpson; ass't, Jas. Johnson; secretary, Ransom Stone; treasurer, Wm. S. Smith; chief engineer, John A. Link; 1st ass't, A. S. Stebbins; 2d ass't, John Ballard; 3d ass't, Edwd. McCready; board of trustees, D. J. Johnston, Wm. E. Thorn, A. T. Becker, Edward Foley, Duncan Munro.

The necessity of securing an increased supply of water had been felt for some time, and early in 1868 a movement was made towards the construction of a new reservoir. A bill was introduced in the legislature directing the water commissioners to make estimates of the cost of obtaining water from the Spring creek at Crescent and also of procuring an increased supply from the Cohoes Co. A vote was to be taken at the spring election; if the result was in favor of the Crescent project the bonds of the village were to be issued for an amount not exceeding $200,000 to defray the expense; and if for the other plan for an amount not exceeding $70,000. A citizens' meeting was held Feb. 11th, of which Murray Hubbard was chairman and Malachi Ball secretary. A communication was read from the Cohoes Co. offering to furnish such additional power as might be necessary for enlarged works at the same rates as were then being paid. A series of resolutions in regard to the matter was read by H. B. Silliman, and adopted by the meeting, to the effect that the citizens disapproved, as impracticable, all plans of bringing water from Crescent, and were in favor of immediately increasing the supply of water from the source then used, and of the construction of a new reservoir or the enlargement of the old one to the necessary size. A committee was appointed to draft a bill in accordance with the spirit of the resolutions, and the act providing for the construction of the new reservoir was passed May 8.

The Harmony Mill No. 3, or Mastodon Mill, begun in 1866, commenced operations this year, the first cotton being taken into the pickers February 1. The building, to which an extension was afterward built, is 565 by 77 feet and five stories high with a fire proof wing of the same height and 50 by 150 feet, in which the pickers are placed. The following figures concerning this mill were published at the time of its completion:

"In its erection the following material was used: 1,000 yards of stone, 3,000,000 brick, 4500 yards of sand, 30,000 bushels of lime, 1,000,000 lbs. cast and wrought iron, 800,000 feet hemlock plank, 500,000 feet pine timber, 450,000 feet southern pine flooring, 400,000 feet pine ceiling, and 1,000 kegs nails. It is lighted by 1,000 gas lights supplied by four miles of gas pipes. The machinery, which is of the most approved kind that could be found in England and America, includes 70,000 yarn spindles and 1,500 looms. When all running it will produce 60,000 yards of cloth per day."

A new enterprise of the year was the cider and vinegar factory of Messrs. Oliver Bros., for which they erected a brick building 35 by 100 feet, and three stories high on the corner of Remsen and Schuyler streets. A new knitting factory was established by Messrs. Wm. Nuttall & Co. who took the Empire Mill, once occupied by L. W. Mansfield, and at a later date by Moore & Hiller.

The number of French Canadians in Cohoes had greatly increased within the last few years, and as they are almost without exception Catholics, they formed an important part of St. Bernard's congregation. The constant growth of their ranks at length compelled a separation of the congregations, and in June arrangements were accordingly made for the establishment of a Canadian church. A census was taken of the number of French Catholics then in the village, under direction of Joseph LaBoeuf, chairman of the committee, resulting as follows: "Heads of families, 387; communicants, 1,470: total number of persons, 2,209." Application was made to Bishop Conroy for the appointment of a French priest, and provision was made for a room in which to hold service until a church could be erected. The pastor, Rev. L. H. Saugon, arrived in Cohoes in August, and at once commenced earnest efforts to raise the necessary building fund. A lot was purchased on Congress street, between White and Hart streets, and on Nov. 22d the corner stone of St. Joseph's church was laid with appropriate ceremonies by Bishop Conroy.

In January, 1869, the project for incorporating Cohoes as a city, which had been under consideration at intervals for several years, assumed definite shape, and a charter was drawn up for presentation to the legislature. Some discussion on the subject arose, and the *Cataract* for several months was occupied with letters on both sides of the question. The principal grounds of opposition, as stated in these communications, was that under the city charter the government would fall into the hands of a political rabble, and that the better class of citizens would have little or no voice in the management of affairs ; it was also held that greater opportunity would be furnished for extravagant expenditure and that taxation would be largely increased. The friends of the bill of course denied that there was any more chance of such calamities befalling Cohoes as a city than there was if the village government continued, and claimed furthermore that the rates of taxation would be in some particulars reduced, since Cohoes would no longer have to contribute to the support of a town government, in which it was allowed to have little share. The *Cataract* was strongly in favor of the bill, and contained a number of articles stating the reasons for advocating its passage, among which was the following :

"Thus far in the existence of Cohoes, there has seemed to be a lack of local pride on the part of its inhabitants. Our proximity to Troy and Albany has lead us, naturally, to depend upon them in a large degree for mercantile facilities, and as a consequence, Cohoes has been looked upon by the outside world more as a suburb of those two cities than as a live, independent municipality of itself. But the moment Cohoes assumes the proportions of a city, and follows it up with a proper — but not overweening sense of its own importance, we shall feel the result favorably. Our citizens will be more self reliant, and pride in our growing city will keep at home hundreds of thousands of dollars which now go to enrich the mercantile trade of adjoining cities."

The bill, which had been considerably modified since the first draft, passed the assembly April 15th, but did not become a law until May 19th. This delay on the part of the senate, and the insertion in the act of a provision by which it was not to take effect until 1870, were due to the efforts of its opposers, as was stated at the time, and were accounted for by political reasons.

The velocipede excitement, prevalent throughout the country during this year, reached Cohoes in the winter, and furnished material for a number of paragraphs in the local paper. The appearance on the streets of the first velocipede was thus described :

"Velocipedism is becoming a mania about these days. On Thursday evening, Feb. 24, Mr. Chas. P. Craig showed himself astride of one on Remsen street, to the great delight of all the people. Shout after shout went up from the gazing multitude, especially when the machine careened and dumped the rider. On Saturday morning he gave us a free exhibition, followed by scores of the *gamins* of Cohoes."

A rink was opened on Factory street, in the hall at the rear of the hotel, which remained in successful operation for some time. Comparatively few of the vehicles were seen on the street, however, and the *furore* in regard to them was much less than in adjoining cities, perhaps because Cohoes streets at the time were not adapted for that sort of travel.

There were during this year several important additions to the manufacturing interests of the place. Two new knitting mills were established, one by Himes & Vail, who leased the building on Mohawk street, which had formerly been occupied by Parsons & Co., and put in operation six sets of machinery ; the other by the Alaska Knitting Co., located in Fuller & Safely's new building. The officers were : Simeon Holroyd, secretary ; Robt. Safely, treasurer ; Horace Fisher, agent.[1] On Courtland street, corner of Canvass, a brick building, 50 by 100 feet and three stories high, was erected by John Land & Sons, for a sawing and planing mill. The foundery and machine shop on Van Rensselaer street near Courtland, was established in the latter part of

---

[1] This establishment was removed to Waterford in the latter part of 1871.

the year by Wm. T. Horrobin. The foundery building is one story high, 100 by 60 feet, and the machine shop is three stories high, 100 by 50 feet. Extensive additions, embracing blacksmith shop, pattern house, etc., were soon afterward made. A number of residences and stores were also erected. Prominent among these new buildings was the block erected by C. H. Adams on Remsen street, below Ontario. It is three stories in height, built of Philadelphia brick, with an ornamental iron front. The plate glass windows in the stores on the ground floor were the first ones introduced in Cohoes. On the site of the old Heamstreet tavern, on Mohawk street one door below Factory, a brick block three stories high was erected by Mr. Witbeck of Troy. Among the public improvements were the engine houses on Main street and Johnston avenue and a new school house corner of Cataract and School streets. Several additions and improvements were also made on church property. An extension was built on the Presbyterian church at a cost of $7,000, by which its capacity was doubled; as enlarged the building is 95 by 48 feet with transepts on the south 59 feet in width, and contains 172 pews, capable of seating 700 people. It was rededicated Jan. 20, 1870. Adjoining St. Bernard's church a parsonage was built 40 by 40 feet, three stories high, at a cost of $15,000. The Baptist congregation also commenced the erection of a parsonage on the lot south of the church, which was completed in the following year, at a cost of about $5,000. St. Joseph's church was dedicated Dec. 12th, with the usual ceremonies. The first mass was celebrated by Rev. Thos. Keveney — the pastor, Father Saugon, being on account of illness unable to attend.

A series of articles appeared in the Albany *Express* during the year on the growth and manufactures of Cohoes. These were revised and expanded by Mr. Edward Fitzgerald, and published in a pamphlet of 55 pages entitled *The City of Cohoes. Its History, Growth and Prospects, Its Great*

Manufactories. The contents were chiefly descriptions of the manufacturing establishments then in operation and statistics of their production. At the close of the publication appeared the following summary:

"At present the city numbers over 16,000 inhabitants. Its manufactories comprise six extensive cotton mills, running 203,000 spindles, eighteen large knitting mills, two foundries, three machine shops, a rolling mill, two axe factories, a planing mill, a sawing and veneering establishment, and many other large and flourishing industrial concerns. The aggregate capital invested in manufacturing operations is estimated at $20,000,000. The mercantile interests of the city are represented by over 300 large and prosperous retail establishments. The religious wants of the community are supplied by six large and magnificent churches. Two splendid steam fire engines of great power are at the service of the fire department."

XI.
1870 TO 1876.

FROM the time that Cohoes assumed the dignity of a city, a marked change was apparent in its general character. A certain degree of local pride became developed, which it must be confessed had previously been wanting, and the results were a wonderful improvement in the appearance of the place, and the provision of many conveniences which had long been needed for the comfort and well-being of its citizens. The gradual accomplishment of these changes, and the evidences of substantial growth which they afford, form a notable feature of the history of Cohoes for the next few years.

The first election under the city charter was held April 12, 1870. It passed off very quietly, and the number of votes polled (1,850), was much larger than at any previous election. The city government was formally organized on the evening of Tuesday, April 19th. After the meeting was called to order and the mayor had administered the necessary oaths of office, the aldermen proceeded to act as a board of canvassers, and the result of the election was officially announced. The privilege of the floor was then obtained by Augustus Ellmaker, late president of the village, who, in behalf of the late trustees, presented an elegant watch to Malachi Ball, who for six years previous had been the efficient clerk of the village and board of education. After this agreeable incident, the mayor delivered his inaugural — a short but comprehensive address, in which were stated the financial condition of the city, and the improvements most needed. The appointments were then made, and the standing committees announced. The meeting was spoken of in the *Cataract* as follows :

"After the transaction of a few minor items of business the board adjourned, having had a session that was remarkable for its unanimity and the good order that prevailed. The new officers seemed to slip into the routine of their positions as easily as if they had been to the manner born; and those who expected a hitch in the proceedings were disappointed in their expectations. The mayor presided with a dignity becoming his high official position, and in the cast of his committees evinced a thorough knowledge of the needs of the several departments and a just estimate of the peculiar qualifications of the gentlemen for the various positions to be filled. We congratulate our citizens upon the auspicious commencement of our career as a city and trust that the most sanguine expectations of the friends of the new system may be realized, and the fears and apprehensions of its opponents prove unfounded."

The capital police law of 1865, though excellent in many of its features, had for some time been made the subject of complaint, and during the winter of 1870, steps were taken by several of the cities and villages which were under its provisions to procure laws creating a different system. Cohoes was one of the last so to do, and it was not until May 6, that the bill under which our present police system is organized was passed. Under this act the government of police affairs was vested in a board of police commissioners, consisting of the mayor and two others, the term of office of the latter being four years. The police force appointed by the board was made to consist of a captain, sergeant, not more than seven patrolmen, a station-house keeper and a surgeon. The first commissioners under this act were chosen at the general election in November.

Soon after the charter went into operation, movements were made towards securing some of the substantial improvements which it was expected would follow as a natural result of the new form of municipal government. The streets, which had so long been a discredit to the place, and had for over twenty years been made the subject for a paragraph in almost every issue of the village newspaper, were among the first objects to which attention was directed. In the early part of June a petition for the pavement of Remsen street from Mohawk to White street was presented to the common council. The committee was unable to decide at once upon the style of pavement which would be most suitable and give greatest satisfaction to the property owners on the street. A long and animated discussion followed, on the merits of the respective pavements — and a number of communications on the subject were published in the *Cataract*. The decision was finally made in favor of a wooden pavement, the Brocklebank and Trainor, and the work of laying it was commenced in October.

The new reservoir, work on which had been commenced in the preceding year, was completed in July, and the water was pumped into it on the 25th of that month. It occupies three and a quarter acres of land, situated at the west of the first reservoir, which were bought in 1869 from Mrs. Jane A. Lansing, for $1,800. It has a capacity of 8,000,000 gallons, and is at an elevation of 28 feet above the old one, and 190 feet above the central portion of the town. The first pump which was constructed for this reservoir did not operate satisfactorily and another was afterward substituted, built under direction of D. H. Van Auken, engineer of the Cohoes Co. This pump is double acting, 16 inch diameter and 6 feet stroke, working 10 strokes to the minute, moving a column of water 16 inches in diameter 120 feet per minute, and elevating it into the new reservoir 118 feet above the pump bed. It is driven by a Jonval turbine water wheel of 100 horse power, made by Fuller & Safely.

On Sept. 17th, the first number of the *Cohoes Weekly Democrat*, a paper about the size of the *Advertiser* of 1847, was issued. It was an outgrowth of a smaller sheet called the *Watchman and Chronicle* which had been published during a few months previous by D. Cady. Mr. Cady's assistant in the editorship of the *Democrat* was John H. Atkinson.

Among the new manufacturing firms which commenced operations this year was the Cohoes Lime, Cement & Plaster Co., which located its works near the Cohoes Co.'s dam. The proprietors were T. G. Younglove, David T. Lamb, Henry I. Dunsbach, G. H. Stewart and L. Dodge.' The first kiln, a Page's Patent Flame Kiln — was put in operation during the summer.[1]

Another establishment, Trost & Bezner proprietors, was located in Land & Son's building on Courtland street; the articles of manufacture being furniture, and fancy articles in wood.[2]

The general improvement of the place during the year was marked. The completion of the new water works, and the addition of two hose companies to the fire department rendered the protection against fire very complete; several important changes were made by the board of education in the method of conducting the schools, and arrangements were made for the erection of the White street school house, a building which had long been needed; many of the streets were graded and repaired, and several sections of country roads, which under the provisions of the charter were included in the city limits, were improved; the construction of sewers, a matter which had formerly been too much neglected, owing to the limited power granted to the village trustees, received the attention of the authorities, and sewers were laid in portions of Remsen, Mohawk, Oriskany, Main

---

[1] A mill for grinding cement and plaster was built in the following year. In 1873 the capacity of the works was increased by the erection of another mill, and two additional kilns. The second mill is located near the Erie Canal, 250 feet from the first, from which the power is obtained by means of a wire cable. The cost of the works was about $50,000. In 1875 this firm was succeeded by the Cohoes Lime & Cement Co., incorporated Aug. 18th with a capital of $70,000. The following were the first officers: president, D. T. Lamb; secretary, T. G. Younglove; treasurer, D. H. Van Auken. D. T. Lamb, H. I. Dunsbach, M. O. Cauldwell, T. G. Younglove, G. H. Stewart, L. Dodge, trustees.

[2] The style of this firm was changed July 21, 1870, to the Trost & Bezner Mfg. Co. John T. Saxe, proprietor.

and Cedar streets. The cost of these various improvements, as shown in the mayor's report, was in the neighborhood of $80,000. The taxes were of course increased, but not so largely as many supposed — the rate being less than a quarter of one per cent greater than that of the previous year. The census of this year indicated the largest five years' growth in the history of the place, there being an increase of 6,578 over the official census of 1865. The male inhabitants over the age of 21 were 2,574, divided as follows : 1st ward, 779 ; 2d ward, 717 ; 3d ward, 728 ; 4th ward, 350. The following statistics in regard to manufactures were given :

Manufacturing establishments,	196
Capital invested,	$4,030,641
Wages paid yearly,	1,839,572
Value material used,	5,084,940
" annual production,	7,889,331

In February, 1871, several amendments to the charter were prepared by a committee from the common council, which were presented to the legislature and passed in May. Among the changes were the following: provision was made for the election of two justices of the peace to serve until 1874 ; the common council was invested with power to pass certain ordinances and regulations for the government of the city, and to appoint commissioners of deeds ; the term of office of the chamberlain was made two years; the power of the recorder was increased, and his salary fixed at $2,000, and the term of office of the overseer of the poor was extended from one to three years. Considerable dissatisfaction was expressed at the last two amendments, which it was claimed were added after the bill had left the hands of the committee in Cohoes.

On Sunday, June 10, the new St. John's church, at the junction of Canvass and Mohawk streets, was formally opened by Bishop Doane, who had laid the corner stone on

June 11th of the previous year. The ceremonies of consecration were postponed until a small debt yet remaining on the building should be liquidated. The customary morning service was read, Bishop Doane, Rev. Ferris Tripp, of Brooklyn, Rev. Chas. Babcock of Greenwood Works, and Rev. J. H. H. Brown, rector of the parish, officiating. The sermon was preached by Bishop Doane. The building, which will accommodate 1,000 persons, is built of Schenectady stone faced with brick, in the modern gothic style, with transept. The nave of the church is 100 feet long, 68 feet wide and 60 feet to the peak of the roof. The ceiling is in blue, and the upper part of the walls has a red ground, diapered. The chancel, which is square, measures 20 by 30 feet, with a large window in the rear. The organ and choir are placed in an alcove a few feet above the level of the transept, on which it opens through an archway. The chapel is 24 by 32 feet and opens on the church and chancel in the same manner as the organ alcove, so that it can be used if desired to make extra accommodations for the church. The Sunday school room, which will seat 450 pupils, is located in the lower part of the building. The rectory, connected with the chapel, is of the same material as the church, and a model of convenience. Besides what is now built, it is the design to have a tower on the south side of the church, with a stone spire 160 feet high. The cost of the structure as far as finished is $40,000, and the completion of it will cost $20,000 more.

Among the additions this year to the business of the city was the Cohoes Warp Mill and Thread Co., incorporated July 23d, with Collins Arnold, president and treasurer, and Stillman Ilsley, secretary. The manufactures of this company are hosiery yarns and cops, seaming thread, chain warps, etc., which are used principally by cotton and woolen mills. The building which is on the site of the Miles White forge shop, on Mohawk street, is of brick, 50 by 80 feet, four stories high, and was completed in July. Another new factory was erected by the Empire Pin Co., on Courtland street, a brick building 40 by 100 feet, and five stories high. With its increased facilities the company did an extensive business, operating 40 machines and producing 46,800 papers of pins per week. These papers average 280 pins each, making a yearly production of 681,408,000.

The Waterford and Cohoes Bridge was burned on the night of the 31st October, but little to the regret of the citizens, if we may judge from the following, from the *Cataract:*

"It was never considered a first class structure and of late years has been a source of constant dread to those who have been obliged to cross it, and a standing insult to public enterprise. During the conflagration, the general expression seemed to be that it were better thus than that the lives of our citizens should be endangered by its longer use."

A steam ferry was established for the accommodation of passengers, and a tug was provided to tow the boats in the Champlain Canal across the river. The new state dam just below the bridge, which had been commenced in June, 1870, was completed this fall, by Sherrill, Strong & Flood, contractors. Its length between the piers is 1,640 feet.

The building of this dam enabled Messrs. Weed, Becker & Co. to obtain an additional head of five feet of water, and add largely to the capacity of their establishment. The improvements connected with these increased facilities were completed during the year at a cost of $20,000.

In October, when the news was received here of the great fires which devastated Chicago, and different places in Michigan and Wisconsin, the citizens were prompt to come forward with substantial expressions of sympathy. A public meeting was at once held in Egberts' Hall to take measures for the relief of the sufferers, at which Mayor Adams presided. Committees of five gentlemen from each ward were appointed to receive subscriptions, who were to report to the following general committee: Hon. C. H. Adams, Murray Hubbard, D. J. Johnston, H. B. Silliman, Wm. Nuttall. The response to the call was general and liberal. About $4,000 in cash were raised, of which $2,500 were sent to Chicago and the balance to the sufferers by the fires in Wisconsin and Michigan. Knit goods and other articles of clothing to the value of $5,000 were also forwarded.

A matter which occasioned considerable discussion in Cohoes during the early part of 1872, was what was known as the Boulevard bill, introduced in January. It provided for the construction of a broad avenue, the line of which was to extend along the Hudson river terrace, beginning at the Newtonville road in Albany and running north, passing a little to the west of the Rural Cemetery and terminating in Cohoes at or near Johnston avenue, affording a straight and level street nine miles in length. The work was to be supervised by seven commissioners, of whom three were from Albany, two from Watervliet, and two from Cohoes, the gentlemen named from this place being David J. Johnston and H. S. Bogue. The expense, estimated at $100,000, was to be defrayed by the localities to be benefited; bonds were to be issued by the city of Albany to the amount of $50,000 and by the town of Watervliet and the city of Cohoes, each for $25,000. The newspapers in the neighborhood were almost without exception in favor of the project, and it had a number of strong supporters among the citizens of Albany and Cohoes. There was, however, from the beginning a strong feeling against it in West Troy, and considerable opposition was soon developed here. Many persons claimed that the bill was a private measure introduced merely to advance the interests of individuals who owned property along the route of the proposed road; and also that in case the latter should be constructed, it would be used merely as a pleasure drive, and, not being suitable for the passage of heavy vehicles, would be of no business advantage. The principal objection, however, which was urged by Cohoes people, was that if the city were to be bonded at all, the money should be expended in making improvements for which there was more pressing necessity. These objections were answered by the friends of the bill, but they failed to entirely overcome the prejudice against it, and it did not go into effect.

A bill introduced during the same month made several changes in the charter of the city, the principal one being in regard to the recorder and overseer of the poor. The former office was abolished, and provision was made that the latter be filled annually by appointment of the common council.

In February, the Cohoes Hospital was established, an institution which for lack of proper support has not had the permanence it deserved. Its officers were: president, Robert Johnston; vice president, Earl L. Stimson; secretary, Wm. E. Thorn; treasurer, Wm. Burton; committee, T. G. Younglove, H. B. Silliman, W. S. Gilbert. A building was hired on Harmony Hill, in which a free dispensary was established, and Drs. Robertson, of Albany, and J. W. Moore and Jas. Featherstonhaugh of this city, gave their services to those in need of them.[1]

With the rapid growth in the business interests of Cohoes, it had for some time been apparent that there was a favorable opportunity for the establishment of a second banking institution, and a movement to this effect was made in January by a number of prominent business men, which resulted in the organization, on March 21st, of the Manufacturers' Bank of Cohoes, with a capital of $100,000. The first officers were as follows: president, Wm. E. Thorn; vice

---

[1] This laudable enterprise was supported for a time almost entirely by the contributions of private citizens. A bill was passed in May, 1873, authorizing the common council to appropriate $1,000 annually for its maintenance. This did not go into effect, however, and, not receiving any encouragement, the gentlemen in charge of the institution were forced to abandon it, not being willing to defray all its expenses from their own pockets.

president, Jno. V. S. Lansing; cashier, N. W. Frost; directors, Wm. E. Thorn, Jno. V. S. Lansing, D. H. Van Auken, Geo. Campbell, J. W. Himes, Jacob Travis, D. J. Johnston, Nicholas J. Clute, Wm. Moore, Alfred Le Roy, P. R. Chadwick. Rooms were fitted up at No. 70 Oneida street, and the institution was opened for the transaction of business, July 8th.

The project of uniting Lansingburg and Cohoes by bridges across the Hudson and Mohawk rivers, which had been agitated in the papers of the vicinity at different times previous, assumed definite shape by the incorporation of the Lansingburg and Cohoes Bridge Co. in March. The bill provided for the construction of "a bridge and the approaches thereto, over the Hudson from some point on Van Schaick's Island, in the city of Cohoes to some point in the village of Lansingburg, south of said ferry."

It was expected that the erection of a bridge across the Mohawk from the island to Cohoes, concerning which Mr. Adams, owner of the island, had made some generous offers, would soon follow, as arrangements had been made the previous autumn. The scheme seemed to meet with approval from all parties concerned. The papers of Troy were earnest in its favor, on the ground that the road distance between that place and Cohoes would be diminished by nearly a mile and communication between the two cities be greatly facilitated; while the Cohoes papers hailed with satisfaction the prospect of beautiful building sites and pleasant drives which was offered to our citizens. As in the case of the Boulevard bill, however, while the value which such an improvement would have was acknowledged on all sides, something occurred to kill the project, and there has been no definite movement towards developing that part of our city until the present year.

The new bridge across the Mohawk above the state dam was completed in September at a cost of about $25,000. It is 704 feet long and consists of four spans of 140 feet and one of 135 feet. The side walks and tow path are each six feet wide, and the trusses twenty-one feet high. It is known as the Combination Bridge, the top chord and posts being of wood, and the lower chord, main and center braces of iron. Belden and Gale of Syracuse were the contractors.

An event of importance in the history of Cohoes manufactures was the completion in this year of the extension to the Harmony Mill No. 3, making the largest complete cotton mill in the country. The extension is five stories high, and 510 feet long by 76 feet wide, making the entire structure 1,185 by 70–76 feet. The junction of the extension with the main building is marked by the central tower, a handsome fire proof structure eight stories in height. A niche in this contains a bronze statue of the late Thos. Garner, for years one of the principal proprietors of the mills, which was cast by the Ames Mfg. Co. of Chicopee, Mass., after a model by Millman. Underneath this tower is the main entrance, substantially built of granite. There are four other entrances to the building, each surmounted by a lofty tower. The building is constructed throughout of the best and most durable materials, and its front is handsomely trimmed with brown-stone. Besides its great importance to the place in a business point of view, the fine architecture of this mill and its complete finish in every detail render it a principal ornament of the city, and it is among the first objects of interest to strangers who visit us.

The Harmony Co. made a further addition to their establishment by the purchase in the early part of the year of the paper mill building on Mohawk street, south of the No. 2 mill, in which the manufacture of jute was afterwards commenced. Messrs. Van Benthuysen & Sons, the proprietors of the paper mill, moved their machinery to Castleton, where they had a similar establishment.[1]

---

[1] The water of the Mohawk was too muddy in the spring and fall for use in their business, and the proprietors had several years before commenced the boring of an artesian well, which was carried down over 2,300 feet before it was abandoned.

An addition to the knitting interests of the place was the establishment of the Globe Mill by Le Roy, Lamb & Co., Wm. Moore being the third partner.[1] The firm took possession of the building on Remsen street between the Diamond and Star Mills, which had been occupied since 1857 by the Harmony Co., and put in operation four sets of machinery. The second mill south of this, a building 30 by 96 feet, and four stories high, was fitted up for knitting purposes early in this year by George Warhurst, of the Atlantic Mill on Mohawk street, who sold both establishments to Thompson & Horrocks, in the fall. Two new knitting mills, the Peerless, and the Sunnyside, were located respectively in the first and second stories of the Empire Pin Co.'s building on Courtland street. The former, Joseph Bullock and Bro. proprietors, ran two sets, and the latter, of the same capacity, was owned by Fisher and Melinda. Neither remained in permanent operation.

A new establishment of the year was a gas and steam pipe factory erected near Courtland street between Saratoga and Van Rensselaer streets, by the Empire Tube Co. The company was incorporated with a capital of $50,000, the following being trustees: Jas. Morrison, Thos. Colwell, Buckley T. Benton, Jas. M. Morehead, W. H. Atwater.[2]

A series of articles, afterward issued in pamphlet form, was published in the *Cataract* during the year, giving a complete and careful account of the manufacturing establishments of the place. The statistics of production may be summarized as follows: The Harmony Mills had in operation 251,000 spindles, and employed 5,170 operatives. The knitting mills, 20 in number, operated 129 sets of machinery, employing 2,503 operatives, at a monthly pay roll of $58,900.

---

[1] Mr. Moore afterward withdrew, selling his interest to the other partners.

[2] The company never commenced active operations, but leased the factory to Albert Smith and Jas. M. Morehead, who ran it a few months. On May 1st, 1874, the present firm, consisting of Albert Smith and A. G. Curtis, was formed.

The annual production was 453,000 doz. goods valued at $3,620,000. The establishments in the iron manufacture, 4 in number, employed 685 men at a monthly pay roll of $35,800. The value of the annual production, consisting of axes, iron and machinery, was $1,680,000. Miscellaneous establishments employed 394 hands at a monthly pay roll of $14,010, and produced goods annually to the amount of $479,000. The annual production stated of other concerns of which no further statistics were given, amounted in the aggregate to $451,000. The total yearly value of manufactured products thus shown was $6,230,000, exclusive of those of the Harmony Mills. A summary of the mercantile establishments, professions, etc., was also given, as follows:

"Groceries, 56 ; dry goods stores, 9 ; clothing stores, 7 ; millinery and fancy goods stores, 25 ; drugs and medicines, 7 ; boot and shoe stores, 15 ; hat and cap stores, 3 ; job printing offices, 1 ; news rooms, 2 ; cigar manufacturers, 5 ; flour and feed stores, 1 ; lumber yards, 3 ; coal dealers, 5 ; junk dealers, 2 ; liquor dealers, 79 ; meat markets, 22 ; jewelers, 3 ; sewing machine agencies, 4 ; insurance agencies, 7 ; fruit and confectionery stores, 6 ; oyster dealers, 4 ; music stores, 1 ; piano rooms, 1 ; marble yards, 1. Of other trades and occupations, we enumerate as follows: dress making establishments, 8 ; attorneys, 12 ; physicians, 11 ; teachers, 34 ; clergymen, 8 ; dentists, 2 ; photographers, 3 ; surveyors, 2 ; architects, 1 ; barbers, 9 ; auctioneers, 2."

Among the improvements of the year was the enlargement of the Baptist church, at a cost of $15,000. The front was extended to the side-walk, a distance of some 20 feet, thus greatly enlarging the seating capacity of the building, and a spire and towers were constructed which much improved its appearance. The interior of the edifice was entirely renovated and its walls and ceiling handsomely frescoed. The church was formally opened on the evening of Jan. 15th, 1873, the dedication services being postponed, until the debt incurred in making the improvements should be liquidated. An historical sermon, giving a detailed account of the organization and progress of the church, was preached by the pastor, Rev. L. S. Johnson, which was followed by the singing of a hymn composed for the occasion, and congratulatory addresses by Revs. C. A. Johnson of Whitehall, Mr. Hanna of West Troy, and C. P. Sheldon, D.D., of Troy. Other clergymen present and participating in the exercises were Rev. Mr. Kenley of Lansingburg, and Rev. Wm. M. Johnson of the First Presbyterian church, Cohoes.

The long period of exemption from serious loss by fire which Cohoes manufacturers had enjoyed was interrupted in February, 1873, by the occurrence of two destructive conflagrations. On the afternoon of the 1st, a fire was discovered in the card room of the Stark Mill, on Courtland street. Efforts were made to extinguish it without giving an alarm, but the whole room was soon in flames, which commenced to spread to adjoining parts of the building, and the operatives throughout the mill were at once informed of their danger. Most of them escaped through the doors but some who were in the upper stories, finding the staircase impassable, were forced to jump from the windows upon the sheds and ground beneath. It is a matter of surprise that only a few persons were injured, and those but slightly— had the building been higher, or the circumstances less favorable, a catastrophe like that at Hurst's Mill might have occurred. The structure was a mass of flames when the firemen reached it, and their efforts were principally directed towards preventing the destruction of the Miller House and other adjoining buildings. The loss of the proprietors, Scott & Stewart, upon machinery and stock, was between $35,000 and $40,000, which was covered by insurance for $22,000. The loss on the building was $3,000.

On the morning of the 14th, a fire broke out in the third story of the Erie Mill, on Erie street, caused by the falling of a small bit of waste, ignited by the gas, into a pile of *laps* upon the floor. It was some fifteen minutes before an alarm could be sounded and when the firemen arrived the two upper stories of the mill were in flames. The department could accomplish but little, for the water was shut off from the reservoir and there was not enough head upon that in the pipes to throw a stream into the second story of the building, and some of the nearest hydrants were besides found to be frozen. Fortunately there was no wind at the time, and the danger to the adjoining mills, Parsons's and Thompson & Horrocks's, was comparatively slight. The loss on the building, which belonged to Wm. Burton, was $12,000 ; Mr. Moore, proprietor of the mill, lost on machinery, etc., between $40,000 and $50,000 of which $25,000 were insured.

The necessity of procuring horses for the *Adams* steamer had been for some time urged in the city papers, but no action was taken on it by the common council. As it was evident, however, at these two fires, that much valuable property could have been saved if the department had been promptly on hand, steps were taken to avoid in future such disastrous delays ; and accordingly a few months later a team of horses was purchased for the steamer and the services of a paid engineer and driver secured.

Among the evidences of the prosperity of the place — at this time at its height — were several movements which were set on foot early in the year, for important public improvements. One of the enterprises proposed was the erection of a new hotel, with all modern conveniences — an institution talked of and desired since the earliest days of the place. The Cohoes Co. were in former years in the habit of holding their annual dinners at the Cohoes Hotel, and in 1840, when the house was managed by the Messrs. Fuller, elaborate plans were made, while the guests were under the warming influence of a generous repast, for the erection of an elegant hotel. It was to be built in the pine grove which was then standing between Courtland street and the river, on the ground now occupied by Fuller's building. The establishment was to be fitted up in the most complete manner, and to have among other attractions, floating baths in the river below, connected with the hotel by a covered passage and a flight of stairs. The nearest this enterprise ever came to completion was the preparation of the plans, which were drawn up by Joshua R. Clarke — for in the next year commenced a period of business depression, the effects of which were severely felt here. Since that time the project had been considered by several different parties, and the columns of the *Cataract*, from almost its first number, contained frequent appeals to the citizens to take some action in the matter.

The first movement of any importance was made in April of this year, when a bill was introduced in the legislature incorporating the Cohoes Hotel Co., of which the following gentlemen (who were to be the first directors), were named as incorporators : T. G. Younglove, Andrew J. Root, John V. S. Lansing, D. J. Johnston, Wm. S. Gilbert, Murray Hubbard, S. E. Stimson, Wm. T. Horrobin, Henry S. Bogue, Thos. Colwell, Otis G. Clark, John Wakeman and Jacob Travis. The capital stock was fixed at $150,000 with liberty to increase to $200,000, to be divided into shares of $100 each. The company had several plans under discussion, but before any definite arrangements were concluded the panic came on, which, as in 1840, put a stop to further proceedings, and at present the long desired hotel is still unbuilt.[1]

---

[1] "The owners of the city hotel property are contemplating the erection of a first-class hotel building on the site of the old building. An Albany firm of architects already have the plans under way. It is to be of brick of modern style in construction, at a cost of from between fifty and sixty thousand dollars. It will front on Mohawk street, and extend back a distance of one hundred and fifty feet, a sufficient depth to be reserved to allow stores being built fronting on Remsen street. The wealthy New York Spanish house which owns this valuable property, is prepared to go ahead, the only obstacle is the lease which the present occupants have."— *Daily News*, Nov., '76.

Another improvement suggested during this year was a fire alarm telegraph, concerning which there was considerable discussion in the common council. The expense of its introduction — $7,000 — was decided to be more than the city could then sustain, and the matter was dropped.

On April 1, a meeting of business men was held at the Manufacturers' Bank to take steps for the formation of a board of trade in this city. Henry Brockway acted as chairman, and N. W. Frost as secretary. A committee was appointed to consider and investigate the matter, consisting of P. R. Chadwick, H. B. Silliman, J. W. Himes, Wm. Acheson and Jno. V. S. Lansing. Subsequent meetings were held, but no permanent organization was ever effected.

Progressive movements of this sort, though they accomplished but little at the time, are worthy of record, for the full development of the above and other similar projects which have been mentioned, will surely come at no distant day, and it will then be of interest to know the time at which their necessity first became apparent and the details of the earliest efforts made in regard to them.

The Mechanics' Savings Bank, which had been incorporated in March, commenced business in May, its office being established in the Manufacturers' Bank rooms on Oneida st. The following were the first officers: president, Robert Johnston; 1st vice pres't, John Clute; 2d vice pres't, Wm. Stanton; secretary, Wm. S. Smith; treasurer, Abner J. Griffin; assistant treasurer, Leonard J. Groesbeck.

On September 22d, was issued the first number of the Cohoes *Daily News*, Edward Monk editor and proprietor, and Clark & Foster printers. The paper was 18 by 13 inches, four columns to the page, and the arrangement of the reading matter was the same as at present. The editors' salutatory was as follows:

" *The Daily News* will be published daily, at noon (Sundays excepted), at No. 1, Granite Hall, Remsen street, Cohoes, N. Y., and can be procured at the news-rooms and at this office or will be delivered to subscribers at one cent per copy. The *News* is especially intended as a local paper and, although a portion of its space may contain a brief summary of general news and miscellaneous matter, its columns will principally be devoted to the doings and transactions daily occurring in our city. With this object in view, items of interest and news about town will be thankfully received at the office of publication; also brief communications of a local nature will be inserted in its columns. Although the *Daily News* goes before the public to-day for the first time unannounced, we hope it will not be entirely unwelcome. With this much of introduction we respectfully present the first number to the citizens of Cohoes with confident expectation that, if deserving, our enterprise will meet with a share of their patronage."

On account of its proximity to Troy and Albany, Cohoes had always been regarded as a poor field for a daily newspaper, and it was prophesied by many that the *News* could not exist more than six months. These predictions have proved false, however, for the circulation of the paper has steadily increased, it has twice been enlarged, and now holds an important position among the newspapers of the city.

During the early part of this season a remarkable business activity had prevailed. A number of buildings were erected in all parts of the city — among them several for manufacturing purposes. Two knitting mills were put up in place of those which were burned in February. Mr. Moore rebuilt the Erie on the same site, and John Scott of the firm of Scott & Stewart, erected the Enterprise Mill, 50 by 50 feet and four stories high, on Courtland street, west of the pin factory, near the site of the old Stark Mill. On Simmons avenue, south of the cemetery, a brick factory 200 by 40 feet and two stories high, was built by Trost & Bezner to accommodate their business, which had increased rapidly since its establishment. Among the blocks erected for business purposes, was that of Campbell & Clute, 100 by 80 feet, four stories high, on Mohawk street south of Courtland, in which they located their machine shop ; and also that of Patrick Rogers, on Remsen street near its junction with Mohawk. A new knitting mill, with six sets of machinery, was established by Fuller & Hay in the foundery building on Courtland street. Another new enterprise was the machine shop of Tubbs & Severson, located in the same building. The station-house of the N. Y. C. & H. R. R. R. at the west of the White street bridge, was completed during the summer, and the local trains to Troy, which were a convenience much appreciated by our citizens, commenced running October 6.

A number of important public improvements were made during the year. Considerable money was expended in grading and opening streets on the hill in the lower part of the city, among them Central ave., Western ave., and Columbia street. The latter street was extended at a width of sixty feet, to the extreme western bounds of the city, at a cost of over $21,000. White, Oneida, and Sargent streets were paved, at the following expense : White street, $13,346 ; Oneida street, $10,709 ; Sargent street, $6,498. The pavement on Mohawk street, which had been commenced in 1872, was also completed. The hill in the southern part of the city, west of the Erie Canal, a locality hitherto undeveloped, was greatly improved and beautified by its owners, Messrs. Crawford & Hubbard. The property was carefully mapped, a number of streets were opened, shade trees were planted, and Grand View Park, on the brow of the hill, was laid out. A *camera obscura*, put in operation during the autumn, afforded an extensive view of the surrounding country, which was enjoyed by a number of visitors.

The degree of growth and prosperity manifested in Cohoes during the early part of this year was greater than any which has since been attained. The financial panic which swept over the country in the fall, paralyzing every branch of business, had the same results here as elsewhere, and the condition of affairs has not since been such as to warrant a general freedom of expenditure. The effects of the panic were first felt here in November, and though they were not, during the following winter, as severe as had been feared, all the manufacturing interests of the city then began to suffer from a continued depression, from which, until the present season, there have been no signs of recovery. During October the various establishments in the city continued running, many of them having reduced the wages and working time of their employés. On the 25th the Harmony Mills were shut down, and the woolen mills ceased operations a few days later, the water being drawn from the Cohoes Co's Canals. For some time there was great anxiety throughout the place. Rumors were afloat that none of the mills would be started until spring, causing apprehensions of the most disastrous effects among all classes of the inhabitants. The local papers were, however, inclined to take a hopeful view of matters. The *Cataract* said:

"There is as yet nothing very discouraging in the prospects before us, and if all will take courage and push ahead as far as their circumstances will allow, everything will come out right, and we shall see a far more favorable winter's business than has been predicted."

Accounts of the condition of business here, most of them favorable, were also published in the New York papers, some of which sent correspondents to the place. The following were some of the views expressed:

"The stoppage of work at the Harmony Mills, Cohoes, is not the unmixed misfortune which the first news led the public to expect. It is a step not unusual at this season and amounts at the very worst, to a few weeks' rest from work. ... If other cotton mills adopt the same remedy the proper relations between demand and supply may become all the more quickly reëstablished, though some little distress must, almost necessarily, be its immediate result."— *New York Daily Times.*

"At Cohoes, which claims a population of 20,000, the reports are more favorable up to the present time, than was to be anticipated. ...Under the present circumstances Cohoes is in as good if not better condition to stand the hard times than any manufacturing town in the United States. The chief hardships and loss are likely to come on the manufacturers and capitalists, who are puzzled to account for the present panic in commercial circles, and like their brethren in New York can see no further reason for it, than a 'lack of confidence.'"— *New York Daily Tribune.*

"Altogether little apprehension exists just now that much suffering is likely to be encountered. By those best informed it is thought that the new year is likely to bring in much increased demand for labor. None of the workers have left, or have even thought of doing so. All are hopeful. But oft has 'hope told its flattering tale,' and why should it alter its habit?"— *New York Daily Herald.*

After a stoppage of two weeks all but two of the woolen mills commenced running, seven of them on full time and the remainder on half or three quarter time. The Harmony Mills were started Nov. 24, an average reduction of 12½ per cent in wages being made. The news of their resumption was gladly received. The *Cataract* published a very hopeful article in regard to it, in which it was stated that the worst of the panic was passed, and that the condition of business would continue to improve during the winter, and be in the following spring as prosperous as ever — a prediction unfortunately not fulfilled. There was no general stoppage of the mills during the season, but the stagnation of the markets, destined to be of long duration, afforded but little encouragement to the efforts of those manufacturers who continued.

A matter which excited much local interest in the early part of 1874, was a dispute which arose in regard to the office of city chamberlain. Mr. C. F. North was appointed to the position at an early meeting of the new common council, and the resolution by which he was appointed was subsequently vetoed as illegal by the mayor, on the ground that the alderman moving it was interested in a city contract.

At a subsequent meeting, Mr. North presented his official bonds for approval and they were signed by Alderman Le Roy acting as mayor *pro tem*. Mr. Cary, however, the incumbent of the chamberlain's office, refused to deliver his books and papers to Mr. North, on the grounds that his appointment was not legal, having been vetoed by the mayor, and that his bonds were not properly signed. A mandamus was accordingly served on him by Mr. North, and the case was argued before Judge Ingalls of Troy. His decision was that the appointment was legal, but that the bonds must be signed by the mayor to be valid. After a delay of some weeks, the mayor on April 27th, signed the bonds, and the matter was thus settled satisfactorily, having furnished material for much animated discussion among our citizens, and numerous articles in the local papers.

As in 1873, two serious fires were among the important events of the early part of the year. The premises of the Ten Eyck Axe M'f'g Co., consisting of three wooden buildings on Courtland street were burned on Jan. 18th. The loss of the owner, John L. Thompson of Troy, was $20,000, of which $9,000 were insured. The buildings were occupied at the time by Sheehan, Jones & Ryan, who lost from $6,000 to $8,000 in manufactured goods besides several thousand dollars' worth of tools and fixtures. The fire was of incendiary origin. Another disastrous fire occurred in Root's Mill on the afternoon of April 2d. The building, which was one of the best appointed of our knitting mills, was, with its contents, completely destroyed, at a loss to the owners of nearly $200,000, which was insured to the amount of $125,000. The bat factory of Edward Walker, situated in the rear, was also destroyed involving a loss of about $5,000. The fire originated in the picking room of the mill and spread with remarkable rapidity. An elevator near the middle of the building was the means of communicating the flames to the upper stories and so quickly that smoke was seen issuing from the cupola within five minutes after the discovery of the fire in the basement. Great excitement prevailed when the conflagration broke out, as it was feared that many of the operatives would be unable to escape from the building, but the fire escapes, which had been provided soon after the terrible fire at Hurst's Mill, proved adequate to the occasion and no injury was suffered by any of the employés. There was great danger at times that the adjoining buildings would be destroyed — the mill of Gregory & Hiller, on the north, being several times on fire — but the exertions of the fire department, assisted by the Knickerbocker Engine Co. of Waterford and the operatives of the mill, prevented its spreading further. These fires caused but a slight interruption of business. Messrs. Sheehan, Jones & Ryan moved their establishment to the pipe factory building on Saratoga street which they now occupy, and the Messrs. Root immediately commenced the erection of their present mill which was finished in the fall. The main part of the building is 150 by 50 feet and five stories high ; on the north side of this is a wing 96 by 20 feet, four stories high, connected with it by arches in every story. On the river bank, entirely disconnected from the principal structure, is a fire proof building 53 by 35 feet, three stories high, containing the pickers, cotton cards, and lappers. The risk of fire is thus greatly diminished. The main building is also provided with every safeguard and means of escape in case of fire, and is in all its appointments one of the most perfectly arranged knitting mills in the place. Its cost, including machinery, was about $150,000. Another large mill just south of Root's was built by Messrs. Bilbrough and Dubuque — the old Mohawk Mill formerly occupied by Mr. Bilbrough having been destroyed by its owners, the Harmony Co., to make room for improvements to the Ogden Mills. The main building is of brick, 120 by 50 feet, and five stories high besides a basement. There are also two wings containing office, store room, etc.

The number of residences erected during the season was notably smaller than in the previous year. Several important buildings for other purposes were, however, constructed.

St. Joseph's French church, built in 1869, had never been considered safe. In the following year its steeple was removed because it threatened to crush the body of the church, and the condition of the edifice became in 1873 so dilapidated that its demolition was resolved upon. The work was commenced in June, 1874, and the corner-stone of the new building, on the site of the first, was laid Aug. 23, under direction of Bishop M'Nierney. The sermon was preached by Rev. Francis Van Campenhouldt of Troy, and the ceremonies were participated in by a number of other clergymen from different localities. The building, which has not yet been completed, was ready for occupancy on Easter Sunday, 1875. Its proportions are: length, 128 feet; width 70 feet; height of nave 60 feet; of tower and spire 206 feet. The cost of the building was $40,000, and it is estimated that as much more will be required to properly finish the interior. Much credit is due to the congregation, for their enterprise and liberality, in thus constructing, within a period of five years, two expensive church edifices, and to Father La Salle whose efforts in behalf of the new enterprise have been indefatigable.

A new church, the German Baptist, was organized during this year, the members being principally employés of Trost & Bezner. Services were for some time held in the First Baptist church, and a small building was afterwards secured on Simmons avenue which the congregation has since occupied. In the certificate of incorporation, filed Feb. 4, 1875, the following were named as first trustees: Herman Bezner, one year; Henry Trost, two years; Conrad Muller, three years.

A noticeable addition to the buildings on Remsen street was the Music Hall Block, 75 by 62½ feet and four stories high, built by Acheson & Masten, at a cost of $60,000.

The two upper stories are occupied by a handsome and conveniently arranged theatre capable of seating 1,000 persons, which was formally opened on the evening of Nov. 23d, by J. W. Albaugh's company from Albany. The entertainment opened with a dedicatory address, delivered by Miss Florence Chase, and the singing of the national anthem by the company. The play of the evening was London Assurance, the leading parts being taken by Mr. and Mrs. Albaugh. The post office was moved into the north end of this building as soon as it was completed, and the city library has since last summer occupied rooms in the second story.

Of the entertainments held in the hall during the ensuing season, those of chief local interest, were eight evenings of social singing, which were well attended. The course, organized through the efforts of L. W. Mansfield, was somewhat similar in plan to that which was held in Mr. M.'s mill, during 1865, and met with such success that it was repeated in the following year.

Several times since its incorporation, the proposition had been made to bond the city for different amounts to defray the expenses of certain public improvements. A project of the sort was submitted to the tax payers in 1872, but some features of the bill which it was proposed to introduce, were distasteful, and it was voted down. In April of this year, another bill was prepared and presented to the legislature which seemed to meet with general approval. The common council was, in this act, directed to issue the bonds of the city whenever it might be requested by the commissioners of construction, for the purpose of opening, extending and improving the following streets : Columbia, from Mohawk to Lancaster; Remsen, from Newark to Saratoga; Saratoga its entire length; Ontario and Oneida streets, the Boght road, and the road leading to Crescent. Of the proceeds of the sale of the bonds, $75,000 were to be expended for the above purposes, and the remainder was to be devoted to the purchase of a site, and the erection of a suitable city building. The commissioners of construction named, were H. S. Bogue, Alfred Le Roy, David J. Johnston, Jas. B. McKee and Malachi Weidman. Unfortunately the bill was not introduced until late in the session, and no action was taken upon it. Several important municipal improvements were, however, completed during the season. Among them were the opening and grading of James street, at a cost of $17,000 ; grading of Central avenue from Columbia street, south to the city line, costing $5,000; grading portions of Saratoga and Howard street at a cost of $3,500, and construction of sewers on Remsen, Lancaster and Orchard streets. The alteration by the state of the course of the Champlain Canal at the junction, and the building of new and improved locks at that point was completed in the early part of the year.

The *Cataract* published at the close of the year a review of the condition of the knitting business, giving the results of interviews with each manufacturer. Most of the establishments were running on full time and expected so to continue during the winter. The conclusions of the *Cataract* were as follows:

"It will be seen that the outlook is anything but discouraging to the operatives at least ... they have thus far known but practically little of the effects arising from the general depression which has existed during the year in all parts of the country. There has been little or no apparent reduction in the production of fabrics, and old prices which have ruled in years past in almost all the mills, have been paid. It is a noticeable fact that Cohoes thus far has never suffered from the strikes that have brought untold misery and want in many portions of the country."

A recapitulation of the figures given in the article compared with those published in 1872, showed a falling off only in the number of operatives employed which was 2,405 as against 2,503 in the former year, while the aggregate of the annual production and monthly wages was even greater.

The discussion of several proposed amendments to the city charter occupied a large share of local attention during the first few months of 1875. The principal changes were in regard to the powers of the common council concerning assessments — authorizing them by a two-thirds vote to raise money for special taxes ; the powers, duties and salaries of the city engineer and city attorney — the compensation fixed for the former being $500, and for the latter $1,000; the duties and salaries of constables, who were to receive $100 per annum, in addition to their fees ; and the organization of a board of fire commissioners who were to have control of a paid department. A meeting of the common council was called Jan. 30, to hear the report of a committee on these amendments, at which a number of citizens were present. After some discussion they were allowed the privilege of the floor, and the following resolution offered by D. H. Van Auken was put to the audience and almost unanimously adopted :

"*Resolved*, That it is the sense of the tax payers at this meeting, in view of the pressure of the times, affecting both business and labor in all departments, it is inexpedient that there should be any amendments to our city charter which shall increase the rate of taxation."

After the passage of a motion requesting the legislature to take no action upon any such amendments that might be presented, the meeting adjourned, but another was immediately organized to consider an amendment creating a fifth ward, concerning which a bill had been introduced during the previous week. The sentiment of the meeting was in favor of such an amendment, and a committee was appointed to attend to its passage. The bill, which also made slight changes in the boundaries of the third and fourth wards, became a law May 1.

On the 20th of May, occurred the most destructive fire that had visited the city since the burning of the Tivoli Mill. The polishing, finishing and handle shops, of the

Weed & Becker M'f'g Co., were destroyed, at a loss of $50,000, throwing nearly 200 men out of employment. One of the buildings destroyed was the original factory of Daniel Simmons, which had been in use since 1835. The company proceeded at once to the erection of a fine brick building on the site, which was completed in the following season. It is of brick, 140 by 50 feet, and four stories high.

The publication of a second daily paper, *The Cohoes Daily Bulletin*, was commenced June 1st. It was a 28 column sheet, democratic in politics, and was conducted by J. H. Atkinson, formerly of the *Democrat*, and J. Barlow Luddy. The office was located in Hayward's building, Ontario street.[1] A further addition to the newspapers of the city, was the *Journal des Dames*, a weekly paper, published in the interests of French Canadian ladies, and edited by Mme. Virginie Authier. The first number appeared Sept. 24.[2] Another French paper, *L'Avenir National*, the publication office of which had formerly been in Troy, was removed here Oct. 15, and located in Silliman's building on Remsen street. The paper, which was a weekly, was conducted by L. G. Leboeuf.[3]

An event of general interest was the consecration of Rev. Dr. J. H. Hobart Brown of St. John's church, who had been called to preside as bishop over the new diocese of Fond du Lac, Wis. The ceremonies, which took place in the church on Wednesday Dec. 15, were attended by a large number of citizens. The presiding bishop was Rt. Rev. Horatio Potter of New York; the sermon was preached by Bishop Welles of Wisconsin, and a number of other eminent clergymen from different localities were present.

---

[1] On Dec. 13, the name of the paper was changed to *The Daily Eagle*, J. B. Luddy being editor, and D. Williams, proprietor. Its publication was discontinued Aug. 12, 1876, and the *Northern Herald*, a Sunday morning paper, established by Williams and Eagan.

[2] This was succeeded Feb. 16, 1876, by *La Patrie Nouvelle*, Authier Bros. editors and proprietors.

[3] Discontinued Aug. 11, 1876.

The dullness of business, continuing during the year, had prevented the outlay of capital to any amount in private improvements, and in municipal affairs the sentiments expressed at the tax payers' meeting in January evidently had their effect. A few public works however, which were greatly needed, received attention. Among them were the grading of North Mohawk and Trull streets and McElwain avenue, at a cost of $5,000, the construction of sewers on McElwain and Johnston avenues and Mohawk street, costing an equal amount, and the ravine sewer near McElwain avenue the expense of which was $13,500. The latter, which is 1,571 feet in length, was an improvement long demanded, and one of great benefit to several portions of the city.

On December 31st, arrangements were made for publicly celebrating the advent of the centennial year. The demonstration, which began in the evening and was continued until about 3 A.M. of Jan. 1st, was thus described in the *News:*

"The celebration of the Centennial New Year in Cohoes was begun by the parade of the Lafayette Guards shortly before the ringing of the bells at midnight. Remsen street was thronged with people, whose patriotism, added to the spirit with which the new year is always welcomed, caused a general turn out and demonstration. Huge bonfires were lighted, red and blue fire burned, cannon thundered, rockets and roman candles were fired and numerous buildings along the route illuminated. The bells of the city churches and factories clanged forth a thousand welcomes in brazen tones to the Centennial New Year, and even the steam whistles on the mills and Adams Steamer did duty on the occasion."

A violent storm, which swept over this section of the country on the morning of Feb. 5, did considerable damage to property in this city. St. Bernard's church suffered the severest injury, in the destruction of its spire, which was over 200 feet high, and one of the handsomest in the neighborhood. It was constructed under direction of Nichols and Brown of Albany in 1866, at a cost of $10,000. The spire was broken off at its brick foundation, and crushing through a portion of the roof, fell upon the rail road track east of the building. The chime of bells, which had been placed in the belfry four years previous at a cost of $5,000, was badly damaged and the total loss to the church reached nearly $20,000. It was expected that the steeples of the Baptist, Presbyterian and French churches which were seen to sway violently in the wind, would be also demolished, but they fortunately were able to withstand the gale, and none of the churches except the Baptist were injured to any extent. A smaller spire on the north side of the latter building was blown over, considerably damaging in its fall the roof, and also the residence of Mrs. H. R. Grant, adjoining the church on the north. A number of small buildings were quite badly damaged, and numerous chimneys in all parts of the city suffered demolition.

In March, bills were introduced in the legislature making a number of important changes in the charter, over some of which followed a long and animated discussion. The law committee of the common council having been directed to draw up needed amendments, reported several, of which the most important were the following: Giving the chamberlain power to collect by sale of property the arrears on taxes since 1870, and allowing him an extra compensation for his services in so doing; authorizing him to set apart $3,000 annually for the use of the water board, instead of allowing them a certain proportion of the moneys raised by highway and other taxes as formerly; empowering the common council to compel the construction and repair of sidewalks, and to appropriate $1,500 for the celebration of the Fourth of July. Two further amendments were prepared — one providing for the appointment of a recorder and fixing his salary at $2,000, and the other known as the "omnibus bill" — giving the mayor power to appoint the city attorney, city clerk, and a number of other officials, whose salaries were in several instances to be increased. The bill in which these were incorporated was drawn up by private parties and was introduced in the legislature without having been submitted to the common council, and it was to these amendments that the greatest opposition was raised. When it was found that the bill had been favorably reported by the assembly committee, a citizens' meeting was called to take action on the matter. This was held at Egberts Hall on the evening of March 28, Henry Brockway presiding. Fifty vice presidents and eighteen secretaries were appointed. Short addresses against the amendments were made by H. D. Fuller, Justice Redmond, Jas. F. Kelly, aldermen Nolan and Ryan, and Chas. Kolb. Resolutions were then adopted protesting against the passage of the bill without further hearing from the citizens, and requesting Senator Harris to use his influence against it. The opposition, especially to the clause appointing a recorder, grew less however, as the people became better acquainted with the provisions of the bill, and the *Cataract* of April 8th, said:

"The signatures of owners of over $2,500,000, of the taxable property in the city have been received to the petition favoring the passage of the charter amendments, and what is the best joke of all, more than two-thirds of the officers of the citizens' meeting, called to protest against them, were among the signers."

None of the amendments were passed, however, except those providing the appointment of a recorder and assigning a fund for the water commissioners, both of which were somewhat changed since their first draft — the sum named in the latter having been raised from $3,000 to $5,000. No general opposition to the passage of several of the others was manifested among citizens but they were "killed" through the influence of a few interested parties. The first recorder appointed by the mayor under the new act was Chas. F. Doyle, who entered upon the duties of his office June 26, holding court in the common council chamber.

Though the bill authorizing an appropriation had failed

to pass, the general feeling throughout the city was, that the centennial year demanded more than an ordinary celebration, and that it would not be to the credit of the place, to be behind other cities in the neighborhood, in such manifestations of patriotism. A special election of the tax payers was accordingly held on May 22, to decide in regard to the matter, which resulted in voting an appropriation of $1,000. A joint committee of members of the common council and Grand Army of the Republic was appointed to make the necessary arrangements, and under its direction, the programme of the exercises was agreed upon. The citizens in general took hold of the matter with earnestness, and the result was a celebration which did credit to the patriotic spirit of Cohoes. At midnight the principal streets were illuminated, and the usual discharge of fire arms, lasting during the day and into the next night, commenced the celebration. The main procession was formed on Remsen street at 9 A.M., and commenced its march soon after in the following order :

FIRST DIVISION.

Marshal and Chief of Column.
Washingtonians.
Green's Band.
Third Separate Company.
Post Lyon, G. A. R.
Hook and Ladder Co. and Truck.
Adams Steamer and Wagon.
M'Intosh Hose Co. and Carriage.
Johnston Steamer Co.
Howarth Hose Co.
Harmony Co's Wagon.
Cannon.

SECOND DIVISION.

Marshals.
Green's Band.
C. H. Adams Zouaves.

St. Bernard's Society.
St. Bernard's T. A. B. Society.
St. Jean Baptiste Society.
St. Joseph's Society.

THIRD DIVISION.

Marshal's Aids.
Drum Corps.
Knights of Pythias.
Delegation of Daniel O'Connell Society.
Ancient Order of Hibernians.
Carriages containing Mayor, Orator, Reader, Common Council, and School Board.
Butchers Mounted.
Merchants, &c.

The houses along the line of march were almost without exception decorated with flags, or appropriate emblems. After the parade, the literary exercises were held on the balcony of the Bret Harte House, on Remsen street, Mayor Johnston presiding. They were as follows:

1. Music by the Glee Club, consisting of Messrs. Targett, Green, Hastings and Taylor.

2. Reading of the Declaration of Independence, by P. D. Niver, Esq.

3. Music.

4. Oration by E. G. Wager.

The features of the afternoon were the parade of the Philibusters, who made some very apt local hits, and the Field Day and Picnic of Post Lyon, held on Simmons's Island. A display of fire works in the evening on the vacant lots east of St. Bernard's church, concluded the public celebration of the day.

It has been before mentioned that a futile movement to extend Remsen street through to Saratoga street, was made as early as 1850. Efforts to carry out this improvement have been made several times subsequent, but with no better result. In 1870, the project came before the common council, who appointed a committee to ascertain its cost, which was reported as $5,000. The question was again agitated in the spring of this year, and received then a larger share of public attention than at any previous time. The following in regard to the matter is from the *Cataract* of June 10th :

"Remsen street is now only open to Newark street, but the city owns the land for 145 feet further south. It is proposed to extend the street through this land and thence at nearly right angles to Saratoga street, intersecting the latter at a point where the state yard bridge crosses the canal. If this is accomplished, a street will be opened across the Van Rensselaer property to the Mohawk river, at which point it is proposed to locate the western end of the Adams' Island bridge. It is claimed that the cost of the proposed extension will be less than $4,000. About one-half the property owners on Remsen street have already signed the petition."

The matter was under consideration some time by the common council, and the final conclusion was that it be dropped, owing to the strong opposition made by interested parties and property owners on the street. Mr. W. L. Adams, who, in despair of ever getting the coöperation of the authorities, had decided to build the bridge from his island to this city at his own expense, was only waiting for some definite action on the part of the common council before commencing operations. As soon, therefore, as it was known that Remsen street would not be extended, work was begun. The bridge was completed during the past autumn at a cost of about $25,000. It rests upon five stone piers, and the superstructure, which is of iron, is 450 feet in length, and fifteen feet above the ordinary level of the water. The approach to the bridge on this side of the river, is by Ship street, south of Travis's lumber yard, which will be opened from Saratoga street east, and a bridge built across the Champlain Canal. The numerous advantages resulting from this improvement render it one of the most important of the year. Our citizens have been afforded the opportunity of purchasing at reasonable figures, pleasant and healthful building sites, located at a short distance from the business centre, and an easy access is offered to a mile frontage on the Hudson river, whenever the growth of the city may make it needed. Fifty acres on this side of the island have been mapped and laid out into city lots, 498 in number, many of which have already been disposed of at good prices, at the auction sales which have been held during the autumn. Mr. Adams owns all the island except 100 acres at the northern end, and intends to dispose of it in lots, as occasion may require. The streets laid out parallel with the river are over a mile long, and are to be crossed by streets running from the Hudson to the Mohawk, a distance of one-half mile. It is expected that the company which was granted a charter to build a bridge from Lansingburg to the island, will commence operations in the spring, and a short and direct road will thus be opened to Lansingburg and the upper part of Troy. The route has already proved popular, though the only means of crossing the Hudson has been a skiff ferry, and will doubtless draw a large share of travel when the bridge is completed.

During the past year, the signs of general activity in the city have been comparatively few. Almost the only addition of importance to the manufacturing interests of the place, is the Ten Eyck Axe M'f'g Co., established Feb. 23, with a capital of $30,000, by the following partners : Abram, Albert and Jonas Ten Eyck and D. H. Clute, Cohoes ; Geo. Carrigan, Bayonne, N. J. A change in the firm will soon be made, and the capital increased. The works, on Saratoga street in the lower part of the city, consist of a building 100 by 32 feet, containing forge shop and polishing shop, and two wings each 60 feet long, containing tempering shop, blacksmith shop, etc. The works are run by a steam engine of 60 horse power. A new factory has been erected by Albert Smith & Co., pipe manufacturers, near the rolling mill, north of Courtland street. The building is of wood, 120 by 95 feet, and cost $20,000. The capacity of the works has been doubled by the construction of a new furnace, just completed.

Among the most important improvements completed by the city authorities, are the paving of Remsen street, from White street south, and the construction of an iron bridge on Johnson avenue, built by the Canton (Ohio) Bridge Co., at a cost of $2,650.

The material growth of the city is, of course, dependent on the fortunes of its leading branches of industry, and as these have been among the interests most severely affected by the panic, it is not to be wondered at that during the past year, and in fact since 1873, there have been so few striking evidences of progress. The panic has not had the result, however, of causing a general retrograde movement in the place. Fortunately for Cohoes, most of its manufacturing concerns have had sufficient capital to enable them to continue operations, though at a loss, during this long period of depression. Much suffering has thus been prevented among the working classes and the mercantile interests of the city. Wages have, of course, been generally reduced, and a number of persons have been, at different periods, without employment ; but the condition of affairs has at no time been so bad as might reasonably have been anticipated. We have had none of those long continued strikes which have caused so much distress elsewhere, and the degree of suffering among the poorer classes has thus far been much less than in neighboring cities.

At present the prospects are by no means gloomy. Nearly all the manufacturing establishments are in operation, and there are no indications as yet that a general stoppage is intended.

The state of affairs on the whole, since 1873, has thus shown the truth of the prediction made at that time, that " Cohoes is in as good, if not better, condition to stand the hard times, than any manufacturing town in the United

States." Its growth has been steady, though less rapid, than heretofore. Although the number of new buildings is small, and little additional capital has been invested in business enterprises, other signs of advancement are apparent. The population has evidently increased, needed public works have been completed, and various important institutions established, all attesting the fact that the business depression of the past three years, though of course retarding, has not seriously interrupted the progress of that substantial development, which became especially noticeable soon after the incorporation of Cohoes as a city ; and which marks the succeeding period as one of the most important in the history of the place.

XII.

Manufactures and Various Institutions.

As a conclusion to the history of Cohoes, now brought down to the close of the present year, a brief account is appended of the manufacturing establishments and various public institutions of the city, showing their condition at present, and stating such facts of importance concerning them as have not been elsewhere mentioned.

The Cohoes Company.— This company has necessarily the most prominent connection with the history of Cohoes. By developing the water power and offering inducements for the settlement here of capitalists, it has been the foundation of all the varied industries of the place; and has, moreover, by the construction of creditable works and improvements, by liberal donations of land for public purposes, and in many other ways, contributed constantly to its growth and prosperity.

The early operations of the company, and the more important improvements made from time to time, have been previously described. No expense or labor has been spared in the development of the material resources of the place, and the facilities now offered for manufacturing are second to none in the state.

The mill privilege which was originally reserved by Mr. I. D. F. Lansing in the sale of his land, was purchased from him in 1859 for $20,000, thus affording the company complete control of the water power of the river from half a mile above, to a mile below the Falls. The supply is always ample, and during the past few years, while other water powers have failed at times, the Cohoes mills have suffered no stoppage. By the construction in 1865 of the present dam and gate house, and the extension, at different times, of other canals besides those already mentioned, the facilities of the company have been greatly increased, and they now have a complete system, in which the same water can be used six different times, and which, when entirely perfected, will be one of the finest in the country. The following is the present arrangement of the canals, as classified by the company.

No. 1. The upper level (canal of 1834), extending from the dam to rear of the Harmony Mills.
No. 2. Mohawk street in front of Harmony Mills.
" 3. From Strong Mill to Clifton Mill.
" 4. Remsen street, formerly known as Basin B.
" 5. Ontario street.
" 6. Courtland street.
" 7. Van Rensselaer street.
" 8. Saratoga street.
" 9. Grove street.
" 10. Remsen street continued.

Nos. 7, 8 and 10 of the above are unfinished.

The total fall is 120 feet, and the available power is established at 10,000 horse power, but little more than half of which is now utilized. The water, together with the necessary quantity of land, is leased to manufacturing firms at much lower rates than prevail elsewhere — the expense of some of the largest mills for water and ground rent scarcely exceeding $1,000 yearly. The company charges $200 for a "mill power," which is 6 cubic feet of water per second, with a 20 feet head and fall — or its equivalent — making an annual rental of about $20 per horse power. The exact quantity of power used by each manufacturer is determined by an accurate system of measurement, the details of which were perfected by officers of the company. Among the most important of the recent improvements of the company, is a tunnel, completed in December, 1876, which adds greatly to the availability of the water power. It extends from the end of Canal No. 1, to a point on the bank of the river, about twenty feet from its bed, opposite the south tower of Harmony Mill, No. 2. Its opening is 6 by 7 feet, its length 360 feet, and the fall from the surface of the canal to the outlet is about 70 feet, affording a pressure capable of moving the entire body of water at least 7 feet per second. By means of this tunnel the necessity of stopping the mills to remove the accumulations of ice and *debris* in the upper canal was entirely obviated. The ice would frequently form to such an extent that the flow of water in the canal was materially obstructed, and the company were compelled to cut it out and remove it by hand, a tedious and expensive process. Under the new arrangement the ice can be floated down to the tunnel gates and then discharged, without interrupting the running of the mills. The work was designed and superintended by D. H. Van Auken, engineer of the company, and was done by Houlihan & Stanton, about six months being required for its excavation.

The officers of the company since its incorporation have been as follows:

President. Canvass White, 1826–1834.
Stephen Van Rensselaer Jr., 1834–1841.
Wm. N. Chadwick, 1841–1847.
Stephen Van Rensselaer Jr., 1847–1849.
Teunis Van Vechten, 1849–1853.
Robert Christie Jr., 1853–1854.
Chas. M. Jenkins, 1854–1859.
Alfred Wild, 1859–1868.
Wm. T. Garner, 1868——.
Secretary. Henry J. Wyckoff, 1827–1828.
Francis Olmsted, 1828–1829.
Henry J. Wyckoff, 1829–1834.[1]
Agent. Hugh White, 1833–1834.
Chas. A. Olmsted, 1834–1835.
Joab Houghton, 1835–1840.
Clarkson F. Crosby, 1840–1841.

---

[1] After this year the agent acted as secretary.

Hugh White, 1841–1847.
Francis S. Claxton, 1847–1850.
T. G. Younglove, 1850–1875.
Wm. E. Thorn, 1875.

The officers elected for the present year were: Wm. T. Garner, president; Wm. E. Thorn, sec'y and treas.; Wm. T. Garner, Wm. W. Niles, Samuel W. Johnson, Jno. Crosby Brown, David J. Johnston, Wm. E. Thorn, Chas. C. Birdseye, directors.

THE HARMONY MILLS.—Proprietors: Garner & Co., New York, D. J. Johnston, Cohoes, Wm. E. Thorn, Cohoes. Chief in importance among the manufacturing concerns of Cohoes is the above, devoted to the production of cotton cloth. The mill erected by the Harmony M'f'g Co., in 1837, was for some years among the most prominent in the place, and after the building of the Ogden and Strong Mills in 1846, this branch of manufacture assumed the leading position here which it has since retained.

The change of proprietorship in the Harmony Mill in 1850 was the beginning of a course of steady prosperity, and its owners, besides erecting several large factories at different times have come into possession of the other two mills, thus founding a mammoth establishment, the most important of the kind in the United States. The existence of a manufacturing concern of such magnitude has of course been of the utmost benefit to Cohoes in a business point of view, and contributed largely to its prosperity. Through its means large accessions have been made to the population, and the constant expenditures made by the corporation in wages, in the erection of buildings and in various improvements have been of marked advantage to the commercial interests of the place. But aside from this Cohoes is under great obligations to the proprietors of the Harmony Mills for the work they have done towards its material improvement. Their factory buildings are all handsomely constructed, and the grounds connected with them tastefully laid out; the streets and sidewalks adjacent to their property are kept in the best condition, and the well built blocks of tenements which have been erected in different localities — more particularly on the West Harmony — are creditable additions to the buildings of the city. Of these tenements, which are nearly 1000 in number, over half have been erected since 1860. Those more recently constructed, at the northwest of Prospect Hill, occupy ground which ten years ago was used as farm land, but is now regularly laid out in well graded and macadamized streets provided with asphalt sidewalks. The tenements are let to the operatives at a merely nominal price, and in this, as in all other respects, the company has manifested a laudable regard for the comfort of those in its employ.

The depression of the past three years has of course severely affected the market for cotton cloths and in this establishment, as in all others of the kind, a general reduction of wages has been found necessary, though it has not been so great as those made in other manufacturing towns. There has, however, been but a trifling reduction in the number of operatives employed, and the mills have almost constantly since the panic been running at their full capacity.

The following statistics show the number of operatives employed, and the amount of machinery in operation at present:

	Operatives.	Looms.	Spindles.
Mill No. 1,	912	912	35,800
" " 2,	703	1,038	47,328
" " 3,	1,639	2,654	125,936
" " 4 (Ogden),	403	632	30,276
" " 5 (Strong),	220	330	14,424
Jute Mill,	97	22	850
Bag Mill,	147	62	3,440
	4.121	5,650	258,054

During the past year 29,250 bales of cotton were consumed, equal to 13,700,000 lbs., and 5,600 bales of jute, equal to 2,240,000 lbs.

The production for 1876 was as follows : 79,500,000 yards printing cloths, percales, wigans, and jaconets. 600,000 seamless bags, 2,130,000 pounds jute goods, 3,000 bales cotton batting. The value of the annual production is estimated at $3,000,000, and the monthly pay roll will average $70,000.

The present officers are : Wm. E. Thorn, agent ; Robert Johnston, general manager ; D. J. Johnston, superintendent; Wm. S. Smith, paymaster.

KNITTING MILLS.— The manufacture of knit goods has always been a distinguishing branch of Cohoes industry. The first machinery for the purpose was here put in operation, and a factory established, which for many years was the only one of the kind in the country ; the most important improvements which have since been made in the process of manufacture are the inventions of Cohoes mechanics, and many of the machines in general use among knitting mills are now constructed here. Though of late years it has been extensively prosecuted in other towns, Cohoes still occupies the foremost position in this branch of manufacture. The factory buildings in this city for substantial construction and perfection of detail are second to none in the country, and the goods produced have a wide reputation and command the best markets. It is impossible at present to give accurately the statistics of production of the seventeen knitting mills which are now in operation. Since the panic many of them have been shut down for greater or less periods, and the number of operatives employed, and amount of wages paid, have varied; the grade and style of the goods manufactured have been changed from time to time to suit the market, so that the amount of annual production cannot be exactly named ; this of course, in connection with the fact that prices have been steadily falling, makes it impossible to fix a definite value on the sales of any one year. The figures given below represent, in the case of almost every establishment, an average year's business.

	Sets in Operation.	Hands Employed.	Monthly Pay Roll.	No. of doz. goods Produced Annually.	Average Value.
The Troy M'f'g Co. David Cowee, prest.; Jno. V. S. Lansing, treas.; Jas. L. Thompson, sec'y.	10	229	$5,500	40,000	$275,000
The Root M'f'g Co. Josiah G. Root, prest.; Samuel G. Root, supt.; Andrew J. Root, treas. and gen. manager; Geo. Waterman, Jr., sec'y.	12	300	8,000	45,000	500,000
J. H. Parsons & Co. J. H. Parsons, Mrs. L. S. Parsons, and W. S. Gilbert.	13	300	9,000	45,000	400,000
The Atlantic Mill. Geo. E. Thompson and John Horrocks.	6	105	2,700	22,000	145,000
The Ranken Knitting Co. Geo. Campbell, prest.; Henry J. Ranken, sec'y. and treas.	7	145	3,500	22,000	200,000
American Hosiery Mill. Wm. M. Gregory and Jonathan Hiller.	6	85	2,600	24,000	120,000
The Victor Mill. — Henry Brockway.	6	105	3,000	20,000	150,000
The Empire Mill. — Wm. & Jno. A. Nuttall.	6	90	2,700	20,000	140,000
The Star Knitting Co. Thos. Coleman, prest.; R. H. Thurman, treas.; O. G. Clark, ag't.	8	140	5,000	27,000	300,000
The Adams Mill. — John Wakeman.	6	125	4,000	25,000	175,000
The Ontario Mill. — Wm. N. Chadwick, Jos. Chadwick, P. R. Chadwick.	6	100	2,000	25,000	150,000
The Mohawk Mill. — Samuel Bilbrough.	5	120	3,000	24,000	150,000
The Erie Mill. — Wm. Moore.	4	75	2,200	17,000	136,000
The Enterprise Mill. — John Scott.	5	110	2,500	20,000	160,000
The Diamond Mill. — J. W. Himes, A. C. Vail.	6	200	3,000	25,000	150,000
The Globe Mill. — Alfred Le Roy, Jas. Lamb.	6	100	3,500	25,000	175,000
The Pine Grove Mill. — H. D. Fuller, Chas. Hay.	6	50	1,500	18,000	100,000
	118	2,379	$63,700	444,000	$3,426,000

IRON MANUFACTURE.— A large amount of capital is here invested in different branches of iron manufacture. The most important interest is the production of axes and edge tools, which from the foundation of the first factory in 1835, by Simmons & Silliman, has always been one of the specialties of Cohoes. The goods turned out are of the first quality and have a world wide reputation.

The figures given below in regard to this, and other branches of manufacture, represent in nearly all cases, an average business. It is difficult to obtain exact statistics, for as a general thing, the works are run according to the orders received, and the production consequently varies greatly. For the past three years, none of the establishments have been run at their full capacity.

The Weed & Becker M'f'g Co.— Officers : Wm. H. Weed, president ; S. A. Becker, vice president ; Jas. E. Place treasurer ; C. Riley, secretary. The producing capacity of the company's works is 100 dozen axes and 75 dozen tools daily. The value of the annual production is from $200,000 to $400,000, and the average pay roll is $9,000.[1]

Empire Edge Tool Works.— M. H. Jones & Co., proprietors. The firm consists of M. H. Jones and A. G. Peck. From 60 to 75 men are employed at a pay roll of $2,000 to $2,500. The annual production is from 10,000 to 15,000 dozen axes and tools valued at from $75,000 to $100,000.

The Ten Eyck Axe M'f'g Co.— Jonas S. Ten Eyck, treasurer. The company employs from 40 to 50 men at an average pay roll of $1,200. The daily production is 500 pieces, including both axes and edge tools.

The Cohoes Rolling Mill.— Morrison, Colwell & Page, proprietors. The firm manufactures bar and band iron. About 200 men are employed at a pay roll of $6,000. The annual production is 6,000 tons of iron at an average value of $60 per ton.

---

[1] Per *month*. This is to be understood in the case of each concern mentioned.

Empire Tube Works.— Albert Smith & Co. proprietors. The firm manufactures gas and steam pipe. About 30 men are employed at a pay roll of $1,250. Five tons of iron are used daily. The annual production of the works is 3,000,000 feet of pipe at an average value of $180,000.

Campbell and Clute.— The firm manufactures chiefly knitting machinery. On an average 40 hands are employed at a pay roll of $2,000. The annual production is valued at $100,000.

William T. Horrobin.— Mr. Horrobin is proprietor of the Cohoes Iron Foundery and Machine shop. He manufactures chiefly cotton, woolen and flouring mill machinery, and architectural iron work. When running full 150 workmen are employed at a pay roll of $6,000, and the annual production is valued at $200,000. The capacity of the furnace is 8 to 10 tons per day.

Tubbs & Severson.— The firm manufactures knitting machinery. On an average 15 hands are employed at a pay roll of $800. The annual production is worth $15,000.

MISCELLANEOUS.

Cohoes Knitting Needle Factory.— Henry Dawson and Chas. Knott, proprietors. The firm employs 15 hands. The annual production is 2,500,000 needles valued at $15,000.

Sash and Blind Factory.— A. J. Griffin, proprietor. On an average 12 men are employed at a pay roll of $600. The annual production is valued at $30,000.

Cohoes Bedstead Factory.— P. S. Holsapple, proprietor. The articles manufactured are bedsteads, cribs and cradles. About 25 men are employed at a pay roll of $1,200. The average annual production is valued at $50,000.

Cohoes Straw Board Co.— Officers: T. G. Younglove, pres't; M. S. Younglove, vice pres't; J. W. Moore, sec'y; Henry W. Edwards, treas. Employment is given to 25 men at a pay roll of $1,350. The daily production is 5 to 6 tons of straw board, the value of which amounts annually to between $75,000 and $125,000. During the year 2,500 tons of straw are consumed.

Flouring Mill.— Jas. McMartin proprietor. Nine hands are employed at a pay roll of $450. The annual production is 40,000 bbls. valued at $280,000.

American Soap Co.— Mrs. H. R. Grant, proprietor. Six hands are employed at a pay roll of $212. The annual production is 395,000 lbs. of soap of different kinds, valued at $21,750.

Cohoes Lime and Cement Co.— Officers: D. T. Lamb, pres't; T. G. Younglove, sec'y; D. H. Van Auken, treas. The company employs 45 hands at a pay roll of $2.000. Annual production is valued at $100,000.

The Trost and Bezner M'f'g Co.— John T. Saxe, proprietor. This establishment manufactures furniture and fancy articles in wood of various kinds. 50 hands are employed at an average pay roll of $2,100. The estimated value of the annual production is $75,000.

The Cohoes Warp and Thread Co.— Collins Arnold, treas. About 60 operatives are employed at a pay roll of $1,400. The annual production is 416,000 lbs. of hosiery yarns, valued at $110,000.

Brick Yard.— Patrick Rogers, proprietor. Annual production at present 1,000,000 brick valued at $8,000, but in a good building season from 5,000,000 to 8,000,000 brick are manufactured.

Paper Box Factories.— Of these there are five, the proprietors being as follows : Isaac Clute, established Aug. 1, 1864 ; David Morris, established 1865 ; F. E. Pennock, established June, 1868; J. C. Sanford, established March 18, 1872 ; J. S. and E. Hughes, Jan. 1, 1876. The specialty of all these establishments is boxes for knit goods for the home trade, though some of them have at times turned out boxes for collars and other purposes. The business, though commenced not long since, has become quite an important feature of Cohoes manufactures. Before the panic, employment was given to from 100 to 125 hands, and nearly 1,000,000 boxes were annually produced. Exact figures of the production at present cannot be ascertained. The above establishments do not vary greatly in capacity, and each employs from 10 to 20 hands, according to the condition of business — at a monthly pay roll of from $400 to $600, producing from 500 to 800 boxes daily at an annual value of from $15,000 to $20,000.

NEWSPAPERS, ETC.

The Cohoes Cataract.— William Bean, proprietor. Size 26 by 38 inches, 8 columns to the page. It is published every Saturday morning, and is republican in politics. The proprietors of the *Cataract* since its foundation have been as follows : Stow & Co., Jan. 1st, to March 1st, 1849 ; Silliman & Miller: to Aug., 1851; James H. Masten: to Aug. 1856; A. F. Onderdonk: to Dec., 1856: Jas. H. Masten: to Dec., 1867 ; A. S. Baker & Co. : to Dec., 1869 ; Jas. H. Masten & Co. : to Dec., 1870 ; Jas. H. Masten : to July 15, 1871; William Bean. The publication office was removed by Silliman and Miller, in Nov., 1850, to the old Presbyterian church, corner Factory and Remsen streets, where it remained for eight years, and was then established by Jas. H. Masten in the third story of Caw and Quackenbush's (now Silliman's) building, the entrance being on Oneida street. In this building it has since remained (though it is now on the ground floor), with the exception of an interval from Jan., 1870, to April, 1875, when it was located in the second story of Adams' block, Remsen street.

The Cohoes Democrat.— Jas. F. Kelly, proprietor. Size 26 by 40 inches, 8 columns to the page. Published every Saturday morning. Mr. Cady's interest in the paper was bought by Jas. F. Kelly, in Nov., 1870, and the partnership of Atkinson and Kelly formed, which was dissolved Aug. 29, 1873, by the retirement of Mr. Atkinson. The publication office of the paper has remained since its establishment in the second story of North's block, Mohawk street.

The Cohoes Daily News.— Edward Monk and Samuel Sault, proprietors. Size 22 by 30 inches 6 columns to the page. Published at noon every day except Sundays. Independent in politics. The name of Mr. Sault first appeared as a partner, June 3d, 1874. The office of the paper was moved from Granite Hall, to the third story of North's block, Dec. 20, 1873, and was established in its present location, Campbell and Clute's block, Mohawk street, April 25, 1874.

La Patrie Nouvelle.— J. B. Authier & Bro., proprietors. Size 18 by 26 inches, 5 columns to the page. Published every Tuesday. Republican in politics. The office has been located since the paper was established, in Lynch's building, Remsen street near Columbia street.

The Northern Herald.— Williams and Eagan, proprietors. Size 30 by 44 inches, 6 columns to the page, quarto. It appears every Sunday morning. Independent in politics. The first number was issued Sept. 4th, from 83 Ontario street, which had been occupied as the office of the *Eagle*.

The People's Railway Guide.— Chas. S. Pease, proprietor, 24 pages. Established Oct., 1875, and is published every fortnight.

BANKING INSTITUTIONS.

The National Bank of Cohoes.— C. H. Adams, president; Murray Hubbard, cashier. Became a National Bank, May 31, 1865. Its capital was increased from $100,000 to $250,000 Aug., 1872. Mr. Hubbard was elected cashier March 5th, 1862, in place of James M. Sill. Mr. Adams became president after the death of Mr. Egberts, in March, 1869.

Manufacturers' Bank of Cohoes.— Wm. E. Thorn, president; Norman W. Frost, cashier. Its capital was increased from $100,000 to $150,000, July 1, 1874.

Cohoes Savings Institution.— Henry D. Fuller, president ; John Hay, secretary; T. G. Younglove, treasurer ; Edward W. Fuller, ass't treas.

Mechanics' Savings Bank.— Robert Johnston, president; William S. Smith, secretary; Abner J. Griffin, treasurer ; Le Roy Vermilyea, ass't treas.

POST OFFICE.

Jas. H. Masten, P. M.; A. W. Adams, Geo. W. Cook, clerks. The first post office was located at Mr. Waterman's, near the junction. On the appointment of Mr. Howe, it was moved to his new store on the canal bank near the present Jute Mill, where it remained for a short time. It was, in 1833, taken to the building just erected by E. L. Miller, on Mohawk street, opposite the City Hotel. When this was burned in 1847, the office was moved to a building on the west side of Mohawk street, between Oneida and St. John's alley. In May, 1851, it was established in a building erected by Dr. Carter, on Oneida street, east of Remsen,[1] where it remained until 1861, with the exception of a few months (August to October), in 1854, when it was moved to a building in St. John's alley, in the rear of J. M. Brown's (now Mrs. I. Terry's) store. On the appointment of I. W. Chesebro, in August, 1861, the office was located in his drug store on Remsen street.[2] In 1865, J. H. Masten transferred it to his building on the site of Music Hall, in which locality it has since remained, except while the new building was in progress of erection — during which time the office was located in Rogers' block.

The postmasters have been as follows :

<pre>
Frederick Y. Waterman, appointed 23d Feb.. 1832.
Hezekiah Howe,   "   13th July, 1833.
Peter F. Daw,   "   28th July, 1854.
Geo. H. Wager,   "   7th June, 1855.
Izrakiah W. Chesebro,   "   7th Aug., 1861.
Jas. H. Masten,   "   16th June, 1865.
</pre>

---

[1] Now A. H. Frink's cigar store. [2] Now occupied by Ten Eyck & Browne.

Samuel D. Trull,[1]   appointed 19th Oct., 1866.
Jas. H. Masten,   "   20th Oct., 1867.

The clerks in the post-office have at different times kept records of the way in which *Cohoes* was spelled on letters received at the office, some of which have been published in the local paper. The following list, recently prepared, presents more varieties of orthography than any of those which have previously appeared:

Kahouse	Kaho	Coughoos	Kehooze
Coohoos	Cuchues	Choswos	Chuhouse
Chosoes	Calhoue	Coehoose	Hachooze
Coahoos	Cughes	Kohouze	Chouhose
Cohoo	Cououse	Cohouse	Choohoo
Coose	Kowhes	Coehoose	Cougheoes
Cauhoose	Cochoes	Koehoughs	Co House
Cowhes	Choess	Chogues	Cousfall
Cowhewes	Couwoos	Cooce	Cohoughs
Cohewes	Gehus	Coohooeas	Coohoo falls
Gohues	Gohose	Calhouse	Choeos
Chohes	Cocose	Coquis	Koihrs
Chohose	Tohoes	Capaes	Choo Has-falls
Chose	Cocuse	Coohuis	Kahouse
Cohyose	Colose	Chaooze	Choohouse
Coheys	Cohoer	Kahahause	Kawoes
Chohous	Cohosa	Keoges	Cowhese
Coughoes	Cayouse	Kooze	Coughows
Clohoes	Cohooes	Caous	Couho
Couhs	Cohosse	Coas	Cohou
Cahos	Gohougs	Cohose	Chooess
Couuse	Dohes	Choose	Cohoos
Caughues	Caehaues	Cahoes	Couhoues
Coohoues	Chiohoe	Cuhuse	Couhouse
Kohoose	Coohooze	Cohooes	Cahoos
Koose	Ceoe	Couos	Coho
Chouse	Kose	Choes	Cohas
Cahous	Koohos	Cohie	Cohous
Cohoze	Coss	Khoose	Chaos
Cahaaes	Kohous	Cohes	Cohues
Chase	Coeys	Crouse	Gohoes
Cahoose	Coehouse	Choze	Cohoase
Gohoeses	Coohooes	Cohooze	Cohaes
Cohees	Choohuse	Cahose	Cohaughes
Cohoe	Cohoise	Couhous	Cahuuse
Cohouse	Chahoos	Cohohoes	Cohois
Cohause	Keoues	Coheas	Chooes
Cohese	Coughies	Choous	Choese
Coheos	Kehoose	Chaus	Cowes

---

[1] Appointed but not confirmed.

Kewes	Cowis	Camoes	Chohoes
Gehoose	Coohooss	Khouse	Cahooes
Cohowus	Coquies	Colcoes	Chehaze
Koohose	Cochoos	Coes	Cohoese
Kohoos	Keuyer	Cohoas	Curhues
Couhoes	Cauauses	Coewes	Cowyous falls
Cookohoves	Coushous	Coloes	Cayousse
Chouscouse	Kahosa	Cawis	Coughy
Cohouth	Chahoose	Keahose	Coughwheeze
Coaches	Chohoose	Cohouches	Cohoes
Cheohes			

CHURCHES, &c.

St. John's Episcopal Church.— The church was under direction of Rev. Orange Clark of Waterford, until 1833, when Rev. Cyrus Stebbins assumed the missionary charge of the parish which he retained until 1841. The subsequent rectors have been as follows: David J. Burger, 1841; Edward F. Edwards, 1844; J. B. Gilson, 1844–49; J. W. Shackleford, 1849–50; James Adams, 1850–53; Theodore Babcock, 1853–59; Alpheus Spor, 1859–1863; J. H. Hobart Brown, 1863–75; Walker Gwynne, 1876. The number of communicants is at present about 500, and twice that number of individuals are connected with the church. The Sunday school, Robert Weir, sup't, has about 300 scholars. Up to 1875, there were entered upon the parish register: baptisms 984, confirmations 502, burials 481.

Reformed Church.— The following have been pastors: William Lockhead, 1838 to 1840; John Van Buren, 1840 to 1841; Gilbert M. P. Myer, 1841 to 1846; John Gray, 1846 to 1848; Chas. N. Waldron, 1849. A fine organ, costing over $5,000, was placed in the church in 1866, a gift from three members: Egbert Egberts, Jno. V. S. Lansing and D. J. Johnston. The present membership is over 300. A large Sabbath school is connected with the church of which Rev. Dr. Waldron is sup't, and D. H. Van Auken ass't supt.

Baptist Church.— The pastors have been as follows: Revs. John Duncan, H. Rounce, J. Eastwood, E. Dwyer, M. Cameron, B. F. Garfield, S. Wilder, D. Round, Ira E.

Kenney, Robert Thompson, David Corwin, W. H. Maynard, A. J. Bingham, C. D. Gurr, C. A. Johnson, L. S. Johnson. The present membership is 380. The Sabbath school, of which P. S. Holsapple is sup't, has 400 scholars.

Presbyterian Church.— The following clergymen have had charge of the church. Those marked with an asterisk were regularly installed as pastors : Revs. Mr. Chamberlin, Dec., 1839 ; Mr. Allen, 1840 ; *John Gray, Oct. 22, 1841 ; L. H. Pease, May 22, 1843 ; Daniel C. Frost, Oct. 3, 1845 ; *R. P. Stanton, Feb. 9, 1848 ; *Stephen Bush, Feb. 1, 1855 ; Villeroy D. Reed, April, 1860 ; H. G. Blinn ; *F. W. Flint, 1864 ; Horatio Pattengill, 1866 ; *Wm. M. Johnson, Oct. 1, 1867. The lecture room east of the church was erected in 1865 at a cost of $3,000. The parsonage, at the corner of Ontario and Mohawk streets, was purchased during the same year, from the estate of Wm. G. Caw for $6,000. During the present season a fine organ, costing $3,150, has been placed in the church, and the lecture room has been greatly enlarged and improved. The membership of the church is 400, and of the Sunday school 420. The superintendent of the latter is H. B. Silliman.

Methodist Episcopal Church.— Until 1845, the church was connected with that in Waterford, as one charge, and was under the direction of the following clergymen : E. Crawford, Oliver Emerson, Benj. Pomeroy, Thomas Armitage, Mr. Tubbs, Mr. Warner. The subsequent pastors have been : G. A. Wells, Cicero Barber, Jacob Leonard, L. Potter, Timothy Benedict, Myron White, Robert Fox, Wm. R. Brown, Ensign Stover, H. L. Starks, J. W. Carhart, D.D., R. R. Meredith, H. L. Sexton, Lorenzo D. Marshall, Horace L. Grant, C. R. Hawley, Wm. H. Meeker. The present membership is 450. The Sabbath school, of which Silas Owen is superintendent, has 500 scholars, and 55 teachers.

St. Bernard's Catholic Church.— Rev. Bernard Van

Reeth, the first pastor, remained in Cohoes until Oct., 1853, and was then succeeded by Rev. Thomas Daly, now of St. John's church, Utica. In June, 1855, the present pastor, Rev. Thos. Keveney, was appointed, who did not commence his duties until the following August, Rev. John Ludden, now of Florence, N. S., officiating meanwhile. Father Keveney is at present assisted by Revs. Thos. Silvester Keveney and Thos. Cullen. There are now in Cohoes over 5,000 Catholics, exclusive of Canadians. The number of infant baptisms recorded in St. Bernard's parish from 1847 to 1876, is over 5,000, and of deaths in the congregation, nearly 4,000.

St. Joseph's Catholic Church (French).— The first pastor, Rev. L. H. Saugon, entered upon his duties Aug. 23d, 1868. The present incumbent, Rev. J. O. La Salle, formerly of Champlain, N. Y., came here after the death of Father Saugon, Dec. 19th, 1869. There are now about 2,500 persons connected with the church, of whom 1,800 are communicants.

German Baptist Church.— The present pastor, Henry Hilzinger, has officiated since the organization of the church. Present membership, 35.

Park Methodist Church.— This was organized Nov. 9, 1876. The building occupied is on the Bowery, north of Columbia street, and was erected by the M. E. church in 1873, as a mission chapel. The first communion was held Dec. 3, 1876. Number of communicants, 51. The Rev. Hiram Blanchard is pastor, and Nathan Thomas is sup't of the Sunday school. The officers are as follows: Trustees: Nathan Thomas, Richard Herell, Monroe Tompkins, Jacob Travis, Aaron Goddard, J. S. Ten Eyck, Chas. Spanswick, John Wilber, John Dunlap. Stewards: Henry Farmilo, Geo. Mink, Henry Watt, Jas. Watt, John Viegle, Henry Van Den Bergh, Jacob Craley, Peter Nelson, W. W. Delanoy.

Harmony Hill Union Sunday School.— The present officers are: D. J. Johnston, superintendent; Joseph Wood, 1st ass't superintendent; Thomas Pillings, 2d ass't superintendent; Wm. S. Smith, secretary; Richard Bolton, ass't secretary; George Dixon, treasurer; Abram Peck, librarian; Robert Campbell, ass't librarian; Wm. R. Brooks, janitor. The number of members at present is 1,124 of whom 203 have been admitted during the past year. The whole number admitted since the organization of the school is 3663.

Public Schools.

Cohoes was one of the first villages in the state to demand an improvement on the old system of district schools, and a special law, passed in 1850, enabled it to enjoy the advantages of free schools before other places in the neighborhood. The interest thus manifested among the citizens in regard to educational matters has since continued, and the public schools have always been among the most creditable institutions of the place.

The principal facts in the history of the system, and the erection of the earliest school houses in the village have been elsewhere mentioned. There are now in the city under the control of the Board of Education, 31 schools, thus arranged: primary 25, intermediate 4, grammar 1, high 1. Eight buildings are occupied, of which seven are the property of the city. They are as follows:

State Yard school.— On Saratoga street. Built about 1835. Is of wood, one story high, 32 by 20 feet.

Columbia Street school.— Corner of Main and Columbia streets. Built 1856. Is of brick, two stories high, 60 by 30 feet. It has been enlarged during the past year, and its capacity doubled at an expense of $5,000.

West Harmony school.— Mangham street. Built 1859–1863. Is of brick, two stories high, 80 by 40 feet.

Egberts High school.— White street. Rented of the trustees of Egberts Institute in August, 1868. Is of brick, three stories high, 38 by 36 feet.

East Harmony school.— School street. Built 1869. Is of brick, two stories high, 43 by 28 feet.

White Street school.— Built 1871. Is of brick, three stories high, 66 by 40 feet.

Pleasure Ground school.— Corner Bowery and Elm streets. Built 1873. Is of brick, two stories high, 70 by 33 feet.

Lincoln Avenue school.— Lincoln avenue north of Spring street. Built 1875. Is of wood, two stories high, and 46 by 26 feet.

The seating capacity of these schools is 1950. The value of the buildings belonging to the city is estimated at $50,000 and that of the lots on which they are situated as $40,000. There are now employed 38 teachers, as follows:

State Yard.— Miss Alice Murray.

Columbia Street.— Miss Sarah Runkle, Miss Etta A. Halstead, Miss Mary A. Winney, Miss L. H. Bowman, Miss E. M'Connel, Miss Wright, Miss O'Reilly.

West Harmony.— Miss Agnes L. Bromley, Miss M. J. O'Reilly, Miss Jennie M. Chisholm, Miss Kitty McMartin, Miss Minnie Stiles, Miss K. E. Hayden, Miss E. L. Murray, Miss Katy Doyle.

Egberts High school.— Mr. Oliver P. Steves, Miss Ella A. Page, Miss Anna E. Brewster, Miss Mary E. Robbins, Miss Clarke.

East Harmony.— Miss Mary E. Hall, Miss Nellie Valley, Miss Louisa Robinson.

White Street.— Miss E. L. Hastings, Miss Elizabeth Humphreys, Miss Belle Z. Van Der Werkar, Miss S. Ella Thomas, Miss Frank McIntyre, Miss Sarah Lawrence, Miss Anna T. Hayden.

Pleasure Ground.— Miss Emma Monk, Miss Harriet J. Monk, Mrs. De Graff, *pro tem.*, Miss Susie Flagler.

Lincoln Avenue.— Miss Ida Van Arnum, Miss Clara Brown. Music teacher, Mr. Otis R. Greene.

The Egberts Institute building on White street was leased in 1868 by the Board of Education, from the trustees of the Institute at a nominal rent, on condition that an academic department, or high school be always taught therein. The Egberts High School was then organized, succeeding the academic department of Egberts Institute. The teachers of this department from its organization, have been as follows:

Rev. Alexander B. Bullions, principal from	July, 1864, to Feb., 1865.
Mr. Charles P. Evans,	" "	Feb., 1865, to July, 1866.
Rev. A. J. Bingham,	" "	Sept., 1866, to July, 1868.
Mr. W. H. Nellis,	" "	Oct., 1868, to May, 1869.
Mr. Robert Hardie,	" "	Aug., 1869, to July, 1870.
Mr. E. H. Torrey,	" "	Aug., 1870, to Dec., 1870.
Mr. Oliver P. Steves,	" "	Feb., 1871.
Miss Emma Osterhout,	Assistant "	Oct., 1872, to June, 1873.
Miss Ella A. Page,	" "	Aug., 1873, to March, 1875.
Miss Mary L. D. Wilson,	" "	April, 1875, to July, 1876.
Miss Ella A. Page,	" "	Aug., 1876.

Evening schools are taught during part of each year in the buildings on the East and West Harmony, Columbia and White streets, with an average attendance of 500. During the year ending Feb., 1876, 2,443 pupils attended the day and evening schools some portion of the year, as follows:

```
In school building No. 1 First Ward,..............  233
    "       "       "   " 2    "    ..............  612
    "       "       "   " 3 Third Ward,..............  459
    "       "       "   " 4    "    ..............  337
    "       "       "   " 5 Fourth Ward,..............  489
    "       "       "   " 6    "    ..............  101
    "       "       "   " 7    "    ..............   65
    "       "       "   " 8 Fifth Ward,..............  147
```

Concerning the expense to the tax payers of maintaining the schools, the following extracts from the last annual report of Mr. Hubbard, president of the Board of Education, will be of interest:

"I think there is not another instance where a city has grown so rapidly as Cohoes, and greatly increased school accommodations have been required, that the cost of the construction of its school buildings has been paid solely from the taxes raised annually. For the erection of new school houses, in other growing cities, money has been raised by the creation of a bonded debt....

In 1875, the *per capita* expense on the number of children enrolled during the year was $9.35; on the average attendance $24.79. I have not the reports of the following cities for 1875, but by reference to their reports for the year prior (and it is, I think, fairly presumable that their expenses have not since been diminished much), I find the expenses of maintaining their schools as follows:

	On No. Enrolled.	On Ave. Attendance.
Albany,	$14.93,	$27.14 per capita.
Kingston,	20.28,	29.92 "
Saratoga Springs,	13.46,	26.04 "
Syracuse,	18.05,	25.74 "
Troy,	14.35,	26.39 "
Utica,	16.14,	25.96 "
Cohoes in 1874,	9.41,	24.50 "

The following table shows the number of children of school age resident in Cohoes, in different years, according to the census:

Years.		Years.	
1855,	1110.	1872,	9200.
1860,	1605.	1873,	9504.
1865,	4055.	1874,	9547.
1870,	7679.	1875,	9607.
1871,	8259.	1876,	8879.

FIRE DEPARTMENT.

Cohoes has suffered from few disastrous fires. Those which have occurred have been at rare intervals, and in nearly every case have been confined to the buildings in which they originated. For the good fortune of the place in the latter respect it is indebted to a fire department, which from its earliest days, has been well organized and efficient, and to the existence in later years of a valuable system of water works. The first organization of the fire department and the substitution of steam for hand engines, have been related elsewhere, as being the most important facts in its history. The department is at present constituted as follows: Martin Redmond, chief engineer; John G. French, 1st ass't; Patrick Hogan, 2d ass't; Elbert E. Richmond, 3d ass't.

Alden Hose Co. No. 1.— James Barter, foreman. Organized June 22d, 1860. First foreman, Daniel Simpson.

Geo. H. Wager Hook and Ladder Co.— Wm. Maby foreman. Organized Oct., 1865. First foreman, Bernard Galligan.

Chas. H. Adams Steamer Co.— Jas. A. Stimson, captain. Organized June 17, 1867. First captain, L. Vredenberg.

Daniel E. McIntosh Hose Co.— M. Platz, foreman. Organized Oct. 10, 1867. First foreman, Chas. N. Green.

Robert Johnston Steamer Co.— Organized Feb. 25th, 1868. First foreman, Daniel Simpson.

Edwin Hitchcock Hose Co.— Michael Larkin, foreman. Organized 1869.

Geo. Campbell Hose Co.— Wm. Dewar, foreman. Reorganized in July, 1870, from the old Cataract Engine Co. No. 1.

Two companies, the Howarth Engine Co., M. Thornton capt., and the Nolan Steamer Co., Jas. Wilson capt., are not in active service. The former was organized in 1870, and for some time took charge of the Old Mohawk engine, their quarters being in the engine house on Johnston avenue. It was relieved from duty by the common council in Nov., 1873, until suitable accommodations could be provided. For the latter company no apparatus has yet been obtained. The buildings occupied by the different companies were erected as follows:

Campbell Hose House,	Cataract alley,	1848
Adams Steamer, Wager Hook & L. Co.	House, Oneida st. cor. Canvass,	1867
Hitchcock Hose House,	Main st. near Columbia,	1869
Alden " "	Johnston ave. cor. Garner st,.	1869
M'Intosh " "	Oneida st. near Canvass	1873

SOCIETIES, ETC.

Masonic.

Cohoes Lodge, No. 116.— Symbolic Masonry. Organized Oct. 21, 1846, and chartered Feb. 5th, 1847, the members at the time being as follows: Ebenezer Wadsworth, W. M.; Geo. Abbott, Sr. W.; John B. Harrison, Jr. W.; Wm. Orelup, Jr. sec'y; Reuben White, treas.; Geo. C., Griffin, Sr. D.; Elbridge G. Mussey, Jr. D.; Stephen Doty, Tyler;— David Wilkinson, Orson Parkhurst, Lewis Valley Darius Parkhurst, Jas. Murray, John Sanderson, Isaac F. Fletcher, Sylvanus Twist. The rooms of the fraternity were first located in the second story of the building on the northeast corner of Oneida and Mohawk streets, then owned by John McDougal, and were afterwards moved to Lansing's building, corner of Factory and Mohawk streets, and still later to Silliman's building, Remsen street. The Masonic Hall in Johnston's Block has been occupied since August, 1871. Present officers: Albert Ten Eyck, W. M.; Charles S. Travis, S. W.; Richard D. Christle, J. W.; Rodney Wilcox, treas.; Paul Game, sec'y; Alfred Gould, S. D.; James Aitkin, J. D.; James Barrie, Sr.; and Anson Tabor, Jr. M. of C.; William Warner, Charles Nealy, stewards; Rev. W. H. Meeker, chaplain; A. S. Targett, organist; Daniel McIntosh, marshal; Kendall Hodgson, tyler; Wm. Clough, Geo. T. Carter, Benjamin Smith, trustees.

Cohoes Chapter, No. 168.— Capitular Masonry, instituted in 1858. Present officers: David Gould, high priest; James Aitkin, E. K.; Richard D. Christle, E. S.; William Clough, treasurer; M. Van Benthuysen, sec'y; John McNiven, C. of H.; G. H. Billings, P. S.; Henry Mills, R. A. C.; Joseph Eccles, M. 3d V.; Kendall Hodson, M. 2d V.; Martin Gilmore, M. 1st V.; George H. Howarth, tiler; Rev. W. H. Meeker, chaplain; Benjamin Coveney, organist.

Mohawk Council No. 29.— Cryptic Masonry. Organized 1867. Present officers: L. D. Sanborn, T. I. M.; W. H. Aiken, R. I. D. M.; Benjamin Coveney, I. P. C. W.; George Neil, recorder; H. Levison, treasurer; Joseph Chadwick, Capt. G.; Geo. Waterman, Jr., Cond. C.; Rev. Geo. C. Thomas, chaplain; Thomas Hatcher, steward; James Durant, sentinel.

Union Board of Relief (Masonic), of Lansingburg, Waterford and Cohoes. Regular meetings, third Friday at Waterford, Lansingburg and Cohoes, consecutively. A. Ten Eyck, president; Geo. E. Shumway, vice president; R. D. Christle, treasurer; John E. Gage, secretary.

ODD FELLOWS.

Spartan Lodge No. 210, I. O. of O. F.— Organized in 1843, surrendered its charter in 1867, and was reörganized March 11, 1869. Present officers: James W. Clark, N. G.; G. G. Black, V. G.; Chas. E. Simons, R. S.; Chas. S. Sault, per. sec.; J. Hiller, treasurer.

Cohoes Encampment, No. 71, I. O. of O. F.— Organized July, 1872. Present officers: Albert Porter, C. P.; George Dean, H. P.; Chas. E. Simons, S. W.; G. G. Black, J. W.; James W. Clark, scribe; Nathan Shaver, treasurer.

TEMPERANCE.

D. J. Johnston Lodge, I. O. of G. T.— Organized April 28, 1868. Present membership, 105. Officers: Deputy G. W. C. Templar, T. C. Collins; W. C. T., Geo. Mather; L. H. S., Ella Rowe; R. H. S., Mrs. Wm. Fletcher; W. V. T., Mary Ferris; W. R. S., H. M. Connelly; W. A. S., Ada Rhodamere; W. F. S., Jas. H. Crossingham; W. treas., Mrs. Margaret Leah; W. chap., T. C. Collins; W. marshal, Wm. Efnor; W. dep. marshal, Eva Frisbie; W. B. G., Lydia Crossingham; W. O. G., Chas. Welles; P. W. C. T., Chas. Skinkle.

St. Bernard's Teetotal Abstinence Benevolent Society.—

Organized May 10, 1868. Present officers : Edward Welch, president ; Wm. Healey, treasurer ; James Caffrey, recording secretary.

Temperance Brethren.— Organized 1870.

D. J. Johnston Temple of Honor.

MILITARY.

C. H. Adams Zouaves.— Organized Sept., 1870. Present officers : captain, J. A. Stimson ; lieutenants: 1st, E. J. Clute ; 2d, E. McCready ; sergeants : orderly, E. J. Foster ; 2d, John Egan ; 3d, P. J. Cannon ; 4th, Thomas Higgins ; 5th, W. H. Nolan ; corporals: first, John Grey ; 2d, H. Tanner ; 3d, James Neary ; 4th, Frank Egan ; 5th, H. McMurray. Membership of company 50, of staff 12.

Third Separate Co. Infantry National Guard S. N. Y. 10th *Brig.* 3d *Div.*— Captain, P. R. Chadwick ; 1st lieutenant, J. W. Brooks ; 2d lieutenant, Samuel Sault ; number of enlisted men 115.

MISCELLANEOUS.

St. Vincent De Paul Society.—Organized 1865 ; William Acheson, president ; Wm. Healey, treasurer ; Patrick Healey, vice president ; Edward Flanigan, secretary ; number of members 40.

N. G. Lyon Post 43, *G. A. R.*— Organized Oct. 14, 1867, with thirty members and the following officers : commander, A. T. Calkins ; senior vice com., Silas Owens ; junior, Malachi Weidman ; adjutant, Le Roy Vermilyea ; quartermaster, Geo. Van Der Cook. Present officers : commander, John Nolan ; senior vice, Chas. McCollough ; junior vice, George Norton ; chaplain, M. Redmond ; quartermaster, P. G. Tymerson ; officer of the day, J. Helmerick ; delegate, M. Redmond ; alternate, Charles Travis.

The Friendly Society of the Sons of Scotia.— Organized

February 12th, 1869. First officers : William Whitehill, president ; John Mc Ewan, secretary. Present membership 80. Present officers : John Campbell, president ; John Buchanan, 1st vice president ; Robert Taylor, 2d vice president ; Malcolm Mc Niven, chaplain; James Hay, treasurer ; Andrew M. Browne, financial secretary ; James D. Scott, recording secretary ; trustees : James Lamb, John Holmes, John Mc Ewan, Andrew M. Browne and James Aitken.

Egberts' Lodge, Knights of Pythias, No. 56.— Instituted June 3d, 1871. Officers: P. C., Geo. Greason; C. C., Chas. P. Craig; V. C., Malcolm McPhail; R. C., A. Hoben; F. C., Jas. Delve; B. K., E. A. Mills. Present officers: P. C., Malcolm McPhail ; C. C., Thomas Page ; V. C., John Groves; P., Anthony Fairchild; K. of R., D. J. Sollinger; M. F., David Williams; M. E., Adam T. Stebbins; M. A., John Hilton; J. G., John M. Geer; O. G., Henry Roberts. Trustees: Thos. Page, Jno. N. Geer, Edward Buckley.

St. Jean Baptiste Society.— Organized Aug. 10, 1871, L. St. Charles, treas.

The Cohoes Medical Society.— Organized August, 1874, with the following officers : president, Dr. J. W. Moore; vice pres't., Dr. L. Boudrias; secretary, Dr. J. D. Featherstonhaugh; treasurer, Dr. C. E. Witbeck. Present officers: pres't., L. Boudrias; vice pres't, Jas. D. Featherstonhaugh; sec'y, O. H. E. Clarke; treas., John U. Haynes; censors, Joseph W. Moore, Thos. S. Parker, Chas. E. Witbeck. Present membership, 13.

St. George's Cohoes Benevolent Society.— Organized June, 1875, with the following trustees: Wm. Clough, Wm. Warner, Thos. Higgins, Lees Wrigley, Wm. H. Gwynn.

St. John's Brotherhood.— Organized Feb. 22, 1876, with the following officers: Pres't, Robert Weir; 1st vice pres., John Horrocks; 2d vice pres't, James Tubbs; 3d vice pres't, Michael Andræ; recording sec'y, M. Van Benthuysen; financial sec'y, Daniel M. Adams; treas., Reuben Lee; precentor, Samuel Horrocks; organist, Harry J. P. Green. Present membership, 50.

The Cohoes Boat Club.— Organized July, 1876, with the following officers: president, Wm R. Benedict; secretary, Geo. H. House; treasurer, Geo. H. McDowell; captain, F. Hastings; lieutenant, Wesley Miller. There are at present 16 members. A boat house, 15 by 50, has been erected by the club on Adams's Island, near Mr. Adams's house.

St. Joseph's Union.— Julian Thibadeau, treas.

Assessed Valuation of Property in Cohoes.

Years.			
1848	$421,452.00	1872	3,010,030.00
1858	1,501,346.00	1873	3,098,630.00
1868	3,249,701.00	1874	3,462,608.00
1870	2,894,335.00	1875	3,606,419.00
1871	3,027,750.00		

Census Table.

Years.	Inhabitants.	Years.	Inhabitants.
1830	150	1855	6,106
1835	750	1860	8,800
1840	1850	1865	8,795[1]
1845	2029	1870	15,373
1850	4229	1875	17,482

The last census in detail is as follows:

	Total Pop.	Voters.		
		Natives.	Naturalized.	Total.
1st Ward,	6,415	274	629	903
2d "	3,233	359	280	639
3d "	5,041	459	559	1,018
4th "	2,793	310	267	577
	17,482	1,402	1,735	3,137

No. of dwellings 1,761, No. of families 3,246.

[1] Private census showed 9,765.

APPENDIX.

NECROLOGICAL RECORD.

THE following record of deaths — except those occurring prior to 1847 — has been taken from the columns of the Cohoes *Advertiser, Cataract, Daily News*, and the *Troy Times*.

In the limits of the present work it is of course impossible to give little more than simple announcements of deaths, except in the case of individuals who have been prominently connected with the history of Cohoes. In almost every instance where an extended notice is given it consists of an abridgement of the obituary article published in one of the above papers at the time.

1834.

Dec. 18, Canvass White, aged 44. Canvass White was born in Whitestown, N. Y., Sept. 8th, 1790. His health, from his infancy, was always delicate, and being unable to share with his brothers the severe labor of farm life, his earlier years were passed as clerk in a country store at Whitestown. His mechanical ingenuity and inventive genius were apparent at an early age, and were turned to practical account in the improvement of many utensils in use on the farm. In 1811, he was compelled on account of poor health to take a sea voyage from which he returned the following year. Soon after, he entered the army with the rank of lieutenant, and saw some months of active service. At the close of the war he returned to his duties as clerk, but his strong taste for mathematical and scientific pursuits rendered this life an irksome one, and he soon left it, to pursue his studies in Fairfield, and afterwards in Clinton. In the latter place he was engaged for a short time in chemical manufacturing, but this proving unsuccessful, he returned home, and assisted in the management of the farm. In the spring of 1816 he joined the corps of engineers for the Erie Canal under Benj. Wright, whose confidential friend and associate he soon became. Mr. White had a most kindly and winning disposition, which won for him the esteem and friendship of all with whom he came in contact, and when in 1817, he made the acquaintance of Gov. DeWitt Clinton, it was but a short time before that gentleman entertained the highest regard for his personal qualities and the utmost confidence in his professional abilities. Little was then known in this country of the actual details of canal navigation and as the information given in English books was vague and unsatisfactory, Mr. White went to England in the autumn of 1817, at the solicitation of the governor, to examine in person the English canal system. During his stay of several months abroad he traveled over 2000 miles on foot, studying closely the construction of every canal, gate, lock and culvert. On his return he brought with him drawings of the most important structures, and the model of the first boat which was built for the Erie Canal.[1]

Considerable difficulty was experienced by the canal commissioners in procuring a cement suitable for use in the construction of locks and it was finally proposed to import the needed article from England, at considerable expense. Mr. White gave his attention to the matter, however, and after repeated experiments, succeeded in manufacturing from a stone found in Madison Co., an hydraulic cement which exactly answered the purpose, and on which he obtained a patent in 1820. He was interested in its manufacture for several years subsequent. Mr. White's share in the construction and development of the Erie Canal was an important one. As regards authority he was second only to Mr. Wright, and every plan or measure of importance was submitted to his judgment before being acted upon.

It was while he was engaged in the construction of the canal that Mr. White's attention was called to the eligibility of this locality as the site for a great manufacturing town. In 1825 he devoted himself to the formation of a company to develop the remarkable water power of the place, and with the assistance of Governor Clinton, succeeded in interesting a number of capitalists in his enterprise. The result was the incorporation of the Cohoes Co., in March, 1826. Mr. White was the first president of the company, and acted as its agent. Though necessarily away a large portion of the time while engaged on other works, he devoted a good deal of his personal attention to the laying out of plans for the development of the company's resources and the formation of a manufacturing town. He was succeeded as agent by his brother Hugh White, in 1830, though continuing to have an active part in the direction of the company's affairs. He never had a residence in Cohoes, but while engaged here, boarded in Troy. From the completion of the Erie Canal, until the time of his death, Mr. White was constantly employed in different parts of the country in public works of importance. Among the principal works which he planned or superintended during these years, may be mentioned the Susquehanna and Schuylkill Canal, the improvements of the Schuylkill Navigation Co., the New Haven and Farmington Canal, the Lehigh Canal, (1827-1828), the Delaware and Raritan Canal (1830), and the Delaware breakwater. Mr. White was induced to take a contract for the completion of the latter structure, and by the mismanagement of others was a loser to a large amount.

In 1834 his failing health compelled him to leave business, and he went to Florida, hoping that the climate would have a favorable effect upon his disease, which was consumption, but the step had been taken too late, and within a month after landing, he died, on December 18th. His remains were brought north and interred at Princeton, N. J., where his family were residing at the time. The estimate in which Mr. White's professional abilities were held by his contemporaries, may be seen by the following remark of Henry Clay, addressed to a gentleman who was seeking an engineer for the Chesapeake and Ohio Canal: " Get Mr. Canvass White; no man more competent, no man more

---

[1] This boat, which was called the "Chief Engineer of Rome" in honor of Benj. Wright, was launched upon the canal between Whitestown and Rome, amidst the greatest rejoicing of the people of the neighborhood. The model was kept in Mr. White's family for fifty years and then presented to the Buffalo Historical Society.

capable. And while your faith in his ability and fidelity increases, your friendship will grow into affection." It was also said by Gen. Bernard, U. S. engineer, "as a civil engineer he had no superior; his genius and ability were of surpassing magnitude." Mr. White's gentle disposition, and the kindly charm of his manner, had endeared him to all whom he chanced to meet, and his early death was mourned by a large circle of friends.

1841.

Nov. 27, Joseph Mudge, aged 57. "Removed to Cohoes in 1833, from Ipswich, Mass, and being a first-class mechanic, he made needles for the first knitting factory started in America, by Egberts & Bailey. He was a man of education and could speak several languages fluently. He invented a system of stenography. His daughter, Caroline Augusta Smith Mudge, who was married to E. G. Mussey, June 8, 1845, was the first female who learned to knit on machines run by water power."
—*Biographical and Historical Account of the name of* MUDGE *in America.*

1844.

June 29, Levi Silliman, aged 59. He was born in Fairfield, Conn., in the year 1786. His ancestors came from Holland in the latter part of the 17th century, and settled in Fairfield, on a place which still bears the name of Holland Hill. About the year 1810 Levi moved to Albany, N. Y., and in 1816, was married to Clarissa Clark. He was a carpenter by trade, and was associated for some years with Jonathan Lyman, then a prominent builder in Albany. Afterward he was superintendent of the Townsend Furnace, and subsequently one of the firm of Rathbone & Silliman, in the furnace in Eagle street. In the year 1835 he formed a partnership with Jonas Simmons, Sen., and under the name of Simmons & Silliman, they built and operated the axe factory so long and widely known as the Simmons axe factory. After remaining in this connection for several years he sold out his interest and purchased a veneer mill owned by Hawes & Baker. Just before his death he sold this property. He died June 29th, 1844, leaving him surviving, his widow Clarissa, and son Horace B (both living 1876), four other children having previously died. Levi Silliman was one whose record is not found among those conspicuous in position among their fellow men, but few had more implicitly the confidence and esteem of the entire community where he lived. He was one gifted with great mechanical ability, and was often consulted by both practical and scientific men, and his opinions, especially when experience and study had been added to his natural powers, were sought and valued by many whose names stand high in the history of mechanical inventions and skill. In all subjects affecting the community where he lived, although never obtruding himself upon the public notice, his wise counsel and discriminating judgment were sought and he never hesitated either to speak or act his convictions. He was an active, earnest, humble Christian, and his religion, underlying every motive and action, made him what he was. To him perhaps more than any other, was due the organization of the Presbyterian church in this city, and the fostering care which nurtured it in its infancy. He always bore it on his heart and aided to hold it up by constant devotion and liberality, and when he heard the summons, "The Master is come and calleth for thee," he was ready to meet Him, and rest from his labors. * *

1847.

April 7, Henry Winans, aged 58. Mr. Winans was the father of W. H S. Winans, editor of the *Cohoes Advertiser*.
May 5, Amos Russell Gay, aged 37.

1849.

Jan. 4, John Jackson, aged 78. Mr. J. was a native of Glasgow, Scotland, and an old resident of Cohoes.
April 8, Thomas Boley, aged 44.
April 19, Reuben P. White, son of Dea. R. White, aged 34.
June 18, James Harris, aged 69.
June 20, Jacob Vanderwerken, aged 72. Mr. V. was born in Saratoga Co., on the 16th day of December, 1777. He moved to Cohoes in 1823, where he resided until his death. He was well known as a charitable, public spirited citizen and was identified with the early history of the place and many of its improvements. Few residents of the village had a larger circle of acquaintances.
Aug. 14, William Martin, aged 41.
Nov. 9, James Yale, aged 88. Mr. Y was a revolutionary soldier and also served in the war of 1812. He left a widow about the same age, 10 children and 23 grand-children.

1851.

March 10, George W. Miller, aged 42.
March 15, John B. Harrison, aged 48. Mr. Harrison was for many years the collector of the village taxes and was much respected in the community.
April 9, James Dodge, aged 63.
Sept. 23, Philip Badgley, aged 27.
Nov. 27, Joseph A. Worden, aged 65.
Dec. 30, Samuel Ketchel, aged 42.

1852.

Feb. 3, at Caledonia Springs, county of Prescott, Canada West, David Wilkinson, aged 81. Mr. Wilkinson was born in Smithfield, R. I., Jan. 5th, 1771. He was the third son of Oziel Wilkinson who was a lineal descendant from Lawrence Wilkinson who came from England and settled in the town of Providence, R. I., in 1645. Oziel Wilkinson had five sons: Abraham, Isaac, David, Daniel and Smith; all of whom like himself, were bred to the blacksmith's trade. David Wilkinson, with his father, removed to Pawtucket in 1783. From his earliest boyhood he had been engaged in the manufacture or supervision of machinery, and his abilities in this direction enabled him while yet a young man to take a prominent position among the business men of Pawtucket. In 1789, Samuel Slater, the father of cotton manufacture in this country, came over from England, and two years later married Miss Hannah Wilkinson, sister of David Wilkinson, and at this time commenced the intimate business relations between the latter and Mr. Slater which continued for a number of years. Mr. Wilkinson then devoted his attention to the production of machinery for the manufacture of cotton and not only the extensive mills in Rhode Island, but most of those throughout the country were fitted out from his machine shop in Pawtucket. He was the originator of many improvements with which his name was never associated. As he said himself, " I was always too much engaged in various business to look after and make profit out of my inventions ; other people, I hope, have gained something by them."

One of the best known and most widely used of Mr. Wilkinson's inventions was the sliding lathe, invented in 1798, for which he received no adequate compensation until 1848, when congress, recognizing the justice of his claims on the country, voted him an appropriation of $10,000, " as a remuneration to him for the benefit accruing to the public service from the use of the principle of the guage and sliding lathe of which he was the inventor,"—(*Report of Com., on Military Affairs*, March 28, 1848)

In 1829, having suffered severe reverses, Mr. Wilkinson was compelled to give up his business, and in 1831, at the earnest solicitation of the Cohoes Company, came to Cohoes. His part in the early history of this place has been elsewhere spoken of. To show the estimation in which he was held in Rhode Island, the following may be quoted : " David Wilkinson became a machinist of great skill and carried on the business in an extensive manner. He is a man of great enterprise and judgment, and his failure in 1829 was very much regretted. The capitalists of Rhode Island ought not to have allowed David Wilkinson to leave the state. But he is now planted at Cohoes Falls, and that place has already felt the benefit of his business talents, and his ardent zeal in internal improvement "— (*History of Cotton Manufacture*, Philadelphia, 1836.)

Mr. Wilkinson did not long remain in active business in Cohoes. He had much to call him away, and in his later years, was here only at intervals. The following, giving an account of some of the enterprises in which he was engaged, is from a letter written by him in Dec., 1846 : " The prospects at Cohoes were flattering for a time. But nullification, Loco-focory, Jacksonism, free trade, and such abominations, killed the new village just born. Europeans who were applying for water power at Cohoes at this time went away, saying, now we were going to have free trade ; they could do their work cheaper ' at 'ome ' than they could in this country and they would build their factories there. We were compelled now to get our living where we could, to go abroad if we could not get work at home. I went to work on the Delaware and Raritan Canal, in New Jersey ; then on the St. Lawrence improvements in Canada ; then to Ohio on the Sandy and Beaver Canal ; then to the new wire bridge on the Ottawa River, at Bytown, Canada, and Virginia. Wherever I could find anything to do, I went."

He was born and bred up in the faith of the Quakers, and always had a great respect for them. In mid life he connected himself with the Episcopal church, of which he was ever after a most active member. He was one of the principal founders of St. Paul's church, in Pawtucket, and one of its largest supporters for years. At Wilkinsonville, Sutton, Mass., where he afterwards had large interests, he built a church, and supported a minister at his own expense ; and on coming to Cohoes, his first achievement was the establishment of St. John's church, of which he and Mr. Howe were the principal founders. He was an active Mason, and one of the founders of Union Lodge, Pawtucket, besides being chiefly instrumental in the establishment of the Cohoes Lodge, in 1846. He was a man of sterling integrity of character, and commanded the respect and affection of a very large circle of friends. His remains were brought to Cohoes, and the funeral took place from St. John's church, Feb. 11th.

Feb. 6, M. C. Kirnan, aged 35.

March 24, Evart A. Lansing, aged 62. Mr. Lansing was an old resident of the Boght — one of a family of six children, of whom two survived him. In his death the community lost an honest and conscientious citizen, the Dutch church of Cohoes a judicious counsellor and an active, zealous member.

April 28, Paul Weidman, aged 30.

May 15, James Abel, aged 54.

July 2, Franklin Waring, aged 38. Mr. W. was for a number of years one of the leading merchants of the place.

Nov. 17, E. D. Gill, foreman in Miles White's axe factory, aged 45.

Dec. 25, Baltheus Simmons, aged 52.

1853.

Jan. 16, Joshua Bailey, Sen., a revolutionary soldier and father of Joshua and Timothy Bailey, aged 90. Mr. B. was born in East Hampton, Conn., in 1763, removed to Meredith, Delaware Co., N. Y., in 1803, and lived in a log cabin seven years, enduring the hardships and privations incident to the life of a pioneer. He removed from Meredith to Cohoes, in 1835, where he continued to reside with his son Joshua until the day of his death.

April 9, Philip Vosburgh, aged 22.

July 31st, John B. Vanderwerken, aged 43. Mr. V. was a son of Jacob Vanderwerken and succeeded to the business so many years conducted by him at the corner of Mohawk and Oneida streets, which he retained until he was appointed gate keeper of the Watervliet turnpike Co., between West Troy and Albany, in which he was a leading stockholder. He held the position until his death.

1854.

July 26, Dewitt D. Slocum, aged 21.

Sept. 27, John D. Perry, aged 72.

Oct. 16, James Manton, aged about 28.

Oct. 27, Alexander Ten Eyck, aged 32.

1855.

March 16, William Pundison Mansfield, aged 80. Mr. Mansfield was born at New Haven, Conn., in 1775, moved with his father's family to Litchfield, South Farms, and was educated at Morris Academy. He subsequently went into mercantile business in Kent, Litchfield Co., where he remained until about 1833, when he came to Saratoga Co., Northside. He married in Kent, Sally, daughter of Bradley Mills, and of four children born there, Mrs. Hugh White and L. W. Mansfield are the only survivors — the other children, a brother and sister, having died at the old home in the Housatonic Valley a few years before the family left it for their new home in this state, and here also, the mother of these children died in Feb., 1842. This family, in both branches, and their own kindred before them, as far back as is known to the writer of this sketch, were all brought up in the faith and practice of the Congregational church, and all who have departed this life died in that faith. Mr. M. was a man of remarkable firmness of character and firmness of principle and of most unquestioned integrity in all his dealings, both with others and with himself. * *

April 12, Asahel Goffe, father of Demas and Augustus J. Goffe, aged 74.
May 24, William H. Vanderwerken, aged 25.
June 3, In Bellevue Hospital, New York, H. N. Pettis, aged 44.
July 22, Samuel Stiles, aged 35.
Sept. 11, in Picton, Canada West, Charles O'Brien, of Cohoes, aged 26.
Sept. 20, Milton, son of Joshua Bailey, aged 28. Mr. B. was secretary of the Bailey Manufacturing Co.
Oct. 14, Christopher White, aged 43.
Oct. 16, Nathaniel Selleck, aged 68.
Dec. 3d, in St. Louis, Mo., Charles H., son of Guy Blakeley, aged 24.

1856.

April 27, Nicholas W. Smith, aged 26.
May 4, Norton T. Raynsford, aged 39.
Aug. 15, Wm. J. Clements, for many years the efficient clerk of the Cohoes Co., aged about 35 years.
Sept. 27, in Meriden, Ct., Elias Howell, only son of Dea. Maltby Howell, aged 44.
Nov. 28, Patrick Mc Entee, merchant, aged about 60.

1857.

Jan. 28, in Albany, Dr. C. F. Goss, formerly a resident of Cohoes, aged 41.
Feb. 3d, in Richmond, Va., William Brooks, printer, formerly of Cohoes, aged 21.
Feb 13, Chas. F. Ferguson, aged 28.
Feb. 19, at the Boght, Cornelius V. Fonda, aged 17.
March 10, Liddell Peverly, foreman of the Cohoes Iron Foundery, aged 37 years.
March 23, Jonathan Hastings, aged 35 years.
June 3, in Shaftsbury, Vt., Benjamin Hutchins, formerly a resident of Cohoes, aged 32 years. He was for some time clerk of the village, and occupied other positions of trust.
July 6, Dr. Henry Adams (father of Hon. Chas. H. Adams), aged 70 years. Dr. Adams was born in Coxsackie, N. Y., on July 6, 1787, and had thus just completed, on the day of his death, three score and ten. He made profession of religion under the ministry of the Rev. Dr. Livingston, and was for many years an active and useful member of the church in Coxsackie, until about 1849, he removed to Cohoes, where he connected himself with the Dutch church. At the time of his death he was an acting elder; an office which for many years he had held in the churches of his earlier and later affection. In his profession, by his kind and sympathizing manner, he gathered around him the affection and confidence of those to whom he ministered, and won for himself the title of the "beloved physician." He was buried in the family burial place at Coxsackie.
Dec. 20, Thomas Brown, aged 62.

1858.

March 8, Douw Vandenburgh, aged 86.
March 1, Daniel Nugent, aged 47.
March 20, in East Paw Paw, De Kalb Co., Ill., John Lansing, father of Deacons Jacob I. and Thomas Lansing, of this city.

June 20, James Barclay, aged 36.

Aug. 19, in Dubuque, Iowa, E. H. Johnston, aged 39. Mr. J. was for some time principal of the Depot school in the 2d ward, but resigned about 1851. The *Galena Daily Courier* in noticing his death said: "In the death of Mr. Johnston, our city has lost a most valuable citizen and an estimable man. He came to Galena in October, 1855, and assumed charge of the Institute, which he conducted successfully up to the present time. Possessed of considerable experience as a teacher, great energy, and devoted to his calling, under his auspices the Institute became at once flourishing. Mr. Johnston was a native of Sydney, Delaware Co., N. Y."

Sept. 20, Garret R. Lansing, aged 45.

Nov. 2, in La Crosse, Wis., Henry, son of Paschal Brooks, M.D., aged 25. For several years Mr. Brooks, with his brother Thomas, was engaged in the drug business.

Nov. 30, at Toboga, in the bay of Panama, Henry E. La Salle, first telegraphic operator in Cohoes.

Dec. 3, John Eastwood, aged 43. Mr. E. was a prominent fireman and an influential member of the masonic fraternity.

Dec. 6, William Dickey, aged 52. Mr. D. was well known as a contractor and prominent citizen of the 3d ward.

Dec. 14, By accident at D. Simmons & Co's axe factory, Thomas Golden, aged 45.

Dec. 31, Robert Leckie, father of William Leckie, Esq., aged 68. Mr. L. was one of the earliest settlers in Cohoes.

1859.

Jan. 28, in Charleston, S. C., David Warren Leland, aged 64.

March 11, Henry L. Landon, M.D., aged about 35. Dr. L. had been for many years a resident of the place and as a citizen had been closely identified with every enterprise that had for its object the welfare and prosperity of the village. For a long time he had been president of the village, and had held other important offices of trust. As a public official he discharged his duties faithfully and conscientiously. From the *Cataract* of March 19, 1859, is taken the following notice of his funeral: "The funeral of Dr Henry L. Landon, which took place in this village on Sunday afternoon last, was one of the largest gatherings of the kind ever witnessed in the village. Besides our citizens, who attended *en masse*, there were large numbers of the friends and acquaintances of Dr. L. from abroad, together with delegations of the masonic fraternity from Waterford, Lansingburg, Troy and Albany. An eloquent and impressive discourse was delivered by Rev. C. N. Waldron, from Isaiah 38: 10: 'I am deprived of the residue of my years.' After the services at the church, the body was taken to the Waterford cemetery, where the masonic rites were conducted by Past Master Geer, of King Solomon's Lodge, assisted by Worshipful Master Ball, of Mount Zion's Lodge, Troy."

March 17, Jacob Upham, aged 53. Mr. U. had been for several years an overseer in the Ogden Mills.

May 3, James Groves, aged 28

Sept. 11, Henry Lyons, aged 40.

Sept. 22, John Downs, aged 41.

Nov. 19, Matthew Fitzpatrick, aged 53. He was one of the oldest and most enterprising residents of the 3d ward, and took a leading part in local affairs.

Dec. 4, Owen Sweeney, aged 36.
Dec. 6, Isaac Fonda, aged 80.

1860.

Feb. 12, Stephen P. Van Woert, aged 40.
August 27, William Penfold, aged 57.
Oct. 22, Nathaniel Wilder, aged 71.
Nov. 1, Jonathan Wightman, aged 69. Mr. Wightman, as a member of the firm of Wightman and Youmans, was for some years prominently connected with the manufacturing interests of Cohoes, and was universally respected.
Nov. 6, James Maitland, aged about 60.
Nov. 10, Octavius Cole, aged 50.
Nov. 14, Aaron L. Ferguson, aged 69. Mr. F., was for many years identified with the business interests of Cohoes, as a contractor and builder.
Nov. 20, Jeremiah Houlihan, aged 68.
Dec. 29, Daniel Simmons, aged 58. Mr. Simmons was one of the first to engage in business in Cohoes, and to his industry and enterprise the place is largely indebted for its reputation as a manufacturing town. Beginning in a small way the manufacture of axes and edge tools in 1835, he, in a few years, succeeded in building up an establishment which was one of the most important of its kind in the country, and in gaining a widespread reputation for energy and ability. The main facts in regard to the connection of Mr. S. with the business history of Cohoes, have been elsewhere mentioned.

1861.

Jan. 1st, John R. Bullock, aged 54. Mr. B. was for many years a resident of the village and was frequently selected by his fellow citizens to represent them in official positions.
Jan. 21, Christopher C. Stow, aged 26.
March 12, Origen Orcutt, aged 64.
April 20, William H. Mead, aged 31.
June 13, John Vandercook, aged 30.
July 3d, Jenks Brown, aged 50. Mr. B. was for several years agent of the Ogden Mills, and in 1859 was president of the village. He died in Indian Orchard, Mass.
July —, Jesse D. Van Hagen, aged 22. Mr. V. H. was a member of Co. K, 34th N. Y. Vols., and was killed at the battle of Fair Oaks, Va.
Nov. 14, John McIntosh, aged 57.

1862.

Jan. 22, A. C. Byrant, aged 46. Mr. B. was a foreman in D. Simmons & Co's axe factory and was widely known and respected.
Feb. 12, William Orelup, Sen., aged 69. Mr. O. had been identified with the interests of Cohoes since its settlement and was known as an enterprising citizen and a prominent member of the M. E. church.
Feb. 27, George M. Howes, aged about 32. Mr. H. was for a long time the only news dealer in the place.
March 10th, Dr. J. H. Tripp, aged 45.
April —, in West Troy, N. Y., Supply F. Wilson, for several years a justice of the peace in Cohoes and a leading politician of the town.
May 31, James Galbraith, killed in battle at Seven Pines, near Richmond.

Aug. 30, Leonard G. Fletcher, aged about 22. This young man was a member of Capt. J. L. Yates' Co., 22d Reg't, N. Y. Vols. He was engaged in the battle before Sharpsburg, Md., and from the fact that no tidings were subsequently heard of his fate, it is probable that he there lost his life.

Sept. 4, William Osterhout, aged 44. He was a foreman in D. Simmons & Co's axe factory, a skillful mechanic and a well known citizen.

Sept. —, James Young, a private in Capt. Wm. Shannon's company, 113th Reg't, died in the hospital at Georgetown, D. C.

Sept. 17, William Orelup, Jr., aged about 45 years. Mr. O. was a member of the Board of Education and a director in the Bank of Cohoes at the time of his death. During a long residence in Cohoes he held many public positions and was much respected as a citizen.

Sept. —, in England, Dr. Blake, for a few years medical practitioner in Cohoes.

Sept. 19, in Newark, Licking Co., Ohio, Col. George I. Abbott, aged about 50. Col. Abbott was one of the earliest citizens of Cohoes and a charter member of Cohoes Lodge, F. & A. M. He is remembered as a gentleman of quiet, unobtrusive manners and possessed of those genial qualities which render a man a true friend and good citizen.

Sept. 22, in hospital, at Washington, D. C., William Long of bilious fever. Mr. Long was a member of Capt. Wm. Shannon's company, 113th Reg't, N. Y. Vols.

Sept. 29, in hospital at Washington, D. C., Lieut. Hiram Clute, of Co. A, 22d Reg't, N. Y. Vols. Lt. Clute was wounded in the foot at one of the battles before Manassas. He lay five days upon the battle field and his limb was not operated upon until he had been in the hospital two days more. An obituary in the *Cataract* said : " Thus ends the career of as brave a soldier and as true a man as ever met death upon the battle field. He was idolized by his company and respected by the regiment to which he belonged, as well as in the community in which he has long resided. He leaves a wife and two children to mourn his loss."

Oct. 17, Peter M. Smith, aged 23. Mr. S. was acting village librarian in 1861.

Nov. 16, Dea. Maltby Howell, aged 77.

Nov. 28, William B. Hitchcock, aged 77.

1863.

Jan. 5, William Padley, aged 51.

Feb. 27, John J. Swartz, aged 58.

Feb. 27, Samuel Maitland, aged 25.

March 31, Michael Farrelly, aged 79.

May 8, George E. Van Vliet, aged 24. Mr. V. V. was a member of Co. H, 177th Reg't, N. Y. Vols. " He was a young man of great promise. He had finished his course of study at Burr Seminary, Manchester, and was about to enter Hamilton College, to prepare for the ministry, when he felt it to be his duty to enlist in the service of his country."

July 1, Lemuel Scott, aged 40.

June 18, killed, at the siege of Port Hudson, John McGaffin, in the 20th year of his age. The following concerning Mr. McG. appeared in the *Cataract :* " There are very few of those who have left our village for the scene of conflict, who were so well known and esteemed as the subject of this notice. He was a youth of great promise. His mind was naturally of a studious, inquiring disposition, which was strengthened by intellectual training, and adorned by the graces of the Holy Spirit. In the 15th year of his age he made profession of his faith in Christ, uniting with the Reformed Dutch church in this village, and was soon after led to commence his preparation for preaching the Gospel. He was a member of the junior class in Rutgers' College, when at the call of his country, he bid farewell for a season to the endearments of his home and the attractions of his studies, and enlisted for nine months as a private in the 177th Reg't, of this state. He stood up manfully in the place of honor and peril; in the forepart of the battle he met with a soldier's death, and has found in a far distant state, a soldier's grave. His death has made another vacant place in the home he loved so well, and has filled with sadness the hearts of a large circle of friends he had gathered around him in this community."

June 16, Robert Taylor, age unknown. He was a member of the 175th Reg't, N. Y. Vols., and was wounded in the engagement before Port Hudson, from the effects of which he died in hospital at Baton Rouge. He was a brother of John Taylor of this place.

July 2, killed, at the battle of Gettysburg, Pa., Lieut. Thomas Walters, of the 97th Reg't, N. Y. Vols.

July 2, William H. Cranston, aged 26. He enlisted as a private in Co. A, 76th N. Y. Vols., and was killed at the battle of Gettysburg, Pa.

July 2, Edward Greason, aged 31. He was born at Hyde, Cheshire, England, and enlisted from Cohoes in Co. A, 76th N. Y. Vols. He was wounded in the battle of Gettysburg, Pa., after which he was missing. It is supposed he died on the field and was buried by the enemy.

July 2, killed at the battle of Gettysburg, Pa., John Wood, John Brierly, Louis Toronto, Hugh Loughry, Wesley Brodt and Wesley Tompkins, ages unknown. These young men were all members of the 76th Reg't, N. Y. Vols.

July 16, James Durham, aged 30, a member of the 3d Reg't N. Y. Vols.

July 22, John N. Meads, aged 65.

July 26, Daniel Ball, aged 80.

July 22, in Nantasket, Mass., William W. Kendrick, formerly of Cohoes, aged 43. Mr. K. was a brother-in-law of Col. Isaac Quackenbush.

Aug. 4, from wounds received in the battle at Gettysburg, Pa. Philip Keeler, of the 50th Reg't N. Y. Vols.

August —, from malaria in the swamps of Bonnet Carré, La., Robt W. Frisby and John Flynn, members of the 10th Reg't N. Y. Vols. Ages unknown.

Sept. 3, Jacob A. Taylor, aged 18. He was a member of Co. H, 177th Reg't N. Y. Vols., and served his country faithfully. He accompanied his regiment on its way home until he reached Rochester, N. Y., where he was taken sick and died.

Sept. —, in Mount Pleasant Hospital, near Port Hudson, William H. Vandenbergh, aged 23. Mr. V. was the only son of Jacob L. Vandenbergh, of the Boght. He enlisted in the 177th Reg't N. Y. Vols. A correspondent said of him: "In his manner he was unobtrusive, in his demeanor amiable and gentle, and possessed, in an eminent degree, those characteristics calculated to inspire the love of those who knew him."

Sept. 28, Abram Lawrence, aged 21. Mr. L. was a son of Geo. Lawrence, of this city, and was for many years deputy postmaster.

Oct. 21, Allen Bordwell, aged about 45

Oct. 29, Patrick Malany, aged 23.

Nov. 17, William Williams, machinist.

Nov. 23, in Troy, Dennis Stow, for many years a prominent inventor and resident of Cohoes, aged 63.

Nov. 21, Isaac F. Fletcher, aged 65. Mr. F. was one of the earliest residents of the place, a prominent member of Cohoes Lodge, F. & A. M., and a conscientious, upright citizen.

Dec. —, James Harvey, a member of the 128th N. Y. Vols. He had served faithfully and honorably in most of the battles of the war, and in consequence of failing health was on his return home, where he hoped to give his mother and friends a pleasant surprise. He lived to enter the harbor of New York, where in sight of his native state, and within a few miles of his friends and home, he yielded up his life.

Dec. 16, Sherman D. Fairbank, aged 50. Mr. F. had been for many years a prominent business man, universally respected for his integrity and excellent traits as a citizen. He held several prominent positions of responsibility in the village, was a leading member of Cohoes Lodge F. & A. M. and a director of the Bank of Cohoes.

Dec. 18, in Syracuse, N. Y., Chauncey Stow, one of the original founders of the *Cataract*, aged about 35.

1864.

Feb. 17, Capt. William Holley, aged 54.

Feb. 20, James R. Wilson, aged 18. Mr. W. enlisted from Cohoes as a private in Co. H, 115th Reg't N. Y. Vols., and was killed by a shell from a rebel battery in the battle of Olustee, Fla. Lt. Clark wrote of him as follows : "The brave young soldier fired his own sixty rounds of ammunition and then sought a fresh supply from a dead companion's cartridge box. He loaded for the sixty-first time and was about firing when the shell exploded that cost him his life."

Feb. 20, Oscar L. Ackley, age unknown. Mr. A. was a member of the 115th Reg't N. Y. Vols. and was killed at the battle of Olustee, Fla.

March 10, Edward O'Reilly, aged 48. He was an upright citizen and conscientious business man and was frequently called upon to represent his ward in public positions.

March 11, in Halfmoon, N. Y., John Oliver, aged 52.

March 23, Edward H. Owen, aged 49.

March 31, Charles Green, soldier, aged about 23.

March 26, Willie H. Howard, aged 21.

April 27, L. Sprague Parsons, aged 55. "Mr. Parsons commenced his preparatory studies in Hamden, Ct., which were afterwards completed in Troy, N. Y. He entered Yale College in the class of 1835, but did not graduate until 1837, having devoted one year to teaching in Bristol, Ct. After graduation he taught for a short time in Norfolk Co., Va., but was obliged to return home on account of ill health. After teaching another year in Bristol, Ct., he moved to Albany, N. Y., in 1839, where with his sister he established a select family school. He was also at the same time principal of the Pearl street Academy for boys, in the same city. In 1845, he was chosen principal of the Albany Female Academy, the duties of which he discharged with success until 1855, when he resigned his office. In the same year he engaged in manufacturing in Cohoes, where he remained until his death."

April 22, in Fort Warren, Boston Harbor, James McCarthy and Matthew Riley, of Cohoes, N. Y. Both were young men.

April 18, Herbert Hastings, aged about 30. Mr. Hastings was a member of the 7th N. Y. Heavy Artillery and died very suddenly in camp from heart disease. He had been a resident of Cohoes from his boyhood and for many years previous to his enlistment was the leading dentist of the place. Of a genial, generous disposition, he had troops of friends who sincerely mourned his early death.

May 5, George Diehl, age unknown, a member of the 77th N. Y. Vols., was killed in one of the battles of the Wilderness.

May 10, killed while on picket duty, John McCarthy, aged 17.

May 25, William Noonan, aged 40.

June 2, Simon O'Dea and Thomas Eastham, members of Battery I, 7th N. Y. Heavy Artillery, both brave and faithful soldiers, were killed in one of the battles of the Wilderness, ages unknown.

June, — James Cole, who faithfully served in all the principal battles of the war, on the peninsula, at Gettysburg and the Wilderness, fell in one of the later engagements. Age unknown.

June 10, Joseph Wickham, aged 39. Mr. Wickham was a member of the 118th Reg't, N. Y. Vols., and was wounded in the shoulder at Bermuda Hundreds, May 16, from the effects of which he died.

June 19, Henry O. Osterhout, aged 17. Enlisted as a private in Co. H, 177th Reg't N. Y. Vols., and was with the army at the siege of Port Hudson. He returned home with his regiment in September, 1863, and died from sickness contracted in the service.

July 9, Daniel D. Tuthill, aged 47. Enlisted as a private in Co. I, 7th Reg't N. Y. Heavy Artillery, and was afterward promoted to the rank of sergeant. He was wounded in the engagement at North Anna Bridge, Va., on May 30th, 1864, and died in the hospital at Washington. Mr. T., was the father-in-law of Capt. William Shannon, now of Pittsburg, Pa., and A. H. Frink, of this city.

July —, Charles Westover, aged 20, a member of the 4th Reg't N. Y. Heavy Artillery, died in hospital at Staten Island.

July 12, George Shipley, aged 43. Mr. S. was a member of Co. I, 7th Heavy Artillery, and died on board the U. S. transport Atlantic, from disease contracted while in the service. His remains were interred in Cypress Hill cemetery, L. I., July 14.

July 22, Sergeant Major E. Raymond Fonda, aged 27. Was a member of the 115th Reg't N. Y. Vols. He was severely wounded May 7th, in one of the battles near Petersburg, Va., from the effects of which he died in the Lady's Home Hospital, New York.

July 29, in Troy, N. Y., John Kerr, aged 62. Mr. Kerr was for several years previous to his death prominently connected with manufacturing interests in Cohoes.

Aug. 1, William G. Caw, aged 48. Mr. Caw came to Cohoes in 1846, and formed a partnership with Isaac Quackenbush, with whom he continued in the grocery business until his death. He was a town supervisor from 1858 to 1861, trustee of the village, water commissioner, director of the Bank of Cohoes, and filled other public positions of responsibility, in all of which the people were faithfully served. In his business relations he was honorable and conscientious, and as a citizen he was enterprising and public spirited. A friend wrote of his death as follows : " The death of William G. Caw makes a great gap in our community. Let it be filled by the renewed devotion of others to those interests to which he gave so freely of his time and his attention, and if the cry of the poor and the needy, the fatherless and the widow, the demands of our country and its brave defenders, the church of Christ, and its overshadowing claims can reach the hearts more forcibly through the remembrance of his character as a business man, a citizen, a politician, a patriot, a philanthropist and a Christian, then indeed, will he, being dead, yet speak to us ; and of the recollections that cluster around his name, it may be truly said, " the memory of the just is precious."

July 18, Nathan Stone, aged 76. Mr. Stone was one of the earliest residents of the place.

Aug. 17, Alfred Phelps, aged about 70. Mr. Phelps was for many years the proprietor of the "old junction" tavern, and had served the people as justice of the peace, and village trustee.

Aug. 11, Peter Forbes, aged 44. Mr. Forbes was for a long time foreman in Fuller and Safely's iron foundery.

Aug. 16, Abbott C. Musgrove, aged 19. Mr. Musgrove was a member of the 115th Reg't N. Y. Vols., and by his bravery, correct deportment and sterling integrity won the esteem of his comrades and left a record that proved him a patriot and heroic soldier. He was killed in the battle at Deep Bottom, Va.

Aug. 16, James K. Himes, aged 18. He was a member of the 115th Reg't N. Y. Vols., and fell in the battle at Deep Bottom, Va., while bearing the colors of the regiment. He was distinguished for his heroic conduct in times of greatest peril, and was beloved by all who knew him.

Sept. 18, Thomas Gooch, son-in-law of John Land, died in St. John's Hospital, Annapolis, Md., from the effects of wounds received in the battle at Ream's Station. He was a member of the 7th Reg't, N. Y. Heavy Artillery.

Oct. 2, Edward Bullock, aged 21.

Oct. 6, Stephen Slocum, aged about 60. Mr. S. was for many years deacon in the Baptist society of the village, and acted as the first superintendent of the Harmony Union Sunday school.

Oct. 12, Adam Turner, aged 41, was born in Castlereagh, Ireland, March 12, 1823. He removed to this country in 1850. He enlisted from Cohoes as a private in Co. I, 4th Reg't N. Y. Heavy Artillery, and died from disease contracted by exposure and fatigue with the army before Richmond.

Oct. —, in Andersonville prison, John Greer and John Ebah.

Oct. 21, John Trull, a veteran of the war of 1812 and father of Stevens V. and Samuel D. Trull of this city, aged 71.

Nov. 6, James K. Stevens, aged 20. He enlisted in Co. H, 4th Reg't, N. Y. Heavy Artillery, and died in the hospital at Annapolis, Md., from sickness contracted in Richmond prison. He was a son of John Stevens of this city.

Nov. 10, Charles T. Cannon, son of Tracy Cannon, aged 33.

Nov. 28, in McClellan Hospital, Philadelphia, Pa., Robert Gormley, a member of the 7th Reg't, N. Y. Heavy Artillery.

Nov. 26, in rebel prisons, John Welch and J. Mangham. Particulars unknown.

APPENDIX.

1865.

Feb. 3, Lt. John C. Carroll, aged 23. Lt. C. belonged to Co. M, 6th N. Y. Cavalry, and was killed near Lovellville, Va.

March 28, John Vandermark, aged 55. Mr. V. was one of the most widely known citizens and belonged to one of the oldest families in the town. He had occupied various public positions, was for a time engaged in manufacturing, and immediately preceding his death was proprietor of the Rock Hotel, on the corner of Mohawk and Howard streets.

May 7, at Chicago, Ill., Patrick O'Brien, son of Lawrence O'Brien, aged 29.

July 6, Nicholas D. Lounsbury, aged 57. Mr. L. was a member of the 30th Reg't, N. Y. Vols.

Sept. 17, Wm. B. Jackson, a member of the 91st Reg't, N. Y. Vols., aged about 45.

Oct. 7, C. F. Ingraham, aged about 42. Mr. Ingraham was for many years principal of the Depot school and superintendent of the Baptist Sunday school.

Oct. 21, Levinus S. Lansing, aged 85. Mr. L. was one of the oldest representatives of the Lansing family, and resided most of his life in the old homestead between this place and West Troy.

Dec. 15, Patrick Neary, aged 26.

Dec. 21, Abram D. Clute, aged 41.

1866.

Jan. 14, John Rafferty, age unknown. He was a member of the 91st Reg't, N. Y. Vols., and his death was occasioned by disease contracted while in the service.

March 1, John Hay, aged 76. Mr. H. was a native of Scotland and emigrated to Cohoes in 1836, remaining a resident until his death. He left a family of ten children, fifty grand-children and three great grand-children. John, James, Charles and Alex. Hay of this place are his sons.

March 31, Peter Manton. At the time of his death Mr. Manton was deputy sheriff and chief engineer of the fire department.

April 19, in Albany, A. E. Stimson, aged 57. Mr. Stimson occupied for some years a prominent position among Cohoes manufacturers, having organized the Clifton Co., in which he held the controlling interest.

May 2, James R. Dickey, aged 22. Mr. Dickey was a printer who served his apprenticeship in the office of the *Cataract*.

May 10, L. G. Forrester, for several years book-keeper at the Harmony Mills, aged about 45.

May 14, George Shires, proprietor of the Miller House, aged 46.

May 14, James Horner, aged 42.

May 28, Edward Packard, aged 38.

June 1st, Lt. Francis Keating, aged 32. Lt. K. was one of the first volunteers from Cohoes and served his country faithfully and honorably.

Aug. 22, Wm. F. Carter, M.D., aged 54. Dr. Carter was born in Newburyport, Mass., and was educated at the old academy of that place. Owing to his father's reverses of fortune by losses at sea, during the war of 1815, and afterwards, his education was not continued as it would otherwise have been, and at 14 years of age he was apprenticed in the drug store of Dr. David Kimball, of Portsmouth, N. H., where he acquired a thorough knowledge of that business. He then became acquainted with Dr. Timothy Upham, who was about removing to Waterford, N. Y., and who being interested in the smart, quick-witted boy, invited him to study medicine with him. The invitation was accepted but not until after the young man had spent some months in the study of Latin. He remained with Dr. Upham one year and afterward attended medical lectures in Boston, going from there to Dartmouth College where he finished his course and received his diploma in 1834. He commenced practice at Hagaman's Mills, Montgomery Co., but not receiving sufficient encouragement there, he removed to Cohoes, in 1835, where he remained in practice of his profession until his death. He was eccentric in manner, and brusque in address but possessed a most tender and sympathetic disposition which was manifested in kindly and charitable acts toward those who were worthy. He was a director in the Bank of Cohoes, and trustee of the Savings Institution and had represented his fellow citizens in local affairs on many occasions.

Dec. 9, John Eastwood, Jr., aged 22. Mr. E. was a member of the 22d Reg't N. Y. Vols., and served his country honorably during the war. He was wounded in one of the battles of Virginia and while in the service contracted the disease from which he died.

Dec. 21, Alexander Bell, aged 89.

1867.

Jan. 2, William Buchanan, aged 44.

Jan. 28, Michael H. Johnson, aged 28. Mr. Johnson enlisted in the U. S. Navy about 1860, and served on board the flag ship Sabine. On an expedition to Paraguay he was sunstruck, from the effects of which he never recovered.

Feb. 25, John Partridge, aged 48, well known as the proprietor for many years of the Cataract House.

Feb. 27, Edward Ayres, aged 40.

July 7th, in Montreal, Ca., Gideon Longley, aged 54. Mr. Longley was born in Tenterden, Kent, England, Dec. 21st, 1813, and came to this country in the spring of 1826, locating in Watervliet. He was one of the earliest members of the M. E. church of Cohoes.

Sept. 21, Abraham L. Smith, a young merchant of the place, aged 30.

Sept. 30, Philip L. Clow, aged 51.

Oct. 16, in New York, Thomas Garner, aged 62. Mr. G. was the principal owner of the Harmony Mills. His connection with this establishment is spoken of elsewhere in this volume.

Nov. 7, Oscar O. Finney, aged 33. Mr. Finney was a leading member of the Masonic Fraternity and for several years was proprietor of the Cohoes Hotel.

Dec. 8, Abraham Lansing, aged 74. Mr. Lansing was one of the oldest inhabitants of Cohoes. The following is an extract from an obituary notice published in the *Cataract*: " A man of an amiable disposition, of the strictest integrity, of a fine and unblemished character, gathering around him the respect and attachment of all who knew him. Beloved in the family, honored as an upright citizen in our community, and in the Reformed church an elder who " ruled well and was counted worthy of double honor." In a good old age, after a long life of Christian usefulness, he has fallen asleep."

Dec. 10, Edward Brennan, aged about 25. Mr. B. was collector of the village.

Dec. 21, Edward Twelvetrees, aged 17.

APPENDIX. 281

1868.

Jan. 27, John Page, aged 22.
Feb. 4, Charles L. Hubbell, aged about 45. Mr. H. was for many years one of the leading mechanics of Cohoes.
Feb. 24, in Flint, Mich., Isaac S. Carter, aged 28. Mr. C. was a son of Thomas C. Carter of Cohoes.
March 26, Alonzo J. M. McKee, aged 23.
April 11, Bernard O'Neil, aged 46.
April 18, William Sullivan, aged 32.
May 15, Col. Dow Fonda, aged 92. Col. F. was one of the oldest residents of the place.
May 28, John Clark, aged 25.
July 6, Louis Valley, aged 54.
Aug. 2, Rev. A. Judson Bingham, aged about 40. Mr. B. came to Cohoes in March, 1865, in response to a call to become the pastor of the Baptist church. He resigned his charge in Feb., 1867, to accept the position of principal of Egberts Institute, in which he continued until his death. As a pastor and teacher he was greatly beloved. He left a wife and three children.
Aug. 3, Daniel Scully, aged 68.
Aug. 17, in Quincy, Ill., Joseph Atwood, formerly a resident of Cohoes.
Aug. 23, James Ryan, aged 47.
Sept. 25, Michael Monahon, aged 28.
Sept. 26, Col. Jacob W. Miller, aged 58. Col. Miller was born August, 1810, in Schaghticoke, Rens. Co., N. Y., and commenced teaching school in his native town when he was 17 years of age. Rev. Ensign Stover, at one time pastor of the M. E. church of Cohoes, and his brother, the late Samuel Stover, Esq., of West Troy, were pupils of his at that time. He afterwards taught school in Halfmoon, N. Y., until his marriage, when he embarked in mercantile pursuits at Visscher's Ferry, Saratoga Co., N. Y., remaining there until the death of his first wife. He then entered the office of Judge Doe at Waterford in the same county, as a law student. Hon. John K. Porter was a student in the office at the same time, and both were admitted to the bar in 1842. It was at this time he married his second wife. In 1844, he came to Cohoes and commenced the practice of law, which he continued up to the time of his death. His first partner was John Van Santvoord, Esq., of New York city, the partnership continuing until the latter left the place in 1852. From this time he continued business alone until December, 1864, when Charles F. Doyle, Esq., a former student, became associated with him. He held many public positions in which he acquitted himself honorably and satisfactorily to his constituents. In 1848, with Mr. Van Santvoord he built the Miller and Van Santvoord Block now owned by H. B. Silliman, and in 1862 erected the Miller House Block, now owned by Frank Brown.
Oct. 8, Samuel H. Foster, aged 52. Mr. Foster was born in Rensselaerville, Albany Co., N. Y., where he resided until his eighteenth year, when he entered Williams College, from which he graduated after completing his course with honor. After teaching for a time, he commenced the study of law in the office of Jonathan Jenkins, at Rensselaerville, N. Y., and was admitted to practice in 1841. He came to Cohoes in 1846, and formed a co-partnership with Stephen C. Miller

36

Esq., a young lawyer of ability and promise. Mr. F., at once took a leading position as a lawyer, which he retained until his death. In 1856, he was the candidate of the American party for district attorney of Albany Co., but owing to loss of prestige by that organization, he was defeated. He afterward served the people as a member of the Board of Education, and in 1866, was chosen chairman of that body, in which position he gave most valuable service to the cause of education.

Nov. 2, Joseph A. Simons, aged 49. Mr. Simons was for many years identified with the business interests of Cohoes, as proprietor of the Cohoes and Troy Stage Line, and as a merchant on West Harmony Hill. He was a leading member of Cohoes Lodge, F. & A. M., and enjoyed the esteem of his fellow citizens in a large degree.

1869.

Jan. 12, John W. Visscher, aged 16.

Feb. 1, Willard A. Bayard, aged 27. Mr. B. was a soldier in the Union army, where he contracted the disease which resulted in his death.

Feb. 8, Edward Knight, aged 26.

Feb. 22, A. F. Safely, M.D., aged 40. Dr. S., was a brother of Robert Safely. He was born in Scotland, and came with his parents to Waterford, N. Y., at an early age. He studied medicine in the Albany Medical College, and graduated in 1852. At the breaking out of the rebellion he enlisted in the 10th N. Y. Vols., and served with it until he was honorably discharged in consequence of wounds received at the 2d battle of Bull Run, from the effects of which he never thoroughly recovered.

March 31, in New York, Thomas Garner, Jr., aged 30. He was for some years connected with the Harmony Co., but retired three years before his death, in consequence of ill health.

March 27, Egbert Egberts, aged 78. Mr. Egberts was born at Coeymans, Albany Co., N. Y., where his father, Anthony Egberts, who was an officer in the revolutionary army, settled at the close of the war. In 1812, he engaged in mercantile business in Albany, with his brother Cornelius, under the firm name of C. and E. Egberts. In 1831, he removed to Cohoes, where he, with Timothy Bailey, first successfully introduced the power knitting frame, and established an extensive manufactory. In 1852, he retired from active business, with a competency which he always used in a spirit of Christian liberality. In that year he was the candidate of the Whig party for congress. In 1858, he organized the bank of Cohoes, and was chosen its president, which office he retained until his death. The "Egberts Institute," received from him an endowment of $20,000, and the Reformed church of Cohoes, of which he was a member, is indebted in a great measure to his taste and liberality for their beautiful house of worship. He was a friend of the poor, and for every good cause he had an open heart and hand.

March 30, A. D. Shepherd, aged about 60. Mr. Shepherd was for many years the proprietor of the extensive flouring mills on the north side of the Mohawk river, known as the Shattemuck Mills.

March 31, in Albany, William Smith, one of the firm of Smith, Gregory & Co. of the American Hosiery Mills of Cohoes.

April 4, John Horan, aged 55.

April 5, at Wappinger's Falls, N. Y., Newton Fowler, aged 22.

April 13, Joseph Atheson, aged 37.

Appendix. 283

April 15, John W. Vandenburgh, aged 30.

May 19, Jerome Sanders, aged 46. Mr. S. was for many years a member of the official board of the M. E. church.

May 20, William Whitehill, aged 84.

June 1, Henry Ashworth, aged 55.

June 14, John Harrison, aged 85. Mr. Harrison was born in Ireland and came to America in 1851. He had been a consistent member of the M. E. church for 68 years.

June 13, Charles L. Benson, aged 36.

July 28, Dr. Ira B. Rose, aged 67.

Aug. 12, John Robertson, aged 31.

Sept. 13, Halsey R. Grant, aged 44. Mr. Grant had for eighteen years previous to his death been prominently connected with the business interests of Cohoes, as a merchant and public official. He frequently represented his fellow citizens in the board of village trustees, and in the board of education where his conscientious discharge of public duties elicited the commendation, and commanded the confidence of the people whom he so faithfully served. He had been for many years superintendent of the water works, a trustee of the Cohoes Savings Institution, and an influential member of Cohoes Lodge, F. & A. M.

Oct. 24, John Lyons, aged 57. Mr. Lyons had resided in Cohoes for many years and was known as a conscientious upright citizen. He frequently represented his fellow citizens as village trustee and in other responsible positions.

Oct. 30, Charles W. Orelup, aged 30.

Oct. 31, at Pulaski, Oswego Co., N. Y., Stephen C. Miller, Esq., aged 47. Mr. Miller was born in Westerlo, Albany Co., N. Y., Feb. 18th 1823. He prepared for college in the Albany Academy and in the fall of 1843 entered the junior class of Union College and graduated in 1845. After graduation he was engaged as a teacher in Kingsley's classical and mathematical military school at West Point, where he remained a year and a half. He then entered upon the study of the law in the office of the late Rufus W. Peckham of Albany, and after finishing his course was admitted to practice in the supreme court. Forming a partnership with the late Samuel H. Foster, Esq., he commenced the practice of his profession, and at the same time was co-editor and proprietor with Horace B. Silliman of the Cohoes *Cataract*. In 1851 he was married to Miss Margaret Wilkinson and about the same time discontinued his law practice and forming a partnership with his father-in-law, Samuel Wilkinson, opened a store where the Empire Mill now stands. This enterprise proving unsuccessful he accepted the position of principal of the Pulaski Academy, which he occupied for three years. He then purchased the office of the *Pulaski Democrat*, and continued the publication of the paper until his death.

Nov. 17, William Ferguson, aged 55.

Dec. 19, Rev. L. H. Saugon, aged 53. Mr. Saugon was the first pastor of St. Joseph's French Catholic church of the village and had presided over his charge but a little more than a year at the time of his death. He was indefatigable in labor for the good of his congregation, by whom he was universally beloved. He was accomplished as a scholar, an eloquent speaker and devotedly attached to his church.

Dec. 12, John E. Damon, aged 29.

1870.

Jan. 17, James Lackin, aged 71. Mr. L. was one of the oldest residents of the 3d ward.

Jan. 15, Thomas Crossley, aged about 40.

Jan. 20, William Nugent, aged 17.

March 26, Joseph Biscornette, aged about 45. Mr. B. was well known as the proprietor of the Union Hotel, on Oneida street.

April 14, Thomas Ryan, aged about 55.

April 30, John Campbell, aged 37.

May 11, Ebenezer Benson, aged 77.

June 24, Dr. Alfred Wands, aged 48. Dr. Wands was an old resident of Cohoes and occupied a prominent position as a citizen and physician. He had on several occasions represented his fellow citizens in local affairs, and in every trust proved himself capable and upright.

July 19, George Grass, aged 56.

Aug. 7, Ira Terry, aged 64. Mr. Terry was for many years the leading druggist of the place, and had occupied a prominent position as a conscientious business man.

Aug. 24, in Watervliet Center, Albany Co., N. Y. Gilbert I. Van Zandt, aged 77. For a long period Mr. Van Zandt had represented the town of Watervliet in the Board of Supervisors and held other positions of trust and responsibility, in which he served his constituents capably and honorably.

Oct. 6, Hon. Hugh White, aged 72. Hugh White was born in Whitestown, N. Y., in December, 1798. His early days were passed upon his father's farm. In 1819, as he approached his majority, he commenced a course of study, preparatory to entering Hamilton College, from which institution he graduated in 1823. On leaving college he went to New York and devoted himself to the law. He was admitted to the bar after a course of study in the office of Col. Chas. G. Haines, but his tastes inclining him more towards commercial life, he embraced an opportunity then offered him by his brother Canvass, of engaging in business. Canvass White had perfected a method of manufacturing an hydraulic cement which was largely used in the construction of the Erie Canal, and had established his works at Chittenango. His brother took charge of these works, and in this occupation he remained for some years, there first manifesting the business ability and sagacity which were his prominent traits in after life. In April, 1830, Mr. White came to Cohoes to take the place of his brother (who was extensively occupied elsewhere), in managing the affairs of the Cohoes Co. Under his supervision the earliest important works of the company were completed. He directed the building of the first dams in '31 and '32, and the construction of the first canal in 1834. He was engaged at the same time in several minor enterprises, which served to occupy his time in the intervals of attention to more important duties. Among these were a saw mill on Harmony Hill, in Cohoes, a flour mill, and mill on the Waterford side of the river in which the manufacture of the cement above referred to was continued. In 1836, Mr. White became interested in the company which built the first Harmony Mill, and its affairs received his attention for some time. Mr. White represented the Saratoga district in congress for three terms, from 1845 to 1851, and though not prominent as a debater, was a most faithful and hard working member, and performed important services on the committees to which he was assigned. Soon after, Mr. White retired from active business, though retaining an interest in a number of business enterprises. At the time of his death he was president of the Saratoga Co. Nat. B'k, with which institution he had long been connected. Mr. White's declining years were passed in the retirement of his home in Waterford, in the enjoyment of the ample fortune which he had amassed. Of his character, the Cohoes *Cataract*, in an article on his death, spoke as follows: " He was essentially an executive man ; what he undertook, he always accomplished, for he was a man of strong indomitable will ; he was generous and large hearted in all his dealings, and many a young man has been started on in the world by his kindness and his means."

Oct. 17, Joseph E. Ballard, aged 22.
Oct. 21, Dr. Joseph Varin, aged about 55.
Oct. 21, William Gledhill, aged 70.
Nov. 2, John Clark, Jr., aged 21. Mr. Clark had entered the Rochester Theological Seminary, with a view to preparing for the ministry. His pure life and genial disposition had endeared him to many friends, and his early death cast a gloom over a large circle.
Nov. 4, Francis Way, aged 60.
Nov. 12, Hiram Chubb, aged 37.
Nov. 17, John Drysdale, aged 71. Mr. D. had been a resident of Cohoes for many years, and was known as an upright, conscientious citizen.
Dec. 7, George Hudson, aged 19.
Dec. 28, Michael Ryan, aged 50.

1871.

Jan. 14, Daniel Keeler, aged 40.
Jan. 20, John Foreman, aged 29.
Jan. 21, Robert Maitland, aged 35.
Feb. 27, James Whalen, aged 67.
Feb. 25, Henry Lyons, aged 21.
March 30, Joseph Moore, aged 63. Mr. Moore was for several years a merchant in Troy, but for some time previous to his death resided with his son Dr. J. W. Moore, of this city.
March 27, Adam Vanderwerken, aged 69.
April 25, Lt. William Buchanan, aged 45. Mr. Buchanan went out as a lieutenant in Capt. Trull's company 30th N. Y. Vols., in October, 1862, and participated with it in the battles of Fredericksburg and Chancellorsville. On the return of that regiment he was transferred to the 76th Reg't, N. Y. Vols. After passing through the battle of Gettysburg and several engagements of less note, he was taken prisoner at one of the battles of the Wilderness and sent to Andersonville prison, where he remained nearly a year. While being removed with other prisoners to a more secure prison he escaped from the cars, and reaching our lines at Knoxville, Tenn., was soon transferred to Washington and discharged. He was one of the first officers appointed under the capital police system and served as captain until he resigned to go into business.
June 5, William Waterhouse, aged 57.
July 24, Michael Latta, aged 68.
July 26, William Green, aged 19.
Aug. 12, William Ballantyne, aged 65.
Aug. 14, Patrick Griffin, aged 37.

Sept. 15, John Russell, aged 24.
Sept. 16, James Wallace, aged 35.
Oct. 30, in Little Rock, Ark., George W. Upham, aged 38.
Nov. 4, in San Francisco, Cal., Joseph Almy, aged 36.
Dec. 2, George W. Hutchins, aged 58.

1872.

Jan. 16, Daniel Whalen, aged 22.
Jan. 18, John Forbes, aged 47.
Jan. 26, James Driscoll, aged 42.
Jan. 27, John C. Mahon, aged 24.
Jan. 29, Michael Lynch, aged 45. Mr. Lynch had been a resident of the 3d ward 25 years and ranked among the leading business men of that part of the place.
Jan. 29, David McLuckey, aged 56.
Jan. 29, John Langtree, aged 37.
March 5, John Ward, aged 33.
March 10, Barent C. Schemerhorn, aged 68, father of the Schemerhorn brothers, dentists, of this city.
March 13, Joseph Phillips, aged 65. Mr. Phillips was formerly a business partner of A. A. Osterhout under the firm name of Osterhout & Phillips; subsequently he did business alone as a grocer in Granite Hall and latterly in company with W. A. McMillan at the corner of Remsen and White streets.
April 1, John P. Steenberg, aged 69. Mr. Steenberg was one of the oldest business men in Cohoes, his store and house on the corner of Remsen and White streets being among the first buildings erected in that part of the city. For many years, in addition to his business in that place, he pursued his profession of engineer and surveyor, and in that capacity was prominently connected with many of the earliest improvements of Cohoes.
April 24, Ezra J. Wheeler, aged 48.
May 1st, Archibald McLean, of the firm of W. D. & A. McLean, aged 32. He was a designer of patterns for shawls in the establishment of Roy & Co., West Troy. Although not a resident of Cohoes, yet through his business relations with his brother, the citizens esteemed and respected him as one of their own number and his unexpected decease cast a gloom over the entire community.
May 11, James Henthorn, aged about 45.
May 31, Henry Cahill, a prominent and influential resident of the 3d ward, aged 40.
June 17, Paul Schmidt, aged 71.
July 16, John Daley, a member of Howarth Engine Co., died from the effects of injuries received while attending a fire at the Clifton Mill.
July 31, William J. Wheeler, aged 50. Mr. Wheeler was a leading democratic politician and business man of the town of Watervliet. He served one term as member of the legislature, five years in the board of supervisors of which body he was chairman four years. In 1870-1, he was superintendent of section No. 1, Erie Canal and occupied other positions of trust and responsibility.
Aug. 9, Daniel Simpson, aged about 45. He was foreman of the Harmony Manufacturing Co's carpenter shop, a member of the board of education, of the Johnston Steamer Co., Alden Hose Co., and various masonic organizations.

August 21, Henry En Earl, aged 86. Mr. En Earl was one of the oldest residents of the city, having moved here from Troy in 1824. He took an active interest in the progress of the place, and in its early days occupied a number of responsible positions in the local government.

Sept. 23, Hezekiah Howe, aged 89. Mr. Howe, the fifth of a family of ten children, was born July 9, 1783, in Killingly, Conn., where his family had resided since 1709. His early years were passed in his native place, and there he obtained his first experience of business life. After his marriage with Miss Lydia Wilkinson, he removed to Pawtucket, R. I., and engaged in business with his brother-in-law David Wilkinson. The firm occupied a prominent position among the manufacturers of the state, and were very successful. At a later period they established a flourishing business at Wilkinsonville, Conn., but in the financial troubles of 1829 their losses were heavy, and they were compelled to discontinue. When Mr. Wilkinson, as elsewhere stated, was prevailed upon to come to Cohoes Mr. Howe decided to accompany him, although every inducement was offered him by his friends to remain in the east, and arrived here May 1, 1831. Here he continued to reside until within a few years of his death. From the history of his connection with Cohoes in its early days, as related elsewhere, it will be seen that he had a most important part in shaping the fortunes of the place, and was prominent among those who established here, in spite of drawbacks and reverses, the foundations of a large and prosperous city. Mr. Howe had contracts for the construction of the first canals of the Cohoes Co.; he was also engaged in general business here at different times and for over twenty years, was postmaster of the village. He was ever an active Christian, and was one of the founders of the first Episcopal church built in Pawtucket, and later of St. John's church of Cohoes. His firm integrity of character, and gentle kindliness of manner, endeared him to a large circle of friends, and his loss was deeply felt.

Dec. 19, in Lansingburg, N. Y., Isaac D. Ayres, one of the originators and founders of the *Cohoes Advertiser* in 1847, and the *Newark Mercury*. The latter years of his life were spent as publisher of the *Lansingburg Gazette*.

1873.

Jan. 10, Dr. J. B. Forrest, aged about 45.
Jan. 12, John O'Neil, aged 79.
Jan. 16, Benjamin M. Alexander, aged 26.
Jan. 19, Hugh Thompson, aged 69. Mr. Thompson came to Cohoes in 1846, and entered into the employ of the Ogden Mills. He afterward established a grocery store on the corner of Remsen and Factory streets, where he continued business until his death. His was the oldest establishment of the kind in the city.

March 8, Wright Mallery, aged 67. Mr. Mallery was one of the early settlers, having removed from West Troy to this place nearly forty years ago. He was widely known and respected.

March 13, N. B. Davis, aged 73.
March 15, Michael J. Collins, aged 27.
March 17, Walter Witbeck, aged 52. Mr. Witbeck came to Cohoes with Daniel Simmons in 1835. He entered the axe factory as overseer of the polishing department, and retained that position in the establishment until his death, a period of over thirty-eight years. Mr. Wit-

beck was one of our best known and most respected citizens. He was closely identified with the growth of Cohoes, and had occupied a number of positions of responsibility in local affairs.

March 22, Henry Schroeder, aged 49.
April 18, John W. Mills, aged 24.
May 12, James Hayden, aged 60.
June 7, Robert Meikleham, for a long time chief book-keeper in the establishment of D. Simmons & Co., aged 62.
June 15, James Brown, aged 39.
July 4, Charles H. Van Schaick, aged 64.
July 18, Francois X. Lauzon, aged 59.
Aug. 11, Rev. John Fitzpatrick, aged 26. " Few young men of our city have commenced life with greater promise than the subject of this notice. Possessing a high order of talent, a peculiarly amiable disposition, and having enjoyed superior educational advantages, he was prepared, at a very early age, to enter upon the active duties of his profession with a bright prospect of usefulness and distinction. He had, however, but just commenced the third year of his ministry at Pompey, Onondaga Co., N. Y., when he was stricken down by disease. His remains were brought to Cohoes for interment, and deeply impressive ceremonies were observed in St. Bernard's, which were attended by a large concourse of the clergy and our citizens."
Aug. 12, Absalom Sharp, aged about 44.
Aug. 13, John Coakley, aged 66.
Aug. 25, Edward Magee, aged 45.
Aug. 27, Bernard McClarey, aged 60.
Aug. 27, Patrick H. Ross, aged 48. Mr. Ross occupied a leading position among the musicians of the place during a long residence in Cohoes. For much of the time he was leader of a band and chorister and organist at St. Bernard's church.
Sept. 20, James McGaffin, aged 70.
Sept. 30, Mark H. Gould, aged 36. Mr. Gould had been a resident of Cohoes about four years and was well known as the manager of the manufacturing establishment of Hon. Wm. T. Horrobin.
Oct. 15, John McCusker, aged 75.
Oct. 28, John Tobin, aged 28.
Dec. 8, Thomas Barclay, printer, aged 17.
Dec. 16, Radcliffe Taylor, aged 50.
Dec. 23, Guy Blakely, aged 71. Mr. Blakely had been a resident of Cohoes since it was a hamlet. He was known as a conscientious, upright citizen and a devoted member of St. John's church, in which he served as warden for many years.

1874.

Jan. 2, in Niles, Michigan, H. S. Reinhart, aged 34.
Jan. 8, William Jones, aged 27.
Jan. 17, Charles T. Carter, aged 64. Mr. Carter, who was a twin brother of Thomas C. Carter of this city, was born in Newburyport, Mass., in 1810. In his early life he was a sailor — but about 1835, abandoned that occupation and came to Cohoes. He entered the employ of Daniel Simmons, and was connected with the axe factory until 1857, when after a short interval, during which he acted as station agent at this place of the Albany Northern RailRoad Co., he established the drug business, which he continued until his death.

APPENDIX. 289

Feb. 7, James L. N. Cranston, aged 39, was killed by the cars of the Rensselaer and Saratoga Rail Road, near Fort Edward.

Feb. 8, Alexander Richmond, aged 38.

March 8, Samuel W. Lovejoy, aged 43. Mr. Lovejoy was born in Oxford, N. H., in 1831. He graduated from Dartmouth College in 1857, and commenced the study of law in the office of Judge Peckham, of Albany. In 1860 he came to Cohoes, where he soon took a prominent position among members of the bar. He was for a number of years deputy U. S. assessor, and at the time of his death was city attorney.

March 17, William Searles, aged 65.

March 29, Elisha T. Green, aged 62. Mr. Green had resided in Cohoes twenty-three years. Most of that time he had been an overseer in the Harmony Mills. He was a man of strong integrity, and was frequently chosen to represent his ward in the village government.

May 28, Jacob J. Lansing, died in Attica, Wyoming Co., N. Y. Mr. L. was a former resident of Cohoes, and well known to many of our older inhabitants. He had been for a number of years previous to his death in the employ of the Erie Rail Road Co.

June 22, Michael Mulholland, aged 56.

June 23, Joseph Taylor, aged 89.

June 26, Louis Falardo, aged 73.

July 2, James M. Campbell, aged 17.

July 11, William Hogben.

Aug. 2, John B. Moulthrop, aged 70.

Aug. 7, John M. Dickson, aged 19.

Sept. 9, Owen McDermott, aged 55.

Sept. 10, William H. Eastwood, aged 19.

Sept. 15, James Dillon, aged 19.

Sept. 29, Edward McArdle, aged 55.

Oct. 1, Michael Lally, aged 68.

Oct. 4, Cornelius O'Keefe, aged 46.

Oct. 5, Daniel Mahar, aged 60.

Oct 14, Peter A. Brown, aged 30. Mr. Brown was a printer, having served an apprenticeship in the *Cataract* office. He entered the army during the rebellion, was taken prisoner and confined seven months in Andersonville, where he contracted the disease which resulted in his death.

Oct. 21, Thomas J. Syms, aged 41. Mr. Syms had been a resident of Cohoes for twenty years. He served in the Union army during the rebellion, was taken prisoner and for seven months confined in Andersonville, where he suffered greatly from exposure and privation.

Oct. 25, Benjamin F. Lovejoy, aged about 44.

Nov. 9, Michael Fallon, aged 88.

Nov. 12, Isaac D. F. Lansing, aged 84. Mr. Lansing was the oldest resident of Cohoes, having been born in 1790, in the brick house still standing near the Cohoes Company's dam, and resided in that locality all his life. As will be seen elsewhere, his ancestors were among the earliest settlers of Cohoes, and were the first to utilize the water power of the Mohawk, having established in 1740, the mills above the falls which remained in possession of the family until a few years ago. Living as he did, outside of the business centre of Cohoes, Mr. Lansing took no very active part in the development of the place, but he was well known in the community, and universally honored and respected.

APPENDIX.

Nov. 18, Edward Cavenaugh, aged 28.
Nov. 19, William N. Crawford, aged 50.
Nov. 27, Thomas Hemphill, aged about 32.
Dec. 2, William Harrison, aged 64.
Dec. 8, Patrick K. Murphy, aged 45.
Dec. 14, William Greason, aged about 32.
Dec. 30, John Short, aged 66.

1875.

Jan. 7, Lucius Doolittle, aged 83.
Jan. 14, Charles H. Vaughan, printer, aged 26.
Jan. 21, Joshua Bailey, aged 75, in Waterford, N. Y. Mr. Bailey was one of the pioneers of Cohoes, and from his connection with the early history of the knitting business, elsewhere spoken of, had a most important influence in the history of the place. He remained in active business until a few years since when he retired to enjoy the ample competence which was the result of his labors.
Jan. 24, Michael Keating, aged 54.
Jan. 27, Owen Garraghan, aged 55.
Feb. 1, Patrick Dennin, aged 77.
Feb. 7, Peter Foley, aged 32.
Feb. 25, John Wesley Howarth, eldest son of Henry Howarth, contractor and builder, aged 32.
March 11, Hugh Laughlin, aged 62.
March 14, Dennis Ryan, aged 49.
March 21, William R. Eagan, policeman, aged 24.
March 25, Myron C. Lansing, youngest son of Jacob I. Lansing, aged 21.
March 26, Thomas McNamara, aged 22.
March 28, James Burns, aged 36.
April 9, Charles W. Carter, son of the late Charles T. Carter, aged 25.
April 13, John Fielding, musician, aged 30.
April 15, John McCormick, aged 64.
April 15, Daniel Fitzpatrick, aged 62.
April 16, John Connors, aged 28.
April 23, Patrick McGraw, aged 60.
April 26, Matthew Bannon, aged 22.
May 5, Thomas Connors, aged 63.
May 11, John Downs, aged 27.
May 13, Thomas Mullin, aged 21.
May 12, Peter Casey, aged 74. Mr. Casey was one of the oldest residents of the place, having been a citizen for 42 years.
May 17, Martin Fitzpatrick, aged 47.
May 18, Richard Ardron, aged 59.
May 22, Daniel B. McClary, aged 29. Mr. McC. was a printer, well-known in the city. He served honorably in the late war as a member of the 12th Reg't N. Y. Cavalry.
May 27, John M. Spencer, aged about 60. For over twenty years Mr. Spencer had lived in Cohoes and on several occasions served the people as census marshal and in other positions.
May 29, George Monk, aged 39.
June 4, John Prairie, aged 55.
June 15, John Belville, aged 36.

June 21, Michael Lawler, aged 67.

June 22, in Albany, Alexander M. Gregory, aged 65. Mr. Gregory, though never residing in this city, had been engaged in the knitting business here for many years and was a prominent business man. He was one of the firm of Gregorys & Hiller.

June 23, Michael Brennan, aged 65.

July 2, Thomas B. Flannigan, aged 29.

July 5, William Parker, aged 20.

July 8, Joseph Mirault, aged 25.

July 9, Patrick Burke, aged 45.

July 10, Charles Hicks, aged 32.

July 16, In Swansea, Mass., John W. Lansing, formerly of Cohoes, aged 61.

August 2, Dennis Normile, aged 29.

August 8, Patrick Quinlan, aged 30.

August 11, William Bindewald, aged 20.

August 31, William S. Southworth, aged 68. Mr. Southworth, who came to this city from Bennington, Vt., was the son of Judge Gordon Southworth of Dorset, in that state. He commenced the study of law at the age of twenty-one and soon became one of the leading members of the profession. He was for some time engaged in manufacturing in Lowell, Mass., and came to Cohoes in 1873. Although he had resided here but a short time, he had endeared himself to all by his kindly manner and upright character.

Sept. 4, Joseph Rousseau, aged 64.

Sept. 11, Thomas A. Hall, aged about 32.

Sept. 18, James M. Hayward, aged 56. Mr. Hayward came to Cohoes in 1850, and commenced the flour and feed business, in which he was engaged until his death. He was one of our best known citizens.

Sept. 21, Peter Ryan, aged 20.

Sept. 29, Thomas Larkin, aged 19.

Oct. 1, William Evers, aged 69.

Oct. 2, Thomas Kenny, aged 75.

Oct. 5, Frank Fitzpatrick, aged 35.

Oct. 5, George Greason.

Oct. 8, James Winterbottom. Mr. Winterbottom had been in the employ of the Harmony Co., nearly 17 years. He served in the army during the rebellion.

Oct. 14, Thomas McTigue, aged 66.

Oct. 30, Robert Barton, aged 51.

Nov. 6, Thomas Page, aged 66.

Nov. 22, Patrick Kennedy, aged 42.

Nov. 27, John Copeland, aged 65. Mr. Copeland came to Cohoes in 1860, and continued the business of slate roofer until his decease. He took an active part in the organization of the Friendly Society of the Sons of Scotia and the Caledonian Club of Cohoes and was one of their most earnest supporters.

Dec.—, Peter Vandercook, Sen., aged 85. Mr. Vandercook had been a resident of Cohoes 39 years. He was born in Pittstown, Rens. Co., N. Y., and in 1836 removed to Cohoes, locating at the head of the four locks, where he lived for many years. He was a farmer and miller by occupation.

Dec. 10, James Durrant, aged 49. Mr. Durrant left home in company with his son, Nov. 29th, on a visit to California, and had nearly reached the end of his journey, when he was killed by accident. He was well and favorably known as a citizen and master builder.

Dec. 20, in Watervliet, Francis Witbeck, aged 57. For many years he was foreman in the finishing department of D. Simmons & Co's axe factory, and was prominent as an active, public-spirited citizen. He was frequently chosen to serve the people in public positions.

Dec. 27, John Owens, aged 49.
Dec. 29, Patrick Reeves, aged 67.

1876.

Jan. 9, Richard Clark, aged 78.
Jan. 17, Joseph Derocher, Sen., aged 75.
Jan. 21, John Bulson, aged 44.
Feb. 3, Charles Lanagan, aged 75.
Feb. 6, John Pierson, aged 56.
Feb. 12, Gabriel Cropsey, aged 70. For many years Mr. Cropsey was one of the leading manufacturers of flour in the place, having been connected with that interest in Cohoes, and in the immediate neighborhood, ever since it assumed any importance as a branch of our local industries. He died in Hibernia, Dutchess Co., N. Y.

Feb. 20, William Fogarty, aged 39.
Feb. 22, Dennis F. Quillinan, aged 20.
Feb. 29, George H. Gregory, aged 28.
March 6, Patrick Holloran, aged 65.
March 22, Edward Connaughty, aged 22.
March 26, Joseph Langlois, aged 23.
March 29, William Hobart, aged 70.
March 30, Joseph De Graff, aged 60.
March 31, William Ferguson, aged 23.
April 6, Joseph Archambault, aged 40.
April 13, John Davis, aged 77. Mr. Davis had been a resident of Cohoes twenty-nine years, and was for a long period superintendent of the Cohoes cemetery.

April 21, Edward Ryan, aged 58.
April 22, Michael Walsh, father of the Rev. John Walsh, pastor of St. John's church at Albany.

April 25, Robert Whittle, aged 70. Mr. Whittle had resided in Cohoes twenty-five years, and although not prominently connected with business interests, was one of the best known citizens of the place.

April 26, William Fleming, aged 76. Mr. Fleming was born in Tipperary, Ireland, emigrated to this country forty years ago, and had been a resident of Cohoes for the past thirty-five years.

May 3, Michael Daly, aged 48.
May 10, William Enos, aged 40.
May 13, William Murphy, aged 34.
May 22, John Lally, aged 21.
May 27, Asahel Carpenter, aged 69. Mr. Carpenter had been a resident of Cohoes thirty-four years, and most of the time was employed in the Simmons axe factory.

May 27, Peter F. Daw, aged 67. Mr. Daw had been a resident of Cohoes nearly thirty years, and had held a number of public positions, among them the offices of justice of the peace, associate justice and post-master. During the last fifteen years of his life he was deputy U. S. marshal of this district.

Appendix.

June 1st, Patrick Keoughan, aged 45.
June 3, Timothy O'Brien, aged 27.
June 8, Patrick McCormick, aged 78.
June 27, Dr. William Boudrias, aged 25. Mr. Boudrias was a young man of fine ability, and though but fairly entered upon the practice of his profession, had taken rank among the foremost dentists of Philadelphia, where he had made his residence. He was the eldest son of Dr. Louis Boudrias of this city.
June 30, Aaron Radcliffe, aged 55.
July 1, John Wesley Frink, aged 50. Mr. Frink, who had been a member of the firm of Alden, Frink & Weston, was for many years one of the most prominent and influential business men of Cohoes. Besides being largely interested in manufacturing, while in active business, he at different times occupied important positions in our local government.
July 10, Thomas Carter, son of Thomas C. Carter, aged 38.
July 18, Thomas Collier, aged 68.
August 13, Arthur Monahon, aged 70.
August 16, Thomas F. Kelly, printer, aged 25.
August 27, Henry J. Vanderwerken, aged 69. He had lived in Cohoes the greater part of his life and as an old resident, was widely known.
Sept. 12, Justus Eastwood, aged about 45.
Sept. 20, John Englestoff, aged 32.
Sept. 21, Patrick Ryan, aged 50.
Sept. 29, William Ryan, aged 60.
Oct. 1, James Mokler, aged 42.
Oct. 8, Alexis Girard, aged 20.
Oct. 13, John Farrell, aged 55.
Oct. 22, William Schofield, aged about 26.
Oct. 25, Michael McGrail, aged 67.
Oct. 26, John Monogue, aged 63.
Nov. 2, James Gill, aged 30.
Nov. 5, Thomas Stanton, aged 85.
Nov. 8, Kossuth Parker, aged 24.
Nov. 9, Isaac Jones, aged 21.
Nov. 17, William Leckie, aged 57. Mr. Leckie was born in Paisley, Scotland, April 20th, 1819, and removed to this country at the age of 9. He located at Williamstown, Mass., and was educated at the Lennox Academy. He had been a resident of Cohoes thirty-five years; was overseer in the Ogden Mill several years and for a short time was principal in what was known as the Depot School of the 2d ward. He subsequently became connected with a firm that operated the Halcyon Mill and was superintendent of that establishment when it passed into the hands of Messrs. Kerr & Knowlson, of Troy. His last business engagement was in the position of superintendent of the Clifton Knitting Mill where he remained six years, closing in 1868. He was trustee of the Cohoes Savings Institution and had been called upon to fill various responsible positions.
Nov. 17, Thomas McDonough, aged 53.
Nov. 18, Dr. Thomas C. Howes, aged 53. Dr. Howes removed from Troy to Cohoes in 1872, and during his residence here was proprietor of the drug store corner of Remsen and White streets. He was an influential member of St. John's Episcopal church.
Nov. 27, William Williams, aged about 70. He was one of the

oldest residents of the first ward and an employé of the Harmony Mills from their establishment.

Nov. 30, Killian F. Winnie, aged 72.
Dec. 4, Timothy Atridge, aged 65.
Dec. 4, Alexander Giard, aged 30.
Dec. 4, Moses Duquette, aged 29.
Dec. 11, William Bowler, aged 25.
Dec. 15, James Hayden, aged 27.

APPENDIX.

Officers of the Village and City of Cohoes.
1848-1876.

Village Officers.

THE following were elected by ballot, except the president, who was chosen by the trustees from their number until 1856.

1848.

President.— Joshua R. Clarke.
Trustees.— Alfred Phelps, Joshua R. Clarke, Geo. Abbott, Henry D. Fuller, Wm. Burton.
Assessors.— Henry En Earl, John P. Steenberg, Wm. H. Hollister.
Treasurer.— Charles A. Olmsted.
Collector.— Jno. B. Harrison.
Clerk.— John Van Santvoord.
Poundmaster.— Isaac F. Fletcher.
Fire Wardens.[1]— Jacob Upham, Henry Van Auken, John McGill, Wm. Osterhout, Abram Ostrom.

1849.

President.—Henry D. Fuller.
Trustees.— Joshua R. Clarke, Miles White, Alfred Phelps, Wm. Burton, Henry D. Fuller.
Assessors.— Wm. Dickey, Bradley Alexander, Matthew Fitzpatrick,
Treasurer.— Wm. H. Hollister.
Collector.— Lawrence S. Fonda.
Clerk.—John Van Santvoord.
Poundmaster.— Isaac F. Fletcher.
Fire Wardens.— Wm. Osterhout, Henry Van Auken, John McGill. Wm. Orelup, Jr.

1850.

President.— Henry D. Fuller.
Trustees.— Henry En Earl, Sr., Henry D. Fuller, Wm. H. Hollister, Wm. G. Caw, Joshua R. Clarke.
Assessors.— Wm. Orelup, Jr., Ralph Buss, Abram Ostrom.
Treasurer.— Franklin Waring.
Collector.— John B. Harrison.
Clerk.— John Van Santvoord.
Fire Wardens.— Lucien Fitts, Henry Van Auken, Wm. K. Lighthall, John Orelup.

1851.

President.— Wm. F. Carter.
Trustees.— Wm. F. Carter, Truman G. Younglove, Joseph A. Simons, John Hay Jr., Wm. H. Hollister.
Assessors.— Wm. Dickey, Alex. Frink, Miles White.
Treasurer.— Henry L. Landon.
Collector.— John B. Harrison.
Clerk.— Abram H. Van Arnam.

---

[1] Elected Sept. 27.

Fire Wardens.— Wm. Osterhout, John Doyle, Geo. N. Ferguson, Elihu M. Stevenson.
Poundmaster.— Wm. Welch.
School Trustees.— No. 13, S. H. Foster, Jacob Travis; No. 5, Wm. Burton, Geo. W. Miller; No. 19, Abram Lansing, Wm. Binns.
Police Justice.— Alfred Phelps.

1852.

President.— Wm. F. Carter.
Trustees.— Wm. F. Carter, John McGill, Egbert Egberts, Lucien Fitts, Jacob I. Lansing.
Assessors.— Wm. Orelup Sr., Jeremiah Clute, Edw'd W. Fuller.
Treasurer.— Henry L. Landon.
Collector.— Nathan L. Benson.
Clerk.— Benjamin Hutchins.
Fire Wardens.— Jno. Eastwood, Elihu M. Stevenson, Stephen Dietz, Geo. Howarth.
Poundmaster.— Samuel Stiles.
School Trustees.— No. 13, Ralph Buss; No. 5, T. C. Carter, Jos. M. Brown; No. 19, Darius Parkhurst, Robert Johnston.

1853.

President.— N. W. En Earl.
Trustees.— Nicholas W. En Earl, Isaac F. Fletcher, Edward O'Reilly, Geo. Lawrence, Henry L. Landon.
Assessors.— Michael Donovan, Jno. P. Steenberg, Walter Witbeck.
Treasurer.— Malachi Weidman.
Collector.— Edward Murray.
Clerk.— Geo. H. Wager.
Fire Wardens.— Peter Powers, John Larkin, Peter Smith, Alex. M'Wha.
Poundmaster.—
School Trustees.— No. 13, John Sullivan; No. 5, John Van Ness; No. 19, Peter Van Der Cook, Sr.

1854.

President.— Wm. F. Carter.
Trustees.— Ralph Buss, C. H. Adams, Wm. Burton, John Henderson, Wm. F. Carter.
Assessors.— Alexander Frink, Wm. Orelup Sr., Stephen Dodge.
Treasurer.— Edward W. Fuller.
Collector—. Ira Kilmer.
Clerk.— Norton T. Raynsford.
Fire Wardens.— Henry Van Auken, Wm. Dutemple, Andrew J. Ballard, E. G. Mussey.
Poundmaster.— Moses House.
School Trustees.— No. 13, Jacob Travis; No. 5, Jenks Brown; No. 19, Elisha T. Green.

1855.

President.— Wm. N. Chadwick.
Trustees.— Henry S. Bogue, Wm. N. Chadwick, Malachi Weidman, Francis Henderson, Wm. Ferrell.
Assessors.— Orson Parkhurst, Geo. Lawrence, Wm. K. Lighthall.
Treasurer.— Edward W. Fuller.
Collector.— Stevens V. Trull.

Clerk.— Wm. Shannon.
Police Justice.— Alex Frink.
Fire Wardens.— H. Van Auken, Wm. Dutemple, Lorenzo Worden, John Welton.
Poundmaster.— Jas. Delve.
School Trustees.— No. 13, Leonard Cary, Matthew Fitzpatrick; No. 5, Leonard Van Derkar, Geo. H. Wager; No. 19, Elbridge Damon.

1856.

President.— Henry L. Landon.
Trustees.— 1st *Ward:* Wm. Orelup, Jr., 2 years; Elisha T. Green, 1 year; 2d *Ward:* John W. Frink, 2 years; Francis Pennock, 1 year; 3d *Ward:* Walter Witbeck, 2 years; Isaac F. Fletcher, 1 year.
Chairman Board of Education.— Truman G. Younglove.
School Commissioners.— 1st *Ward:* Samuel H. Foster, 2 years; David Aiken, 1 year; 2d *Ward:* G. H. Vermilyea, 2 years; Jonathan Hiller, 1 year; 3d *Ward:* John R. Bullock, 2 years; Jno. P. Steenberg, 1 year.
Assessors.— Jonas Simmons, Alex. Frink, Sheffield Hayward.
Treasurer.— Isaac Quackenbush.
Collector.— Henry Lyons.
Sealer of Weights and Measures.— Wm. Beeman.
Poundmaster.— Jno. Westover.

1857.

Trustees.— 1st *Ward:* Jas. F. Crawford. 2d *Ward:* Isaac Van Natten. 3d *Ward:* G. H. Wager.
Treasurer.— Henry S. Bogue.
Collector.— John Van Ness.
Assessor.— Geo. Lawrence.
School Commissioners.— 1st *Ward:* Wm. C. Carroll. 2d *Ward:* John Little. 3d *Ward:* Henry Lyons.
Sealer of Weights and Measures.— Francis Keating.

1858.

President.— Henry L. Landon.
Trustees.— 1st *Ward:* D. J. Johnston. 2d *Ward:* S. D. Fairbank. 3d *Ward:* Joseph Chadwick.
Assessor.— Joshua R. Clarke.
Treasurer.— Francis Henderson.
Collector.— Malachi Ball.
Chairman Board of Education.— Truman G. Younglove.
School Commissioners.— 1st *Ward:* Rob't Rogerson. 2d *Ward:* Jenks Brown. 3d *Ward:* John Van Der Mark.
Sealer of Weights and Measures.— Wm. Beeman.

1859.

Trustees.— 1st *Ward:* Geo. Lawrence. 2d *Ward:* Wm. G. Caw. 3d *Ward:* John Fulton.
Assessor.— Almon C. Bryant.
Treasurer.— Francis Henderson.
Collector.— Malachi Ball.
School Commissioners.— 1st *Ward:* G. H. Vermilyea. 2d *Ward:* J. V. S. Lansing. 3d *Ward:* Geo. Jackson.
Police Justice.— Peter D. Niver.
Sealer of Weights and Measures.— Wm. Beeman.

1860.

President.— Sidney Alden.
Trustees.— 1st ward: D. Fitzpatrick. 2d ward: P. Smith. 3d ward: Walter Witbeck.
Assessors.— Jonas Simmons, Robert Whittle.
Treasurer.— Egbert J. Wilkins.
Collector.— Jas. Waters.
Chairman Board of Education.— Geo. H. Wager.
School Commissioners.— 1st ward: A. T. Calkins. 2d ward: John Van Ness. 3d ward: Jas. H. Masten.
Sealer of Weights and Measures.— Edward McCarthy.

1861.

Trustees.— 1st ward: Cornelius Houlihan. 2d ward: Wright Mallery. 3d ward: S. Stiles.
Assessors.— Abram Van Der Werken, Wm. H. Hollister.
Treasurer.— John Lyons.
Collector.— Nathan L. Benson.
School Commissioners.— 1st ward: Wm. Orelup, Jr. 2d ward: Jno. V. S. Lansing; 3d ward: N. W. En Earl.
Sealer of Weights and Measures.— Daniel B. McIntosh.
Poundmaster.— George Cummings.

1862.

President.— Wm. F. Carter.
Trustees.— 1st ward: John Land. 2d ward: C. H. Adams. 3d ward: Benj. F. Clarke.
Assessor.— Jno. P. Steenberg.
Treasurer.— Jno. W. Frink.
Collector.— Edward Welch.
Chairman Board of Education.— James H. Masten.
School Commissioners.— 1st ward: Geo. Dixon. 2d ward: David J. Johnston. 3d ward: Halsey R. Grant.
Sealer of Weights and Measures.— D. B. M'Intosh.
Poundmaster.— Joseph Simpson.

1863.

Trustees.— 1st ward: Geo. Lawrence. 2d ward: Alfred Rider 3d Ward: H. Brockway.
Assessor.— Daniel Simpson.
Treasurer.— Walter Witbeck.
Collector.— Thomas Keefe.
Police Justice.— Harvey Clute.
School Commissioners.— 1st ward: Wm. S. Smith. 2d ward: Gilbert H. Vermilyea. 3d ward: John Van Ness.
Police Constables.— Wm. Stanton, Peter Manton, M. Bowler.
Street Superintendent.— Jas. Hay.
Sealer of Weights and Measures.— Patrick Sheridan.

1864.

President.— Geo. H. Wager.
Trustees.— 1st ward: John Fulton. 2d ward: T. R. Howard. 3d ward: Sherebiah Stiles.
Assessor.— John Brady.

Treasurer.— Walter Witbeck.
Collector.— Michael Keeden.
Chairman Board of Education.— Samuel H. Foster.
School Commissioners.— 1*st ward:* Reuben S. Calkins. 2*d ward:* Spencer Frink. 3*d ward:* Halsey R. Grant.
Constables.— Wm. Stanton, Peter Manton, Patrick H. Kelly.
Street Superintendent.— Michael Long.
Sealer of Weights and Measures.— Thos. Nagle.
Poundmaster.— Jno. Cavanaugh.

1865.

Trustees.— 1*st ward:* S. G. Root. 2*d ward:* Wm. H. Stevenson. T. P. Hildreth (to fill vacancy). 3*d ward:* Henry Brockway.
Assessors.— John Baker, Jno. McMullen.
Treasurer.— John W. Frink.
Collector.— Thomas Gaffney.
School Commissioners.— 1*st ward:* Wm. S. Smith. 2*d ward:* J. W. Moore. 3*d ward:* Norris North.
Constables.— Jas. Clark, Peter Manton, Chas. Muldowney.
Street Sup't.— Wm. Smead.
Sealer of Weights and Measures.— Richard Clark.
Poundmaster.— Nicholas D. Lounsberry.

1866.

President.— Murray Hubbard.
Trustees.— 1*st ward:* Lewis W. Land. 2*d ward:* Daniel McIntosh. 3*d ward:* Daniel Wilder.
Assessor.— Geo. Lawrence.
Treasurer.— John Wakeman.
Collector.— Robert Frost.
Chairman Board of Education.— Samuel H. Foster.
School Commissioners.— 1*st ward:* D. J. Johnston. 2*d ward:* R. S. Calkins. 3*d ward:* H. R. Grant.
Constables.— Pat'k Thornton, Garret Robbins, Chas. Muldowney.
Street Sup't.— John Foley.
Sealer of Weights and Measures.— Martin Garrigan.
Poundmaster.— John Rossiter.

1867.

Trustees.— 1*st ward:* John F. Simpson. 2*d ward:* Alfred LeRoy. 3*d ward:* Jas. Lamb.
Assessor.— Sheffield Hayward.
Treasurer.— Gilbert H. Vermilyea.
Collector.— Edward Brennan.
Police Justice.— Harvey Clute.
School Commissioners.— 1*st ward:* Jno. S. Crane. 2*d ward:* M. S. Younglove. 3*d ward:* Jno. M. Spencer.
Street Sup't.— John Drysdale.
Constables.— Robert Frost, John McCullick, Moses House.
Sealer of Weights and Measures.— Patrick McGrath.
Poundmaster.— John Rossiter.

1868.

President.— Augustus Ellmaker.
Trustees.— 1*st ward:* Wm. Stanton. 2*d ward:* Wm. Warner. 3*d ward:* Edwin Hitchcock.

APPENDIX.

Assessor.— Guy Blakeley.
Treasurer.— Geo. H. Wager.
Collector.— Geo. Van Der Cook.
Chairman Board of Education.— Samuel H. Foster.
School Commissioners.— 1st *ward:* Daniel Simpson. 2d *ward:* Chas. Rogers. 3d *ward:* Harvey Ferris.
Constables.— John O'Brien, John Long, Henry Morrison.
Street Sup't.— Andrew Cox.
Sealer of Weights and Measures.— Patrick McGrath.
Poundmaster.— John Rossiter.

1869.

Trustees.— 1st *ward:* John S. Crane. 2d *ward:* Wm. S. Smith. 3d *ward:* Jas. B. McKee.
Assessor.— Anthony Russell.
Treasurer.— Geo. H. Wager.
Collector.— Thomas Nolan.
School Commissioners.— 1st *ward:* Jas. E. Place. 2d *ward:* T. P. Hildreth. 3d *ward:* Wm. C. Travis.
Constables.— Jas. O'Brien, Peter McAvinia, Michael Bowler.
Street Sup't.— Peter Powers.
Sealer of Weights and Measures.— Patrick McGrath.

During the years when the street superintendent, village clerk and police constables were appointed by the trustees, those officers were as follows:

Street Superintendents.

1849, Frederick W. Upham.
1850, Elbridge G. Mussey.
1851, Lewis Wells.
1852, Adam Van Der Werken.
1853, Daniel Nugent.
1854, Adam Van Der Werken.
1855, Chas. T. Carter.
1856, 1857, Samuel Steenberg.
1858, Leonard Van Der Kar.
1859, R. G. Smith.
1860, John Doyle.
1861, Francis Keating.
1862, Jas. Hay.

Clerks.

1856, D. S. Ostrom.
1857, '58, '59, P. B. Ferguson.
1860, Michael Monahon.
1861, Wm. Shannon.
1862, '63, Wm. H. Stevenson.
1864–1870, Malachi Ball.[1]

Police Constables.

1849, Alexander Frink.
1850, 51, John M. Brownson.
1852, Joseph M. Brown.
1853, Justus Eastwood.
1854, Abner Deyo.
1855, Frederick S. Uhl.
1856,'57,'58, Peter Van Der Cook, Jr.
1859, '60, Hugh O'Hare.
1861, Michael Long, Hugh O'Hare, Wm. Stanton, Richard Hurst.
1862, Jas. T. Hemphill, Peter F. Daw, Daniel E. M'Intosh.

Chief Engineer of Fire Department.
1852–1876.

1852, Joshua R. Clarke.
1853, Wm. Osterhout.
1854, Henry D. Fuller.
1855, Wm. Burton (resigned).
1856, Joseph Gould, Jr.
1857, John Eastwood.
1858, Herbert Hastings.
1859, Thos. V. Brown.

---

[1] Mr. Ball held the position of city clerk till June, 1871.

APPENDIX.   301

1860, Malachi Ball.
1861, '62, H. B. Silliman.
1863, Timothy Atridge, Jr.
1864, '65, Peter Manton.
1866, Daniel M'Intosh.
1867, Joseph C. Dodge.
1868, '69, Michael Redmond.

1870, '71, Jas. Coleman.
1872, Miller Hay.
1873, Richard Powers.
1874, Miller Hay.
1875, James Cavenagh.
1876, Martin Redmond.

Water Commissioners.
1856–1876.
1856.

Chas. H. Adams. } 6 years.
Truman G. Younglove. }

Alfred Wild. } 2 years.
Wm. F. Carter. }

Joshua Bailey. } 4 years.
Henry D. Fuller. }

1858.

Jas. F. Crawford.

John W. Frink.

1860.

Wm. Burton.

Henry D. Fuller.

1862.

Sherebiah Stiles.

Daniel M'Elwain.

1864.

Wm. G. Caw.[1]
A. M. Harmon (to fill vacancy).

John Land.

1866.

James H. Masten.[2]

Cornelius Houlihan.

1868.

Wm. E. Thorn.

Jas. Lamb.

1870.

John Clute.
Henry Brockway.

A. M. Harmon (to fill vacancy).

1873.

Jacob Travis.

CITY OFFICERS.
(Elected.)
1870.

Mayor.— Chas. H. Adams.
Justice of the Peace.— Joseph Le Boeuf.
Poormaster.— Jno. H. Ring.
Assessors.— T. Moore, 3 years. J. O'Neil, 2 years. O. Garrahan, 1 year.
Supervisors.— 1*st ward:* Joseph Coleman. 2*d ward:* Wm. T. Dodge. 3*d ward:* John Scully. 4*th ward:* Solomon Dotter.
Aldermen.— 1*st ward:* D. J. Johnston, 2 years. E. W. Lansing, 1 year. 2*d ward:* Geo. Campbell, 2 years. M. S. Younglove, 1 year. 3*d ward:* B. Mulcahy, 2 years. Walter Witbeck, 1 year. 4*th ward:* C. F. North, 2 years. C. Hay, 1 year.
School Commissioners.— 1*st ward:* Frank C. Reavy, 2 years. Daniel Simpson, 1 year. 2*d ward:* Wm. Burton, 2 years. E. N.

---

[1] Died.

[2] Resigned.

Page, 1 year. 3d *ward:* A. M. Harmon, 2 years. J. Hiller, 1 year. 4th *ward:* W. C. Travis, 2 years. W. S. Crane, 1 year.

Constables.— 1st *ward:* Chas. Wilcox. 2d *ward:* J. M'Culloch. 3d *ward:* M. M'Guire. 4th *ward:* Robt. P. Jones.

Inspectors of Election.— 1st *ward:* Matthew Keough, Richard Nagle. 2d *ward:* Rodney Wilcox, S. W. Lovejoy. 3d *ward:* Jno. Fitzpatrick, Jno. B. Latta. 4th *ward:* J. Brown, P. Nagle.

Police Commissioners.— (Elected Nov. 8.) Geo. Z. Dockstader, Wm. Bamerick.

(By appointment.)

Excise Commissioners.— Henry D. Fuller, Edwin Hitchcock, Geo. H. Wager.

Street Superintendent.— Norris North.
Supt. of Cemetery.— Daniel Manning.
Chamberlain.— Leonard Cary.
City Physician.— C. E. Witbeck.
Trustee of Sinking Fund of Water Loan.— H. B. Silliman.
Poundmaster.— Alexander Brown.
Sealer of Weights and Measures.— Chas. Egan.
Fire Wardens.— Wm. Clough, Wm. Doty, E. S. Gregory, Richard Shannon.

1871.
(Elected.)

Recorder.— James F. Kelly.
Overseer of Poor.— John H. Ring.
Assessor.— Roger M'Garry.
Supervisors.— 1st *ward:* Joseph Coleman. 2d *ward:* Wm. T. Dodge. 3d *ward:* John Scully. 4th *ward:* Solomon Dotter.
Aldermen.— 1st *ward:* Cornelius Horan. 2d *ward:* David Morris. 3d *ward:* Jas. B. M'Kee. 4th *ward:* Alfred Le Roy.
School Commissioners.— 1st *ward:* Daniel F. Simpson. 2d *ward:* Edward N. Page. 3d *ward:* Geo. Ducharme, 2 years. Edward Keeler, 1 year. 4th *ward:* Wm. Benedict.
Constables.— 1st *ward:* Terrence Reeves. 2d *ward:* John M'Culloch. 3d *ward:* Michael M'Guire. 4th *ward:* Robt. P. Jones.
Inspectors of Election.— 1st *ward:* Wm. Stanton, F. C. Reavy, Absalom Sharp. 2d *ward:* S. W. Lovejoy, A. K. Dixon, Martin Brennan. 3d *ward:* Thos. Slavin, T. A. Murphey, Thos. Gleason. 4th *ward:* Wm. C. Travis, Jno. P. Webber, Francis Keegan.

(By appointment.)

Excise Commissioner.— Wm. Whitehill (to fill vacancy).
Street Superintendent.— Norris North.
Supt. of Cemetery.— Amos T. Calkins.
Health Officer.— Chas. E. Witbeck.
Poundmaster.— Thos. Larkins.
Sealer of Weights and Measures.— Abraham N. Poole.
City Clerk.— I. W. Lansing.

1872.
(Elected.)

Mayor.— David J. Johnston.
Assessor.— Alexander Frink.
Police Commissioner.— Amos. T. Calkins.
Supervisors.— 1st *ward:* Michael Sherlock. 2d *ward:* Wm. T. Dodge. 3d *ward:* Jas. M'Guirk. 4th *ward:* Wm. Nelligan.

Aldermen.— 1st *ward:* John W. Howarth. 2d *ward:* Geo. Campbell. 3d *ward:* John E. Land. 4th *ward:* Wm. C. Travis.

School Commissioners.— 1st *ward:* Frank C. Reavy. 2d *ward:* Geo. T. Carter. 3d *ward:* Sherebiah Stiles, 2 years. Wm. S. Gilbert, 1 year. 4th *ward:* Edward S. Carpenter.

Constables.— 1st *ward:* James Burns. 2d *ward:* Chas. Egan. 3d *ward:* Michael M'Guire. 4th *ward:* Robert P. Jones.

Inspectors of Election.— 1st *ward:* Michael Cummins. Patk. English, Thos. Smith. 2d *ward:* A. K. Dixon, J. H. Egan, P. H. Ross. 3d *ward:* Thomas Slavin, John Quinan. 4th *ward:* Chas. S. Travis, Jas. H. Masten, Michael Travis.

(By appointment.)

Street Superintendent.— Benj. Coveny.
Supt. of Cemetery.— John Van Deusen.
Chamberlain.— Leonard Cary.
Health Officer.— Chas. E. Witbeck.
Sealer of Weights and Measures.— John Moulthrop.
Fire Wardens.— Absalom Sharp, Alexander Arthur, John Horrocks, Timothy Atridge, Jr.
City Clerk.— John H. Egan.
City Attorney.— S. W. Lovejoy.
City Engineer.— John W. Ford.
Overseer of Poor.— Thos. Newby.

1873.

(Elected.)

Assessor.— Edward Heffern.
Supervisors.— 1st *ward:* Silas Owen. 2d *ward:* Geo. E. Simmons. 3d *ward:* Jas. M'Guirk. 4th *ward:* C. Van Der Cook.

Aldermen.— 1st *ward:* Michael Noonan. 2d *ward:* David Morris. 3d *ward:* Thos. Nolan. 4th *ward:* Alfred Le Roy.

School Commissioners.— 1st *ward:* Jas. D. Featherstonhaugh. 2d *ward:* James A. Stimson. 3d *ward:* Jonathan Hiller. 4th *ward:* Wm. R. Benedict.

Constables.— 1st *ward:* John Coleman. 2d *ward:* Alfred Brault. 3d *ward:* John H. Condley. 4th *ward:* Robt. P. Jones.

Inspectors of Election.— 1st *ward:* Michael Cummins, Edward Barret, D. Munro. 2d *ward:* A. K. Dixon, W. F. Jones, P. H. Ross. 3d *ward:* Michael Sheehan, John Scully, T. A. Murphey. 4th *ward:* Jas. H. Masten, P. E. Marshall, P. D. Niver.

(By appointment.)

Excise Commissioners.— Joshua R. Clarke, Henry D. Fuller, Geo. Higgins.
Street Superintendent.— James Hay.
Supt. of Cemetery.— Dennis Daley.
Health Officer.— Geo. H. Billings.
Sealer of Weights and Measures.— John Moulthrop.
Poundmaster.— Abram H. Fonda.
Fire Wardens.— Henry Humphreys, Nelson White, Alex. Brown, Frank Fonda.
City Clerk.— John H. Egan
City Attorney.— S. W. Lovejoy.
City Engineer.— John W. Ford.
Overseer of Poor.— Thos. Newby.

1874.
(Elected.)

Mayor.— Henry S. Bogue.
Police Commissioner.— John Slavin.
Justices of the Peace.— Michael Redmond, Jas. B. Sweeney.
Assessor.— John Quirk.
Supervisors.— 1st ward: Thos. O'Dea. 2d ward: Geo. E. Simmons. 3d ward: Jas. M'Guirk. 4th ward: Maurice Fitzgerald.
Aldermen.— 1st ward: Wm. Stanton. 2d ward: Jno. V. S. Lansing. 3d ward: John Scott. 4th ward: Philip E. Marshall.
School Commissioners.— 1st ward: Michael M'Garrahan. 2d ward: Geo. H. Graves. 3d ward: Jas. B. M'Kee. 4th ward: John S. Crane.
Constables.— 1st ward: John Coleman. 2d ward: Henry Shepard. 3d ward: John H. Condley. 4th ward: Michael J. Burke.
Inspectors of Election.— 1st ward: Michael Meagher, Amos Crapo, Edwin Clough. 2d ward: W. F. Jones, D. M. Adams, Abram Van Der Werken. 3d ward: Jas. Hayden, Bernard Acheson, Myron Van Benthuysen. 4th ward: Thos. H. Kelly, Edgar H. Stiles, Jas. H. Masten.

(By appointment.)

Chamberlain.— Chas. F. North.
Sealer of Weights and Measures.— Bernard Ryan.
City Attorney.— Peter D. Niver.
City Engineer.— John W. Ford.
Overseer of Poor.— Michael Breen.

1875.
(Elected.)

Assessor.— James Rabbit.
Supervisors.— 1st ward: Thomas O'Dea. 2d ward: Frank Brown, Jr. 3d ward: Thomas Golden. 4th ward: Solomon Dotter.
Aldermen.— 1st ward: Silas Owen. 2d ward: Nathan Shaver. 3d ward: Thomas Nolan. 4th ward: Thomas Ryan.
School Commissioners.— 1st ward: Jas. Doherty. 2d ward: Geo. T. Carter. 3d ward: Matthew Fitzpatrick. 4th ward: Malachi Ball.
Constables.— 1st ward: Patrick Hanly. 2d ward: John Hay. 3d ward: John H. Condley. 4th ward: Edward Kenney.
Inspectors of Election.— 1st ward: Edward J. M'Alear, M. Meagher, Jno. H. Graves. 2d ward: Jas. Van Benthuysen, A. K. Dixon, Hugh Cahill. 3d ward: Thos. Scott, Michael Sheehan, Chas. D. Gilman. 4th ward: Geo. Whitney, Francis Keegan, Wesley Miller.

(By appointment.)

Excise Commissioner.— Daniel M'Intosh (to fill vacancy).
Fire Warden.— Henry C. Hibbard (to fill vacancy).

1876.
(Elected.)

Mayor.— David J. Johnston.
Police Commissioner.— Edwin Hitchcock.
Assessor.— Timothy Moore.
Supervisors.— 1st ward: Thos. Murphy. 2d ward: Frank Brown, Jr. 3d ward: Thos. Golden. 4th ward: Joseph Stewart. 5th ward: Geo. E. Simmons.
Aldermen.— 1st ward: Eugene Conway. 2d ward: Jno. V. S. Lansing. 3d ward: Daniel E. M'Intosh. 4th ward: Philip E. Mar-

shall. *5th ward:* Daniel M'Elwain, 1 year, Michael English, 2 years.

School Commissioners.— *1st ward:* Patrick J. M'Kee. *2d ward:* Theodore W. Pease. *3d ward:* Edward Monk. *4th ward:* Geo. Van Der Cook. *5th ward:* Peter Murray, 1 year, Geo. C. Daley, 2 years.

Constables.— *1st ward:* John Coleman. *2d ward:* Lees Wrigley. *3d ward:* John Crowley. *4th ward:* Henry R. Dickey. *5th ward:* John Doran.

Inspectors of Election.— *1st ward:* Jas. Deecher, Edward Ward, Frank Simpson. *2d ward:* Burton W. Crandall, John McEwan, R. J. Powers. *3d ward:* Thomas Scott, Louis G. LeBoeuf, Charles D. Gilman. *4th ward:* Wm. C. Demarest, Wesley Miller, Bernard Linnen. *5th ward:* Edmund Barret, John Kennedy, John Cooley.

(By appointment.)

Excise Commissioners.— Wm. Whitehill, Chas. S. Longley, John Carter.

Street Superintendent.— James Hay.
Health Officer.— Geo. H. Billings.
Poundmaster.— Abram H. Fonda.
Sealer of Weights and Measures.— Bernard Ryan.
Fire Wardens.— Harry Hibbard, Nelson White, Alex. Brown, Frank Fonda.
City Clerk.— John H. Egan.
City Attorney.— Peter D. Niver.
City Engineer.— John W. Ford.
Overseer of Poor.— Michael Breen.

MEMBERS OF THE LEGISLATURE FROM COHOES.

Assembly.

1858, Charles H. Adams.
1866, James F. Crawford.
1872, Charles H. Adams.

1869, '70, John Tighe.
1875, Alfred Le Roy.

Senate.

MEMBER OF CONGRESS.

1873, Charles H. Adams.

INDEX.

Abbey, Chas. E., 160.
Abbey, Wm , 161.
Abbott, Geo. I., 88, 91, 260, 274, 295.
Abel, James, 270.
Aberhart, John, 161.
Ablett, James W., 160.
Ablett, Wm. H., 160.
Acheson, Bernard, 304.
Acheson, James, 159.
Acheson, John, 161.
Acheson, Wm., 136, 155, 217, 225, 262.
Ackley, Oscar L., 161, 276.
Adams, A. W., 250.
Adams, C. H., 78, 110, 115, 119, 129, 130, 134, 136, 140, 148, 159, 175, 178, 193, 194, 201, 208, 249, 271, 296, 298, 301, 305.
Adams, Cortland, 161.
Adams's Block, built, 199.
Adams's Mill, 132, 175, 244.
Adams, Daniel M., 160, 263, 304.
Adams, Geo. M., 160.
Adams, Henry, 271.
Adams, James, 38.
Adams, Rev. James, 252.
Adams Steamer Co., 194, 259.
Adams Steamer, 229; horses for, 215.
Adams, Stephen H., 110.
Adams, Wm. L., 23, 29, 234.
Adams' Zouaves, 232, 262.
Adams's Island. See *Van Schaick's Island.*
Agan, John, 161.
Aiken, David, 297.
Aiken, W. H., 261.
Aitkin, James, 260, 263.
Alaska Knitting Co., 198.
Albany Pin Co., 127, 142.
Albany water supply, 129.
Alcombrack family, 45.
Alcombrack, Jacob, 161.
Alden & Frink, 153.
Alden, Frink & Bingham, 131, 132, 134, 174.
Alden, Frink & Weston, 175, 176, 190, 191.
Albion, James, 160.
Alden, Sidney, 85, 131, 132, 141, 148, 298.
Alden Hose Co., 259.
Alexander, Andrew, 88.
Alexander, Benj. M., 287.
Alexander, Bradley, 295.
Allen, Campbell, 113.
Allen, Lester, 116.
Allen, Rev. Mr., 253.
Almy, Joseph, Jr., 141, 286.
Alston, William, 160.

American Hosiery Mill. See *Smith, Gregory & Co., Gregory & Hiller.*
Andrae, Michael, 161, 263.
Andrews, Captain, 54, 58.
Anthony, Israel, 40, 54.
Anthony, Jacob, 69.
Archer, G. R., 137.
Ardron, Richard, 290.
Archambault, Joseph, 292.
Armitage, Rev. Thos., 253.
Arnold, Collins, 206, 247.
Arnold, Jonathan D., 160.
Artesian well, 211.
Arthur, Alex., 303.
Arthur, Wm. Jr., 141, 160.
Ashdown, Arthur, 161.
Ashworth, Henry, 283.
Assemblymen, from Cohoes, 305.
Atheson, Jos., 282.
Atkinson, John H., 203, 228.
Atlantic Mill, 192, 212, 244.
Atridge, Thomas C., 16.
Atridge, Timothy, 294.
Atridge, Timothy, Jr., 301, 303.
Attorney of city, 227, 230.
Atwood, Joseph, 281.
Augsburg, David, 160.
Authier Bros., 228, 249.
Auringer, Isaac, 155.
Austin, Geo., 161.
Axe factories, production of, 1847, 87; enlarged, 115; statistics of, 1876, 245.
Axe factory, 119, 120, 128, 146, 175, 176, 207; burned, 222, 227, 228; established, 64, 76, 235.
Ayres, Alexis, 83, 99.
Ayres, Edward, 280.
Ayres, Isaac D., 98, 99, 287.

Babcock, Rev. Theodore, 252.
Badgley, Philip, 268.
Bagley, William, 161.
Bailey, Gustavus, 181.
Bailey, Joshua, 61, 62, 63, 72, 113, 115, 119, 120, 127, 128, 129, 134, 148, 161, 290, 301.
Bailey, Joshua, Sen., 270.
Bailey M'f'g Co., 115, 119.
Bailey, Milton, 271.
Bailey, Timothy, 61, 62, 63, 72, 78, 80, 87, 104, 132.
Baker, A. S., 248.
Baker, Chas. H., 161.
Baker, John, 58, 65, 82, 120, 137, 142, 299.
Baker, John A., 161.
Baldwin, Samuel, 53, 57, 82.

INDEX.

Baldwin & Baker, 82.
Ball, Daniel, 275.
Ball, Jerome, 161.
Ball, Malachi, 98, 114, 156, 195, 297, 300, 304.
Ballard, A. J., 296.
Ballard, John, 194.
Ballard, Joseph E., 285.
Ballentyne, Wm., 285.
Bank of Cohoes, 140, 249.
Bank, The Manufacturers', established, 209.
Bannon, James, 161.
Baptist church, damaged, 229; enlarged, 213; history of, 252; organized, 72; built, 93; parsonage of, 199; rebuilt, 115, 116.
Baptist German church, 254.
Barber, C. P., 128, 132.
Barber, Rev. C., 253.
Barber & Leckie, 128.
Barclay, James, 272.
Barclay, Thos., 288.
Barker, Calvin, 38, 50.
Barlow, Samuel, 161.
Bamerick, Wm., 302.
Bartlett, Ebenezer, 72.
Barrett, Edward, 303, 305.
Barrett, Edward S., 162.
Barrett, John, 162.
Barrett, Wm. B., 98.
Barrie, James, 260.
Barter, James, 259.
Barton, Robert, 291.
Base-ball club, 141.
Basin, A., 76; constructed, 58, 63; B., constructed, 58.
Bassett, Rev. J., 33.
Bat factory burned, 105, 222.
Battin, J., 119.
Baxter, Wm., 120.
Bayard, Augustus Willard, 161.
Bayard, Wm. II., 282.
Beach, Josiah H., 72.
Bean, Wm., 248.
Beaver, Lawrence, 162.
Becker, Arthur T., 127, 141, 175, 194.
Becker, S. A., 64, 145, 148, 157, 245.
Bedell, Moses, 122.
Bedford, Henry, 156.
Bedstead factory, 75, 80, 87, 93, 120, 124, 137, 142, 246.
Beecher family, 43.
Beeman, Wm., 297.
Bell, Alexander, 280.
Belville, John, 290.
Bemis, Luke, 81, 88, 91, 92, 97, 100.
Bender, C. W., 127.
Benedict, Rev. T., 253.
Benedict, Wm. R., 139, 156, 264, 302, 303.
Bennett, John, 161.
Bennett, Lyman, 190.
Bennett, Napoleon, 161.
Benson, Chas. L., 283.
Benson, Ebenezer, 284.
Benson, Egbert C., 161.
Benson, Nathan L., 296, 298.
Bentley, A. C., 69.
Bentley, Chas., 161.
Benton, Buckley T., 212.

Bezner, Herman, 204, 218, 224.
Bilbrough, Samuel, 120, 190, 244.
Bilbrough, Sam'l & Dubuque, 223.
Billings, Dr. Geo. H., 141, 260, 303, 305.
Billings, H. C., 92, 104.
Bills & Sage, 147.
Bindewald, William, 291.
Bingham, Rev. A. J., 159, 253, 257, 281.
Bingham, Willard, 131.
Binns, Wm., 296.
Birdseye, Chas. C., 241.
Biscornette, John, 155.
Biscornette, Jos., 284.
Bisschof, Jacob, 155.
Black, G. G., 261.
Blair, Frederick, 161.
Blair, John, 133.
Blake, Dr., 274.
Blake & Sons, 146.
Blakely, Chas. H., 271.
Blakely, Guy, 288, 300.
Blakely, W. I., 156.
Blanchard, Rev. Hiram, 254.
Blinn, Rev. H. G., 253.
Blower, Joshua, 52.
Blum, William H., 161.
Board of Health, appointed, 104.
Board of Trade, proposed, 217.
Boat Club, Cohoes, 204.
Bobbin factory, 120, 128, 137, 142.
Bogardus, Rev. C., 33.
Boght, the, 15, 17; church, 32, 33, 39; road, 225. See also *Manor avenue*.
Bogue, H. S., 122, 142, 143, 148, 178, 182, 190, 208, 216, 226, 296, 297, 304.
Boley, Thomas, 268.
Bonce, John G., 49, 121.
Bonding the city, 225.
Boomhower, Edward, 156.
Booth, Joseph, 155.
Bordwell, Allen, 276.
Bortell, H., 144.
Bortell, Wm. H., 107.
Boss, Chas., 161.
Bolton, Richard, 255.
Bouchard, Frank, 162.
Boucher, Geo., 161.
Boudrias, Dr. Louis, 263, 293.
Boudrias, Dr. William, 293.
Boulevard bill, 208.
Bowler, Michael, 298, 300.
Bowler, Robert, 156.
Bowler, William, 294.
Bradford, Geo. S., 78.
Bradley, Wm. J., 188.
Bradshaw, Geo., 161.
Brady, John, 298.
Brault, Alfred, 303.
Bray, Geo., 43.
Bray, Joseph, 161.
Bray, William, 161.
Breen, Michael, 304, 305.
Brennan, Dennis, 161.
Brennan, Edward, 280, 299.
Brennan, Martin, 302.
Brennan, Michael, 291.
Brewery, built, 173.
Bricks, first made, 61; manufacture, 247.
Bridge on Johnston ave., 236; at White street, 191; to Lansingburg, 234;

INDEX.

Bridge, to Van Schaick's Island, 210, 234; Waterford, completed, 210; to Waterford, 39, 45; the first built, 33; described, 34; laws concerning, 35, 36; burned, 207; rebuilt, 49, 121, 122.
Bridges, repairs of, 108, 109.
Bridgeford. John, 182.
Brierly, John, 161, 275.
Brigamuel, Fred., 156.
Briggs, R. T., 82.
Brigham, Origen S., 96.
Brockway, Geo. E., 161.
Brockway, Henry, 143, 148, 159, 178, 194, 217, 231, 244, 298, 299, 301.
Brodt, Wesley, 161, 275.
Bronk, Rev. Robt., 33.
Brooks, Geo., 192.
Brooks, Henry, 272.
Brooks, Jno. W., 262.
Brooks, Thomas, 192, 272.
Brooks, William, 161, 271.
Brooks, Wm. R., 255.
Brower, Geo., 161.
Brown, Albert M., 156, 161.
Brown, Alex., 302, 303, 305.
Brown, Frank, 304.
Brown, Henry, 114.
Brown, J., 302.
Brown, Jas., 128, 288.
Brown, Jenks, 128, 135, 140, 146, 273, 296, 297.
Brown, John, 70.
Brown, Jno. Crosby, 241.
Brown, Joseph M., 93, 98, 106, 110, 113, 296, 300.
Brown, Peter A., 161, 289.
Brown, Rev. J. H. H., 188, 205, 228, 252.
Brown, Rev. W. R., 253.
Brown, Thomas, 271.
Brown, Thos. V., 300.
Browne, Andrew M., 263.
Brownson, Jno. M., 88, 90, 300.
Bryan, Hugh, 161.
Bryan, John, 155.
Bryant, A. C., 273, 297.
Buckley, Edward, 263.
Buckley, James, 161.
Buchanan, Geo., 161.
Buchanan, John, 263.
Buchanan, John C., 161.
Buchanan, William, 161, 181, 280, 285.
Buildings, statistics of. 134.
Bulletin. See *Cohoes Daily B.*
Bullions, Rev. A. B., 180, 257.
Bullock, Edward, 156, 278.
Bullock, John R., 132, 273, 297.
Bullock, Joseph, 212.
Bulson, Geo., 161.
Bulson, John, 292.
Bump, Alonzo, 162.
Buregard, Oliver, 161.
Burger, Rev. David J., 252.
Burke, Michael J., 304.
Burke, Patrick, 291.
Burnap, John G., 84.
Burns, James, 290, 303.
Burton, Wm., 80, 85, 87, 113, 120, 128, 131, 132, 148, 152, 153, 173, 182, 209, 295, 296, 300, 301.
Bush, Lewis, 161.

Bush, Rev. Stephen, 126, 253.
Buss, Ralph, 295, 296.
Butt factory, 81.

Cady, D., 203, 248.
Cady, Peter V., 162.
Caffrey, James, 262.
Cahill, Henry, 286.
Cahill, Hugh, 304.
Cahill, James, 162.
Cahill, John, 155.
Cain, John, 162.
Caisse, Joseph, 162.
Calkins, A. T., 153, 159, 162, 262, 298, 302.
Calkins, R. S., 299.
Camera obscura, 219.
Cameron, Rev. M., 252.
Campbell, Geo., 175, 194, 210, 244, 301, 303.
Campbell Hose Co., 259.
Campbell, James M., 289.
Campbell, John, 263, 284.
Campbell, Robert, 255.
Campbell & Clute, 175, 246.
Campbell & Clute's Block, 219.
Canal boat, first, 266; first to pass through, 42.
Canal enlargement, 68, 73, 76; the Erie, 52.
Canal street. See *Main street.*
Canals, construction of, 41, 42, 265; courses of, 43, 44.
Candly, Samuel, 156.
Cane, Patrick, 156.
Cannon, Chas. T., 278.
Cannon, P. J., 262.
Canvass street, 116.
Carhart, Rev. J. W., 253.
Carleton, Chas. M., 137.
Carpenter, Albert F., 162.
Carpenter, Asahel, 292.
Carpenter, Edwd. S., 303.
Carpenter, Lorenzo, 162.
Carpenter, Philip H., 162.
Carpenter, William G., 162.
Carpet factory, 59.
Carr, Albert, 156.
Carr, T., 162.
Carrigan, Geo., 235.
Carroll, John C., 162, 279.
Carroll, Wm. C., 297.
Carter, Chas. T., 118, 288, 300.
Carter, Charles W., 290.
Carter, Dr. Wm. F., 104, 111, 113, 119, 129, 140, 144, 157, 178, 189, 279, 295, 296, 298, 301.
Carter, Geo. T., 260, 303, 304.
Carter, Isaac S., 281.
Carter, John, 176, 305.
Carter, Michael, 156.
Carter, Thomas, 293.
Carter, T. C, 121, 281, 288, 293, 296.
Cartwright, Thomas, 134.
Cary, Leonard, 107, 222, 297, 302, 303.
Casey, Peter, 290.
Casey, Thos. B., 162.
Cassidy, John, 155.
Cataract Alley, 103.
Cataract engine, 104; purchased, 97; company for, 98, 259; house built for, 99.

Cataract House, 4, 177.
Catholic church. See *St. Bernard's church.*
Cavan, Washington, 54.
Cavanaugh, John, 299.
Cavenaugh, Edward, 290.
Cavenagh, John V., 162.
Cauldwell, M. O., 204.
Caw, Wm. G., 84, 87, 108, 112, 113, 121, 140, 148, 152, 157, 178, 253, 277, 295, 297, 301.
Caw & Quackenbush Block, 92.
Cedar street, 204.
Cement Mill. See *Lime.*
Cemetery, presented to village, 122, 123.
Census of 1855, 125; of 1860, 147; of 1865, 183; of 1870, 205; tables of, 261.
Centennial celebration, 229.
Central avenue, 219, 226.
Chadwick Guards. See *Third Sep. Co.*
Chadwick, Joseph, 133, 136, 152, 159, 141, 162, 163, 175, 192, 244, 261, 297.
Chadwick, P. R., 149, 152, 162, 175, 210, 217, 244, 262.
Chadwick, Wm. N., 26, 81, 93, 95, 97, 101, 111, 113, 128, 148, 175, 240, 244, 296.
Chamberlain, 205; dispute in regard to, 221; powers of, 230.
Chamberlin, Rev. Mr., 72, 253.
Chambers, John, 162.
Charter, a city, proposed, 178; amended, 112, 125, 205, 209, 227, 230; for city, passed, 197; of village drawn, 95.
Chesebro, I. W., 142, 150, 250.
Chicago fire, relief for sufferers by, 208.
Childs, John, 156.
Cholera, in 1832, 59; in 1849, 104.
Christie, James, 162.
Christie, Robt. Jr., 240.
Christie, Rich'd D., 260, 261.
Chubb, Hiram, 285.
Churches, organized, 32, 41, 56, 71, 72, 91, 196, 221, 254; built, 60, 73, 91, 101, 116, 141, 176, 189, 196, 205, 224; improvements in, 145, 199, 213; damaged, 229; history of, 252-255.
Cider mill, 196.
Claffey, Wm., 155.
Clark, Alvin, 156.
Clark, Asa, 142.
Clark, Bayard, 26.
Clark, J. B., 162.
Clark, James, 299.
Clark, Jas. W., 261.
Clark, John, 281.
Clark, John, Jr., 285.
Clark, Joseph, 162.
Clark, Otis G., 190, 216, 244.
Clark, Rev. Orange, 56, 252.
Clark, Richard, 217, 292, 299.
Clarke, Benj. F., 298.
Clarke, Dr. O. H. E., 263.
Clarke, Joshua R., 53, 57, 59, 65, 67, 80, 88, 96, 101, 111, 113, 120, 140, 148, 216, 295, 297, 300, 303.
Clancy & Co , 192.
Claxton block, 106.
Claxton, Col. F. S., 92, 100, 104, 129, 241.
Cleacham, Robt., 155.

Clements, Wm. J., 271.
Clerk of city, 230.
Clifton Company, 127.
Cline, William H., 162.
Clinton, Gov., 265.
Clough, Edwin, 304.
Clough, Wm., 260, 263, 302.
Clow, Philip L., 280.
Clute, Abram D., 279.
Clute, Adam, 162.
Clute, D. H., 235.
Clute, E. J., 262.
Clute family, 8, 22; farm, 18, 29.
Clute, Gerardus, 33.
Clute, Gerrett, 30, 31, 32, 40.
Clute, Harvey, 298, 299.
Clute, Hiram, 153, 162, 274.
Clute, Isaac, 179, 247.
Clute, Jeremiah, 91, 95, 113, 124, 137, 296.
Clute, John, 155, 175, 194, 217, 246, 301.
Clute, Nicholas J., 210.
Coakley, John, 288.
Cockroft, Wm., 82.
Cohoes, derivation of name of, 1; manner of spelling, 251; settlement of, 15, 18; in 1813, described, 39; in 1824, 45, 46; in 1831, 53-56; 1836, 66; 1847, 85; incorporated as a village, 94, 95, 96; incorporated as a city, 197; movement to incorporate, 178; to be part of the city of Watervliet, 192; charter of, amended, 112, 205, 209, 227, 230; statistics of, 200, 264; officers of, 295-305; census of, 125, 147, 183, 205, 264; farms and farm houses in, 18-29; bonding of city proposed, 225; history of, published, 199, 212; first directory of, 193; first election, as a city, 201; expenses of, in 1849, 103; war record of, 148-172.
Cohoes Falls, 45, 48; early accounts of, 2, 3, 4, 6, 7, 8, 9, 10, 11, 12, 14; dimensions of, 4, 12; pictures of, 10, 12; described, 39.
    Hospital, 209.
    Hotel, 59, 69, 85.
    House, 43, 54.
    Iron foundery. See *Foundery.*
    Manufacturing Co., 37, 38, 39, 46, 50, 65.
    Savings Institution. See *Savings Inst.*
    & Troy Rail Road, 88, 89, 114.
Cohoes Company, 28, 29, 37, 50, 65, 100, 101, 123, 131, 143, 215, 266; canal of, 68, 69; dam of, 73, 182; disputes of, with village, 108, 109; foundation of, 47, 48; first operations of, 51, 52, 58, 63; sketch of, 238-241; works of, 66, 76, 239, 240; water supply from, 130, 195.
Cohoes Advertiser, the, described, 83, 84, 85.
Cohoes Cataract, the, established, 102; sketch of, 248, 249; discontinued, 180.
Cohoes Daily Bulletin, 228.
Cohoes Daily News, established, 217; sketch of, 249.

INDEX.   311

Cohoes Democrat, established, 185; sketch of, 248.
Cohoes Journal, 99.
Cohoes Weekly Democrat, established, 203.
Cole, Aaron, 163.
Cole, Abram V., 262.
Cole, George, 162.
Cole, James, 162, 277.
Cole, Lorenzo S., 262.
Cole, Octavius, 273.
Coleman, James, 301.
Coleman, John, 163, 303, 304, 305.
Coleman, Joseph, 163, 301, 302.
Coleman, Morris, 163.
Coleman, Silas B., 162.
Coleman, Thos., 163, 244.
Colgrove, David, 155.
Colgrove, John B , 81.
Collier, Thomas, 293.
Collier, William, 162.
Collins, George Z., 143.
Collins, L. D., 193.
Collins, Michael J., 287.
Collins, T. C., 261.
Collin and Jones, 41.
Columbia street, 44, 55, 219, 225.
Colwell, Thos., 179, 212, 216, 245.
Commissioners of Deeds, 205.
Common Council, first meeting of, 201; powers of, 205, 227.
Condley, John H., 303, 304.
Condron, James, 162.
Condron, William, 162.
Congressman from Cohoes, 305.
Conley, John, 155.
Conliss, Wm., 151, 156, 159, 176.
Conliss & Carter, 176; mill of, burned, 180.
Connaughty, Edward, 292.
Connaughty, Mr., 91.
Connoly, James, 162.
Connolly, Samuel, 162
Connors, John, 162, 290.
Constables, 227.
Constant, Joseph D., 67.
Conway, Eugene, 304.
Cook, Alfred, 61.
Cook, Alanson, 72.
Cook, Geo. W., 250.
Cook, Samuel, 74.
Cooley, John, 305.
Coon, John M., 85.
Cope, William, 162.
Copeland, John, 291.
Corcoran, J., 162.
Corwin, Rev. D., 252.
Costello, Joseph, 162.
Cotton factory, 41, 45, 46, 47; of E. L. Miller, 59; of Harmony M'f'g Co., 67.
Cotton flax mill, 120.
Cotton mills, condition of, in 1857, 134; erected, 80, 81; production of, 81; statistics of, in 1847, 86; in 1853, 119; in 1855, 128. See also *Harmony, Strong & Ogden* Mills.
Court room, built, 107.
Coveney, Benj., 260, 261, 303.
Cowden, Geo., 162.
Cowee, David, 176, 244.

Cox, Andrew, 162, 300.
Coyle, Nicholas, 105.
Craig, Chas. P., 198, 263.
Craig, F. B., 162.
Craig, William, 162.
Craley, Jacob, 254.
Cramer, John, 101.
Crandall, Burton H., 162, 305.
Cranston, James L. N., 155, 162, 289.
Cranston, Wm. H., 162, 275.
Crapo, Amos, 304.
Crane, J. H., 116.
Crane, John S., 155, 299, 300, 304.
Crane, W. S., 302.
Crescent, water supply from 131, 195; road to, 225, 229.
Crawford, J. F., 131, 144, 174, 178, 219, 297, 301, 305.
Crawford, Rev. E., 71, 253.
Crawford, William N., 290.
Crocker, M. L., 69.
Crookley, Thomas, 234.
Cropsey, Gabriel M., 147, 292.
Crosby, Clarkson F., 240.
Crossley, Robert, 162.
Crossingham, Jas. H., 262.
Crowley, John, 305.
Crowner family, 43, 54.
Cullen, Rev. Thos., 251.
Cummings, Geo., 298.
Cummings, Michael, 303.
Curtis, A. G., 212.
Curtis, Joseph, 50.
Curtis, Robert, 81.
Cushman, John P., 27.

Dailey, Jeremiah A., 163.
Daily Eagle, the, 228.
Daily News. See *Cohoes Daily News*.
Daley, Dennis, 163, 303.
Daley, Geo. C., 305.
Daley, John, 163.
Daley, Michael, 292.
Dallas, Thomas, 155.
Daly, Rev. Thos., 254.
Dam, of Cohoes Co., 73, 182; built and rebuilt, 51, 58.
Dam, the state, built, 207.
Damon, Elbridge, 297.
Damon, John, 156.
Damon, John E., 283.
Danaher, Maurice, 163.
Darrow, David M., 163.
Davenport, Chas., 163.
Davenport, Geo., 163.
Davenport, James, 163.
Davenport, John, 163.
Davids, Elias, 155.
Davis, John, 292.
Davis, N. B., 287.
Davis, Thos., 163.
Daw, Peter F., 107, 250, 292, 300.
Dawson, Henry, 133, 192, 246.
Dean, Geo., 261.
Dearborn, John, 114.
Deecher, Jas., 305.
De Graff, Joseph, 292.
De Haas' patent, 15.
Delahanty, Joseph, 194.
Delanoy, W., 254.
Delany, John, 163.

312 INDEX.

Delve, James, 181, 263, 297.
Demarest, Rev. John, 32, 33.
Demarest, Wm. C., 305.
DeMilt, B. & S., 41, 50.
Democrat. See *Cohoes Democrat.*
Denio, Henry, 163.
Dennis, Nicholas, 163.
Dennin, Patrick, 290.
Derby, William, 163.
Deroche, ———, 163.
Deroche, James, 163.
Derocher, Joseph, 292.
Deuel, George, 163.
Dewar, Wm., 259.
Deyo, Abner, 300.
Deyo, Marcus S., 98.
Diamond Mill, 244.
Dickey, James R., 279.
Dickey, Henry D., 305.
Dickey, Wm., 140, 272, 295.
Dickson, John M., 289.
Diehl, Geo., 163, 277.
Dietz, Sidney, 156.
Dietz, Stephen, 163, 296.
Dillon, James, 289.
Directory, published, 193.
Dixon, A. K., 302, 303, 304.
Dixon, Geo., 255, 298.
Dockstader, Geo. Z., 69, 302.
Dodge, Jacob, 82, 85, 87.
Dodge, James, 208.
Dodge, Joseph C., 163, 300.
Dodge, Levi, 143, 175, 204.
Dodge, Stephen, 296.
Dodge, Wm., 71.
Dodge, Wm. T., 139, 301, 302.
Donahue, William, 163.
Doncaster & Hay, 102.
Donnelly, Catherine, 176.
Donovan, Michael, 90, 163, 296.
Doolittle, Lucius, 290.
Doran, John, 305.
Dorr, David, 163.
Dotter, Solomon, 301, 302.
Doty, Stephen, 260.
Doty, Wm. H., 98, 302.
Dougherty, James, 304.
Dowd, Luman, 109.
Dowd, Patrick, 163.
Downey, Margaret, 176.
Downing, Michael, 163.
Downs, John, 272, 290.
Doyle, Chas. F., 163, 231, 281.
Doyle, Geo. H., 163.
Doyle, John, 114, 156, 157, 296, 300.
Doyle, M., 163.
Doyle, Mrs. Sarah, 74
Draft in 1862, 151, 152; in 1863, 154.
Driscoll, James, 286.
Driscoll, Simon P., 163.
Drysdale, Geo., 163.
Drysdale, John, 163, 285, 299.
Dubois, Henry, 113.
Dubois, Rev. John, 33.
Dubuque, L. R., 179, 223.
Ducharme, Geo., 302.
Dudley, Chas. E., 48.
Dudley, Henry, 67.
Dumell, Alfred, 163.
Duncan, Rev. John, 72, 252.
Duncan, Thos., 192.

Dunlap, John, 254.
Dunn, Edward, 163.
Dunn, Thos., 163.
Dunsback, Henry I., 204.
Duquette, Moses, 294.
Durham, Henry, 163.
Durham, James, 163, 275.
Durrant, James, 261, 291.
Dutemple, Wm., 296, 297.
Dwyer, Rev. E., 252.

Eagan, Kyran, 156, 164.
Eagan, William R., 290.
Eastham, Henry, 164.
Eastham, Thos., 163, 277.
Eastwood, J., 114.
Eastwood, John, 98, 272, 296, 300.
Eastwood, John H., 164.
Eastwood, John Jr., 280.
Eastwood, Justus, 293, 300.
Eastwood, Rev. J., 252.
Eastwood, William H., 289.
Ebah, John, 164, 278.
Eccles, Francis T., 163.
Eccles, J., 126.
Eccles, Joseph, 260.
Eccles, Samuel P., 163.
Edwards, Henry W., 246.
Edwards, Rev. Edw'd F., 252.
Egan, Chas., 302, 303.
Egan, John, 262.
Egan, John H., 303, 305.
Egan, Owen, 164.
Egberts, Egbert, 61, 62, 63, 91, 95, 97, 101, 104, 110, 111, 113, 115, 119, 123, 127, 128, 140, 145, 148, 152, 180, 249, 252, 282, 296.
Egberts & Bailey, 62, 74, 86, 91, 100; block, 106; dissolved, 115; factory of, 77, 79.
Egberts Hall opened, 138.
Egberts Institute, 255; established, 180; teachers of, 257.
Egnesperry, Francis, 164.
Election districts changed, 136.
Election, first under city charter, 201; first under village charter, 96.
Ellis, Elisha, 164.
Ellison, Robert, 164.
Ellmaker, Augustus, 201, 299.
Elmore, J. C., 133.
Emerson, Rev. Oliver, 253.
Empire Mill, 174, 182, 196, 244; built, 142.
Empire Pin Co., 127, 207.
Empire Tube Works, 212, 246; enlarged, 235.
En Earl, Henry Jr., 88, 91.
En Earl, Henry Sr., 43, 49, 54, 287, 295.
En Earl, John H., 164.
En Earl, Merrit D., 164.
En Earl, N. W., 296, 298.
Engineer of city, 227, 230.
Engine houses built, 90, 114, 199, 259.
Englestoff, John, 293.
English, Michael, 305.
English, Patrick, 303.
Enlistments of soldiers, 149, 150, 156, 157.
Enos, W. C., 133.
Enos, William, 292.
Ensign, H. A., 164.

INDEX.   313

Ensign's Mill, 41.
Enterprise Mill. 218, 244.
Episcopal church. See *St. John's church*.
Eric Mill, 182, 190, 244; burned, 214; rebuilt. 218.
Evans, Joel, 164.
Evans, Rev. C. P., 257.
Evers, William. 291.
Everts, J. D., 164.
Excelsior Fire Engine, 96, 97, 98.

Fabyan. H. G., 164.
Fairbank, David, 164.
Fairbank, J. W., 164.
Fairbank, Sherman D., 63, 98, 139, 175, 276, 297.
Fairchild, Anthony. 263.
Falardo, Daniel, 164.
Falardo, Dennis L., 164.
Falardo, John, 164.
Falardo, Joseph. & De Villiers, 105.
Falardo, Louis, 289.
Falardo, Onesime, 164.
Fallon, Michael. 289.
Fallon, Peter, 164.
Farmhouses, location of, 18–29.
Farmilo, Henry. 254.
Farms, boundaries of, 24 to 29.
Farnam, F. W., 84, 93, 100, 115.
Farrell, Edward, 164.
Farrell, John, 293.
Farrell, Matt, 164.
Farrelly, Michael, 274.
Farthing, F. E., 164.
Faulkner's tavern, 53.
Fay, Patrick, 155.
Featherstonhaugh, Dr. J. D., 209, 263, 303.
Felthousen, Herman D., 98.
Ferguson, Aaron L, 93, 114, 273.
Ferguson, Chas. F., 271.
Ferguson, Geo. N., 296.
Ferguson, P. B., 140, 300.
Ferguson, Wm., 164, 283, 292.
Fero, David, 32.
Fero, Peter & Henry, 29.
Ferrell, Wm., 98, 296.
Ferris, Harvey, 300.
Fielding. John, 290.
Fifth ward bill. 227.
Finney, Oscar O., 69, 280.
Finlay, Charles, 164.
Finlay, John, 164.
Finnigan, James, 156.
Fire alarm telegraph, proposed, 217.
Fire, in post office, 84; at Clute Paint Mill, 91; at T. Bailey's Mill. 104; in Strong Mill. 123; in Harmony Mill, 136; in Wilkinson Machine Shop, 137; at horse car barn, 184; at Eric Mill, 214; at Stark Mill, 214, at Harmony Mills, 173; at Burton's Mill, 173; at Paper Mill, 173; at Hurst's Mill, 176; at old Junction, 178; at Conliss & Carter's Mill, 178; at Van Rensselaer House, 104, 105; at Ten Eyck Axe Factory, 222; at Root's Mill, 222; at Weed & Becker's, 227.
Fire commissioners, 227.

Fire Department, 113; organized, 96, 97, 98; chief engineers of, 300; improvements in, 181, 182, 194; sketch of, 258, 259.
Fisher, Horace, 198, 212.
Fitts. Lucien. 98, 295, 296.
Fitz Gerald, Edward, 200.
Fitz Gerald, Lawrence, 156.
Fitz Gerald, Maurice, 304.
Fitz Patrick, Daniel, 164, 290, 298.
Fitz Patrick, Frank, 291.
Fitz Patrick, John, 302.
Fitz Patrick, Martin, 290.
Fitz Patrick, Matthew, 123, 272, 295, 297, 304.
Fitz Patrick, Rev. J., 286.
Flag raisings, 149.
Flannigan, Dennis, 57.
Flannigan, Edward, 262.
Flannigan family, 43.
Flannigan, Geo., 164.
Flannigan, John, 164.
Flannigan, Thomas B., 291.
Fletcher, Isaac F., 54, 131, 164, 260, 276, 295, 296, 297.
Fletcher, Isaac V., 141.
Fletcher, Leonard G., 164, 274.
Fletcher, Thos., 164.
Fletcher, William, 164, 292.
Flint, Rev. F. W. 180.
Flour Mill, 75, 124, 146, 147, 247.
Flynn, John, 164, 275.
Fogarty, William, 292.
Foley, Edward, 104.
Foley, John, 299.
Foley, Peter, 290.
Fonda, Abraham D., 32.
Fonda, Abram H., 305.
Fonda, Col. Dow, 281.
Fonda, Cornelius V., 271.
Fonda, Douw, 22.
Fonda, Douw A., 29, 122.
Fonda, E. Raymond, 164. 277.
Fonda family, 17. 18, 29, 32.
Fonda, Frank. 303. 305.
Fonda, Geo. F., 164.
Fonda, Gilbert M., 164.
Fonda, Isaac. 32, 273.
Fonda, Isaac J., 30.
Fonda, Jacob D., 26, 29.
Fonda, Jesse, 33.
Fonda, Lawrence S., 97, 295.
Fonda, Wm., 153.
Foote, Wm., 137.
Forbes, John, 286.
Forbes, Peter, 273.
Foreman, John, 285.
Ford, John W., 303, 304, 305.
Forrest, Dr. J. B., 287.
Forrester. L. G., 279.
Fort family, 12, 17.
Forth's tavern, 12.
Forward, John, 164.
Foster, E. H., 217, 262.
Foster, James G., 85.
Foster, Samuel H., 81, 87, 88, 104, 113, 281, 296, 297, 299, 300.
Foster, Wm., 164.
Foundery, established, 64, 199; the Cohoes. 87, 120; removed, 192.
Fountain, Theophilus, 156.

314 INDEX.

Fourth of July celebration, appropriation for, 230; account of, 232; of 1850, 109, 110; of 1865, 159.
Fowler, Newton, 282.
Fowler, Ralph, 164.
Fowler, Thos., 115, 119, 127.
Fowler, T. S., 164.
Fox, Joseph, 38.
Fox, Rev. Robert, 253.
Franklin, Benj., 98.
Frazier, P., 164.
Freeman, Wm. L., 98.
French church. See *St. Joseph's church*.
French, John G., 258.
Frink, Alex., 295, 296, 297, 300, 302.
Frink, Alexander H., 155, 277.
Frink, John W., 131, 132, 144, 293, 297, 298, 299, 301.
Frink, Spencer, 299.
Frisby, Robert W., 164, 275.
Frost, James, 164.
Frost, Norman W., 164, 178, 210, 217, 249.
Frost, Robert, 164, 299.
Frost, Rev. Daniel C., 253.
Fry, Edwin A., 164.
Fuller & Safely, 203.
Fuller & Safely's building, 192.
Fuller, Edward W., 69, 70, 88, 118, 119, 120, 133, 135, 148, 192, 250, 296; & H. D., 215.
Fuller, Henry D., 64, 69, 70, 88, 90, 95, 100, 107, 110, 113, 119, 120, 128, 129, 140, 148, 192, 231, 244, 249, 295, 300, 301, 302, 303; & Hay, 219.
Fuller, Mr., 59.
Fulton, John, 114, 121, 122, 156, 297, 298.
Furniture factory, 204, 218, 247.

Gaffney, Thos., 299.
Gage, William, 165.
Gaine, Henry M., 188.
Gaine, Paul, 260.
Galbraith, James, 165, 273.
Gallapo, Joseph, 165.
Galligan, Bernard, 259.
Galvin, John, 156.
Garfield, Rev. B. F., 252.
Garner, Thomas, 112, 135, 211, 280.
Garner, Thos. Jr., 282.
Garner, Wm. T., 240, 241.
Garraghan, Owen, 290, 301.
Garrigan, Martin, 299.
Gas Light Co., organized, 119.
Gauthier, F., 165.
Gauthier, Joseph, 164.
Gauthier, Peter, 165.
Gay, Amos R., 268.
Geer, John N., 263.
Genoie, J. H., 165.
German Baptist Church, 254.
Gilbert, Wm. S., 209, 216, 244, 303.
Gill, E. D., 270.
Gill, James, 293.
Gilligan, Pat'k, 155.
Gillis, J., 165.
Gilman, Chas. O., 304, 305.
Gilmore, Martin, 260.
Gilson, Rev. J. B., 252.
Giard, Alexander, 294.
Girard, Alexis, 293.

Gleason, Thos., 302.
Gledhill, Wm., 285.
Glines, B. A., 142.
Globe Mill, 212, 244.
Goddard, Aaron, 254.
Goffe, Asahel, 72, 271.
Goffe, Augustus J., 72, 105, 132, 207.
Goffe, Demas, 133, 271.
Golden, Thos., 272, 304.
Gooch, Thomas, 164, 278.
Goodfellow, James H., 165.
Goodrich, Frederick S., 165.
Goodwater, Vital, 165.
Gordon, Van Olinda, 165.
Gormley, Robt., 165, 278.
Goss, Dr. C. F., 84, 110, 271.
Gould, Alfred, 155, 260.
Gould, David, 260.
Gould, Joseph, 71, 114.
Gould, Joseph Jr., 300.
Gould, Mark H., 288.
Grand Army of Republic. See *Post Lyod*.
Grand View Park, 219.
Granite Hall Block, 92.
Grant, F. W., 147.
Grant, H. R., 130, 136, 283, 298, 299.
Grant, Mrs. H. R., 229, 247.
Grant, Rev. H. L., 253.
Grass, George, 284.
Graves, Geo. H., 304.
Gray, John, 262.
Gray, Rev. John, 252, 253.
Greason, Edward, 165, 275.
Greason, Egbert, 165.
Greason, George, 263, 291.
Greason, William, 290.
Gregory, Alex. M., 132, 291.
Gregory & Hiller, 223.
Gregory, C. N., 139.
Gregory, Chas., 155.
Gregory, Dr. O. H., 141, 145.
Gregory, E. S., 302.
Gregory, George H., 292.
Gregory, Rev. Dr., 145.
Gregory, Wm. M., 132; & Hiller, 244.
Green, Chas., 276.
Green, Chas. D., 165.
Green, Chas. N., 165, 259.
Green, Elisha T., 280, 296, 297.
Green, Geo., 165.
Green, H. J. P., 264.
Green, John, 165.
Green, Otis R., 165, 256.
Green, Wm., 98, 285.
Greer, John, 165, 278.
Greenman, L., 137, 192.
Greenwood, William, 165.
Grierson, Geo., 156.
Griffin, A. J., 93, 137, 142, 178, 217, 246, 250.
Griffin, Francis, 67.
Griffin, Geo. C., 260.
Griffin, Patrick, 285.
Griffenty, Thos., 156.
Groesbeck, Leonard, 217.
Groves, James, 272.
Groves, John, 263.
Grist Mill, Lansing's, 29, 45; Clute's, 30; Heamstreet's, 30.
Gugerty, Patrick, 134, 189.
Gurr, Rev. C. D., 253.

Index.   315

Gwynne, Rev. Walker, 252.
Gwynn, Wm. H., 4, 263.

Haggerty, Wm. C., 112.
Hahn, Joseph, 98.
Hart, Richard P., 25, 27.
Halcyon Mill, 128, 132; sold, 175, 191.
Haley, John, 286
Haley, Joseph, 165.
Halfmoon, 39.
Hall, Henry, Jr., 98.
Hall, Thomas A., 291.
Hallenbeck, Jacob H., 114.
Halpin, James, 165.
Halve Maan or Half Moon, 12, 16, 17, 33.
Hamilton, David, 101.
Handy, Chas. O., 67.
Handy, Isaac F., 165.
Hanley, Patrick, 304.
Hanson, G. W., 166.
Hardenbrook, Chas. C., 165.
Hardie, Robert, 257.
Harmon, A. M., 301, 302.
Harmony Company, 181, 182. See also *Harmony Mills*.
Harmony Hill, growth of, 133, 242, 190.
Harmony Hill U. S. S. See *Sunday School*.
Harmony M'f'g Co., 57, 81; organization of, 67. 68.
Harmony Mills, 119, 146, 194; additions to, 179, 183; fire in, 136, 173; condition in 1857, 134, 135, 136; in panic of 1873, 220, 221; ownership of changed, 11; No. 2, erected, 133; No. 3 commenced, 185; completed, 195, 211; statistics of, in 1847, 86; in 1866, 190; in 1872, 212, 213; in 1876, 242, 243; sketch of, 241, 243.
Harmony, Peter, 67.
Harrington, John W., 189.
Harris, E. S. and H. W., 127.
Harris, James 268.
Harrison, John, 283.
Harrison, John B., 260, 268, 295.
Harrison, William, 290.
Hart, Richard Jr., 165.
Hartness woolen mill, 120.
Hartnett, Daniel Jr., 166.
Harvey, James, 166, 276.
Harvey, Ruel, 165.
Haskins, Joseph, 120.
Hastings, Frank, 233, 264.
Hastings, Herbert, 139, 165, 277, 300.
Hastings, Jonathan, 271.
Hastings, Wm., 181.
Hatcher, Thomas, 165, 261.
Haver Island, 16, 17, 32.
Hawes & Baker, 65, 70, 80, 81.
Hawley, Rev. C. R., 253.
Hay, Alex., 98, 279.
Hay, Chas., 132, 219, 244, 279, 301.
Hay, Francis, 166.
Hay, James, 263, 279, 298, 300, 303, 305.
Hay, John, 250, 304, 279.
Hay, John, Jr., 295.
Hay, John W., 165.
Hay, Miller, 301.
Hayden, James, 148, 288, 294, 305.
Hayes, John, 99.
Haynes, Dr. J. U., 263.

Hayward, Charles, 165.
Hayward, James M., 124, 291.
Hayward, John, 165.
Hayward, Sheffield, 136, 178, 183, 297, 299.
Heady, William, 166.
Healey, Patrick, 262.
Healey, Wm., 189, 262.
Health, Board of, appointed, 104.
Heamstreet, Albert, 30.
Heamstreet, Chas., 26, 30, 37, 42.
Heamstreet, Jacob, 41.
Heamstreet, John, 45, 55.
Heamstreet, Richard, 27, 36, 43, 53, 54, 55, 85.
Heamstreet family, 18, 21, 27.
Heffern, Christopher, 165.
Heffern, Edward, 303.
Helmerick, J., 262.
Helmerick, Joseph, 165.
Hemstreet, James, 71, 136.
Hemphill, Henry, 165.
Hemphill, James T., 165, 300.
Hemphill, John, 166.
Hemphill, Thomas, 166, 290.
Hemstreet, Russell, 165.
Henderson, Francis, 136, 148, 296, 297.
Henderson, John, 296.
Henry, John, 114.
Henthorn, James, 286.
Herell, Richard, 254.
Herkimer family, 43.
Hewson, Edward, 165.
Hibbert, Henry C., 165, 303, 304, 305.
Hicks, Charles, 291.
Higgins, Geo., 303.
Higgins, Michael, 155, 165.
Higgins, Thos., 262, 263.
Higley, H. E., 106.
Hildreth, T. P., 137, 142, 300.
Hill, Barney, 166.
Hill, Joseph, 165.
Hiller Jonathan, 120, 132, 182, 244, 261, 297, 302, 303.
Hilton, John, 263.
Hilzinger, Rev. Henry, 254.
Himes, Jas. K. P., 166, 278.
Himes, Jehial W., 152, 165, 178, 198, 210, 217, 244.
Himes & Vail, 198.
Hines, Patrick, 114.
Hitchcock, Edwin, 114, 194, 299, 302, 304.
Hitchcock, Wm. B., 274.
Hitchcock Hose Co., 259.
Hitchens, Thomas, 74.
Hobart, William, 292.
Hoben, A., 263.
Hodgson, John, 166.
Hodgson, Kendall, 166, 260.
Hodgson, Lester, 166.
Hogan, Patrick, 258.
Hogben, William, 289.
Hogg, Thos., 155.
Holley, Wm., 276.
Hollister, D. Cady, 120.
Hollister, Wm. H., 84, 92, 110, 120, 295, 298.
Holloran, Patrick, 292.
Holmes, John, 263.
Holsapple, P. S., 137, 246, 253.
Hopkins, John, 165.

Horan, Cornelius, 302.
Horan, John, 282.
Horner, James, 279.
Horrobin, Wm. T., 192, 199, 216, 246.
Horrocks, John, 212, 263, 244, 303.
Horrocks, Samuel, 264.
Horse Rail Road Co., Cohoes and Troy, incorp., 173; road of, completed, 177; stables of, burned, 184; suits against, 184.
Horse Rail Roads to Waterford, 178.
Hospital, established, 209.
Hotel, the first, 59.
Hotel, the Cohoes, 59, 85, 215; company organized, 215; proprietorship of, 69.
Houghton, Joab, 67, 240.
Houlihan, C. & Stanton, 240.
Houlihan, Cornelius, 159, 298, 301.
Houlihan, Jeremiah, 273.
House, Geo. A., 264.
House, Moses, 296, 299.
House, Rosen J., 165.
House, Theodore M., 165.
Howard, Geo. W., 165.
Howard, T. R., 298.
Howard, Wm. H., 276.
Howard street, 185, 226.
Howarth Engine Co., 232, 259.
Howarth, Geo., 296.
Howarth, Geo. H., 260.
Howarth, Henry, 107, 142.
Howarth, John, 165.
Howarth, John Wesley, 290, 303.
Howe, E. C., 85.
Howe, Hezekiah, 53, 56, 57, 58, 60, 70, 75, 100, 250, 269, 287.
Howe & Ross, 84, 85.
Howe, Miss E, 152.
Howe, Miss M., 57.
Howell, Elias, 271.
Howell, Maltby, 72, 274.
Howes, Dr. Thomas C., 293.
Howes, Geo. M., 273.
Hubbard, Murray. 148, 178, 194, 195, 208, 216, 219, 247, 257, 299.
Hubbard, Oliver C., 44, 58, 73, 74, 96.
Hubbell, Chas. L., 281.
Hude, John, 156.
Hudson, Benj., 166.
Hudson, Geo. 285.
Hughes, J. S. & E., 247.
Hughes, Michael, 165.
Hume, Geo., 156.
Hunt, Henry, 155.
Hurst, Richard, 120, 132, 300.
Hurst's Mill, burning of, 176; sold, 190.
Hutchins, Benj., 114, 271, 295.
Hutchins, Geo. W., 286.

Ilsley, Stillman, 206.
Incorporation, as a city, discussed, 196, 197; movement towards, 94, 95, 96.
Indian legends, 4, 5.
Ingraham, Chas. F., 139, 279.
Irish famine, 90.
Israel, Wm. P., Jr., 100.
Ivory, Michael, 189.

Jackson, Geo., 98, 297.
Jackson, John, 133, 166, 268.

Jackson, Robert, 155.
Jackson, Samuel, 156.
Jackson, Thos., 156.
Jackson, Wm. B., 166, 279.
James street, 226.
Jones, Elisha, 38.
Jenks, Willard, 69.
Jenkins, Chas. M., 128, 240.
Jerome, Joseph, 166.
Jerome, Louis, 166.
Johnson, Hugh, 156.
Johnson, James, 194.
Johnson, John, 156.
Johnson, J. H., 98.
Johnson, Michael H., 166, 260.
Johnson, Rev. C. A., 214, 253.
Johnson, Rev. L. S., 214, 253.
Johnson, Rev. Wm. M., 214, 253.
Johnston avenue, 236, 239.
Johnston, D. J., 131, 135, 139, 148, 153, 178, 181, 194, 208, 210, 216, 226, 233, 241, 243, 252, 255, 297, 298, 299, 301, 302, 304.
Johnston, E. H., 113, 272.
Johnston Lodge, 261.
Johnson, Samuel W., 166, 241.
Johnston, Robert, 112, 127, 140, 194, 209, 217, 243, 250, 296.
Johnston Steamer Co., 194, 232, 259.
Jones, Hiro & Southworth, 84.
Jones, Isaac, 293.
Jones, M. H., 222.
Jones, M. H. & Co., 176, 245.
Jones, Robert, 302, 303.
Jones, Wm., 288.
Jones, Wm. F., 155, 194, 303, 304.
Jones & Ryan, 176.
Journal des Dame, 228.
Juber, Adolphus, 156.
Judge, John, 74.
Judge, Patrick, 74, 107.
Jump, Joseph, 166.
Jump, Joseph E., 166.
Junction, the, of canals, 42, 43, 45, 46.
Justice of peace, 205.
Jute Mill, 242.

Kaffa, Wm., 156.
Keating, Lieut. F., 149, 159, 166, 279, 297.
Keating, Michael, 290.
Keeden, Michael, 299.
Keefe, John, 166.
Keefe, Thos., 166.
Keegan, F., 166.
Keegan, Francis, 302, 304.
Keeler, Daniel, 285.
Keeler, Edward, 302.
Keeler, Philip, 166, 275.
Kellogg, Giles B., 192.
Kelly, Jas. F., 231, 248, 302.
Kelly, John, 166.
Kelly, Michael, 166.
Kelly, Patrick, 166.
Kelly, Patrick H., 299.
Kelly, Thos. F., 293.
Kelly, Thos. H., 304.
Kemp, James, 155.
Kendrick, Edward E., 113.
Kendrick, P., 84.
Kendrick, Thos. H., 98.
Kendrick, Wm. W., 275.

INDEX. 317

Kennedy, John, 305.
Kennedy. Patrick, 291.
Kenney, Edw'd, 156, 304.
Kenney, Rev. Ira E., 252.
Kenny, Thomas, 291.
Keough, Matthew, 302.
Keoughan, Patrick, 293.
Kerr, John, 277.
Keveney, Rev. Thos., 148, 176, 199, 254.
Keveney, Rev. T. S., 244.
Ketchel, Samuel, 268.
Kilmer, Ira, 296.
King, John M., 40.
Kimball, Geo. H., 53.
Kirnan, M. C., 270.
Kittle, Joseph C., 98.
Kinder, Wm., 156.
Knight, Edward, 282.
Knights of Pythias, 233, 263.
Knitting business, growth of, 78, 79.
Knitting, by power, invention of, 61, 62.
Knitting machinery, of Cohoes inventors, 132, 133.
Knitting Mills, condition of in 1874, 226; condition of in 1857, 134; established, 61, 77, 111, 115, 127, 128, 131, 132, 142, 174, 175, 176, 182, 190, 191, 192, 198, 212, 218, 223; sketch of, 243, 244; statistics of, 212, 213; in panic of 1873, 220, 221; statistics of in 1853, 110; statistics of in 1847, 87; statistics of, in 1855, 128; statistics of, in 1876. 244.
Knitting needle factory, 133, 192, 246.
Knott, Chas., 246.
Knower, Benj., 67.
Knox, Geo., 166.
Kolb, Chas, 231.

Labe, Cilem, 156.
Lackey, James, 156.
Lacy, Patrick, 156.
Ladies Aid Society, organized, 149; work of, 151.
Lake, Hulet, 69.
Lally, John, 292.
Lally, Michael, 289.
Lamb, D. T., 122, 143, 204, 247.
Lamb, James, 212, 244, 263, 299, 301.
Lamb, Levi W., 155.
Lambert, Wm., 33.
Lamey, Michael, 167.
Lanagan, Charles, 292.
Lanahan, John, 166.
Lancaster street, 226.
Land, John, 278, 298, 301.
Land, John E., 166, 303.
Land, John, & Sons, 198.
Land, Lewis W., 299.
Landon, Dr. Henry L., 111, 133, 138, 140, 272, 295, 296, 297.
Laudon, Mr., 113.
Langtree, John, 286.
Lanigan, M., 166.
Lannigan, Daniel, 156.
Lannigan, Thos., 166.
Lansing, Abraham, 113, 280.
Lansing, Abram, 129, 148, 296.
Lansing, Abram G., 26, 42, 45, 49, 110.
Lansing, Andrew, 28, 110.
Lansing, Andrew D., 113, 128.

Lansing, Col. F., 76.
Lansing, Douw, 32.
Lansing, Erbert W., 22, 301.
Lansing, Evert, 28.
Lansing, Evert A., 270.
Lansing, F. A., 166.
Lansing families, 18, 21, 22, 24, 29, 32.
Lansing, Frans, 22.
Lansing, Gerret, 20, 24, 29.
Lansing, Gerret I., 32.
Lansing, Gerret R., 143, 272.
Lansing, Henry, 20, 25.
Lansing, Isaac D. F., 24, 29, 51, 52, 109, 113, 131, 143, 238, 289.
Lansing, I. W., 302.
Lansing, Jacob H, 25, 41.
Lansing, Jacob I., 74, 80, 98, [110, 111, 113, 114, 145, 289, 296.
Lansing, Jacob L., 38.
Lansing, James, 123.
Lansing, John, 22, 271.
Lansing, John V. S., 22, 28, 128, 194, 209, 216, 217, 244, 252, 297, 304.
Lansing, John W., 291.
Lansing, Levinus S., 279.
Lansing, Myron C., 290.
Lansing, Rutger, 24, 29, 33.
Lansing, Thomas, 72.
Lansingburg Bridge Co., 210.
Lansingburg, bridge to.
Lar Patrie Nouvelle, 228, 249.
Larkins, John, 114, 296.
Larkins, Michael, 114, 259.
Larkins, Thos., 291, 302.
La Salle, Henry E., 133, 272.
La Salle, Rev. J. O., 224, 254.
Latta, John, 166.
Latta, John B., 302.
Latta, Michael, 285.
Latta, Thos., 166.
Laughlin, Hugh, 291.
Laughlin, Michael, 292.
Lauzon, F. X., 288.
L'Avenir National, 228.
Lawler, Michael, 291.
Lawrence, Abram, 276.
Lawrence, Geo., 296, 297, 298, 299.
Lawrence, Robt. W., 166.
Lebard, Frank, 155.
Le Boeuf, Francis, 155.
Le Boeuf, Joseph, 196, 301.
Le Boeuf, Louis G., 228, 305.
Le Boeuf, Peter, 189.
Le Bron, & Ives, 67.
Leckie, Robert, 53, 272.
Leckie, Wm., 63, 88, 110, 128, 151, 293.
Lecture course, 121.
Lee, John, 166.
Lee, Reuben, 263.
Lefferts, Geo., 166.
Lefferts, Geo. Jr., 166.
Leland, D. W., 84, 272.
Leonard, Rev. Jacob, 253.
Leonard, Timothy, 38.
Le Roy, Alfred, 210, 222, 226, 244, 290, 302, 303, 305.
Le Roy, Lamb & Co., 212.
Levison, H., 261.
Lieverse or Lievense family, 17, 18, 22.
Lieverse, Peter, 29.
Lightthall, Nicholas, 71,

318 INDEX.

Lighthall, Wm. K., 295, 296.
Lime, Cement & Plaster Mill, 204.
Lime & Cement Mill, 247.
Limerick, Samuel, 156.
Lincoln, A., funeral of, 158.
Link, John A., 194.
Link, Peter, 72.
Link, Wm., 40, 54.
Linnen, Bernard, 305.
Linnen, Thos., 166.
Little, John, 297.
Lockhead, Rev. Wm., 71, 252.
Locks, enlargement of, 48, 49; location of, 44, 45.
Long, John, 300.
Long, Michael, 167, 181, 299, 300.
Long, William, 166, 274.
Longley, Chas. S., 305.
Longley, Gideon, 71, 280.
Longhery, Hugh, 166, 275.
Lounsberry, Charles, 167.
Lounsberry, Jas., 167.
Lounsberry, Nicholas D., 166, 279.
Lounsberry, Richard D., 299.
Lounsberry, Robt., 167.
Lovejoy, Benjamin F., 289.
Lovejoy, Samuel W., 148, 289, 302, 303.
Loveland & Palmer, 82, 105.
Lowe, Chas., 166.
Luckin, James, 284.
Ludden, Rev. John, 254.
Luddy, J. B., 228.
Luffman, John D., 85, 100.
Lynch, Bartholomew, 167.
Lynch, John, 166.
Lynch, John A., 155.
Lynch, Michael, 286.
Lyon, Heber T., 127.
Lyons, Anna, 176.
Lyons, Henry, 272, 285, 297.
Lyons, John, 148, 283, 298.

McAlear, Edwd. J., 304.
M'Alpine, Wm. J., 70.
McArdle, Edward, 289.
McCabe, ——, 168.
M'Calla, Alex., 98.
McCarthy, Edward, 298.
McCarthy, James, 277.
McCarthy, John, 168, 277.
McCarty, John, 167.
McClary, Bernard, 288.
McCleary, Daniel B., 168, 290.
McCormick, John, 168, 290.
McCormick, Patrick, 293.
McCready, Edward, 168, 194, 262.
McCready, Geo. B., 167.
McCready, John, 167.
McCulloch, Chas., 167, 262.
McCulloch, J., 302.
McCulloch, John, 299, 302.
McCulloch, William, 167.
McCusker, John, 167.
McConn, John, 155.
McLean, Archibald, 286.
McDermott, John, 141, 181.
McDermott, Owen, 289.
McDermott, Patrick, 167.
McDonald, D. P., 90.
McDonald, Frederick, 168.
McDonald, James, 167.

McDonough, Thomas, 293.
McDowell, Geo. H., 264.
McDowell, Robert, 167.
McElroy, Alex., 156.
McElwain avenue, 229.
McElwain, Daniel, 88, 141, 175, 191, 301, 305.
McEnerny, John, 98, 140.
McEntee, Patrick, 84, 271.
McEvenia, Peter, 300.
McEwan, John, 263, 305.
McGafferny, James, 156.
McGaffin, James, 167, 288.
McGaffin, John, 167, 274.
McGarrahan, M., 304.
McGarry, Robt., 302.
McGill, John, 107, 113, 295, 296.
McGovern, Robt., 167.
McGrail, Michael, 293.
McGrath, Pat'k, 299, 300.
McGray, Timothy, 114.
McGuire, John, 155, 168.
McGuire, M., 302.
McGuire, Michael, 156, 302, 303.
McGuire, Thos., 168.
McGuirk, Chas., 155.
McGuirk, James, 302, 303, 304.
McIntosh, Daniel, 156, 260, 304.
McIntosh, Daniel E., 298, 299, 300.
McIntosh Hose Co., 232, 259.
McIntosh, John, 273.
McKee, Alonzo J., 281.
McKee, Jas. B., 178, 236, 300, 302, 304.
McKee, Pat. J., 305.
McKernan, M., 102, 105.
McKinnon, William R., 167.
McLuckey, David, 286.
McMahon, Patrick, 167.
McManus, James, 167.
McMar, Frank, 156.
McMartin, James, 147, 247.
McMillan, Wm. A., 286.
McMullen, ——, 168.
McMullen, John, 209.
McMurray, James, 155.
McNamara, Thomas, 290.
McNiven, John, 260.
McNiven, Malcolm, 263.
McPhail, Malcolm, 263.
McTigue, Thomas, 291.
McVey, Patrick, 167.
McWha, Alex., 296.
Maby, Wm., 259.
Machine shop, 57, 82, 101, 128, 219; established, 175, 199; statistics of, 1876, 246.
Magee, Edw'd, 288.
Maguire, Samuel, 156.
Mahar, Daniel, 289.
Mahar, John, 167.
Mahar, Thos., 155.
Mahon, John C., 286.
Main street, 43, 116, 204.
Maitland, James, 273.
Maitland, Robert, 285.
Maitland, Samuel, 274.
Major, Rev. John W., 83.
Malany, Patrick, 276.
Mallery, Willard, 167.
Mallery, Wright, 58, 159, 287, 298.
Mangham, J., 168, 278.

INDEX. 319

Mangham, Michael, 167.
Mann, Francis N.,191.
Manning, Daniel F., 167, 179, 302.
Manning, Egbert A., 167.
Manning, James F., 167.
Manning, Wm., 98, 106, 121, 159, 167, 193.
Manor avenue, 15.
Mansfield, L. W., 131, 174, 225, 270.
Mansfield, Wm. P., 270.
Mansfield & Hay, 131.
Manton, James, 270.
Manton, Patrick, 168.
Manton, Peter, 149, 153, 175, 189, 279, 299, 300.
Manufacturers' Bank, 209, 249.
Manufactures, statistics of, 81, 86, 87, 119, 120, 147, 205, 213; in, 1876, 242, to 248.
Marshall, P. E., 303, 304.
Marshall, Rev. L. D., 253.
Martin, Wm., 268.
Masonic organizations, 260.
Masta, Peter, 155.
Masten, James H., 139, 148, 181, 225, 248, 250, 251, 298, 301, 303, 304.
Mastodon, discovery of, 185 to 189.
"Mastodon Mill," commenced, 185; completed, 195; extension completed, 211.
Mather, Geo., 167, 261.
Maxwell, John, 131, 133.
Mayhew, Geo., 168.
Mayhew, Geo. Sr., 167.
Maynard, Rev. W. H., 180, 253.
Mead, Wm. H., 273.
Meads, John N., 275.
Meagher, Michael, 305.
Mechanic's Savings Bank, 217, 250.
Medical Society, Cohoes, 263.
Meeker, Rev. W. H., 253, 260.
Meikleham, Robt., 288.
Melahy, Michael, 167.
Meredith, Rev. R. R., 253.
Merrifield, R., 119.
Methodist church, 54, 92; organized, 71; built, 73; 41, 101; dedicated, 145; history of, 253; Park church, 254; the present, commenced, 141.
Miggins, James, 156, 167.
Milestones, location of, 41.
Military companies, 262.
Miller, E. L., 59.
Miller, Geo. W., 98, 268, 296.
Miller, Jacob W., 84, 88, 93, 118, 148, 149, 281.
Miller, John A., 98.
Miller, Lyman, 167.
Miller, Mrs., farm of, 29.
Miller, Stephen C., 102, 110, 283.
Miller, Wesley, 264, 304, 305.
Miller & Van Santvoord's Block, 92.
Mills, E. A., 263.
Mills, Henry, 260.
Mills, John W., 288.
Mills's saw mill, 81.
Mills, Wm., 167.
Mills & McMartin, 147.
Mink, Geo., 254.
Mirault, Joseph, 291.
Mitchell, John, 155.

Mohawk Engine Co., organized, 114.
Mohawk mill, 120, 190, 244; built, 92; destroyed, 223.
Mohawk River Mills, 127, 132.
Mohawk street, 204, 229; line of, 143, 144; paved, 219.
Mokler, James, 293.
Molamphy, Hugh, 167.
Molamphy, Rody, 167.
Monahon, Arthur, 293.
Monahon, M., 148, 151, 159, 185, 281, 300.
Monk, Oliver, 167.
Monk, Edward, 168, 217, 249, 305.
Monk, Geo., 168, 290.
Monk, J. H., 168.
Monogne, John, 293.
Monroe, Gordon, 168.
Mooney, Daniel, 167.
Mooney, Peter, 167.
Mooney, Peter B., 168.
Mooney, Thomas, 168.
Moore, Dr. J. W., 168, 209, 246, 263, 299.
Moore, Joseph, 285.
Moore, John, 167.
Moore, Patrick H., 98.
Moore, Robt. B., 114.
Moore, S. C., 114.
Moore, Thomas at Cohoes, 12, 13, 14.
Moore, Timothy, 156, 301, 304.
Moore, Wm., 182, 210, 212, 215, 218, 244.
Moore & Hiller, 182, 196.
Moran, James, 168.
Moran, Peter, 114.
Morehead, Jas. M., 212.
Morris, David, 247, 302, 303.
Morris, G. M., 127.
Morrison, Colwell & Page, 179, 245.
Morrison, Henry, 300.
Morrison, James, 212, 245.
Morrison, William, 167.
Mouselin de laine Block, 82.
Moulthrop, John, 303.
Moulthrop, John B., 289.
Mudge, Joseph, 63, 71, 74, 267.
Mulcahy, B., 180, 301.
Mulcahy, Wm., 156.
Muldowney, Chas., 299.
Mulholland, Michael, 289.
Muller, Conrad, 224.
Mullin, Thomas, 290.
Munro, Duncan, 194, 303.
Munro, Thos., 168.
Murphey, Thos. A., 167, 302, 303, 304.
Murphy, Martin, 167.
Murphy, William, 167, 292.
Murphy, Patrick K., 290.
Murray, Edward, 296.
Murray, Henry, 167.
Murray, James, 260.
Murray, M., 167.
Murray, Michael, 167.
Murray, Peter, 305.
Musgrove, A. C., 152, 168, 278.
Music Hall Block, 225.
Mussey, E. G., 83, 260, 296, 300.
Myer, Rev. Gilbert M. P., 252.

Naery, Peter, 168.
Nagle, P., 302.
Nagle, Richard, 302.
Nagle, Thos., 299.

320 INDEX.

Nealey, Chas., 260.
Neary, Patrick, 279.
Neil, Geo., 261.
Nelligan, Wm., 302.
Nellis, W. H., 257.
Nelson, Nicholas, 168.
Nelson, Peter, 254.
Newark street, opened, 111.
Newby, Thos., 303.
Newspapers, established, 83, 185, 203, 217, 228; changes, 99, 102, 180, 248, 249.
Nichols, A., 168.
Nichols, Edward, 155, 168.
Niles, Wm. W., 241.
Niskayuna, 15, 16, 17, 19, 33.
Niver, Peter D., 141, 147, 156, 175, 233, 297, 303, 304, 305.
Nolan, John, 262.
Nolan, John, B., 168.
Nolan Steamer Co., 259.
Nolan, Thos., 231, 300, 303, 304.
Nolan, W. H., 262.
Noonan, Michael, 303.
Noonan, Wm., 277.
Normile, Dennis, 291.
North, Chas. F., 178, 221, 301, 304.
North, Norris, 142, 299, 302.
North Mohawk St., See *Crescent road*.
Northern Herald, The, 228, 249.
Notrhside, 52.
Norton, Geo. H., 168, 262.
Norton, Hiram C., 168.
Norton, William P., 168.
Notman, James, 168.
Novelty Works, 120.
Nugent, Daniel, 271, 300.
Nugent, Thos., 168.
Nugent, Wm., 284.
Nut factory, 192.
Nuttall, John A., 244.
Nuttall, Samuel, 194.
Nuttall, Thomas, 156.
Nuttall, Wm., 139, 208, 244.
Nuttall, Wm. & Co., 196.

O'Brien, Chas., 74, 68, 271.
O'Brien, J., 168.
O'Brien, James, 300.
O'Brien, John, 3 0.
O'Brien, Michael, 169.
O'Brien, Patrick, 169, 279.
O'Brien, Timothy, 293.
O'Brien, William, 169.
O'Day, Simon, 168, 277.
O'Day, Thos., 304.
O'D anel, Thos., 168.
O'Hare, Hugh, 168, 300.
O'Hare, James, 153, 159, 168.
O'Hare, M., 137.
O'Hearn, Timothy, 168.
O'Keefe, Cornelius, 289.
O'Leary, Cornelius, 189.
O'Neil, Bernard, 281.
O'Nell, J., 301.
O'Neil, John, 168, 287.
O'Neil, Thos., 168.
O'Reilly, Edward, 148, 276, 296.
Odd Fellows, 261.
Ogden Mills, 86, 119, 242; building of, 80, 81, 82; Co. formed, 81; enlarged, 179; sold, 146; strike in, 105, 136.

Oliver Bros., 196.
Oliver, John, 276.
Olmstead, Francis, 48, 67, 240.
Olmstead, G. T., 97.
Olmsted, Chas. A., 63, 64, 76, 81, 82, 85, 89, 91, 93, 95, 96, 97, 100, 105, 113, 137, 143, 240, 295.
Omnibus bill, 230.
Onderdonk, A. F., 248.
Oneida street, 40, 55, 116, 225; paved, 219.
Ontario street, 225; arched, 80, 116, 225; opening of, 191.
Orchard street, 226.
Orcutt, Origen, 273.
Orelup, Chas. W., 155, 283.
Orelup, John, 74, 295.
Orelup, Wm. Jr., 140, 260, 274, 295, 297, 298.
Orelup, Wm. Sen., 273, 296.
Oriskany street, 204.
Osterhout, A. A., 286.
Osterhout, Henry, 168.
Osterhout, Henry O., 277.
Osterhout, Wm., 274, 295, 296, 300.
Ostrander, Lorenzo, 168.
Ostrom, Abram, 295.
Ostrom, D. S., 300.
Ouderkirk family, 18, 21.
Overpaugh, I. F., 98.
Overpaugh, I. F. & Childs, 105.
Owen, Edward H., 276.
Owen, S., 153, 155, 169, 253, 262, 303, 304.
Owen, Silas, Sen., 71.
Owens, John, 292.

Packard, Edward, 279.
Padley, Wm., 274.
Page, Edward N., 179, 245, 302.
Page, John, 281.
Page, Thomas, 263, 291.
Paint mill burned, 91.
Paisley, John, 169.
Paisley, Thos., 169.
Palmer, Wm T., 82, 98, 105, 111.
Panic, of 1857, effects of, 134, 125, 136; of 1873, effects of, 220, 221, 236.
Paper box manufacture, commenced, 179; statistics of, 247.
Paper mill, of Gerret Clute, 40, 45; built and rebuilt, 173; enlarged, 179; sold, 211.
Parker, John, 116.
Parker, Joseph, 155.
Parker, Kossuth, 293.
Parker, Dr. Thos. S., 263.
Parker, William, 291.
Park Methodist Church, 254.
Parks, James, 169.
Parks, Robert, 169
Parkhurst, Darius, 88, 98, 113, 260, 296.
Parkhurst, Orson, 75, 260, 296.
Parkhurst, O. & D., 80, 87, 93, 100, 120.
Parmelee, Elias, 38.
Parmelee Engine Co., 98, 113.
Parsons, J. H., 146.
Parsons & Co. J. H., 192, 215, 244.
Parsons, L. S., 127, 128, 146, 149, 151, 152, 276.
Partridge, John, 280.
Pattengill, Rev. H., 253.
Pattrie, Sylvian, 155.

INDEX. 321

Paul, A., 175.
Pavement, laid, 203, 219, 236.
Paxton, Thos., 169.
Pense, Chas. S., 249.
Pease, Theo. W., 305.
Pease, Rev. L. H., 253.
Peck, Abram, 139, 255.
Peck, A. G., 245.
Peck, B. R., 105, 120.
Peck, William, 169.
Peebles, Gerret, 37, 38.
Peerless Mills, 212.
Penfold, Wm., 273.
Penniman, Wm. C., 39.
Penniman, Sylvanus J., 38.
Pennock, Artemus, 156.
Pennock, F. E., 247, 297.
People's Railway Guide, 249.
Perham, C. O., 114.
Perham & Pettis, 88.
Perry, John D., 270.
Pettis, H. N., 114, 271.
Peverly, Liddell, 271.
Phelps, Alfred, 43, 54, 96, 112, 179, 278, 295, 296.
Phelps, A. L., 85.
Phelps, Francis, 192.
Phelps, Russell, 63.
Phillips, Joseph, 286.
Pickering, Moses, 181.
Pierce, John, 38.
Pierson, John, 292.
Pillings, Thomas, 255.
Pin factory, established, 127; moved, 142; new building for, 207.
Pindar, Thos., 169.
Pine Grove mill, 219, 244.
Pine street, 103.
Pipe factory, 212; enlarged, 235; statistics of, 246.
Pitcher, D., 169.
Pitcher, Rev. Wm., 33, 110.
Place, Jas. E., 245, 300.
Plank road built, 106.
Plantz, Geo. H., 169.
Plaster mill. See *Lime*.
Platz, M., 259.
Pohlman, Rev. Dr., 141.
Police, force established, 181; change in, 202.
Police justice elected, 112.
Pomeroy, Rev. Benj., 253.
Poole, Abram, 302.
Poor, overseer of, 205, 209.
Porter, Albert, 261.
Porter, Jonathan G., 169.
Porter & Hall, 137.
Post Lyon, G. A. R., 232, 262.
Post Office established, 58; burned, 84; history of, 250.
Potter, Lewis, 169.
Potter, Rev. L., 253.
Powers, David, 169.
Powers, Peter, 296, 300.
Powers, Richard, 189, 301.
Powers, R. J., 305.
Prairie, John, 290.
Presbyterian church, 92, 101; organized, 72; enlarged, 199; history of, 253.
Prescott, Col., 39, 46.
Prescott, Joseph B., 98.

Pruyn, Robert H., 118.
Pulver, W. H., 169.
Pumpelly H, 113, 119.
Punnett, Henry, 67.
Purdy, John, 156.
Putnam, Lewis, 169.
Pynes, Thos., 169.

Quackenbush, Isaac, 84, 85, 139, 148, 178, 297.
Quillinan, Dennis F., 292.
Quinan, John, 303.
Quinlan, Patrick, 291.
Quinliven, Michael, 169.
Quirk, John, 304.

Rabbitt, James, 304.
Rabbitt, Pat'k, 156.
Radcliffe, Aaron, 293.
Rafferty, John, 169, 279.
Rail Road, Troy & Schenectady, 73, 74, 88, 114; Albany & Cohoes, proposed, 100, 101; opened, 117, 118; trains to Troy, 219.
Railway Guide, 249.
Ranken, Henry S., 192, 244.
Ranken Knitting Co., 191, 244.
Ranken, Hugh, 191.
Ranken, Wm. J., 192.
Raymond, Rev. H. A., 33.
Raynsford, Norton T., 271, 296.
Reamer, Benj., 33.
Reavy, Frank C., 301, 302, 303.
Recorder, 205, 209, 230, 231.
Recruiting. See *Enlistments*.
Redmond, J., 169.
Redmond, Martin, 258, 301.
Redmond, Michael, 169, 231, 262, 300, 304.
Reed, Rev. V. D., 148, 253.
Reed, William, 169.
Reeves, Patrick, 292.
Reeves, Terrence, 302.
Reformed Dutch church, organized, 71; destroyed, 140; rebuilt, 141; dedicated, 145; history of, 252.
Reinhart, H. S., 288.
Reinhart, Harvey, 169.
Remsen, Peter, 48, 65, 67.
Remsen street, 55, 73, 103, 116, 204, 225, 226; arched, 80, 116; extension of, proposed, 110; paved, 203, 236; extension of, 233.
Rensselaerswyck, Manor of, 15, 20.
Renwick, Wm., 71.
Reservoir, estimates for, 129; authorized, 195; commenced, 131; completed, 139, 203.
Revolutionary war, Cohoes soldiers in, 32.
Reynolds, John, 169.
Rhodes, Mr., 71.
Richard, Henry, 169.
Richmond, Alexander, 289.
Richmond, Elbert E., 258.
Richmond, John, 181.
Rider, Alfred, 298.
Rider, Earl D., 169.
Rider, Geo. B., 155.
Rider, Henry C., 114.
Rignor, Alfred, 169.
Riley, C., 245.
Riley, Hugh, 169.

41

Riley, James, 169.
Riley, Jeremiah, 169.
Riley, Lawrence, 169.
Riley, Matthew, 277.
Ring, John H., 301, 302.
Riverside Mill, 182, 190.
Roach & Jones, 59.
Robbins Garret, 299.
Robbins, Henry E., 98.
Roberts, Henry, 169, 263.
Roberts, Wm., 169.
Roberts, Wm. Jr., 49.
Robertson, John, 156.
Robinson, James, 169.
Robinson, Joseph, 169.
Robinson, Mr., 54.
Rock Alley, 103.
Rockfellow, Henry, 74.
Rockwell, A. F., 98.
Rogers, Chas., 300.
Rogers, Patrick, 61, 247.
Rogers's Block, 219.
Rogers's Woolen mill, 81.
Rogerson, Robt., 297.
Rolling mill, 124, 179; statistics of, 245.
Rollowine, Frederick, 169.
Rooney, Bryan, 169.
Root, A. J., 146, 191, 216, 244.
Root, J.G., 127, 140, 146; & Sons, 146, 244.
Root, S. G., 146, 194, 244, 299.
Root's mill, 149, 244; burned, 222; rebuilt, 223.
Rose, Dr. Ira B., 283.
Ross, Patrick H., 288, 203.
Rossiter, John, 299, 300.
Rounce, Rev. H., 252.
Round, Rev. D., 110, 252.
Rousseau, Joseph, 291.
Roy's butt factory, 81.
Runkle, Isaac F., 114.
Russell, Anthony, 300.
Russell, James, 289.
Russell, John, 169, 286.
Russell, Joseph, 169.
Russell, W. D., 84.
Ryan, Bernard, 304, 305.
Ryan, Dennis, 290.
Ryan, Edward, 156, 292.
Ryan, James, 169, 281.
Ryan, Michael, 285.
Ryan, Patrick, 293.
Ryan, Peter, 291.
Ryan, Thomas, 231, 284, 304.
Ryan, William, 293.

St. Bernard's church, organized, 91; completed, 188; damaged, 229; parsonage of, 199; the present, commenced, 176; history of, 254.
St. Bernard's T. A. B. Society, 261.
St. Charles, L., 263.
St. George Society, 263.
St. Jean Baptiste Society, 233, 263.
St. John, Chas. E., 98.
St. John, H., 64.
St. John's Brotherhood, 263.
St. John's church, organized, 56, 57; built, 60; alterations in, 145; opening of, 205; history of, 252.
St. Joseph's church, commenced, 196; dedicated, 199; hist., 254; rebuilt, 224.

St. Joseph's Union, 264.
St. Onge, Treffle, 170.
St. Vincent de Paul Society, 262.
Safely, Dr. A. F., 170, 282.
Safely, James, 71.
Safely, Robert, 64, 140, 198.
Sager, Alexander, 170.
Sager, Staats A., 170.
Sailors. See *Soldiers*.
Salisbury, James, 82.
Sanborn, Lorenzo D., 155, 261.
Sanders, Jerome, 283.
Sanderson, John, 260.
Sanford, J. C., 247.
Saratoga street, 225, 226; surveyed, 49.
Sargent street, paved, 219.
Sash & blind factory, 82, 87, 105, 120, 137, 142, 246.
Sangon, Rev. L. H., 196, 199, 254, 283.
Sault, Samuel, 249, 261, 262.
Savings Bank, Mechanics, 250; organized, 217.
Savings Institution, Cohoes, 249; incorporated, 113; opened, 119.
Savoid, Lewis, 114.
Saw Mill, Hugh White's, 57, 68; Lansing's, 29, 45; of Hawes & Baker, 65; of Mills, 81.
Saw works, 146.
Sawyer, Mason, 61.
Saxe, John T., 247.
Sayres, John, 46, 50.
Schenck, P. H., 67.
Schermerhorn, Barent C., 286.
Schenectady, 9, 11, 17.
Schmidt, Paul, 286.
School act of 1850, 106.
School established, 40, 50.
School houses built, 40, 98, 126, 199, 204, 255, 256.
Schools, changes in, 106; organization of, in 1851, 113; in 1855, 125, 126; in 1876, 256; sketch of, 255 to 258.
School teachers, 256.
Schoonmaker, John, 71.
Schouten, Wm., 69.
Schroeder, Henry, 288.
Schuyler, Col., 25.
Schuyler, Philip, 27.
Scofield, Joseph, 170.
Schofield, William, 293.
Scott, Jas. D., 263.
Scott, John, 132, 218, 244, 304.
Scott, Lemuel, 142, 274.
Scott, Roger, 170.
Scott, Thos., 155, 304, 305.
Scott, Wm., 170.
Scott & Stewart, 214.
Scovill, Chas., 170.
Screw factory, 38, 39, 41, 46.
Scully, Daniel, 281.
Scully, John, 301, 302, 303.
Scully, John H., 170.
Scully, M. H., 170.
Scully, Patrick, 156.
Seaport, Christ'an, 170.
Searles, William, 289.
Seelye, Seth, 38.
Seiler, Daniel, 156.
Selleck, Nathaniel, 271.
Senator, from Cohoes, 305.

Seneca street bridge, 109.
Sewers constructed, 204, 226, 229.
Sexton, Rev. H. L., 253.
Seymour, Geo. R., 176.
Shackleford, Rev. J. W., 252.
Shaffer, Fred., 170.
Shannon, James, 71, 74.
Shannon, Richard, 170, 302.
Shannon, Wm., 98, 114, 149, 150, 151, 153, 159, 170, 277, 297, 300.
Sharp, Absalom, 170, 288, 302, 303.
Shaughnessy, John, 170.
Shaver, Nathan, 261, 304.
Shaw, Albert, 170.
Shaw, Christopher, 170.
Shaw, Isaac, 170.
Sheehan, Jones & Ryan, 220, 222.
Sheehan, Michael, 303, 304.
Shepard, Chas., 170.
Shepard, Edward, 175.
Shepard, Henry, 114.
Shepard, Joseph, 170.
Shepherd, H. D., 282.
Sheppard, Henry, 304.
Sheridan, Bernard, 170.
Sheridan, Patrick, 298.
Sheridan, Wm., 155.
Sherlock, Michael, 302.
Shields, John, 170.
Shields, Peter, 170.
Shields, Thos., 170.
Shipley, Geo., 170, 277.
Ship street, 234.
Shires, Geo., 279.
Short, John, 290.
Shortsleeves, John, 170.
Shortsleeves, Joseph, 170.
Shovel factory, 41.
Sidewalks, bad condition of, 107; laid, 116, 142.
Silcocks, John E., 171.
Sill, James M., 140, 249.
Silliman, H. B., 102, 106, 123, 131, 135, 139, 148, 149, 150, 153, 154, 181, 194, 195, 208, 209, 217, 248, 253, 267, 283, 301, 302.
Silliman, Levi, 64, 70, 72, 80, 81, 245, 267.
Silliman, Mrs. Clarissa, 72.
Silliman's Block, 92.
Simmons, Baltheus, 71, 270.
Simmons, Daniel, 64, 71, 87, 113, 115, 120, 133, 134, 136, 140, 141, 245, 273.
Simmons, Geo. E., 303, 304.
Simmons's Island, 87; dyke to, built, 141.
Simmons, Jonas, 124, 175, 179, 267, 29 298.
Simons, Chas. E., 261.
Simons, J. A., 114, 177, 282, 295.
Simons & Ives, 114.
Simpson, Clark, 170.
Simpson, Daniel, 156, 194, 259, 286, 298, 300, 301, 302.
Simpson, Frank, 305.
Simpson, John F., 299.
Simpson, Joseph, 298.
Sinclair, Wm., 67.
Sinophy, Matthew, 156.
Sisters of St. Joseph, 145, 146.
Sitterly, Abram, 170.
Sitterly, G., 170.

Sitterly, Henry, 170.
Sitterly, Martin, 170.
Skating Parks, 174, 175.
Skinkle, Chas., 261.
Skinkle, A. W. L., 170.
Slater, James, 170.
Slater, Samuel, 268.
Slaveholding, 30, 31.
Slavin, John, 304.
Slavin, Thos., 302, 303.
Slocum, De Witt D., 270.
Slocum, G. A., 97.
Slocum, G. J., 90.
Slocum, Stephen, 123, 278.
Slocum & Granger, 75.
Smead, Wm., 156, 299.
Smith, Abram L., 280.
Smith, Albert, 212; & Co., 235, 246.
Smith, A. W., 170.
Smith, Benj., 260.
Smith, Gregory & Co., 132.
Smith, Harvey, 190.
Smith, John H., 170.
Smith, Martin, 171.
Smith, Michael, 170.
Smith, Nicholas W., 271.
Smith, Peter, 296, 298.
Smith, Peter M., 274.
Smith, R. G., 300.
Smith, Thos., 303.
Smith, Waterman, 146.
Smith, Wm., 132, 155, 282.
Smith, Wm. S., 187, 194, 217, 243, 250, 255, 298, 299, 300.
Snell, Joseph, 170.
Soap factory, 147, 247.
Social singing in Mansfield's Mill, 174; in Music Hall, 225.
Sofa factory, 82, 87.
Soldiers, letters from, 152; return of, 153, 154; enlistment of, 149, 150, 156, 157; list of, 160-172.
Solon, Louis, 155.
Sons of Scotia, 262.
Soup house established, 136.
Southworth, Wm. S., 291.
Spafford, Horatio, 39.
Spain, Roger, 170.
Spanier, Louis, 127.
Spanswick, Chas., 254.
Specie, scarcity of, 153.
Spencer, A. C., 194.
Spencer, John M., 290, 299.
Spor, Rev. Alphens, 148, 252.
Sprague, Otis, 50, 57.
Sprinkling cart, 137.
Staats, Francis S., 156, 181.
Stacy, D. H., 170.
Stage line, change in, 114; established, 44, 70, 89, 90; sold, 177.
Station House, location of, 181.
Stanton, Rev. R. P., 253.
Stanton, Thomas, 293.
Stanton, Wm., 217, 240, 298, 299, 300, 302, 304.
Stapleton, John, 170.
Star Knitting Co., 190, 244.
Stark mill burned, 214.
Starks, Rev. H. L., 180, 253.
Steam fire engines presented to village 193, 194; purchase of, proposed, 181

Stebbins, A. S., 194, 263.
Stebbins, Rev. Cyrus, 252.
Steele, Rev. John B., 33.
Steenberg, John P., 74, 84, 95, 286, 295, 296, 297, 298.
Steenberg, Marvin, 170.
Steenberg, Samuel, 300.
Steer, G., 119.
Stephens, Joseph, 156.
Stevens, C. A., 88.
Stevens, James K., 170, 278.
Stevens, John, 170.
Stevenson, Elihu M., 59, 114, 296.
Stevenson, Geo., 170.
Stevenson, James, 67.
Stevenson, John, 59, 63.
Stevenson, Wm. H., 299, 300.
Steves, O. P., 257.
Stewart, Geo. H., 143, 204.
Stewart, John, 38, 101.
Stewart, Joseph, 132, 304
Stiles, Edgar H., 304.
Stiles, Samuel, 271, 276.
Stiles, Sherebiah, 178, 298, 301, 303.
Stimson, A. E., 127, 279.
Stimson, E. L., 127, 178, 209.
Stimson, Jas. A., 259, 262, 303.
Stinson, S. Edward, 216.
Stone, Almon E., 152.
Stone, Nathan, 277.
Stone, Rawson, 194.
Stone, Winsor, 127, 174.
Storer, Chas., 170.
Stover, Rev. Ensign, 253, 281.
Stoves, manufacture of, 70.
Stow, Chauncey, 102, 248, 276.
Stow, Christopher C., 273.
Stow, Dennis, 276.
Straw Board Factory, 128, 143.
Straw Board Mill, statistics of, 246.
Street lamps erected, 116.
Strikes in 1857, 136; in Ogden Mills, 105, 136; scarcity of, 226, 236.
Strong Mill, 86, 119, 128, 243; building of, 81; burned, 123; sold, 182.
Strover, Geo., 63.
Sullivan, John, 296.
Sullivan, Wm., 281.
Sumner, Clark, 50.
Sunday School, the first, 57; H. H. Union, 123, 187, 255. See also in hist. of *churches*.
Sunnyside Mill, 212.
Swart, S. M., 98.
Swartz, John B., 170.
Swartz, John J., 274.
Sweeney, Jas. B., 304.
Sweeney, Owen, 273.
Sword presentations, 153.
Syms, Chas., 156.
Syms, Thos. J., 170, 289.

Tabor, Anson, 260.
Tanner, H., 262.
Tape factory, 192.
Tapler, Alonzo, 171.
Targett, A. S., 233, 260.
Taverns established, by R. Heamstreet, 36, 85; Dyer & Williams, 43; Van Der Mark, 43, 44.
Taylor, Alonzo, 171.

Taylor, Ammon, 171.
Taylor, Edward, 50.
Taylor, Jacob A., 171, 275.
Taylor, John H., 171.
Taylor, Joseph, 299.
Taylor, Radcliffe, 288.
Taylor, Rev. Geo. I., 33.
Taylor, Robert, 171, 263, 275.
Telegraph established, 133.
Telfair, Wm. H., 171.
Temperance Societies, 261, 262.
Temple, Capt. F., 149.
Ten Eyck, A., 261.
Ten Eyck, Abram, 235.
Ten Eyck, Albert, 155, 181, 235, 260.
Ten Eyck, Alexander, 270.
Ten Eyck Axe Manufacturing Co., 190, 222, 235, 245.
Ten Eyck, Geo., 155.
Ten Eyck, Jacob H., 67.
Ten Eyck, Jonas, 235, 245, 254.
Ten Eyck, W. J. & Co., 176, 179.
Tenney, A. & J., 81.
Tenny & Cowles, 81.
Terry, Ira, 133, 234.
Thayer, H. B., 126.
Thibadeau, Julian, 264.
Third Separate Co., 232, 262.
Thomas, Nathan, 254.
Thomas, Rev. Geo. C., 261.
Thompson, F., 139.
Thompson, Geo., 156.
Thompson, Geo. E., 244; & Horrocks, 212.
Thompson, Hugh, 153, 180, 287.
Thompson, Jas. L., 244.
Thompson, John, 155.
Thompson, John L., 222.
Thompson, R. H., 176.
Thompson, Rev. R., 126, 253.
Thorn, Wm. E., 194, 209, 210, 241, 243, 249, 301.
Thornton, Pat'k, 299.
Thread factory, 115, 120.
Thurman, R. H., 190, 214.
Tighe, John, 173, 305.
Tillinghast, John, 53, 63.
Tivoli Mill. See *Root*.
Tobacco factory, 120, 128.
Tobin, John, 288.
Tobin, Robert, 171.
Tompkins, Monroe, 171, 254.
Tompkins, Wesley, 171, 275.
Torongeau, Louis, 171, 275.
Torrey, Geo. W., 171.
Tourville, Chas., 171.
Town Hall proposed, 192, 193.
Tracy, Dr. L. M., 54, 57.
Tracy, John, 171.
Tracy, Pat'k, 171.
Traver, James, 156.
Travers, Michael, 171.
Travis, Chas. S., 171, 260, 262, 303.
Travis, Jacob, 113, 123, 135, 210, 216, 254, 296, 301.
Travis, Michael, 303.
Travis, Wm. C., 300, 302, 303.
Tremain, John M., 80.
Trim, John, 155.
Tripp Dr. J. H., 273.
Tripp, Wm., 171.

INDEX.   325

Trojan Alley, 103.
Trost, Henry, 224.
Trost & Bezner. 204, 218, 247.
Troy, John, 171.
Troy Manufacturing Co., 77, 115, 179, 244.
Trull, John, 278.
Trull, S. D., 278.
Trull, Stevens V., 148, 150, 151, 171, 278, 296.
Trull street, 229.
Trustees, Board of, first elected, 96; deadlock in, 174.
Tubbs, James, 263; & Severson, 127, 219, 246.
Tubbs, Rev. Mr., 253.
Tunnel, of Cohoes Co., 239.
Turner, Adam, 171, 278.
Tuthill, Clarence, 171.
Tuthill, Daniel D., 171, 277.
Tuthill, Edward, 171.
Twelvetrees, Edward, 280.
Twichell property, 180.
Twining & Alden, 85.
Twist, Sylvanus, 260.
Tymerson, P. G., 262.

Uhl, Fred'k S., 300.
Underhill, L., 156.
Upham, Fred'k W., 300.
Upham, Geo. W., 171, 286.
Upham, Jacob, 272, 295.
Upham, Willard, 171.

Vail, A. C., 198.
Vail, Chas., 156.
Valley, Louis, 260.
Van Arnam, Abram H., 295.
Van Arnam, Alonzo, 155.
Van Auken, D. H., 139, 143, 156, 157, 182, 203, 204, 210, 227, 240, 247, 252.
Van Auken, Henry, 99, 107, 295, 296, 297.
Van Benthuysen, Chas., 101, 173, 179, 211.
Van Benthuysen, Jas. D., 152, 171, 304.
Van Benthuysen, Myron, 152, 171, 260, 263, 304.
Van Buren, Rev. John, 252.
Van Brunt, Rev. R., 141, 145.
Van Denberg, Douw, 271.
Van Denberg family, 15.
Van Denberg, Henry, 254.
Van Denberg, Jacob, 33.
Van Denberg, John W., 283.
Van Denberg, Wm. H., 171, 275.
Van Dercar, Leonard, 95, 131, 297, 300.
Van Dercar, Thos., 137.
Van Dercook, C., 303.
Van Dercook, Geo. 171, 262, 300, 305.
Van Dercook, John, 273.
Van Dercook, John H., 171.
Van Dercook, Peter, Jr., 300.
Van Dercook, Peter, Sen., 291.
Van Der Mark, A., 69.
Van Der Mark family, 29, 54.
Van Der Mark, G., 155.
Van Der Mark, James, 171.
Van Der Mark, John, 98, 279, 297.
Van Der Mark, Sylvester, 57.
Van Der Werken, Abram, 298, 304.

Van Der Werken, Adam, 122, 285, 300.
Van Der Werken, Henry J., 293.
Van Der Werken, Isaac, 55.
Van Der Werken, Jacob, 49, 54, 55, 70, 268.
Van Der Werken, James, 171.
Van Der Werken, John B., 57, 70, 71, 270.
Van Der Werken, Wm. H., 98, 271.
Van Deusen, John, 303.
Van Dwyer, ———, 78.
Van Hagen, Jesse D., 171, 273.
Vanlouven, Nathaniel, 171.
Van Natten, Isaac, 297.
Van Ness, John, 296, 297, 298.
Van Ness, Zalmon, 152.
Van Noorstrand, J. J., 17.
Van Olinda family, 15, 18.
Van Rensclaer block, 92, 116.
Van Rensselaer House, fire at, 104.
Van Rensselaer, Stephen, 28, 46, 47, 48, 65, 67, 101, 240.
Van Reeth, Rev. Bernard, 91, 254.
Van Santvoord, John, 84, 88, 95, 100, 107, 110, 112, 281, 295.
Van Schaick, C. H., 288.
Van Schaick family, 16, 17, 22.
Van Schaick house, 22, 24, 32.
Van Schaick's Island, 16, 17, 29, 32; bridge to, 210, 234; bridge to, proposed, 90.
Van Schaick patent, 52.
Van Schoonhoven, Guert, 17, 52.
Van Schoonhoven, Jacobus, 37, 46.
Van Steenberg W., 171.
Van Vechten, Teunis, 67, 113, 240.
Van Vliet, Geo. E., 171, 274.
Van Vliet, Isaac, 114.
Van Woert, Stephen P., 273.
Van Zandt, Gilbert I., 284.
Varin, Dr. J., 285.
Vaughan, Charles H., 290.
Velocipedes, introduced, 198.
Veneering mill, 65, 80, 120, 128.
Vermilyea, Gilbert H., 297, 298, 299.
Vermilyea, Le Roy, 152, 171, 250, 262.
Viegle, John, 254.
Vincent, Hiram, 171.
Visscher, John W., 282.
Vosburgh, Philip, 270.
Vredenberg, L., 194, 259.

Wadsworth, Ebenezer, 260.
Wager, E. G., 233.
Wager, Geo. H., 156, 182, 190, 192, 250, 296, 297, 298, 300, 302.
Wager Hook & Ladder Co., 232, 259.
Wakeman, John, 175, 178, 216, 244, 299.
Walbridge, E. W., 38.
Walker, Isaac, 172.
Waldron, Rev. C. N., 110, 145, 180, 252, 272.
Wall, J., 172.
Wallace, James, 286.
Walsh, Michael, 292.
Walsh, Wm., 155.
Walters, Thos., Lieut., 172, 275.
Wands, Dr. A., 284.
Wands, Jas. B., 172.
Ward, Edward, 305.

INDEX.

Ward, John, 286.
Ward & Robinson, 132.
Wards, constituted, 125; changes in, 227.
Warhurst, Geo. 175, 192, 212.
Warhurst, Samuel, 171.
Waring, Franklin, 114, 270, 295.
Waring & Robbins, 85.
War meeting, in 1861. 148; in 1862, 151; in 1863, '65, 157, 158.
Warner, Rev. Mr., 253.
Warner, Wm., 260, 263, 299.
Warp & Thread Mill, 206, 247.
Warwick, John P., 98.
Water act passed, 129.
Water Commissioners, suits of, 144.
Waterford, 16.
Waterford & Cohoes H. R. R., 178.
Water fund, 230, 231.
Waterhouse, Job. 172.
Waterhouse. Wm., 285.
Waterman, F. Y., 43, 54, 58, 250.
Waterman, Geo. Jr., 244, 261.
Waters, James, 298.
Watervliet, city of, 192.
Watervliet Mill, built, 111, 115; leased, 175, 191.
Water Works, company formed, 128; completion of, 139; enlargement of, 195, 203; established, 99, 100; of Cohoes Co., sold, 131.
Watt, Henry, 254.
Watt, James, 254.
Way, Francis, 285.
Webber, Chas., 156.
Webber, John P., 155, 302.
Weed, Becker & Co., 64, 207.
Weed & Becker M'f'g Co., 227, 245.
Weed, Wm. H., 64, 245.
Weidman, Abram, 71.
Weidman, Malachi, 153, 156, 159, 172, 226, 262, 296.
Weidman, Paul, 270.
Weidman, Wm., 172.
Weir, Robert, 252, 263.
Welch, Edward, 262, 298.
Welch, John, 172, 278.
Welch, Nicholas, 172.
Welch, Wm., 296.
Wells, Chas., 261.
Wells, Lewis, 114, 300.
Wells, Rev. G. A., 253.
Welton, Fred'k, 172.
Welton, John, 297.
Western avenue, 219.
Weston, S. J., 132.
Westover, Charles. 277.
Westover, Chas. E., 172.
Westover, J., 171, 297.
Whale, stranded in river, 5, 6.
Whalen, Daniel, 286.
Whalen, James, 285.
Wheel factory, 120, 128, 176; established, 115.
Wheeler, Ezra J., 286.
Wheeler, Nathaniel, 53, 64.
Wheeler, Wm. J., 192, 286.
Whipple, Madison, 172.
White, Canvass, 28, 47, 48, 52, 65, 116, 240, 265, 266, 284.
White, Christopher, 271.

White, G. K., 115.
White, Hugh, 27, 50, 52, 57, 61, 67, 101, 113, 128, 133, 178, 240, 241, 266, 284.
White, John, 172.
White, Miles, 76, 91, 97, 96, 100, 110, 113, 115, 116, 117, 295.
White, Mrs. Hugh, 270.
White, Nelson, 303, 305.
White, Olmsted & Co., 76, 84, 85, 87.
White, Reuben, 260.
White, Reuben P., 268.
White, Rev. Myron, 253.
White street, 103; bridge, 191; paved, 219.
White, Wm. M., 151, 178.
Whitchill, Wm., 263, 283, 302, 305.
Whiting, Mr., 59.
Whiting's Factory, 45.
Wheelwright, David, 156.
Whitman, Pardon, 53.
Whitney, Geo., 172, 304.
Whitney, James, 172.
Whitney, Morris, 156.
Whitney, Sheldon, 172.
Whitney, Silas, 139.
Whittle, Robert, 292, 298.
Wickes, Van Wyck, 67.
Wickes, Eliphalet. 67.
Wickham, Jos., 172, 277.
Wightman, Jonathan, 115, 120, 273.
Wilber, John, 254.
Wilcox, Alex., 172.
Wilcox, Chas., 302.
Wilcox, Rich'd, 156.
Wilcox, Rodney, 175, 260, 302.
Wild, Alfred, 112, 128, 129, 143, 144, 152, 187, 240, 301.
Wild, Nathan. 112.
Wild, Wm., 156.
Wilder, Daniel, 299.
Wilder, Nathaniel, 273.
Wilder, Rev. S., 252.
Wildricks, Thos., 172.
Wilkins, Egbert J., 149, 298.
Wilkins, J. R., 69.
Wilkinson, Albert S., 57.
Wilkinson, David, 48, 53, 56, 57, 60, 64, 96, 260, 268, 287.
Wilkinson, John L., 64.
Wilkinson Machine shop, 57, 82; burned, 137.
Wilkinson, Miss, 57.
Wilkinson, Samuel, 97, 98, 100, 283.
Williams, David, 228, 263; & Eagan, 249.
Williams, Jones & Ryan, 176.
Williams, Mathias, 57.
Williams, Robert, 69, 85, 95.
Williams, Wm., 139, 156, 276, 293.
Wilmot, Alonzo, 98.
Wilson, James, 172.
Wilson, James R., 276.
Wilson, Supply F., 40, 97, 273.
Winans, Henry, 268.
Winans, W. H. S., 88, 97.
Winnie, Ammon, 155.
Winnie, Jacob, 34.
Winnie, Killian F., 294.
Winnie, Illis, Jr., 67.
Winterbottom, James, 291.
Winters, John, 172.
Wiswall, Ebenezer, 27, 28.

Witbeck's Block, built, 199.
Witbeck, Dr. C. E., 263, 302, 303.
Witbeck, Francis, 292.
Witbeck, Gerret, 27.
Witbeck, G. L., 131, 136.
Witbeck, Walter, 287, 288, 296, 297, 298, 299, 301.
Wolcott family, 43.
Wolford, E., 133.
Wolford & Stephenson, 111.
Wood, Giles B., 172.
Wood, John, 172, 275.
Wood, Joseph, 255.
Woolen Mill, 81.
Woolhizer, Fred'k, 172.
Worden, Joseph H., 268.
Worden, Lorenzo, 297.
Wormwood, C. F., 171.
Worsted Co., 81, 87.
Worthen, Wm. E., 182.

Wrigley, Lees, 263, 305.
Wycoff, H. J., 48, 67, 240.
Wyckoff, Rev. I. N., 145.

Yale, James, 268.
Yates, Capt. J. L., 149, 172.
Yates, O. P., 85.
Youmans, E. L., 115.
Young, James, 172, 274.
Young, Wm. H., 193.
Younglove, M. S., 143, 246, 299, 301.
Younglove, T. G., 113, 117, 119, 120, 121, 123, 127, 128, 129, 136, 140, 142, 143, 148, 152, 178, 182, 204, 209, 216, 241, 246, 247, 250, 293, 297, 301.
Young Men's Association, officers of, 1847, 188.
Young Men's Christian Association, 121, 138, 187.

www.ingramcontent.com/pod-product-compliance
Lightning Source LLC
Chambersburg PA
CBHW021158230426
43667CB00006B/451